SOA Security

W9-CLG-716

SOA Security

RAMARAO KANNEGANTI
PRASAD CHODAVARAPU

MANNING

Greenwich
(74° w. long.)

For online information and ordering of this and other Manning books, please go to www.manning.com. The publisher offers discounts on this book when ordered in quantity. For more information, please contact:

Special Sales Department
Manning Publications Co.
Sound View Court 3B   Fax: (609) 877-8256
Greenwich, CT 06830   Email: orders@manning.com

©2008 by Manning Publications Co. All rights reserved.

No part of this publication may be reproduced, stored in a retrieval system, or transmitted, in any form or by means electronic, mechanical, photocopying, or otherwise, without prior written permission of the publisher.

Many of the designations used by manufacturers and sellers to distinguish their products are claimed as trademarks. Where those designations appear in the book, and Manning Publications was aware of a trademark claim, the designations have been printed in initial caps or all caps.

♾ Recognizing the importance of preserving what has been written, it is Manning's policy to have the books we publish printed on acid-free paper, and we exert our best efforts to that end. Recognizing also our responsibility to conserve the resources of our planet, Manning books are printed on paper that is at least 15% recycled and processed elemental chlorine-free.

Manning Publications Co.   Copyeditor: Benjamin Berg
Sound View Court 3B   Typesetter: Denis Dalinnik
Greenwich, CT 06830   Cover designer: Leslie Haimes

ISBN: 1-932394-68-0

Printed in the United States of America
1 2 3 4 5 6 7 8 9 10 – MAL – 11 10 09 08 07

To my family: Madhavi, Kamala, and Mallika,
and to my colleagues at HCL
                                              —*R.K.*

To all my teachers: family, friends, and colleagues
                                              —*P.C.*

brief contents

contents

preface

Security is everyone's business.

It is especially so if you are in IT. At some point, you will have had to implement, or at least understand, the security aspects of applications. As an application designer, you might have been asked to come up with a security model for your application. If you are an IT administrator, you might have been charged with the task of configuring security for an application. It has been our experience that every architect, designer, developer, administrator, and information officer needs to understand the basics of security technologies.

Most practitioners of IT pick up the basics of security on the job. Almost everyone who has worked for a few years in IT has an intuitive feel for username/password–based authentication. A decade of practice with HTTPS has made many in the IT community familiar with PKI as well. However, the security concepts required for SOA cannot be learned by osmosis. Not only are there new security concepts and technologies that need to be understood, some of the most popular security practices turn out to be counterproductive when used in SOA implementations.

The fact that so few people understand SOA security poses a danger to the success of SOA. In our work as SOA consultants, we encounter too many customers and fellow practitioners who make poor choices about security, with the mistaken assumption that they can apply traditional application security strategies in SOA. It is in this context that we decided to write this book.

We started working with SOA security in 2003 quite by accident. In order to solve a problem of one of our clients, we had to research the state of SOA security and its evolution. As part of that work, we ended up creating a prototype security service that used WS-Security, SAML, SOAP intermediaries, and WS-Addressing. Later, through our work for other clients, including projects involving "SOA appliances," we came to understand the evolution of SOA security better. In the process three things became very clear:

1 SOA security is an important topic that the global IT community needs to understand.

2 The material available on the Web is fragmented, and it is not easy for even experienced IT practitioners to learn by themselves.

3 The few books available on the topic introduced the standards but did not help general SOA practitioners who are not security experts to put those standards into practice.

When Manning asked if we were interested in writing a book about SOA security, we knew that it was a great opportunity for us to fill the void: a book that could be read and understood by all SOA practitioners, without a need for a formal introduction to security topics. We took up the challenge and here's how we approached it.

- We made sure that nonexperts could follow this book. We tried to provide all the prerequisites so that you will be able to understand the book without any external resources.

- We provided theory together with working examples. We wanted to make sure that you understood how and why a security solution works so you can modify it to suit your needs. We provide only the essential details of theory to keep it simple.

- We explained how each concept is useful in the real-world and pointed out its limitations and extensions.

- We provided a list of references for readers interested in digging deeper.

In short, we wrote a book for all practitioners of SOA, and not just security specialists, with relevant technical details and lessons from the field. This book is not a comprehensive tome on the topic of SOA security. Instead it is a book that will teach you the 20% of SOA security topics that you will need 80% of the time. We hope this book will deliver value that our peers will appreciate.

acknowledgments

We'd like to thank our publisher at Manning Publications, Marjan Bace, as well as our editor, Lianna Wlasiuk, for helping us understand in very specific ways how to improve our first drafts of the manuscript. Thanks to Lianna's detailed feedback and patience, the book you see is in much better shape than it would otherwise have been. We'd also like to thank Cynthia Kane, who helped us to finish the book, by providing valuable input in the last stages of development. There were numerous other editors who worked with us along the way. We thank each and every one of them!

The rest of the staff at Manning is also to be thanked for their hard work and professionalism. That includes review editor Karen Tegtmeyer, design editor Dottie Marsico, copyeditor Benjamin Berg, proofreader Elizabeth Martin, typesetter Denis Dalinnik, project editor Mary Piergies, cover designer Leslie Haimes, and webmaster Gabriel Dobrescu. We also thank Ron Tomich for his help in promoting the book and getting the word out into the community.

Sincere thanks to our peer reviewers who read the manuscript at different times in the writing process and who provided us with much constructive feedback on how to improve it. We thank them for taking time to help us out. They are Craig Borysowich, Kunal Mittal, Nikhilesh Krishnamurthy, Srikanth Sundararajan, Patrick Steger, Vivek Awasthi, TVS Murthy, Jeff Machols, Scott Shaw, Nikolaos Kaintantzis, Andrew Nash, Doug Warren, Paul Williams, and Tom Valeksy. Special thanks to our technical proofreader, Sunil Kumar, who read the book one last time, shortly before it went to press, checking it for any remaining errors and inconsistencies. Thanks also to our MEAP readers who posted their feedback on early versions of the manuscript.

Ramarao Kanneganti

First, I'd like to thank my colleagues at HCL, Vikram Duvvoori, Kiran Somalwar, and Sundar Varadarajan, for their constant encouragement in this undertaking, that took more time and energy than I had ever anticipated. I also would like to acknowledge the support HCL gave us as we wrote this book by providing a great work environment.

Next, I'd like to thank my daughters, Kamala and Mallika, for letting me sacrifice playtime with them for this book. We will be able to make up for lost time now!

Finally, thanks to all of our customers—too many to name here—from whom we learned so much.

Prasad Chodavarapu

I am a "work in progress," put together by everyone around me, and this book would not have come about without their influence. I am fortunate to have come into contact with a great number of people, each of whom loved me and enriched me in his or her unique way. I wish to thank all of them from the bottom of my heart for their affection.

I cannot list every one of them by name, but I would like to identify the following people: my parents, my late grandmother, and my brother and his family. My mentors, Vijaya Venkatesh, Adam Grove, and Rama. And my friends, Shailesh, Hari, Subbu, Sharath, Gangadhar, Sridhar, Madhavi, and their families. Also, all of my colleagues at HCL and Savera, especially Vikram, Hari, Rod, Krishna, Ramana, Ram Mohan, Sunil, Sowmya, Suresh, and Sandeep, who supported me directly in the writing of this book. And finally, my customers, especially Pankaj Srivastava of Cisco Systems.

about this book

This book is about SOA security. The focus of the book is neither SOA nor security. Instead, it focuses on the intersection between security and SOA implementations.

SOA, or Service-Oriented Architecture, is a new and popular paradigm of IT. SOA uses services as building blocks to organize and architect the applications in an enterprise. There are several different ways these services can be built, put together, and offered.

Security is a well-understood concept, at least in the context of applications. You secure an application against various threats: network eavesdroppers, users (both internal and external), and other programs. There are various techniques, libraries, packages, and best practices you use to achieve this goal.

In the context of SOA, instead of securing a single application, you should secure the architecture. On one hand, you need to keep the services—the building blocks—open so that applications, both internal and external, can easily reuse them. On the other hand, unless these services are properly secured, they can be misused to cause security breaches. How do we secure services without reducing reusability?

There are additional questions to answer as well. How do we ensure security when services from different providers are brought together to create higher-level services? How can we make management, including changes to the security, cost-effective when a large number of services need to be secured?

This book provides concrete answers to these questions and more. It is intended to be of use to multiple audiences: architects, designers, developers, and IT managers. Its explanation of theoretical underpinnings and concise description of standards is helpful to architects and designers. Through its use of code examples, it provides material for developers to tinker with and learn from and to use in their code. Through its description of enterprise-level SOA security architecture, it helps IT managers to deploy SOA security solutions in practice.

How this book is organized

Since this book is meant for a diverse audience, we have divided it into three parts: the basics of SOA, the building blocks of SOA security, and enterprise SOA security.

The first part teaches you the basics of SOA. It is not meant as a comprehensive guide to SOA, but it has enough details for you to follow the rest of the book. We introduce you to some of the best practices, toolkits, and techniques through simple solutions. Developers may find this part useful, even if they are familiar with SOA.

The second part deals with the nuts and bolts of SOA security. We introduce you to each aspect of SOA security: authentication, authorization, nonrepudiation, and so on, in isolation. This part is self-contained and provides the theory as well as the code which illustrates the theory. Developers and designers will benefit from these chapters.

The last part is about building real SOA security solutions using the techniques we built up in the previous parts. We outline several real-life problems and discuss possible frameworks that can solve them. Since these chapters use code developed in earlier chapters, they do not contain listings. This part will be accessible to all readers, even to those without hands-on experience. It will be particularly useful for architects as well as IT managers.

How to use this book

To make most of this book, we expect users to be familiar with the following:

- *SOA:* We only provide basics of SOA that help you follow the text. To internalize the lessons taught in this book, you would have to have some experience with SOA.

- *Java:* All our examples are shown in Java. To understand the examples in depth, it is assumed that you can follow the code presented in the book. These code snippets will help you even if you are using a different platform such as .NET, since the concepts work similarly in all platforms.

In other technical matters, this book is self-sufficient and self-explantory. We provide all the definitions and explanations needed to understand the material presented in all the chapters.

This book addresses not only different audiences, it also presents a wide range of uses, from casual to complex. Whether you need simple security for just a few services or a framework for all of your enterprise services or to extend a vendor solution, this book has information that you can use to address any of those needs.

For people using "do-it-yourself" solutions

If you are a developer of a simple web services-based application, you will benefit from reading parts I and II. You will understand different aspects of security that need to be addressed and will be able to quickly ascertain the appropriate solution and implement it in your application.

If you are developing SOA security frameworks, you will benefit from parts II and III. Since developing such frameworks requires more grounding in SOA than this book provides, we assume that background in these sections.

For people using packaged frameworks

Not everybody develops security solutions from the ground up. Some may be using security frameworks available with a commercial service bus or application server such as WebLogic or WebSphere. These frameworks can simplify several tasks. For example, some come with full-fledged implementations of authentication frameworks; all you need to do is configure them appropriately.

If you are using such a framework, this book provides valuable theoretical background for practical issues. For example, you will learn the basics of encryption and its limitation. You will learn about digital certificates and their limitations. Framework facilities may reduce the direct applicability of the code in the examples, but the essential lessons remain the same.

In addition, the book fills the gap in the completeness of the solutions provided by the packaged frameworks. This book will help you to figure out whether a packaged framework is good enough for your needs and how to implement the missing functionality.

For people using complete platforms

A new breed of frameworks is evolving into complete SOA security platforms. They provide complete working solutions that only need to be configured to get a full-fledged solution. They often come in the form of an appliance.

However radically different these platforms may be, they still use the open standards illustrated in this book. The example code may not be needed on these platforms, but the understanding of the standards they provide is going to be useful to leverage the platform for solving practical problems.

Typographical conventions

The following conventions are used throughout the book:

- Courier typeface is used in all code listings.
- Code annotations are used when directing your attention to a particular line of code.
- Courier typeface is used within text for code words and class and method names.
- *Italics* are used to introduce new terms.

Source code downloads

The source code for all the examples in the book can be downloaded from the publisher's website at http://www.manning.com/kanneganti or http://www.manning.com/SOASecurity. To run the source code, you will need a Windows XP or 2000 machine with 256MB or more of RAM. To download the prerequisites for running the source code, you will need access to the Internet. You will not need access to the Internet in order to run them.

Author Online

Purchase of *SOA Security* includes free access to a private web forum run by Manning Publications where you can make comments about the book, ask technical questions, and receive help from the authors and from other users. To access the forum and subscribe to it, point your web browser to http://www.manning.com/kanneganti or http://www.manning.com/SOASecurity. This page provides information on how to get on the forum once you are registered, what kind of help is available, and the rules of conduct on the forum.

Manning's commitment to our readers is to provide a venue where a meaningful dialogue between individual readers and between readers and the authors can take place. It is not a commitment to any specific amount of participation on the part of the authors, whose contribution to the book's forum remains voluntary (and unpaid). We suggest you try asking the authors some challenging questions, lest their interest stray!

The Author Online forum and the archives of previous discussions will be accessible from the publisher's website as long as the book is in print.

About the cover illustration

The illustration reused on the cover of *SOA Security* is simply labled "Soldier." It is from a collection of costumes of the Ottoman Empire published on January 1, 1802, by William Miller of Old Bond Street, London. The title page is missing from the collection and we have been unable to track it down to date. The book's table of contents identifies the figures in both English and French, and each illustration bears the names of two artists who worked on it, both of whom would no doubt be surprised to find their art gracing the front cover of a computer programming book...two hundred years later.

The collection was purchased by a Manning editor at an antiquarian flea market in the "Garage" on West 26th Street in Manhattan. The seller was an American based in Ankara, Turkey, and the transaction took place just as he was packing up his stand for the day. The Manning editor did not have on his person the substantial amount of cash that was required for the purchase, and a credit card and check were both politely turned down. With the seller flying back to Ankara that evening the situation was getting hopeless. What was the solution? It turned out to be nothing more than an old-fashioned verbal agreement sealed with a handshake. The seller simply proposed that the money be transferred to him by wire and the editor walked out with the bank information on a piece of paper and the portfolio of images under his arm. Needless to say, we transferred the funds the next day, and we remain grateful and impressed by this unknown person's trust in one of us. It recalls something that might have happened a long time ago.

The pictures from the Ottoman collection, like the other illustrations that appear on our covers, bring to life the richness and variety of dress customs of two centuries ago. They recall the sense of isolation and distance of that period—and of every other historic period except our own hyperkinetic present.

Dress codes have changed since then and the diversity by region, so rich at the time, has faded away. It is now often hard to tell the inhabitant of one continent from another. Perhaps, trying to view it optimistically, we have traded a cultural and visual diversity for a more varied personal life. Or a more varied and interesting intellectual and technical life.

We at Manning celebrate the inventiveness, the initiative, and, yes, the fun of the computer business with book covers based on the rich diversity of regional life of two centuries ago—brought back to life by the pictures from this collection.

Part I

SOA basics

Part III: SOA Security in the Enterprise

Part II: Building Blocks of SOA Security

Part I: SOA Basics

XML, Namespaces, and Schema		XPath		SOAP		WSDL

	JAXP and DOM		Apache Axis		JAX-RPC	

In part I, we introduce the basics that you need to know before embarking on a study of SOA security. We will also help you set up the tools and environment needed for running the examples in this book.

In chapter 1, we introduce the basic ideas behind SOA security by contrasting it with traditional application security. While doing so, we define what we mean by SOA, what we mean by security, and what we mean by SOA security. We also briefly introduce the options you have when implementing SOA security and describe how this book will help adopters of each option.

In chapter 2, we introduce the basics of SOAP-based web services. We cover the essentials of XML, XML namespaces, XML schemas, XPath, WSDL, and

SOAP. We also show how you can set up Apache Axis and use JAX-RPC (along with JAXP and DOM) APIs to create and consume SOAP-based web services.

In chapter 3, the focus is on how SOAP can be extended to take care of additional concerns, such as security. We show how you can use JAX-RPC handlers to process SOAP extensions in Apache Axis.

While part I will make sure you are familiar with all the basics needed to understand the SOA security techniques discussed in the rest of the book, it is by no means intended as an authoritative and exhaustive introduction to SOA and its technology underpinnings. The suggestions for further reading at the end of each chapter will tell you how you can obtain a more thorough understanding of SOA basics.

SOA requires new approaches to security

This chapter covers

- Functional and nonfunctional aspects of security
- New security approaches for SOA
- SOA security implementation choices

Since you are reading this book, you should be a developer, designer, or an architect. But let's, for a moment, pretend that you are the CEO of a firm.

As a CEO, you want to innovate and raise the top line of your firm. You can do several things. For instance, you can increase sales by understanding customer needs better and creating self-service channels that induce customers to buy more of your products. You can work with your partners better and make it easier for them to sell your products as part of their offerings. Or, you can make your offerings more compelling by bundling them with offerings from your partners. You can also reach out to new customers through targeted campaigns and venues.

As a CEO, you also want to reduce costs and boost the bottom line. Depending on your business, there are several ways you can approach this problem. Like most other CEOs, you can make it mandatory for your CIO and COO to outsource all noncore competencies and reduce IT and operational costs. To meet this mandate, your CIO can consolidate your firm's application portfolio, outsource day-to-day IT operations and infrastructure management, pay for infrastructure more on a "per use" basis instead of spending a lot of money up-front buying and setting up infrastructure, and move more things out of applications into infrastructure. Similarly, your COO can outsource low value-added operations.

All of these strategies face several common problems during execution. Your enterprise relies on a large number of applications, each developed in a different silo, assuming particular business models. Every time you want to change your firm's business model—either to innovate or to cut costs—the assumptions built into your firm's IT applications get in your way and impede your efforts. To add to your woes, every time you try to open up your firm to partners and customers, technology differences between your IT applications and those of your partners/ customers get in the way.

To rectify this situation, enterprises are now turning to a new IT architectural approach called Service-Oriented Architecture (SOA). SOA suggests new ways of thinking about how IT systems are designed, used, managed, and combined.

Now that you understand the business motivations for SOA, put your technology hat back on and imagine the consequences of making a fundamental change in your enterprise IT architecture. As you may expect, you will have to review all aspects of building enterprise IT systems, including requirements gathering, design, and testing of applications. One very important aspect you will need to review is security,[1] and that is what we will help you do in this book.

---

[1] By security, we mean application security. Security in IT can be broadly classified as network security, platform security, and application security. SOA has little bearing on the first two. The discussion

In this opening chapter, we will briefly review traditional approaches to security and evaluate them in the context of changes SOA is expected to bring in IT. We will find that traditional approaches to security don't work well with SOA. We will identify the specific challenges that need to be solved and suggest new approaches that you can use to solve them.

The rest of this book will greatly elaborate and dig into detail on each of the new security approaches we identify in this chapter. Understand the big picture described in this chapter clearly so that you do not get lost in the detail of later chapters.

One important prerequisite for understanding the motivation behind the new security approaches required by SOA is an understanding of the motivation behind SOA itself. We start this chapter by explaining the need for SOA, what SOA is, and how it accomplishes the goals it is intended for. Once we do that, we will briefly describe traditional approaches to different aspects of security and explain why those approaches are not good enough in SOA. We will then introduce to you new security approaches that address the security challenges introduced by SOA. We will close the chapter with a quick overview of the choices you have today to take care of security in your SOA implementations.

1.1 SOA lowers long-standing barriers

Enterprise IT architectures have been evolving organically for quite some time—as business needs grew, different kinds of applications and application infrastructure evolved. All along, the goal of IT was to enable enterprises to take on complex sets of human activities on a large scale in a very efficient way. IT promised businesses that it will enhance productivity and provide competitive differentiation. Somewhere along the way, IT stopped being part of a solution and became more of a problem.

Enterprises with huge investments in IT found to their dismay that their existing investment locked them into specific ways of carrying out business and created barriers to their succes:

---

in this book is limited to application security. The difference between network security and application security is becoming blurred, with the network starting to take on some of the security tasks traditionally handled by applications. We will discuss more about this in chapter 8 when we introduce Application-Oriented Networking (AON).

- Applications, developed independently of each other, provided functionality that can only be used within the boundaries of each application.

- Differences between platforms, programming languages, and protocols created technology boundaries that are not easy to cross.

- Security technologies relied too much on enterprise boundaries and created barriers for cross-enterprise cooperation.

All these barriers slowed changes required in business models to react to market changes and increased costs. SOA seeks to solve this problem and return to enterprises the flexibility and the agility they need to win in the marketplace and maximize the return on investments. What magic allows SOA take on this ambitious goal? The magic comes from a few simple principles—basic tenets—that underlie the idea of SOA.

1.1.1 *Basic tenets of SOA*

SOA seeks to solve several issues that come with an application-centric view of IT. The basic principles it enunciates toward this end are:

- Applications must open up their capabilities for use by other existing/new applications. It must be possible to combine the services offered by different applications to create higher-level services or composite applications.

- Technology differences must not matter and interoperability must be a key goal.

- Open standards must be adopted to enable integration across enterprises. Orchestration of business processes across multiple suppliers, partners, and customers must be possible.

- Attention must be paid to governance and manageability in order to make sure that flexibility granted by the first three principles does not lead to chaos.

In other words, SOA insists that traditional barriers to reuse must be lowered. This, of course, has huge implications for security. But before we go into detailing the implications of SOA for security, we should tell you a little more about SOA. We won't go into too much detail, as this book is about SOA security and not SOA. We will simply give you a high-level overview of how it is possible to satisfy the basic tenets of SOA described here.

1.1.2 *Idea of a service*

Traditionally, applications are designed mainly for use by people. Any provisioning for use of one application's capabilities by another is often an afterthought, and is usually not backed up by standards. When enterprises need to bring together the capabilities of two or more applications to meet their changing needs, the approaches traditionally used were mostly ad hoc. No one consistent approach was followed. Figure 1.1 depicts this scenario.

The problem with this approach is that it becomes extremely time-consuming and costly to reuse one application's functionality from another. This limitation severely impacts the ability to combine capabilities of different applications into a new application that may be needed to meet changing business needs.

SOA solves this problem by looking at IT systems as collections of units called *services*, and not as collections of applications. A service is functionality encapsulated in a form that is readily consumable by other applications and services.

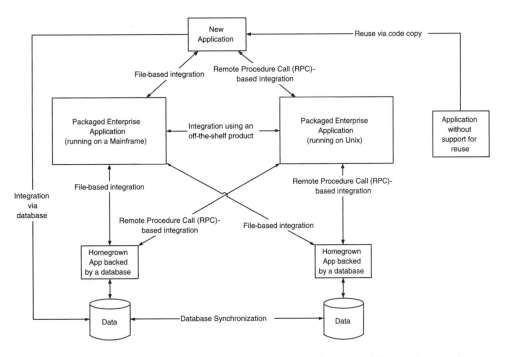

Figure 1.1 In a typical enterprise, applications are built for end users and the mechanisms for applications to interact with each other are ad hoc: database, RPC, files, and so on.

NOTE   *What qualifies as a service?*   Services, if defined correctly, possess desirable attributes that come in handy in overcoming the drawbacks of organizing IT along application boundaries. Some of these attributes are as follows:

- A service is defined at the right level of granularity, from the point of view of a service consumer. In other words, convenience of the consumer drives the service definition.

- A service is self-describing. Potential consumers can learn by themselves how to invoke the service. Service descriptions should include service interface, wire format, transport, location, policies, and SLAs (service level agreements).

- A service is technology-agnostic. Potential consumers are not constrained from using the service because of a mismatch in hardware or software platforms. In other words, an ideal service "interoperates" with every possible consumer.

- A service is discoverable. Consumers looking for a service can discover its presence, usually by looking up a service registry (á la the yellow pages in a phone directory).

- A service can be composed with other services to create a higher-level service. In fact, often several "technical services" are composed into "business services."

- A service is context-independent. That is, it is usable irrespective of what the caller did before invoking the service.

- A service is stateless, making it easy for service providers and service consumers to create and consume services, respectively.

In contrast to the application-centric view, where application interaction is an afterthought, in SOA, applications are concerned with how to expose services and which services to expose. This allows you to build new applications by pulling together services provided by other applications.

Figure 1.2 shows the state of SOA implementations in enterprises today. Capabilities of existing applications, be they packaged applications or home-grown ones, are exposed as services. Quite a few application vendors are beginning to expose some of their applications' capabilities as services out of the box. A number of Software as a Service (SaaS) providers such as Sales-force.com are also offering hosted services that enterprises can take advantage of. All of these services are being brought together and managed by a new class of IT infrastructure known as *Enterprise Service Bus (ESB)*. ESB is a term used for distributed omnipresent infrastructure within an enterprise that provides

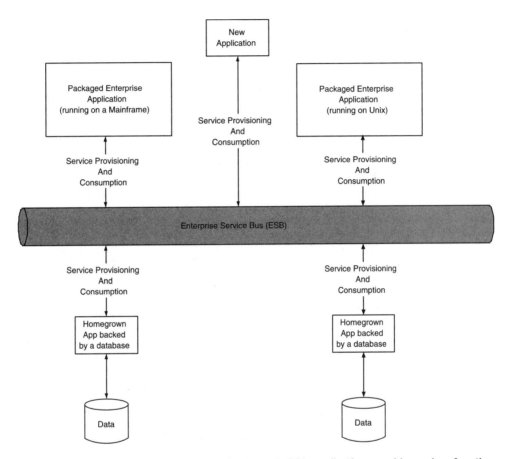

Figure 1.2 **Instead of ad hoc mechanisms for reuse, in SOA, applications provide services for other applications. Some applications may be only consumers. Services are brought together and managed by an ESB.**

routing, security, visibility, and other facilities commonly needed in large-scale SOA implementations.

As you can see, SOA shifts IT from an application-centric view to a service-centric view. This shift lets IT build applications that make use of other applications (via the services they provide), making it easy to meet changing business needs by combining functionality from different applications.

    NOTE   *Web services and SOA*   The idea of a service, as discussed so far, can be implemented in multiple ways. Currently, most service providers prefer to implement their services as web services.

A *web service* can be defined as any software offering that can be described using the Web Services Description Language (WSDL). WSDL specifies these details about a service:

- What operations the service provides.
- How to invoke those operations, specifically: the format and protocols we can use to send the data for those operations.
- The location (address) of the service.

There is a companion standard awkwardly called UDDI (Universal Description, Discovery, and Integration) that provides for discovery of services and retrieval of their WSDL descriptions. Together, these standards let applications discover and use web services. Several frameworks use the details from WSDL at runtime, providing loosely coupled integration between service consumers and service providers.

The most popular data format and protocol in use for web services are, of course, XML and SOAP, respectively. In chapter 2, we will describe XML and SOAP at the level needed for following the rest of the book. There are alternatives for XML and SOAP that are capable of providing web services, the most popular being REST, described by some of the references provided at the end of this chapter. In our book, we are going to focus on SOAP-based web services exclusively, as they are the most popular ones. There are also other, less-popular ways web services can be implemented. For example, EJBs and database queries can be exposed as services described using WSDL.

Now that we understand what SOA is and what its building blocks are, let's return to the security problems introduced by SOA's lowering of traditional barriers to reuse—application boundaries, technology boundaries, and enterprise boundaries.

1.2 Lowering of barriers forces us to rethink security

Barriers may be good for security, but they get in the way of business. That does not mean security can be compromised to meet the business goals; we just have to find smarter ways to secure our applications. Traditional security approaches assumed and took advantage of barriers. Since SOA lowers barriers, we must rethink the security approaches.

Figure 1.3 shows the traditional application security architecture. An application manages its own security and relies on secure channels to protect data it exchanges with client applications.

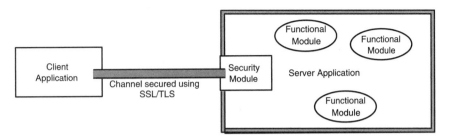

Figure 1.3 A single server application may have several independent functionalities to offer to the clients, but has only one security module. All the security decisions are taken by the application only and are centralized.

What's wrong with this picture? The answer is nothing! At least in the context of the traditional application-centric view, this kind of security works well. Before seeing what aspect of this security breaks in SOA, we can observe that there are two implicit assumptions being made here.

- The server application is assumed to know what the appropriate security model is. By security model, we mean who makes the decisions regarding security, and when and how.
- The server application is assumed to be trustworthy enough to see all the data, including any sensitive data that the client is sending.

Now, let us consider an application that is composed of services from multiple applications, as shown in figure 1.4.

First, let us see how the server applications in figure 1.4 differ from the server application in figure 1.3.

- Thanks to SOA, the functionality within an application can be easily recombined with functionality in other apps to create composite applications (such as composite application 1 in figure 1.4).
- Some of these composite applications (such as composite application 2 in figure 1.4) may even combine services in an enterprise with services of partners.
- In addition, services of an enterprise may be invoked directly (like the way client application 3 invokes service 2b) or by partner applications (like the way a partner service p2 in figure 1.4 invokes service 2b).

It is difficult for an application designer to foresee all possible situations in which a service may be invoked. For instance, how is service 2b invoked? It is

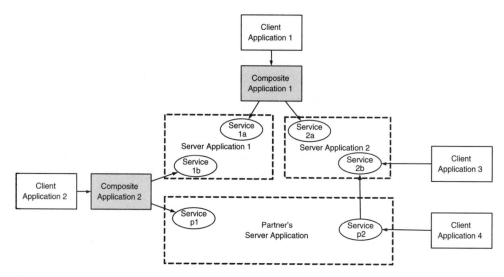

Figure 1.4 Here are three server applications, including one from a partner. The client applications can make use of services from any of these applications. Naturally, no single application controls or has a complete view of the security model.

invoked in different contexts by different client applications, which means it can never tell how it should handle security. *Applications can no longer be in charge of security.* That is, security models cannot be hard-coded into applications, as shown in figure 1.3.

Because some or all parts of a message intended for one enterprise's application may end up in another's applications, we need to correctly limit the data exposed to each application. For example, parts of messages submitted by client application 4 in figure 1.4 may be sensitive, intended for use only by service 2b. In such cases, a secure channel between client application 4 and service p2 will not be enough, as service p2 will get to see everything submitted by client application 4.

In other words, as application and enterprise boundaries are no longer impediments to reuse, traditional approaches to security no longer suffice. We need to rethink how we secure our applications.

Of course, any new security approaches we come up with should be in alignment with the philosophy of SOA. That is, security should keep the services as open as possible, and as easy to use as possible. Technology boundaries should not be re-erected. Interoperability should not suffer because of security.

Going one step further, it'll be even better if security architecture is itself service-oriented. To be specific, security infrastructure should be accessible independent of technology, using open standards. It should be manageable, preferably via *policies,* a SOA standard.

So far, we are talking in abstraction about security. What exactly are the security concerns we need to address? We can broadly classify them into two groups:

1 Functional aspects of security: These aspects of security are standard in the sense that they exist even with traditional applications as well. These are:

   a Authentication—Verifying identity of users.
   b Authorization—Deciding whether or not to permit action on a resource.
   c Data confidentiality—Protecting secrecy of sensitive data.
   d Data integrity—Detecting data tampering and making sure neither the sender nor the receiver can deny the message they sent or received.
   e Protection against attacks—Making sure attackers do not gain control over applications.
   f Privacy—Making sure the application does not violate the privacy of the users.

2 Nonfunctional aspects of security: These aspects are nonfunctional in the sense that they do not directly relate to security. Instead, they are required to make sure that a security solution works well in an enterprise setting. These are:

   a Interoperability—This concern is specific to SOA, where different security solutions must not break compatibility of services that are otherwise compatible.
   b Manageability—This concern is bigger for SOA, as a security solution needs to protect many different services.
   c Ease of development—This concern is common for any security solution. Be it SOA or traditional application development, complexity reduces adoption of any security solution.

In the next section, we will study the functional aspects of security. In each subsection, we will look into a specific security concern, see how it is traditionally solved, and see why the same approach will not work for SOA.

1.3 *Functional aspects of security: With and without SOA*

As explained earlier, the functional aspects of security in SOA are the same as in traditional applications. For the most part, they are well understood in the context of traditional applications. While the security functions themselves do not change with SOA, the approach needed to address each functional aspect is certainly impacted by SOA. Let us discuss these in detail, one by one.

1.3.1 Authentication

Applications need to verify that only legitimate users are trying to use them. The process of verifying the identity of users is referred to as *authentication*. Broadly speaking, there are three kinds of evidence a user can present to an application to prove identity, as described in table 1.1.

Table 1.1   Evidence you, the user, can present to prove your identity to an application

Evidence Type	Description	Examples
What you know	You present one or more secrets that the application expects you to know	You may present the username and password that you previously registered with. Alternatively, you may respond to a challenge question that can be only answered correctly by one who knows the secret
What you have	You prove that you are in possession of something the application expects you to have	You may prove that you are possess a special hardware token such as an RSA token by presenting the number displayed on the token at the time of authentication
What you are	You prove your identity with biometric evidence	You may present a fingerprint or retina scan

First, let us see the strategy that applications have traditionally used for authentication. Next, we will see how that strategy is inadequate for securing SOA.

Traditional authentication strategy

No matter which type of evidence users present to an application, the burden of examining that evidence and validating it traditionally fell on the application.

To fulfill this responsibility, applications need to possess a master copy of the evidence legitimate users are going to present. For example, in order to verify a username/password (or a retina scan), an application needs to know all the correct username/password combinations (or what retina images of all legitimate users look like) up front. Or, if users are using an RSA token, the application needs to know an algorithm that can verify whether the number presented by the user matches the number that is displayed on the user's RSA token at the time of authentication.

In other words, every single application that needs to authenticate user identity will need a copy of true user credentials. To reduce the administrative complexity, most enterprises store these credentials in a *directory server*, a repository for user credentials. Most enterprise applications readily integrate with directory servers using a standard protocol named *Lightweight Directory Access Protocol (LDAP)*. LDAP allows applications to consult the directory server for validating user-provided evidence of identity.

Even with the use of directory servers, the onus of ensuring that authentication is carried out still lies with the applications. Based on configuration, most applications contact one or more directory servers and deny access to unauthenticated users.

Authentication strategy in the context of SOA

If a service is invoked in different ways, how can we do authentication? For instance, if the service is invoked within the same enterprise, we can use the corporate directory. But, if it is invoked from outside the enterprise, that repository is of no use.

Moreover, when a service uses another service, how does it provide the credentials? Can we trust the authentication done by one service and reuse it? How do we make sure we communicate the results of authentication between services? All these questions are complex, and have no answers that work well in every situation. Table 1.2 presents a few scenarios and possible authentication strategies in each scenario.

Table 1.2 Possible authentication strategies in different service invocation scenarios

Scenario ID	Scenario description	Possible authentication strategies
1	Service is directly invoked by a client app belonging to the same enterprise as the service	Authenticate against the corporate directory
2	Service is invoked by another service or composite app in the same enterprise	If the caller is another service with the same authentication requirements, the called service can rely on the authentication carried out by the calling service. Otherwise, called service may re-authenticate user identity against the corporate directory. If the caller app is a composite app, the called service may rely on the composite app for authentication or do authentication by itself against the corporate directory.
3	Service is invoked by a partner's app	Rely on partner app's assertion of user identity

As you can see, the traditional authentication strategy will not work for SOA. Next, we see what authorization means, how it is tackled traditionally, and why the same mechanisms will not work for SOA.

1.3.2 Authorization

Once a user is authenticated with or without the help of a directory server, an application needs to determine whether the identified user is *authorized* to access the functionality she is requesting. Authorization is also commonly referred to as *access control*.

The decision to grant access may depend on multiple criteria, such as the action that is being requested, the resource on which the action is being requested, and the groups to which the authenticated user belongs or the roles that the user plays. For example, the superuser or the administrator may access all the files in a system, but a user belonging to the HR group can access only those files that are allowed for that group.

You can avoid the confusion between "authorization" and "authentication" this way: authentication establishes who you are (like your photo ID may establish who you are) and authorization determines what you are allowed to do (your age and local laws may determine whether you can legally take a drink).

Traditional authorization strategy

Most applications come with their own access control model; that is, the logic for deciding whether or not to grant access for a particular action on a resource is hard-coded into the application. Some of the information used to decide whether to grant access is often pulled from a directory server or a configuration repository.

The two most common access control models are *Role-Based Access Control (RBAC)* and *Access Control List (ACL)*.

In RBAC, permissions for each action on a resource are granted to one or more *role*. For example, in an e-learning application, a teacher role is required to grade a test. Information on what roles are granted to which users can be maintained in an LDAP directory.

ACL-based access control works differently. Administrators associate a list of rules with each resource. A rule declares whether to grant or deny permission for a specific action on a specific resource. For instance, in an e-learning application, each test may be associated with a set of rules describing which user can do what actions.

Authorization strategy in the context of SOA

Think of a composite application that stitches together the capabilities of multiple services. As an action in the composite app may consist of multiple actions in constituent services, the composite app should ideally check the access control rules of all constituent services before initiating an action. But this is only possible if the access control rules of each constituent service are also available to the composite application. This is not possible, in general; traditionally, access control rules are built into each application in an opaque way.

There is another reason why we cannot hard-code a specific access control strategy into each application. The reusability of the service may be drastically reduced for use cases that require a different access control model. Any authorization strategy for SOA will have to address these issues.

Next, we will see how data confidentiality is impacted by SOA.

1.3.3 Data confidentiality

Data exchanged over a network needs to be safeguarded from prying eyes.[2] Unauthorized parties can otherwise gain access to data over the network by using sniffer tools.

Traditional strategy to ensure data confidentiality

Encryption is the standard technique used to safeguard confidentiality of data exchanged over a network. Without encryption, web commerce would never have succeeded, as it would have been unsafe to transmit credit card information over the wire. Part II of this book will introduce the fundamentals of encryption. For now, it is enough to note that encrypted data can only be understood by parties that know the encryption scheme and the decryption key.

Traditionally, applications that care about data confidentiality establish a secure channel for data exchange using *Secure Sockets Layer (SSL)/Transport Layer Security (TLS)*. SSL/TLS encrypts all the data exchanged over a channel.

Data confidentiality protection strategy in the context of SOA

SOA makes it easier for enterprises to integrate their service offerings with those of partners, and this of course fulfills a real business need. There is now additional complexity: customer information will now cross enterprise boundaries. That will

---

[2] Data stored by an application—be it in memory or in files/databases—also needs to be secured against unauthorized access. We don't discuss this aspect here, as SOA does not in any way impact the strategies used to secure stored data.

make the traditional data confidentiality strategy less useful. Consider the example shown in figure 1.5.

In this example, the ACME brokerage firm is integrating with a bank to make it easier for customers to pay for their stock purchases. Customers who wish to take advantage of this integration will have to trust ACME with their bank account information, which is not a good idea, in general. It imposes security risks, responsibilities, and even legal obligations that those enterprises (the ACME brokerage, as well as the bank in this example) are not willing to accept.

Observe that SSL/TLS is not enough to address the data confidentiality concerns in this use case. SSL/TLS can protect the confidentiality of a customer's

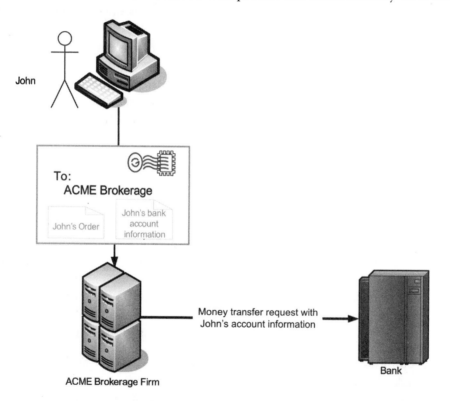

Figure 1.5 John, a customer of the ACME brokerage firm, is placing an order. As ACME has integrated its applications with the payment services offered by John's bank, John can pay for his order directly from his bank account. John attaches his bank account information to his order and sends both securely to ACME. ACME then places a money transfer request with John's bank. Note the security hole in this arrangement. ACME knows the details of John's bank account and an administrator at ACME may be able to misuse this information.

message when it is passing over the wire, but once the message reaches the brokerage application, SSL/TLS's responsibility ends and the application is free to read and use all the data in the message. Clearly, we need better techniques to ensure data confidentiality.

Now, we will examine how the data integrity aspect of security becomes complex with SOA.

1.3.4 *Data integrity and nonrepudiation*

When an application receives a message, it needs to make sure that the message received is exactly what the sender sent and not something that is fabricated/ tampered with by a man in the middle. In other words, applications are responsible for verifying integrity of data received over a network. Furthermore, the sender should not be able to "repudiate" or deny having sent a message.

These requirements are important for both senders as well as receivers of data over a network. Suppose you authorized the withdrawal of a certain amount from your bank account for purchases at an online merchant. You, the sender, must be sure that the merchant, or even the bank, did not modify the amount in your authorization.

From a recipient's point of view, you must protect yourself, as a merchant, against customers who falsely report fraud claims against you. As a recipient of a sensitive email, you must be sure that the message was indeed sent by the person whose address appears in the mail headers.

Traditional strategy to ensure data integrity and nonrepudiation

SSL/TLS, used by most applications to ensure confidentiality of data exchanged over a network, also helps in verifying the integrity of data received over the network and ensuring nonrepudiation. In part II we will describe the underlying techniques that help verify data integrity and guarantee nonrepudiation.

Data integrity protection strategy in the context of SOA

As with data confidentiality, the traditional strategy of using SSL/TLS to protect data integrity and nonrepudiation is not enough when higher-level services bring together lower-level services from different parties. To understand this easily, consider the use case illustrated in figure 1.5. A secure channel provided by SSL/ TLS cannot prevent the brokerage application from claiming a different amount from the bank than what the customer authorized. We need new and better ways of ensuring data integrity and nonrepudiation.

1.3.5 *Protection against attacks*

Every network application needs to be protected against attacks. Broadly, attacks seek to exploit three kinds of vulnerabilities:

- Vulnerabilities in application code: For example, failure to vet user input before using it in an SQL query can allow attackers to trick the application into executing arbitrary SQL code.[3]

- Vulnerabilities introduced by poor administrative practices: For example, if an administrator does not change the default superuser password for a publicly exposed server application, attackers can walk right in through the front door and take charge.

- Vulnerabilities inherent in computing/networking infrastructure: TCP/IP has many known weaknesses. In addition, TCP/IP implementations and operating systems often come with their own set of vulnerabilities that can be exploited by attackers.

Let's see how we can address these vulnerabilities in traditional applications as well as in SOA.

Traditional strategy for protection against attacks

Traditional strategy for protection against attacks is multifold

- Using firewalls, isolate publicly exposed applications from internal applications as much as possible.

- Run applications within sandboxes (such as `chroot` jails) to limit damage of compromise.

- Carefully audit application code.

- Use intrusion detection systems to monitor application activity.

How well do these techniques work for SOA?

Strategy for protection against attacks in the context of SOA

With SOA, more and more code gets exposed—directly or indirectly—to external parties, and attack opportunities multiply. The very openness of services can make it vulnerable to denial of service (DoS) attacks. There is nothing inherently special about SOA that makes it more vulnerable to these kinds of attacks. We will not focus on much on this kind of security concerns in this book.

---

[3] This kind of attack is known as SQL Injection attack and is described in more detail in chapter 10.

1.3.6 Privacy protection

Businesses are often prohibited by law or by contract from disclosing the personal/private information of customers/partners to third parties. This prohibition applies as much to applications as it does to humans. In other words, business applications must be carefully designed and managed to avoid leakage of users' private information.

Traditional strategy to protect privacy

Leakage of private information happens primarily due to two simple reasons.

- Flaws in access control rules: for example, an e-learning application screen that exposes the social security numbers of students enrolled for a class should not be openly accessible; only administrators should be allowed. Traditionally, flaws in access control rules were eliminated by careful reviews and security audits.

- Vulnerabilities exploited by attackers: vulnerabilities may lie in application code or may result from poor administrative practices. For example, failure of application code to vet user input may be exploited by attackers to inject SQL that queries sensitive information from a database. Or, the failure of an administrator to change the default superuser password may open up all the data managed by an application. Traditionally, damage from vulnerabilities is contained by good security management practices, security audits, and intrusion detection tools.

In addition to these two simple ways, there are several complex ways (such as triangulation) in which privacy can be compromised. We will not go into them in this book.

Privacy protection strategies in the context of SOA

With SOA, privacy protection is lot more challenging. Since SOA makes it easier to compose services from multiple parties, the chances of unwittingly sharing your customers' private information with external parties are increased.

Privacy protection is not a topic we focus on too much in this book, so we will give away right here the basic idea behind privacy protection strategies in SOA.

When invoking a third-party service, service providers can the mask real identities of users using pseudonyms. Holding back real identities is not enough. It is possible to guess identity based on patterns of usage. Protecting against such leaks is difficult and is not often attempted.

We have now completed a review of the different functional aspects of security, all of which are impacted by SOA. New strategies are needed to address these aspects in the context of SOA.

The impact of SOA on security extends beyond the functional aspects of security. SOA forces us to pay more attention to some nonfunctional aspects of security as well. We will describe this impact next.

1.4 *Nonfunctional aspects of security*

For a security solution to be successful, it is not enough to take care of all the functional aspects of security. We need to address a few nonfunctional concerns as well, so that the solution is scalable, manageable, and usable. While these concerns exist even for the traditional applications, for SOA, they are very pronounced. We will explain why in the next subsections.

1.4.1 *Interoperability*

As described in section 1.1.1, one of the basic tenets of SOA is that technology differences must not matter. A service should be usable by any service consumer, regardless of what technology platforms the service and service consumer run on. In other words, interoperability of services and service consumers is a major promise of SOA. Security approaches we adopt for SOA must not break that promise. If everyone adopts a different approach for securing services and service consumers, interoperability will certainly break. But even with standardized approaches, interoperability is not guaranteed because, for good reasons, standards have to leave some choices to implementers. For example, the choices of authentication mechanism and cryptographic algorithm have to be left to the implementers, otherwise the standards run the danger of not being applicable in all situations.

Traditional strategy to ensure interoperability

As interoperability between applications was itself not guaranteed, interoperability of security implementations was traditionally not a topic of great interest. Interoperability needs have been addressed to varying degrees in traditional security strategies. For example:

- Most applications supported only one form of authentication.
- HTTP supported a few standard authentication schemes.
- SSL/TLS allowed for dynamic negotiation of cryptographic algorithms.

As you can see, this issue is not very important in application security as it is self contained.

Interoperability needs in SOA security

With SOA, interoperability not only becomes an important goal, but also a tougher goal to accomplish. Expectations will be that a service implemented on any platform can be secured without affecting interoperability with a wide variety of service consumers. Also, as SOA allows composition of services from a number of parties, the likelihood of interoperability problems will be higher.

Another important nonfunctional aspect of security is manageability, which is of particular importance to SOA. Let us examine that next.

1.4.2 Manageability

Manageability refers to the ease with which a security implementation can be managed. By "managing," we mean all aspects of dealing with a security implementation, including configuration, provisioning, auditing, and maintenance.

Traditional strategy to ensure manageability

Manageability of application security solutions has traditionally been poor to fair. The most pressing pain points in application security management have been user account provisioning and password synchronization. The common strategy to tackle these problems is:

- Where possible, modify applications to authenticate against a common credential store such as a directory
- Otherwise, use tools that synchronize user accounts and passwords across multiple applications

One additional management concern that has become commonplace recently is auditing. Recent regulations in the U.S. and Europe have made it necessary to not just secure but also prove that enterprises are doing all that they can to secure their applications. Traditionally, there is no easy solution to this problem. It has proved quite expensive for enterprises to install auditing controls in existing applications.

Manageability needs in SOA security

As interactions between applications multiply with SOA, it becomes difficult to prove that the security decisions being made by all the applications are correct and comprehensive. In other words, security audits now become much more difficult unless we improve on the traditional approaches to manageability.

In addition, provisioning of users and user privileges in applications becomes difficult due to the increase in the number of ways applications can be used.

1.4.3 *Ease of development*

Usually, security is seen as an esoteric topic that is better left to experts. While it is true that security requires expert attention, everybody, including software developers, designers, architects, IT administrators, and managers, needs to do tasks that require a good understanding of security topics. If a security strategy is not easy to understand and develop, it cannot be successful.

Traditional strategy to ease burden on developers

Fortunately, traditional security techniques have been around long enough for designers, developers, and architects to understand and apply them in practice. In addition, a number of libraries, frameworks, and other facilities reduce the burden on developers. For example, J2EE application containers assume a lot of the responsibility for security.

Ease of development needs in SOA security

If you followed this far, you understand that any solution for SOA security is bound to be more complex than any traditional security solution. Therefore, it becomes more important than ever to make sure that SOA security solutions are easy to use. Thankfully, this is not a subjective measure; there are specific steps, which we'll show in the next section, to make SOA security solutions easy for developers to use.

Now that we have discussed the different ways SOA security can be more complex than traditional security, it is time to offer a few words of optimism. Despite all these difficulties, SOA security is not impossible—thanks to the support of standards, tools, and technologies. As tools and frameworks mature, SOA security becomes easier to understand and implement.

In the next section, we will describe three approaches to SOA security. They solve different aspects of security, and can be combined. In fact, any framework or solution you develop or buy will have some elements of these approaches.

1.5 *New security approaches for SOA*

It is clear from the discussion so far that traditional approaches to various aspects of application security will no longer suffice. By lowering long-standing barriers between applications, SOA forces us to rethink how we approach security. At the same time, SOA fortunately allows a few new approaches, thanks to the standards it supports, that fit the changed requirements of application security discussed previously. In this section, we describe three such new security approaches:

- Message-level security
- Security as a service
- Policy-driven security

Let's start with a description of message-level security.

1.5.1 *Message-level security*

As you might recall from sections 1.2.3 and 1.2.4, SOA brings changes in the requirements for data confidentiality and data integrity. As illustrated in figure 1.5, when a message sent to party 1 (brokerage) contains parts intended for party 2 (bank), we need the ability to differently encrypt and/or sign the part that is intended for use only by party 2. Clearly, traditional transport layer security mechanisms such as SSL/TLS are not good enough here, as they cannot stop party 1 from reading and/or tampering with the message part intended for party 2.

Message-level security (as opposed to transport-level security) is a new approach to solve this problem. With this approach, different parts of a message can be protected differently, to make them usable only by intended parties in the message path. Figure 1.6 illustrates this idea in the context of the brokerage and bank example introduced by figure 1.5.

In this figure, John separately protects a part of the message he is sending to the brokerage, as he wants that part to be usable only by his bank. This idea of protecting different parts of a message differently to make each part usable only by intended parties is what is commonly referred to as message-level security.

Part II describes how a standard named WS-Security allows message-level security to be implemented with SOAP.

Remember that wish we made at the beginning of the chapter? We wanted our SOA security solution to be in line with the basic principles of SOA—the security solution itself should be usable as a service. We will describe this approach next.

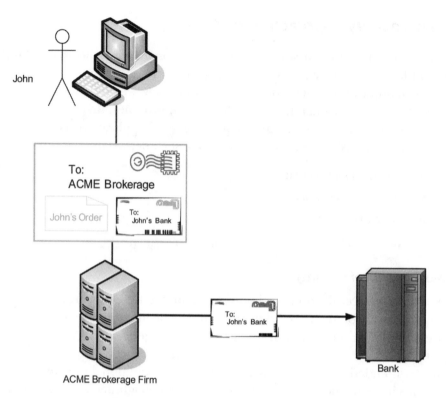

Figure 1.6 The message from John to the bank is in a different envelope inside the envelope to the ACME firm. ACME can only open its envelope, so the letter to the bank is safe from everybody else.

1.5.2 *Security as a service*

In sections 1.3.1 and 1.3.2, we discussed how applications can no longer be in charge of authentication and authorization, for they might not know the context in which they are being used. The natural question is: who else can do authentication and authorization? The answer, in keeping with the spirit of SOA, is a *security service*.

A security service can offer applications the ability to authenticate, authorize, encrypt/decrypt messages, sign messages/verify signatures, and log messages. It may also scrub messages to protect applications against known and unknown vulnerabilities. Applications might still need to know a little bit about security—for example, they may need to know how to invoke a security service and use the information provided by the security service in return—but the meat of the security logic can be executed by a central security service.

The idea of a security service is in some ways similar to the idea of an application service, and in some ways different. Like an application service, a security service should be usable by any application; technology differences should not be a barrier. Unlike an application service, a security service is infrastructural and may come into play even if it is not explicitly invoked. For example, as shown in figure 1.7, the security service may be implemented as part of the ESB or by application-aware network devices.

As a security service is central, and not a part of any application, its security model can evolve in-line with business needs, without affecting any of the applications. Treating security as a service helps offload much of the burden of security enforcement from developers of business services, allowing them to focus on business logic.

Implementing security as a service was not possible until recently because of the absence of technologies and standards for communicating with a security service. While LDAP did enable applications to rely on a central directory server for authenticating users and retrieving user attributes, applications still had to implement their own logic for authorization and other aspects of application security that we discussed earlier in this chapter.

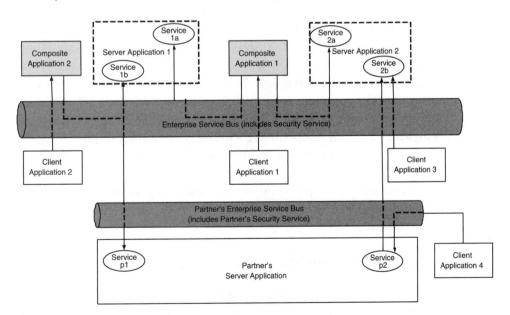

Figure 1.7 Security can be implemented as an infrastructure service, for example, offered by the ESB. This approach avoids the problems that arise when particular security models are hard-coded into applications. See also figure 1.4.

SOA supports standards such as *Security Assertion Markup Language (SAML)* and WS-Trust that can be used to implement such a service. Chapter 8 describes SAML, WS-Trust, and other technologies that help offer security as a service in web services implementations.

No matter how good a solution is, unless it is easy to use and manage, it will not be successful in the enterprise. In the next section, we will describe an emerging approach to make SOA security easy to develop and manage.

1.5.3 *Policy-driven security*

In sections 1.4.1 to 1.4.3, we discussed the nonfunctional needs of SOA security solutions. Policy-driven security is a new approach that is evolving to address those needs.

The idea behind policy-driven security is simple. Security requirements and mechanisms must not be hard-wired into applications. Instead, security requirements of an enterprise should be declared separately as a "security policy."

A security policy declaration becomes handy in many ways: It separates security logic from business logic, leaving the former to security specialists. It becomes easier to ensure consistency of security enforcement across multiple applications. Most importantly, interoperability is enhanced as policies of involved parties can be compared to figure out how to make their security implementations compatible.

Chapter 9 describes the WS-SecurityPolicy standard that is emerging to make this new approach possible.

In this section, we have introduced three new approaches that address the impact of SOA on various aspects of security. As a SOA practitioner, you need to know how you can put these approaches into action to tackle SOA security. If you are an application developer using a web services toolkit in Java, .Net, or a legacy platform, you need to know if and how your toolkit supports these approaches. If you are an IT administrator or an enterprise solution architect, you need to know about products that help you implement frameworks based on these approaches across the enterprise. We will discuss what's available in current generation SOA products next.

1.6 *Current SOA security implementation choices*

This book will teach you the details of each of the three new approaches described in the previous section. You will see sample Java code that helps you to understand how most of the relevant standards can be implemented.

While you can definitely write custom code based on the samples shown in this book, there are better options. Table 1.3 lists the options you have under various scenarios.

Table 1.3   Currently available options for implementing SOA security in different scenarios

Scenario	Options	Examples
Securing a single service built using a web services toolkit that supports policy-driven security	Select one of the precrafted security policies offered by your web services toolkit, if it meets your needs.	BEA WebLogic Server (WLS) 9.1 provides three "simple" policies and .NET WSE 3.0 provides five policies (called turnkey security profiles). While prepackaged policies in WLS 9.1 support authentication using username/password and digital certificates, those in WSE 3.0 also support authentication using Kerberos tickets. Both restrict encryption/signing to the whole message body; if you want to encrypt/sign different parts of the message differently, you cannot use the prepackaged policies. You also cannot use other forms of authentication (such as SAML assertions, introduced in chapter 8) in either case.
	If none of the precrafted policies offered by your web services toolkit meets your needs, declaratively specify your own security policy using a toolkit vendor-specific policy language that is usually a variation of WS-SecurityPolicy (described in chapter 9). Toolkit vendors also allow you to extend what you can enforce with a policy by coding your own assertions.	BEA WLS 8.1 and .NET WSE 2.0 are examples of web services toolkits that offer this level of support.
Securing a single service built using other web services toolkits	Look for extensions or code your own extensions.	If you are using Apache Axis, an open source web services toolkit, publicly available extensions named Apache WSS4J (for Axis 1.x) and Apache Rampart (for Axis2) will let you handle, with a combination of declarations and code, usernames/passwords and encryption/signing of entire message bodies. For everything else, you will have to code your own extensions.

continued on next page

Table 1.3 Currently available options for implementing SOA security in different scenarios *(continued)*

Scenario	Options	Examples
Securing a large number of services within an enterprise	Consider deploying security infrastructure that takes care of security for your services. A natural place for such security infrastructure is in your ESB. But, not many ESB implementations currently offer comprehensive implementations of SOA security standards. You will need to augment your ESB with a security appliance that specializes in SOA security. Or, you can extend the vendor implementations with your own code.	Examples of ESB are BEA AquaLogic Service Bus and IBM WebSphere ESB. Example of specialized security appliances are IBM DataPower XML Security Gateway, Cisco AON Modules, Reactivity XML Gateway, Layer 7 SecureSpan XML Firewall.

These are only some of the options. No doubt as the tools and frameworks mature, you will have even more options. You will need a good understanding of security issues and the strengths and weaknesses of different security strategies in order to pick the right tools and technologies. That understanding is what we seek to provide in this book.

1.7 *Summary*

SOA is changing long-standing assumptions about how applications are used and combined, and these changes impact the ways in which we can secure applications.

Traditionally, functional capabilities of an application were by and large only available within the context of that application. Other applications could not easily reuse them, either because they were not designed to be reusable or because technologies used by different applications did not work well together. This fact slowed the pace at which IT departments in enterprises can respond to ever-changing needs of businesses.

SOA fixes this problem by asserting that the capabilities of an application must be exposed as "services" that can be easily reused by other applications. But in the process, SOA opens a new can of worms with respect to security. As we explained in this chapter, traditional approaches to addressing different aspects of security do not work well in a world where application, technology, and enterprise boundaries are rendered insignificant by SOA.

Security becomes a serious concern for enterprises seeking to adopt SOA on a large scale. To guarantee security, people naturally tend to be conservative and impose cumbersome restrictions on the use of services. Such an approach negates the benefits of SOA. Fortunately, there are new approaches enabled by SOA that can ensure security without diluting the advantages SOA can bring.

In this book, we present three new approaches to security. The first uses message-level security instead of transport-layer security to ensure confidentiality and integrity of data even when multiple parties are involved in a message exchange. The second looks upon security itself as a service in order to decouple security logic from applications. The third uses declarative security to guarantee interoperability and manageability. Elements of these approaches are present in most commercial, open-source, or home-grown solutions.

Naturally, you need to know about the new tools, standards, and technologies that make these three new approaches possible. In the rest of the book, we will introduce all of these with working examples. Along the way, we will also describe several simple techniques that solve specific small problems.

In the next chapter, we will cover the basics of SOA, where you will create and execute your first service. As explained earlier, you will learn the theory followed by actual code that you can modify and see in action.

Suggestions for further reading

- "Reference Model for Service Oriented Architecture," OASIS Committee Draft 1.0, February 2006, is available at http://www.oasis-open.org/committees/download.php/16587/wd-soa-rm-cd1ED.pdf.

- "Web Services Architecture," a W3C Working Group Note, is available at http://www.w3.org/TR/2004/NOTE-ws-arch-20040211/.

- *Understanding Enterprise SOA*, by Eric Pulier and Hugh Taylor, published by Manning Publications in November 2005. ISBN: 1932394591.

- "Security in a Web Services World: A Proposed Architecture and Roadmap," a white paper published in 2002 by IBM and Microsoft, is available at http://www.ibm.com/developerworks/library/ws-secmap/.

- Support for declarative security and WS-Policy in BEA WebLogic Server 9.1 is described at http://edocs.bea.com/wls/docs91/webserv/security.html# 210122.

- Support for declarative security in Web Services Enhancements (WSE) 3.0 for Microsoft .NET is described by http://msdn.microsoft.com/webservices/default.aspx?pull=/library/en-us/dnwse/html/newwse3.asp and http://msdn.microsoft.com/webservices/default.aspx?pull=/msdnmag/issues/06/02/wse30/default.aspx.

- Apache WSS4J, a publicly available extension of Apache Axis 1.x to add limited support for security, is available at http://ws.apache.org/wss4j/.

- Apache Rampart, a publicly available extension of Apache Axis2 to add limited support for security, is available at http://ws.apache.org/axis2/modules/rampart/1_0/security-module.html.

- Cisco's Application-Oriented Networking (AON) product page is at http://www.cisco.com/go/aon.

- DataPower (acquired by IBM), Sarvega (acquired by Intel), Layer 7 Technologies, Reactivity (acquired by Cisco), and Forum Systems are some of the firms selling XML security devices. The home pages of these firms are at http://www.datapower.com/, http://www.sarvega.com/, http://www.layer7tech.com/, http://www.reactivity.com/, and http://forumsys.com/ respectively.

2

Getting started with web services

This chapter covers

- XML, SOAP and WSDL basics
- Web services with Apache Axis
- Choices in service design

Chapter 1 described why and how SOA security is different from traditional application security. In this chapter, we are going to learn some of the foundational technical details of SOA, namely web services and SOAP.

Web services provide the most popular approach for implementing SOA. SOAP is the most-supported protocol in web services. It should be no surprise then that security solutions are more widely researched, developed, and implemented for SOAP-based web services. The principles behind the techniques for SOAP security hold good for wider SOA security as well, and the first two parts of this book will almost exclusively assume SOAP-based web services. Therefore, you need to have a good understanding of SOAP and other basic technologies that SOAP relies on to follow this book.

In this chapter, we will introduce the required technology, along with the tools and environment assumed in the sample code included with this book. We will get going by describing how you can set up the tools and environment required by our first example. The example consists of a sample SOAP-based web service and its clients, all developed using Apache Axis, an open-source web services toolkit. After showing you how to run the example, we will dig into the basics needed to understand the example—XML, SOAP, and WSDL. Once you understand the basics, we will return to the example and explain the code. We will then demonstrate interoperability between different web services platforms by showing how you can invoke the sample service (running on Apache Axis) from a client running on a different web services platform (.NET WSE). We will conclude the chapter with a discussion of the choices and challenges frequently faced by architects, designers, and developers when doing real-life SOA implementations.

This chapter is mostly about getting started with SOAP. It does not address any of the security issues in SOA. Readers with hands-on experience in creating and consuming SOAP-based web services can skim through this chapter merely to gain familiarity with the tools.

2.1 Setting up tools and environment

What do we need to create and use a basic web service?

To begin, we need to understand the technologies that make web services possible. XML and SOAP provide the basic technical foundation for web services. Next, we need to choose a programming platform and a toolkit for creating/consuming web services. In this section we will focus on the latter, so that we can illustrate technology basics of web services through hands-on examples in subsequent sections.

2.1.1 *Choosing a platform and a toolkit*

The programming platform you choose for web services depends on a number of factors such as the following:

- Previous experience with the platform
- Availability of toolkits for web services on the platform
- Availability of trained developers at affordable rates
- Synergy with other choices made for the project

The choice of a programming platform for web services is not as critical as in traditional application development, since no matter what choice we make, we expect our services/clients to interoperate well with those written on other platforms. After all, that is the promise of open standards-based web services.

In fact, you may even decide to use multiple platforms and toolkits in your implementations. For example, you may decide to use .NET for your clients and J2EE for your service implementations.

The current mainstream choices for the programming platform are .NET and J2EE. For the purposes of this book, we are interested in choosing open-source tools that allow you, the reader, to try out all the examples by yourself. That restricts our choice to the J2EE platform.

Apache Software Foundation (ASF) provides many of the popular open-source tools needed for implementing and consuming web services in Java. Apache Axis is at the center of those offerings. Axis implements SOAP and makes it possible to plug in support for protocols built on SOAP. All the examples in this book will assume Axis as the SOAP engine. There are of course other J2EE-based implementations that support SOAP. Most J2EE application servers come with one. For example, BEA WebLogic and IBM WebSphere come with their own SOAP engines.

The Java Community Process (JCP) is working to standardize on vendor-neutral Java APIs for web services. Most of these standards, except for the basic ones such as Java API for XML-based RPC (JAX-RPC), Java API for XML Messaging (JAXM), and SOAP with Attachments API for Java (SAAJ), are still on the drawing board. We will use Java vendor-neutral APIs in our examples as much as possible, but when we cannot, we will rely on particular open-source implementations. For example, instead of using Axis native APIs, we will stick to the standard JAX-RPC API when illustrating RPC with SOAP.

Even if you are not using the J2EE platform or Apache Axis, the examples in this book should still be useful to you as guidance in creating similar solutions. First, let's get started with Axis.

2.1.2 *Getting started with Apache Axis*

In this section we provide you with the information needed to quickly set up Apache Axis and run an example web service. All it takes is a few steps. First, we will install the prerequisites. Next, we will install Apache Axis. Finally, we will show how to run the example. We will explain the inner workings of the example in the subsequent sections. For the present, we will only concentrate on getting the example running.

Installing the prerequisites

Apache Axis needs JDK and Tomcat. In addition to these, our example needs JUnit and Ant. Table 2.1 shows the details required to download and install the correct version of all these.

Table 2.1   Prerequisites for running examples in this book

Tool	Version	URL to download from	Notes
Java SE Development Kit (JDK)	5.x (also referred to as 1.5.x)	For Windows/Linux /Solaris: http://java.sun.com/j2se/ 1.5.0/download.jsp For Mac OS X: http://developer.apple.com/ java/download/	JDK 1.4.x would work as well; axis configuration just becomes more complex.
Tomcat	5.5.x	http://tomcat.apache.org/	You have the option of downloading the .exe (for Windows) or .zip for all the platforms, including Windows. These instructions assume that you downloaded a zip and extracted it to a directory of your preference. 1. Open a command prompt and change directory to `apache-tomcat-*` 2. To start Tomcat, run `bin/startup.bat` if you are on Windows. On other platforms, run `bin/startup.sh` instead. 3. You can verify that tomcat is running by visiting http://127.0.0.1:8080/ as tomcat listens on port 8080 by default.
Ant	1.6.x	http://ant.apache.org/	Download a zip archive containing Ant's binary distribution and extract files to a location of your preference. Then: 1. Complete the installation using instructions found in `docs/manual/ install.html`. 2. Test Ant by running the command `ant -help`

continued on next page

Table 2.1 Prerequisites for running examples in this book *(continued)*

Tool	Version	URL to download from	Notes
JUnit	3.8.x	http://sourceforge.net/ projects/junit	Extract JUnit zip archive into a directory of your preference. Copy `junit.jar` to the `lib` folder under Ant.

Once the prerequisites are set up, the next step is to install Axis.

Installing Axis

Table 2.2 provides the instructions for setting up Axis.

Table 2.2 Instructions for installing Axis

Step	Action	How to
1	Set up the prerequisites	See table 2.1 for instructions
2	Download Axis 1.x	Download a binary distribution of Axis as a zip file from http://ws.apache.org/axis/. Extract the archive to a location of your preference.
3	Add Axis as a web application in Tomcat	1. Copy or move the `webapps/axis` folder found under your Axis location as a subfolder of `webapps` under your Tomcat location. 2. Restart Tomcat by running `shutdown` and `startup` scripts (`.bat` files if you are using Windows and `.sh` files if you are on Linux/Soaris/OS X) found in the `bin` directory of Tomcat.
4	Validate Axis installation	1. Open http://127.0.0.1:8080/axis/happyaxis.jsp in your web browser. This web page will tell you if you are missing any of the required or optional jars. 2. Axis provides a link for downloading a jar whenever a required or optional jar is found to be missing. Download the missing (required) jars and add them to `webapps/axis/WEB-INF/lib/` under your Tomcat location. 3. Restart Tomcat and check again to make sure that the installation is successful.

Now that Axis is installed, the next step is to set up the examples.

Setting up the examples

All the examples in this book come packaged with an Ant script. Use the instructions in table 2.3 to set up the examples.

Table 2.3 Instructions for setting up examples

Step	Action	How to
1	Download examples archive	Download the examples archive from http://www.manning.com/kanneganti/. Extract it to a location of your choice.
2	Configure build script	Edit the `build.properties` file in the top level directory and customize as necessary. The questions that precede each property assignment and the sample values will guide you in choosing the right values.
3	Deploy examples in Axis	Run the command `ant deploy`.
4	Restart Tomcat	Run `shutdown` and `startup` scripts (`.bat` files if you are using Windows and `.sh` files if you are on Linux/Solaris/OS X) found in the `bin` directory of Tomcat.

Let's now see how you can run the first example.

Running the first example

We now have Axis up and running with all the examples deployed. Table 2.4 shows how we can invoke our first sample web service.

Table 2.4 Instructions for running example 1

Step	Action	How to
1	Set up a monitoring mechanism to record and display all the network traffic to and from Tomcat.	1. Run the command `ant tcpmon`. It will run a proxy on port 8000 that relays requests and response messages to their respective destinations after displaying them in a GUI. 2. In tcpmon window, check the box marked "XML format" since we are going to be looking at the XML traffic.
2	Invoke example web service	Run the command `ant demo -Dexample.id=1`. This results in the invocation of an example web service via the proxy we set up in the step 1.

If all went well, you should see the message BUILD SUCCESSFUL along with some recorded network traffic in the tcpmon window. Look at the recorded network traffic to figure out what exactly happened. If this is the first time you are looking at SOAP, you will get a general feel for how SOAP over HTTP looks.

Figure 2.1 shows a screenshot of tcpmon after you are done with the example.

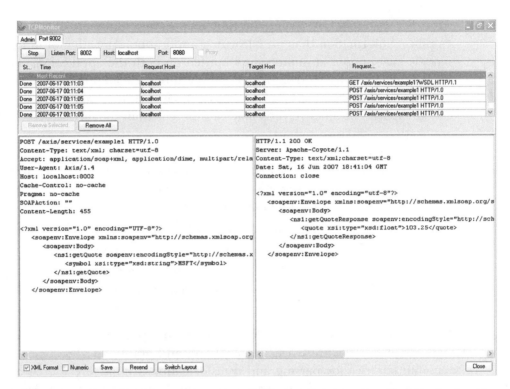

Figure 2.1 Screenshot of `tcpmon` showing the SOAP request and response messages captured in example 1. `tcpmon` is a tool available with Apache Axis to inspect messages received and sent by a service. It acts like a proxy, relaying requests and responses to their respective destinations after displaying them in the GUI.

The rest of this chapter will take advantage of this example to dig more into basic XML and SOAP concepts.

2.2 XML basics

Given that you are reading a book on SOA security, you may already be familiar with XML. XML is everywhere we look in modern integration practice. XML is quite often introduced and seen as a document format—as a generalization of HTML or as a variant of SGML (a standard format for encoding electronic texts). But that is not the most interesting way to look at XML for SOA practitioners.

For us, XML is the common denominator format for data exchange between applications. Mismatch of data models and data formats is one of the biggest challenges of integration. Different applications will have different models of data. For example, an HR application may have a different data model for employee information than an e-learning application. Any attempt to unify the models may impose an unnecessary burden on both the applications. Furthermore, when exchanging data between applications, each application needs data in a format of its own liking. For example, the format in which your CRM application exports customer records may be different from the format your logistics application accepts for import.

When we integrate different applications, we may need to translate data from one model and format into another. If the data formats are arbitrary, we will be forced to write parsers for each data format, which requires good programming skills. So, what we need is a standard format that has two properties:

1   The format should be expressive enough to serve multiple applications. That is, the data structures that the format can express (lists, trees, graphs, maps, and so on) should be sufficient for any application.

2   The format should allow generic and reusable libraries for parsing and transformation.

XML is a format that solves both these problems to a large extent. It supports standard data structures such as lists, trees, and graphs. It allows generic and reusable libraries for parsing and transformation. Almost every programming language in use for business applications supports at least two varieties of XML parsers and one standard mechanism for transforming XML. We will elaborate on these parsing and transforming mechanisms in the later section.

In this section, we will introduce all aspects of XML that are required for understanding the material in the rest of the book. We're going to cover quite a bit in this section, so if you are new to XML, get ready for a whirlwind tour. We'll discuss:

- Use of XML to represent arbitrary data structures
- How to avoid naming conflicts using XML namespaces
- XML Schema Definition (XSD)
- XML processing with DOM API
- XPath expressions to query XML content

We will begin our tour with a description of how XML can be used to format arbitrary data structures.

2.2.1 *XML data format*

Consider the following XML:

```
Listing 2.1   A sample XML document
```

```
<Envelope>
  <Header>
    <Security>
      <UsernameToken>
        <Username>              A start-tag
          roy                   starts an
        </Username>             element        Text value within
        <Password                              an element
          Type="PasswordDigest"
        >                       An end-tag ends an element
          YmVycjFrYWJ1cw==
        </Password>             An attribute is a
      </UsernameToken>          name-value pair
    </Security>
  </Header>
  <Body>
    <getQuote>
      <symbol>TOW</symbol>
    </getQuote>
  </Body>
</Envelope>
```

It is easy to see that this XML document in listing 2.1 resembles a tree, as shown in figure 2.2. All the items that make up an XML document can be thought of as nodes in a tree. This includes elements, attributes, text values within the elements, and whatever else you find in XML documents. For example, comments too are nodes in the tree.

The two constraints that a *well-formed* XML document must satisfy are completely analogous to the two constraints a tree must satisfy. A tree should have:

1 One and only one root node.
2 One and only one path from the root to every node in the tree.

A well-formed XML document should have the following properties:

1 It should have only one root element.
2 If an element's start tag lies within the content of another element, its end tag must also lie within that element.

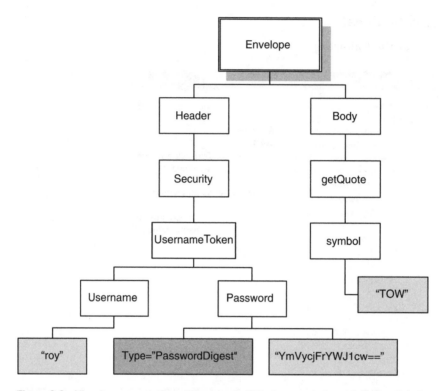

Figure 2.2 **Visual representation of the sample XML document shown in listing 2.1. A well-formed XML document can always be represented as a tree. Text literals in the elements become leaf nodes. So do attributes. An attribute node, such as the** Type **node shown here, holds a name and a value. All other items permitted in an XML document become nodes as well. For example, comments become leaf nodes too.**

We can see that the second rule of well-formedness, also known as the containment rule, is equivalent to the second rule that a tree should satisfy. Note the second rule of well-formedness can be reworded as "every non-root element lies completely within the content of one and only one element." That is, every non-root element is a child of one and only parent. There can be one and only one path from the root element to any other element with the XML document.

But is a tree good enough to express more complex data structures such as graphs? For example, can XML be used to represent a dictionary in which terms can be hyperlinked to their meanings every time they appear? The answer is yes—let's see how.

```
<Dictionary>                    | Each entry is
   <entry id="1">          ⊲⏋ identified by an id
      <term>nonplussed</term>
      <meaning>
         To be at a loss as to what to think, say, or do
      </meaning>
   </entry>
   <entry id="2">          ⊲⏋ Start of another entry
      <term>perplexed</term>                              | Cross-reference to
      <meaning>same as <termref ref="1"/></meaning>   ⊲⏋ entry with id=1
   </entry>
</Dictionary>
```

An XML document only looks like a tree syntactically; it may however be capturing semantically more complex structures. A common trick to achieve this is the use of identifier (ID) and identifier reference (IDREF) attributes. In the preceding example, the `ref` attribute of `termref` is an IDREF pointing to an `entry` element by its `id`. So, it is possible to represent using XML data structures more complex than a tree.

2.2.2 XML namespaces

When we use XML as data format, especially for multiple applications, one issue we face is conflicts in names. For example, two data formats might use the `<account-number>` tag to mark up different items. One application may use the tag to mark up a person's bank account number, whereas another may use the same tag to mark up the person's brokerage account number. When we are integrating these data formats into a unified format, we need to disambiguate our usage of such tags. XML namespace provides such a facility.

What is a namespace? Think of it as a clearly identifiable partition of a set of names. Two names, coming from different namespaces, are distinct even if the names are literally the same. This is made possible in XML by letting us prefix every tag name with a namespace identifier. For example, we can distinguish between the bank and brokerage account numbers if the tags that mark them up are prefixed appropriately as in `<bank:account-number>` and `<brokerage:account-number>`.

How can we ensure that two different namespaces aren't identified by the same prefix? For example, more than one banking firm may employ the `bank` prefix to identify its tags. To make sure that the prefix itself is not ambiguous, we bind each namespace prefix to a *Uniform Resource Identifier (URI)*. URIs, by definition, are guaranteed to be globally unique identifiers. For example, in the following XML, the `soapenv` prefix is bound to an URI containing a registered domain name to make sure that the namespace identification is unambiguous.

```
<soapenv:Envelope
  xmlns:soapenv=
    "http://schemas.xmlsoap.org/soap/envelope/"
>
  <soapenv:Body>
    ...
  </soapenv:Body>
</soapenv:Envelope>
```
> **The soapenv prefix is bound to the shown URI**

Namespace prefixes are bound to URIs using attributes prefixed with xmlns. Think of a URI as an opaque string that's unlikely to be chosen by someone else to define their namespaces as well—a globally unique id. Often, people use strings that look like *Uniform Resource Locators (URLs)*. This is primarily because registered domain names are a good way to generate readable globally unique IDs. However, there's no requirement that a URI should look like a URL.

Namespace prefixes can qualify more than just element tags. Attribute names can be qualified as well, as shown for the encodingStyle attribute in the next example.

```
<soapenv:Body>
  <ns1:getQuote
    soapenv:encodingStyle=
      "http://schemas.xmlsoap.org/soap/encoding/"
    xmlns:ns1=
      "http://manning.com/xmlns/samples/soasecimpl">
    ...
  </ns1:getQuote>
</soapenv:Body>
```
> **encodingStyle attribute is in soapenv namespace**

Note that the binding for a prefix is scoped. A binding is only valid within the element on which the binding is shown and its descendants. So, the ns1 prefix in the previous example is only bound to the shown URI within the getQuote element.

It is perfectly acceptable to rebind a previously bound prefix to a new URI. The rebinding will only be effective within the child element on which the binding is shown and its descendants. This scenario occurs when you combine different XML documents into a single document.

A default namespace can be defined as well. A default namespace within an element is defined by setting the xmlns attribute. Let us see how this works using an example.

```
<Envelope
  xmlns="http://schemas.xmlsoap.org/soap/envelope/"
  xmlns:xsd="http://www.w3.org/2001/XMLSchema"
  xmlns:xsi="http://www.w3.org/2001/XMLSchema-instance">
  <Body>
    <ns1:getQuote
```
> **❶ Default namespace declaration**

```
xmlns:soapenv=
  "http://schemas.xmlsoap.org/soap/envelope/"
soapenv:encodingStyle=
  "http://schemas.xmlsoap.org/soap/encoding/"
xmlns:ns1=
  "http://manning.com/xmlns/samples/soasecimpl">
<symbol xmlns=""
  xsi:type="xsd:string">MSFT</symbol>
  </ns1:getQuote>
</Body>
</Envelope>
```

❷ Attributes in soapenv namespace still need prefixes

❸ Previous default namespace declaration is cleared

❶ We can now omit the namespace prefix for `Envelope` and `Body` tags, as the namespace they come from is declared as the default namespace.

❷ The default namespace definition does not apply to attributes. Unqualified attributes always lie in an undefined namespace. That is why we are forced to still define and use the `soapenv` prefix for the `encodingStyle` attribute on `ns1:getQuote`.

❸ What if we want to have an element without any namespace if we already set a default namespace in one of the ancestors? We can do that too, by resetting the default namespace to an empty string, as in the example, where the unqualified `symbol` element has no namespace.

Namespaces no doubt make XML less readable. SOA standards make extensive use of namespaces, and it will be difficult to read and comprehend web services messages without a good understanding of namespaces. One technique is to practice reading XML by filtering out the namespace tags mentally. For example, the preceding XML data without the namespaces will look like this:

```
<Envelope>
  <Body>
    <getQuote encodingStyle=".../soap/encoding/">
      <symbol type="string">MSFT</symbol>
    </getQuote>
  </Body>
</Envelope>
```

Obviously, this snippet of data is not of much use to the computer—but for SOA practitioners, being able to read without the namespaces baggage can be helpful to understand XML data.

2.2.3 *XML schema*

Before we move on, let's back up and remember how we got here. We now have two of the conceptual underpinnings needed to make XML suitable as a common-denominator data format in integration.

1 The concept of "well-formed" XML helps us define the constraints that every XML document from every domain should always satisfy. These constraints help us create tools such as parsers that can deal with all XML documents uniformly.

2 If we think of a collection of all the element and attribute names within an application as its XML vocabulary, the concept of namespaces helps us distinguish terms of one XML vocabulary from another. Namespaces help eliminate confusion when XML is exchanged between applications.

Two additional constructs are clearly needed to ensure applications can indeed integrate via XML exchange.

1 We need a way to clearly specify the contract that an application demands (or provides) when consuming (or producing) XML. Without such a contract, we cannot know if a particular XML document is fit for consumption by an application. Obviously, an application cannot make sense out of arbitrary XML.

2 We need a way to transform (or map) the XML produced by one application to make it fit for consumption by another. Such mapping should support semantic translation from one format to another format.

The first requirement is easy; XSD language and other XML schema languages such as DTD and RELAX NG meet this requirement substantially. XSD, described in detail later, provides a language for specifying the contract an application demands from its XML providers. It answers questions such as what elements can appear, in what hierarchy, and with what content. XSD cannot explicitly spell out the semantics, of course. It cannot express all the constraints on the content either. However, it provides a starting point for assessing the *validity* of an XML document.

The second requirement, namely mapping, is a difficult issue. It involves lot more than simple inferences based on element and attribute names. To map one XML vocabulary into another, we need to know not only the terms but also the semantics of each element and attribute.

Obviously, mapping wouldn't be needed if both applications used the same XML vocabulary and semantics. That usually happens to be the case if both applications are from the same vendor or if adequate standardization of XML vocabularies and semantics has happened within a particular domain. You can see such a standardization with SOAP, which pins down the vocabulary and semantics for use in SOAP servers and clients.

Listing 2.2 shows an extract from an XML schema describing a SOAP 1.1 envelope. We will be discussing SOAP later in this chapter.

Listing 2.2   Extract from the XML schema[1] describing a SOAP 1.1 envelope

```
<xs:schema
  xmlns:xs=
  "http://www.w3.org/2001/XMLSchema"
  xmlns:tns=
    "http://schemas.xmlsoap.org/soap/envelope/"
  targetNamespace=
    "http://schemas.xmlsoap.org/soap/envelope/"
>

  <!-- Envelope, header and body -->
  <xs:element name="Envelope"
    type="tns:Envelope/>

  <xs:complexType name="Envelope" >
    <xs:sequence>
      <xs:element ref="tns:Header"
        minOccurs="0"/>
      <xs:element ref="tns:Body"/>
    </xs:sequence>
    <xs:anyAttribute namespace="##other"
      processContents="lax"/>
  </xs:complexType>

  <xs:element name="Header"
    type="tns:Header"/>

  <xs:complexType name="Header" >
    <xs:sequence>
      <xs:any namespace="##other"
        minOccurs="0" maxOccurs="unbounded"
        processContents="lax"/>
    </xs:sequence>
    <xs:anyAttribute namespace="##other"
      processContents="lax"/>
  </xs:complexType>

  <xs:element name="Body"
    type="tns:Body"/>

  <xs:complexType name="Body" >
    <xs:sequence>
      <xs:any namespace="##any"
        minOccurs="0" maxOccurs="unbounded"
```

1 The targetNamespace declaration

2 Envelope element declaration

3 Envelope type definition

---

[1] This schema is sourced from http://schemas.xmlsoap.org/soap/envelope/ and is copyrighted by Martin Gudgin.

```
        processContents="lax"/>
    </xs:sequence>
    <xs:anyAttribute namespace="##any"
        processContents="lax" >
        <xs:annotation>
          <xs:documentation>
              Prose in the spec does not specify that attributes
              are allowed on the Body element
          </xs:documentation>
        </xs:annotation>
    </xs:anyAttribute>
  </xs:complexType>
  ...
</xs:schema>
```

Here is how you should read this listing.

The `targetNamespace` attribute ❶ on the `schema` element declares the namespace to which types and elements defined by this schema belong. The other two attributes on the `schema` element are simply namespace prefix bindings, as described in the previous section.

The contents of the `schema` element are either element declarations or data type definitions. In ❷, the `Envelope` element is declared as an instance of the `Envelope` data type. The `Envelope` data type is itself defined in ❸. According to the definition shown in ❸, an instance of the `Envelope` data type (such as the `Envelope` element declared in ❷) can have a optional `Header` element before a `Body` element that must always be present in an envelope. (Note that `minOccurs` and `maxOccurs` attributes on an `xs:element` default to 1.) In addition, any attribute from a namespace other than the `targetNamespace` of this schema is allowed on an instance of the `Envelope` data type.

Subsequent to ❸, we see the same pattern repeating. The `Header` and `Body` elements are declared to be of types `Header` and `Body`, respectively. The definitions for the `Header` and `Body` types describe the attributes and the content instances of these data types can/must have.

We also see that XSD allows in-line annotations that can be used to describe the contents of a schema.

As you can see, XSD specifies the syntactic structure of an XML document only. For example, the preceding specification does not tell us what goes in the body and what goes in the header. It is good enough for several purposes—notably for specifying abstract types in WSDL, which we will be using later for describing web services.

2.2.4 *Processing XML*

A common denominator data format such as XML should be easy to create, parse, and modify. In this section, we will very briefly mention some of the options available to application developers for processing XML. We will also show an example using W3C DOM, an API almost all the examples in this book rely on for XML processing. The material in this section is too brief to be sufficient if you have no prior experience in processing XML. The "Suggestions for further reading" section at the end of this chapter lists books and online resources you can use to learn more about XML processing.

Different applications will have different needs when processing XML. Performance may be critical for some applications, whereas ease or speed of development may be more important for others. Given this, multiple XML processing libraries are available from which application developers can pick the one that best fits their needs.

Broadly, XML processing libraries can be classified into two categories.

- Those that create or load the entirety of data in an XML document into memory. Document Object Model (DOM) APIs standardized by W3C (across multiple languages including Java) are most popular for libraries that create or load the entirety of the XML document in memory.

- Those that produce/consume the documents incrementally. These are commonly referred to as *stream-based* or *streaming* processors. Simple API for XML (SAX) and Streaming API for XML (StAX) are two different standard APIs for libraries that allow incremental parsing of documents.

DOM-based processors are obviously heavy on memory usage and not particularly suitable for server-side applications that need to concurrently process a large number of XML documents. However, they are still used in a large number of server-side applications, because processing logic in most applications is too complex to be implemented using a pure stream-based processor. For example, Apache Axis 1.x, the SOAP toolkit we introduced in section 2.1, uses DOM processing. Axis 2.x (which is still in the works at the time of writing this chapter) moves away from DOM to provide better performance.

Because most example code in this book relies on DOM APIs, we provide a very brief overview of DOM APIs here. This introduction is limited to the bare minimum required to understand the sample code in this book. You should refer to other books and online resources for a more comprehensive introduction to DOM APIs.

Basic DOM classes and interfaces can be found in the `org.w3c.dom` package. DOM looks upon an XML document as a tree of `Node` instances. Everything in a document tree is a `Node`—be it an element, attribute, text, comment, or the document itself. To be more precise, `Node` is a Java interface implemented by classes such as `Element`, `Attr` (attribute), `Text`, `Comment`, and `Document`.

The root element of the tree can be accessed using the `getDocumentElement()` method of a `Document` instance. You can traverse from any node in the tree to every other node using methods such as `getParentNode()`, `getChildNodes()`, `getPreviousSibling()`, and `getNextSibling()`.

Attributes are not considered to be child nodes of the element they belong to. To get the attributes defined for an element, use the `getAttributes()` method to get a `NamedNodeMap`. To find the element node an attribute node belongs to, use the `getOwnerElement()` method.

Namespace URI and local name of an element or an attribute can be queried using `getNamespaceURI()` and `getLocalName()`. The `getNodeValue()` method returns the character data in text or comment nodes, and attribute value in the case of `Attr` nodes. To get the text content in an element, one needs to iterate through the child nodes and concatenate the text content under each of them unless they happen to be comments or processing instructions. The type of a node can always be determined using `getNodeType()`.

Here is some sample code to give you a taste of DOM-based XML processing. The method in listing 2.3 locates a child element given its parent and name.

Listing 2.3 Locating a named child element under a given DOM element

```
public static Element locateChildDOMElement
    (Element parent, String childNsUri,
     String childLocalName) {
    NodeList children =  parent.getChildNodes();      ❶ Get child
    int numChildren = children.getLength();              node list

    for (int i=0; i < numChildren; i++) {    ◁─┘  ❷ Iterate over
                                                     child node list

        Node child = children.item(i);
        if (child.getNodeType() != Node.ELEMENT_NODE) {    ❸ Filter out
            continue;                                         children that are
        }                                                     not elements
        Element childElement = (Element) child;

        if (childNsUri.equals(child.getNamespaceURI()) &&    ❹ Match child
            childLocalName.equals(child.getLocalName())) {      element name
            return childElement;                                against given
        }                                                       name
```

```
        }
        return null;
    }
```

In this example, we are defining a helper method named `locateChildDOMElement` to locate a child element with the given name (that is, with the given namespace URI and given local name) under the given parent.

We first get the list of child nodes using the `getChildNodes()` method ❶. This method returns a `NodeList` whose length can be determined using `getLength()`. We then iterate over each of the child nodes ❷ to find the desired child element.

As we are looking only for a child element, we need to skip over child nodes (such as comments) that are not elements ❸. We retrieve the i-th item in the `children NodeList` using `item(i)` and check its type using `getNodeType()`.

For each child element, we compare its namespace URI and the local name against the desired values. `getNamespaceURI()` and `getLocalName()` retrieve the namespace URI and local name of a node ❹. If a matching element is found, it is returned. If we exhaust all the child elements without finding a match, we return `null`.

As you can see, the DOM API is quite simple to use. However, it is quite verbose, not to mention tedious to work with, especially when all you want to do is identify and extract a specific item from an XML document. XPath, an expression language for identifying specific parts of an XML document, can remove some of this tedium. We will introduce XPath next.

2.2.5 *XPath*

When developing XML applications, one often encounters the need to clearly identify specific portions of an XML document. For example, when we selectively encrypt or sign parts of a SOAP message, there is a need to declare exactly which parts of the message have been encrypted/signed. The same need arises when transforming an XML document or selectively validating a portion of it. When transforming, we need to identify which portions of the source document need to be mapped into the destination document. When selectively validating portions of an XML document, we need the ability to point out exactly which fragment or set of fragments needs to be validated.

XPath provides a standard mechanism for identifying parts of an XML document. It takes advantage of the fact that XML documents resemble trees structurally. A *node* in a document can be identified using the *path* to that node from the root or any other previously identified node. If the path is from the root node, it is known as an *absolute path*. Otherwise, a path is said to be *relative* to the *current context*. Let us look at a few easy examples.

- `/soapenv:Envelope/soapenv:Header` is an absolute path because it provides the path from the root (represented by the leading `/`) to the `Header`.
- If `soapenv:Body` is the current context, `ns1:getQuote/@soapenv:encoding-Style` refers to the `encodingStyle` attribute on the `Quote` element. The symbol `@` is used to refer to attributes.

As you can see, a path is made up of a series of steps. In both examples, the steps are away from the tree's root toward the leaves. As trees in programming books are always drawn with the root at the top and leaves at the bottom, we can say that each step in these examples is down the tree. Can we go up as well? Of course!

- To go one step up, to the parent of the current node, use `..` (two dots).
- To get to any ancestor, prefix the step with `ancestor::`. For example, to reach the `Body` node from anywhere beneath it, you can say `ancestor::soapenv:Body`. Prefixes such as this that allow you to specify the direction of traversal are referred to as *axis specifiers*.
- Similarly, you can go sideways using the axis specifiers `sibling::`, `following::`, and `preceding::`.

Notice that the axis specifiers not only allow you to traverse the tree in directions other than down, but also to travel more than one node at a time. When we search for the `Body` element from anywhere beneath it using `ancestor::soapenv:Body`, we may be traveling over multiple nodes to reach the `Body` node. Can we gallop the same way down the tree?

- We can travel one or more levels down the tree using two slashes instead of one. For example, `//ns1:getQuote` searches the `getQuote` element anywhere below the root.
- Just as in the case of other axes, we can use the `descendant::` axis specifier. For example, `/descendant::ns1:getQuote` is equivalent to `//ns1:getQuote`.

We now have the machinery to move around the tree and identify elements and attributes by their names. What if we want to select a particular element when there is more than one element with the same name in the current context? For example, how do we choose a particular `Security` element in the following `Header`?

```
<soapenv:Envelope
  xmlns:soapenv="http://schemas.xmlsoap.org/soap/envelope/"
  xmlns:wsse="http://schemas.xmlsoap.org/ws/2002/04/secext">
  <soapenv:Header >
    <wsse:Security>
      ...
    </wsse:Security>
    <wsse:Security
      soapenv:actor="http://schemas.xmlsoap.org/soap/actor/next">
      ...
    </wsse:Security>
    <wsse:Security
      soapenv:actor="http://manning.com/xmlns/samples/soasecimpl/hub">
      ...
    </wsse:Security>
  </soapenv:Header>
  <soapenv:Body>
    ...
  </soapenv:Body>
</soapenv:Envelope>
```

We can pick a `Security` element by its position. For example, if `/soapenv:Envelope/soapenv:Header` is the current context, use `wsse:Security[1]` to pick the first `Security` element.

But the selection criteria we need to express are often much more complicated. XPath provides a detailed expression syntax that can be used to specify predicates. For example, to select a `Security` element whose `actor` attribute has a particular value, we can use the XPath:

```
wsse:Security[
  @soapenv:actor="http://manning.com/xmlns/samples/soasecimpl/hub"
]
```

We can use `Boolean` algebra as well. To select all `Security` elements whose `actor` attribute has one of two values, we can use the XPath:

```
wsse:Security[
  @soapenv:actor="http://manning.com/xmlns/samples/soasecimpl/hub"
  or
  @soapenv:actor="http://schemas.xmlsoap.org/soap/actor/next"
]
```

XPath also defines a few functions to help in creating more complex expressions. To select `Security` elements that do not have an `actor` attribute, we can use `wsse:Security[count(@soapenv:actor)=0]`, or more succinctly, `wsse:Security[not(@soapenv:actor)]`.

A more exhaustive description of XPath is outside the scope of this book. The description found here should, however, be sufficient for understanding its use in the rest of the book.

This concludes our discussion of XML basics. XML seems simple at first glance, yet is surprisingly rich and complex. In spite of this complexity, XML has gained popularity, as a number of libraries and tools are available in almost every programming language to help tackle the complexity in XML.

The near-universal acceptance of XML as a common denominator data format led to the development of XML-based integration technologies. The B2Bi[2] community was the first one to adopt XML in a big way for integration. Several B2Bi protocols such as RosettaNet and ebXML use XML messaging for integration between trading partners. Their success caught the attention of the distributed computing[3] community as well. This led to the development of XML-based distributed computing protocols such as XML-RPC and SOAP. With the backing of industry heavyweights such as Microsoft and IBM, SOAP gained a lot of momentum. Over time, SOAP became independent of its roots in distributed computing and is currently used for distributed computing as well as message-based integration. SOAP inspired the idea of web services, which in turn inspired the idea of SOA. As you can see, XML played a very influential role in the evolution of SOA.

Some of the material you have seen in this section, such as XML namespaces, is essential for anyone trying to understand SOAP and related technologies such as WSDL. The rest of the material we have covered in this section will be helpful for you to follow the code listings in this and later chapters. Now that we have covered XML basics, we can turn our attention to understanding the basics of SOAP.

---

[2] B2Bi stands for Business-to-Business integration. B2Bi involves integration of the applications in an enterprise with the applications of its supply chain partners—be they suppliers, distributors, or other businesses that are customers. B2Bi is almost always implemented through exchange of messages (commonly referred to as "documents" in B2Bi) over transports such as FTP and HTTP. Popular B2Bi protocols are EDI, AS2, RosettaNet, and ebXML.

[3] Distributed computing technologies strive to make code in one application usable by code in another application running on a remote machine. Examples of distributed computing technologies include DCOM (Distributed Component Object Model) and CORBA (Common Object Request Broker Architecture).

2.3 SOAP basics

SOAP is the core protocol that underlies most web services implementations. In this section, we'll cover basic SOAP concepts. In particular, we will describe:

- SOAP message exchange model
- Anatomy of a SOAP message
- RPC with SOAP[4]
- Use of SOAP for document exchange between applications
- Error (fault) handling in SOAP

Let's start with the first of these—the SOAP message exchange model.

2.3.1 SOAP message exchange model

SOAP provides a standard model for exchange of messages between applications. Key elements of this model are:

- A SOAP message is a transmission from one endpoint to another. Two tranxxsmissions can be combined synchronously or asynchronously to make a request/response. Similarly, multiple transmissions can be combined to make a conversation.

- A SOAP message is created by wrapping any application message with a standard XML-based envelope structure. The envelope structure enables applications to express semantics such as what is in the message and how it is encoded.

- All error handling is carried out using a standard SOAP Fault mechanism.

- When making RPC calls and responses, application messages are structured using the conventions defined by SOAP.

- Data within the application message may be serialized using a standard SOAP-defined encoding. Other encodings may be declared and used as well.

---

[4] RPC is one of the first technologies that simplified distributed computing. It provides a way to invoke a function on the remote machine, as though it were available in the same process. Toolkits generate the code that does the heavy work: argument marshaling, sending over the wire, getting the response, and returning to the function. Since XML did not exist at that time, the protocol between RPC server and RPC client is implementation-specific.

As you can see, SOAP is a higher-level protocol than application-layer transport protocols such as Hypertext Transfer Protocol (HTTP). A SOAP message can hence be carried as a payload of any application transport. For example, applications can exchange SOAP messages using Java Messaging Service (JMS) or even File Transport Protocol (FTP).

The current version of the SOAP specification is 1.2. WS-I, an organization working to enhance interoperability among web services implementations, is basing its work on SOAP 1.1. They are tightening the specifications of basic web services standards under the name Basic Profile. Given that more than 170 organizations including Microsoft and IBM are driving WS-I, it is quite likely that the focus will remain on SOAP 1.1 for a while to come. For good reason, the examples shown here are all based on 1.1. We will point out any major changes from 1.1 to 1.2 as we discuss the details.

2.3.2 *Anatomy of a SOAP message*

SOAP messages are XML documents with the following structure:

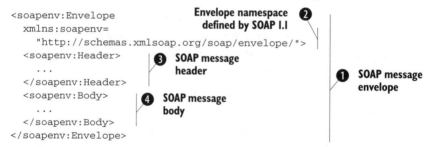

The root element of a SOAP message must always be an Envelope ❶ element that is defined in a namespace whose URI ❷ is defined by the SOAP specification. The Envelope element consists of an optional Header element ❸ followed by a mandatory Body element ❹.

The Header element ❸ may contain one or more entries that can be used to extend SOAP and/or express additional application semantics. For example, user credentials and security assertions may be carried using header entries to extend SOAP for security. Similarly, a correlation identifier may be carried within a Header element to provide request/response semantics. We'll discuss the use of Header entries extensively in the next chapter.

The Body element ❹ is where the application messages are carried. The only constraint on the content of a Body element cannot carry free text by itself. It should have only XML elements as its content. It is also possible to have no text at all. In other words, the `Body` element cannot carry free text by itself; at least, the text to be carried should be encapsulated in an XML element.

How to interpret the content of a SOAP message `Body` is up to the receiving application. In the next two sections, we will describe two popular ways of interpreting SOAP `Body` content.

2.3.3 *RPC with SOAP*

As we discussed in chapter 1, SOA makes distributed computing possible with services that can be invoked anywhere. Traditionally, such distribution happened with RPC. In this section, we will see how SOAP can be used for RPC. In the next section, we will see how SOAP can be used for message-based integration.

In SOA, applications make it possible for their capabilities to be integrated with those of others by exposing their capabilities as services. For the sake of simplicity, let's say that an application wants to expose one of its functions as a service that other applications can invoke. What should it do so that other applications can invoke such a function?

- It must specify a function name.
- It must specify the *signature* of the function. The signature specifies the types of the arguments and the return value.
- It must specify the application instance. Remember that there can be many instances of the same application providing the service.

Obviously, the service and clients need to agree on a consistent way of representing or *encoding* this information. Let us see how this works with an example.

Consider the following request/response transmissions:

```
<soapenv:Body>
  <ns1:getQuote
    soapenv:encodingStyle="..."
    xmlns:ns1="...">
    <symbol xsi:type="xsd:string">MSFT</symbol>
  </ns1:getQuote>
</soapenv:Body>
```
Body of a SOAP request

```
<soapenv:Body>
  <ns1:getQuoteResponse
    soapenv:encodingStyle="..."
    xmlns:ns1="...">
    <quote xsi:type="xsd:float">103.25</quote>
  </ns1:getQuoteResponse>
</soapenv:Body>
```
Body of a SOAP response

What these messages do is self-evident. The first message is a remote call to get the quote for the symbol MSFT, and the second message is the result of that call.

The target instance in which a function is to be invoked is identified by a URI. The SOAP message itself does not carry the URI. The underlying application transport is relied upon to carry the URI instead. For example, if we use HTTP to carry these messages, the URI may be carried using the target URL of the request and/or an additional header named SOAPAction, as shown in listing 2.4.

Listing 2.4   A SOAP RPC request sent over HTTP

```
POST /axis/services/example1 HTTP/1.0                    ◁─┐  HTTP command,
Content-Type: text/xml; charset=utf-8                       target URI, and
SOAPAction: ""                        │ HTTP headers         protocol version
Content-Length: ...

<soapenv:Envelope ...>
  <soapenv:Body>
    <ns1:getQuote ...>
      <symbol xsi:type="xsd:string">MSFT</symbol>       SOAP message as
    </ns1:getQuote>                                      payload of POST
  </soapenv:Body>
</soapenv:Envelope>
```

The function call is represented as a single structure. The function name becomes the name of the structure, and each of the function's input and in/out parameters become top-level members of the structure. For example, in listing 2.4, getQuote is the function name, symbol is an input parameter, and there are no in/out parameters.

Similarly, the function's response is modeled as a single structure. The return value along with the function's out and in/out parameters, if any, become top-level members of the response structure. The names, types, and order of parameters in the function's signature are preserved within the call/response structures. The return value is always the first top-level member of the response structure.

SOAP encoding

When using SOAP for RPC, the function call and response structures can be encoded using any scheme understood by the service and its clients. The scheme used for encoding data within any element of the SOAP message may be indicated by adding the SOAP-defined encodingStyle attribute to that element. The value of this attribute should be a list of one or more URIs that indicate the encoding schemes used within the element. When decoding, the receiver should try each of the schemes listed in the same order as they appear.

Just like XML namespace prefix bindings, an encoding style holds good for all content within the element unless it is specifically overridden by a different or empty `encodingStyle` attribute on a subelement. No encoding is assumed by default.

SOAP defines one possible RPC encoding. It is identified by the URI: `http://schemas.xmlsoap.org/soap/encoding/` and is referred to as *SOAP encoding*. For example, the RPC request and response payloads shown in the beginning of this section use SOAP encoding.

SOAP encoding defines rules for serializing[5] simple and compound values. Compound values are formed by combining simple values that can be addressed by index (as in arrays) or by name. Serialization of complex object graphs is made possible by what are known as `multiRefs`. The easiest way to understand `multiRef` is by looking at an example, such as the one in listing 2.5.

Listing 2.5   Example illustrating the use of `multiRef` in SOAP encoding

```
<soapenv:Body>
  <ns1:createMarketOrder
    soapenv:encodingStyle=                          Declaring SOAP encoding
      "http://schemas.xmlsoap.org/soap/encoding/"    as encodingStyle
    xmlns:ns1="...">
    <symbol xsi:type="xsd:string">GOOG</symbol>
    <buy href="#id0"/>              ◁─┐  Referring to multiRef
    <quantity href="#id1"/>      ❶      with id=id0
  </ns1:createMarketOrder>
  <multiRef
    id="id0"
    soapenc:root="0"
    soapenv:encodingStyle="..."
    xsi:type="xsd:boolean"
    xmlns:soapenc=
      "http://schemas.xmlsoap.org/soap/encoding/">
    true          ◁─┐  Value of multiRef
  </multiRef>   ❷      with id=id0
  <multiRef
    id="id1"
    soapenc:root="0"              ◁─┐  Node is not a
    soapenv:encodingStyle="..."  ❸      true root
```

---

[5] Serialization (or marshaling) is the process of converting a data structure into a sequence of bytes or characters.

```
        xsi:type="xsd:int"
        xmlns:soapenc="...">
        200
      </multiRef>
    </soapenv:Body>
```

In this example, note the use of the `id` attribute ❷ to assign an identifier to a `multiRef` and `href` attribute to refer to it elsewhere ❶. The `soapenc:root` attribute is used ❸ to distinguish true roots of the encoded object graph from others. That is, when it is 0, the node is assumed to not be the root of the object.

As you might already have observed, use of `multiRefs` clearly makes SOAP messages hard to read and understand by simple inspection. However, if we allow the serialization of complex data types commonly found in real-world applications, we find a need for `multiRefs`. Obviously, the use of tools is a must for managing encoding and decoding data structures in RPC calls. Still, tools cannot solve all problems. Data structures created in one programming language may not have good equivalents in other programming languages. In such cases, RPC is clearly not the best way to integrate two applications via SOAP. In the next section, we present an alternative technique to RPC.

2.3.4 *Document exchange with SOAP*

As we discussed earlier, message-based integration is as popular as RPC, if not moreso, for application integration. SOAP accommodates both approaches to integration under one model. The body of a SOAP message can carry any XML-based content as the payload. For example, a RosettaNet document can be embedded as the body of a SOAP message.

Let us rewrite the SOAP Body from the RPC example in the previous section (see listing 2.5) to use document exchange instead. The document we are submitting is called `MarketOrderSubmission`, which specifies what stock to buy or sell and in what quantity. It might appear similar to the RPC example—however, the model of programming is different. In RPC, applications invoke functions *on* endpoints, whereas here, the document is sent *to* the endpoint. As such, a data-centric model of processing would use document exchange.

```
    <soapenv:Body>
      <ns2:MarketOrderSubmission>
        <ns2:symbol>GOOG</ns2:symbol>
        <ns2:buyOrSell>buy</ns2:buyOrSell>
        <ns2:quantity>200</ns2:quantity>
```

```
      </ns2: MarketOrderSubmission>
    </soapenv:Body>
```

Request-response is possible too. For example, here is how the SOAP Body may look in response to the MarketOrderSubmission document.

```
<soapenv:Body>
  <ns2:MarketOrderReceipt>
    <ns2:orderId>72379</ns2:orderId>
  </ns2:MarketOrderReceipt>
</soapenv:Body>
```

How should an application respond to a SOAP message if it encounters an error while processing it? You'll find out next.

2.3.5 *SOAP Fault*

SOAP defines a standard SOAP Fault mechanism to communicate error information back to a caller. The mechanism can be used in RPC as well in messaging. Let us start with an example.

```
<soapenv:Envelope ...>
  <soapenv:Body>
    <soapenv:Fault>
      <faultcode>soapenv:Server</faultcode>
      <faultstring>Internal Server Error</faultstring>
      <detail>
        <e:exception
          xmlns:e=
            "http://manning.com/xmlns/samples/soasecimpl/exception">
          <class>java.sql.SQLException</class>
          <message>Database connection lost</message>
        </e:exception>
      </detail>
    </soapenv:Fault>
  </soapenv:Body>
</soapenv:Envelope>
```

As you can see, a Fault element is returned within the Body to indicate that an error has occurred. Contents of the Fault element provide more information about the error.

The faultcode element is a machine-readable indication of what went wrong. A namespace-qualified name is what SOAP 1.1 mandates as the value. Table 2.5 shows the four faultcode values predefined in the SOAP 1.1 envelope namespace.

Table 2.5 The four `faultCode` values predefined by SOAP 1.1 specification

SOAP faultcode value	Description
`soapenv:VersionMisMatch`	The SOAP envelope element is not in the expected namespace. This might happen if the sender is assuming a different version of the SOAP spec.
`soapenv:MustUnderstand`	A `Header` entry that was marked as `mustUnderstand` is not understood by the receiver. We will revisit this more in depth when we discuss headers in the chapter 3.
`soapenv:Client`	The client made a mistake in composing the message. For example, the client may have provided no value for a mandatory parameter in a RPC method call.
`soapenv:Server`	The server encountered an internal error. For example, a database connection needed to provide the service might be temporarily down.

SOAP 1.1 allows for a hierarchy of `faultcode` values. To specify an error subclass along with a more generic `faultcode`, SOAP 1.1 recommends the `ns:generic-FC.specificFC` convention. Interoperability experts will discourage you from attempting to extend the four predefined `faultcode` values because two applications can easily use the same subclass to express two semantically different errors. Hierarchical `faultcode` values are however encouraged for `faultcode` values defined in custom namespaces. Listing 2.6 is an example.

Listing 2.6 Example of a SOAP 1.1 Fault

```
<soapenv:Envelope ...>
  <soapenv:Body>
    <soapenv:Fault xmlns:e="...">
      <faultcode>e:Server.Recoverable</faultcode>        Hierarchical faultcode
                                                          in a custom namespace

      <faultstring>
        Recoverable Internal Server Error               ❶ Human readable
      </faultstring>                                       description of the fault

      <detail>
        <e:exception>
          <class>java.sql.SQLException</class>
          <message>                                     ❷ Hierarchical
            Database connection lost. Retry later.         faultcode in
          </message>                                       a custom
        </e:exception>                                      namespace
      </detail>
```

```
    </soapenv:Fault>
  </soapenv:Body>
</soapenv:Envelope>
```

The `faultstring` element ❶ is a description of the error. It is mandatory. An optional `faultactor` element (not shown in the listing, as we have yet to define the concept of an actor; chapter 3 will discuss this concept) takes a URI value to indicate the source of the error. The `detail` element ❷ is reserved and mandatory for errors related to `Body` content.

The SOAP fault mechanism has seen substantial refinement from SOAP 1.1 to SOAP 1.2. Listing 2.7 shows how it looks in SOAP 1.2.

Listing 2.7   Example of a SOAP 1.2 Fault

```
<soapenv:Envelope
  xmlns:soapenv=                                          ❶ SOAP l.2 namespace
    "http://www.w3.org/2003/05/soap-envelope"
  xmlns:e=
    "http://manning.com/xmlns/samples/soasecimpl/exception"
  xmlns:xml=
    "http://www.w3.org/XML/1998/namespace">
<soapenv:Body>
  <soapenv:Fault>

      <soapenv:Code>
        <soapenv:Value>
          soapenv:Sender
        </soapenv:Value>
        <soapenv:Subcode>            ❷ Machine-readable
          <soapenv:Value>              fault description
            e:SQLException
          </soapenv:Value>
        </soapenv:Subcode>
      </soapenv:Code>

      <soapenv:Reason>
        <soapenv:Text xml:lang="en">   ❸ Human-readable
        Internal server error           fault description
        </soapenv:Text>
      </soapenv:Reason>

      <soapenv:Detail>
        <e:exception>
          <class>java.sql.SQLException</class>
          <message>Database connection lost</message>
        </e:exception>
      </soapenv:Detail>
```

```
      </soapenv:Fault>
    </soapenv:Body>
  </soapenv:Envelope>
```

Notice the change in namespace URI ❶ between listings 2.6 and 2.7 to indicate that the latter is a SOAP 1.2-compliant envelope. SOAP 1.1 `faultcode` gives way to a more elaborate `Code` element ❷ in SOAP 1.2.

SOAP 1.1 `faultstring` ❸ gives way to a more elaborate `Reason` element that allows for multilingual error messages through the use of the `xml:lang` attribute.

The `Code` element is a machine-readable indication of what went wrong. The SOAP 1.2 spec adds one more value, `soapenv:DataEncodingUnknown`, to the four predefined `faultcode` values in SOAP 1.1. This code is used if one of the data encodings, declared with URIs as shown previously, is not understood by the application that needs to process the encoded data. In addition, SOAP 1.2 renamed the `soapenv:Client` and `soapenv:Server` values as `soapenv:Sender` and `soapenv:Receiver`, respectively.

Hierarchical error codes are supported by one or more nested `Subcode` elements. There are a few other changes from SOAP 1.1 to SOAP 1.2, some of which can be observed from the previous example. For example, the `soapactor` element is replaced with `Node` and `Role` elements. We'll talk more about them in chapter 8.

So far we have seen how SOAP can be used to communicate between two applications. How does an application know what kind of message to send? In our `getQuote` example, how does the client know that it is supposed to send a stock symbol as a string? We need a way of specifying what the server expects—a contract that the server publishes for the client to use. WSDL serves that purpose for SOAP, and it is the subject for the next section.

2.4 WSDL basics

Formally describing a service helps establish a clear contract between the service and its clients. To describe a service, we need a declarative language. It is common practice in programming systems to generate required procedural code from a single declarative description. Interface Definition Language (IDL) did this job for CORBA and WSDL does it for the web services world. WSDL has a role in SOA security as well, by providing a possible vehicle to carry the security (and other) policies for a service.

WSDL builds upon several other abstractions such as endpoints, ports, and services. All these abstractions support a generic way of specifying the protocols and data formats. To make it easy to understand, we will provide a top-down example-driven explanation for WSDL. Specifically, we'll cover:

- How to declare a service
- The concepts of port type and port
- The concept of a binding

Although WSDL can be used to describe services offered using any protocol and data format (see the callout at the end of this section), we will only focus on the use of WSDL with SOAP as the protocol.

2.4.1 Describing a service with WSDL

The example we use here is available in the examples archive under `code/wsdl/example1.wsdl`. The first point to note from this example is that WSDL uses `<wsdl:definitions>` as the root element. Coming from the bottom of the file, here is the last element:

```
<wsdl:service name="BrokerageService">    ←—❶
  <wsdl:port
    binding="impl:example1SoapBinding"      ❷
    name="example1">
    <wsdlsoap:address
      location="http://..."/>    ←—❸
  </wsdl:port>
</wsdl:service>
```

This element is declaring a service named `BrokerageService` ❶. It contains details about a *port* ❷, and an *address* ❸. WSDL defines a service as collection of *related* ports.

2.4.2 Understanding ports and port types

Think of a port as a specific implementation of an interface (port type), available at a particular address using a particular protocol and a particular data format.

What are related ports? A service may offer the same interface over different protocols. It may even offer a set of complementary interfaces over one or more protocols. Any logical grouping of ports qualifies as a service as long as they are not interdependent.

In the example `BrokerageService`, we can see the address at which a port named `example1` is available ❷, but where's the rest of the information, such as interface (port type) name and protocol used? The `binding` attribute on the `<wsdl:port>` element refers to a previously declared binding element that provides this information.

2.4.3 Understanding bindings

A binding defines the protocol and data format details for all the methods (operations) defined in an interface (port type).

Listing 2.8   WSDL binding in action

```
<wsdl:binding                          ❶ Binding
  name="example1SoapBinding"             definition
  type="impl:Brokerage">

  <wsdlsoap:binding
    style="rpc"                        ❷ Transport
    transport=                           specification
    "http://schemas.xmlsoap.org/soap/http"/>

  <wsdl:operation name="getQuote">     ❸ Details of
                                         operations
    <wsdlsoap:operation soapAction=""/>  ◁─┘

    <wsdl:input name="getQuoteRequest">
      <wsdlsoap:body use="encoded"
        encodingStyle=
          "http://schemas.xmlsoap.org/soap/encoding/"
        namespace=
          "http://manning.com/xmlns/samples/soasecimpl"/>
    </wsdl:input>

    <wsdl:output name="getQuoteResponse">
      <wsdlsoap:body use="encoded"
        encodingStyle="..."
        namespace="..."/>
    </wsdl:output>

  </wsdl:operation>
  ...
</wsdl:binding>
```

In listing 2.8, we see how a binding is defined ❶. The example defines a binding named example1SoapBinding for the impl:Brokerage interface (port type). The binding specifies that it uses SOAP RPC over HTTP ❷ as the transport protocol for operations defined by the interface.

In addition, this binding defines per-operation details such as SOAPAction ❸ and input/output data formats. SOAPAction is an HTTP header that may be used to succinctly convey the intent of a SOAP message. It is useful for HTTP infrastructure elements such as load balancers and routers to act on an HTTP request without having to look into the SOAP message itself.

Although it is obvious from this binding as to what operations constitute the impl:Brokerage interface, it is helpful to define the interface separately. This helps in detecting erroneous bindings, especially if there are multiple bindings for the same interface that can contradict each other as to what operations make up the interface. WSDL refers to an interface and its methods as *port type* and *operations*, respectively. Listing 2.9 shows how a port type is declared.

Listing 2.9 Declaring a port type

```
<wsdl:portType name="Brokerage">           ◄─❶  Declaring port type
   <wsdl:operation name="getQuote"                         ◄┐
      parameterOrder="symbol">                              │
      <wsdl:input message="impl:getQuoteRequest"            │
         name="getQuoteRequest"/>                           │
      <wsdl:output message="impl:getQuoteResponse"       ❷  Declaring each
         name="getQuoteResponse"/>                          operation
   </wsdl:operation>                                        │
                                                            │
   <wsdl:operation name="createLimitOrder"             ◄────┘
      parameterOrder="symbol buy quantity priceLimit">
      <wsdl:input message="impl:createLimitOrderRequest"
         name="createLimitOrderRequest"/>
      <wsdl:output message="impl:createLimitOrderResponse"
         name="createLimitOrderResponse"/>
   </wsdl:operation>

   ...

</wsdl:portType>
```

In this example, we are defining the operations provided by the Brokerage port type ❶. For each operation ❷, we are identifying the input and output message types by reference, indicating that these are request-response operations. We would have omitted the output definition if any of the operations were one-way. For request-response operations, we can add a fault message type as well.

A message defines a named collection of typed parts.

```
<wsdl:message name="createLimitOrderRequest">
   <wsdl:part name="symbol" type="xsd:string"/>
   <wsdl:part name="buy" type="xsd:boolean"/>
   <wsdl:part name="quantity" type="xsd:int"/>
   <wsdl:part name="priceLimit" type="xsd:float"/>
</wsdl:message>
```

In this example, we are defining the names and types of parts that constitute a createLimitOrderRequest message. All the parts in this message use basic types defined in the XSD specification. User-defined types can be used as well, provided they are declared within WSDL by embedding an XSD schema under a <wsdl:types> element.

```
<wsdl:types>
  <xsd:schema>
    ...
  </xsd:schema>
</wsdl:types>
```

Now that you understand how WSDL is written, in the next section we are going to show you how to use WSDL to generate skeletal code for web service implementations and invocations.

> **NOTE** *WSDL is not just for SOAP-based services* WSDL can be used to describe services bound to any protocol and data format, not just SOAP. For example, WSDL can be used to describe the services offered by an Enterprise JavaBean (EJB). WSDL makes this possible by explicitly allowing extensions to describe protocol and data format bindings. Anyone can extend WSDL to describe services provided by existing applications using native protocols and data formats.

2.5 Web services in action with Apache Axis

Now that we understand the basics of XML, SOAP, and WSDL, let's revisit the example in figure 2.1 (hereafter referred to as example 1). The goal is not only to better understand what happened in example 1, but also to see how we went about creating it. In this section, we will walk you through the process of creating and consuming a web service with Apache Axis.

2.5.1 Creating a web service

Example 1 illustrates RPC with SOAP. It illustrates the services a stock brokerage may offer to its customers. We will describe all the steps in creating web services:

- Defining the Java interface for brokerage services
- Converting the service interface into WSDL
- Implementing the service
- Deploying the service

We will also show you, as required, snippets of code for each of these steps.

Defining the service interface

The first step in the process is to identify the interfaces for services we want to offer. In other words, we want to create the WSDL for brokerage services. We can hand-code WSDL, but often, it is more convenient to generate WSDL using a tool. This is especially the case if we have pre-existing applications whose interfaces we wish to make available via SOAP.

Axis provides a `Java2WSDL` tool to generate WSDL from Java interfaces. So, let's first create a Java interface describing the services we want to offer as a brokerage, as shown in listing 2.10.

Listing 2.10 Sample brokerage service

```
package com.manning.samples.soasecimpl.example1;
public interface Brokerage extends java.rmi.Remote {

    public float getQuote(String symbol)      ❶ Provides a quote for
        throws java.rmi.RemoteException;          given symbol

    public String createLimitOrder            ❷ Places a limit order
        (String symbol, boolean buy, int quantity, float priceLimit)
        throws java.rmi.RemoteException;

    public String createMarketOrder           ❸ Places a market order
        (String symbol, boolean buy, int quantity)
        throws java.rmi.RemoteException;
}
```

In this interface, we are describing three methods: getQuote ❶, createLimitOrder ❷, and createMarketOrder ❸. Some methods ❷, ❸ need additional information such as the person placing the order, which is assumed to be available from MessageContext. Because we want to use this interface as the basis for a JAX-RPC service, we follow the JAX-RPC rules by making the interface extend java.rmi.Remote and by declaring that all of the interface methods can potentially throw a java.rmi. RemoteException.

NOTE *Interfaces involving complex data types* Note that all of the methods in the interface defined by listing 2.10 use simple data types such as String and int for input and output. A more realistic implementation would:

- Involve objects such as Quote, Order, and OrderInstruction.
- Provide a lot more methods such as getOrderStatus(orderId) and modifyOrder(orderInstruction).

The use of complex objects as opposed to simple types certainly complicates the process of invoking them via SOAP. In some cases, custom serializers and extractors may have to be written to help Axis determine how to marshal and unmarshal such data types. But as this is simply a brief introduction and not an exhaustive reference on how to do RPC with SOAP using Axis, we will keep it simple.

Now that we have the `Brokerage` interface defined in Java, let's convert it into WSDL.

Converting the interface to WSDL

The Ant script available in the examples archive provides a `java2wsdl` target. Run it with the command `ant java2wsdl`. You should now be able to find the produced `example1.wsdl` under the `build/generated` folder.

The `Java2WSDL` functionality in Axis comes with a minor limitation. As Axis relies on Java reflection to determine the methods declared in the interface, it does not have access to the parameter names in each method. All it can figure out using reflection are the method parameter types and order. So, Axis-produced WSDL uses manufactured names such as `in0` and `in1` for the parameters. If we want to restore the appropriate parameter names so as to make the resulting WSDL more human-readable, we will need to hand-edit the generated WSDL and fix the parameter names. You can observe this by comparing the generated `build/generated/example1.wsdl` with `wsdl/example1.wsdl` found in the examples archive.

Implementing the service

Now that we have declared what the service provides through its interface definition, it is time to implement it. Axis provides a `WSDL2Java` tool to assist in implementing the service and testing it. The Ant script available in the examples archive provides a `wsdl2java` target to use this tool. Run it using the command `ant wsdl2java`. This will produce:

- Server-side artifacts we can use to implement the service
- A deployment descriptor needed to deploy the service on Axis
- Client-side stubs we can use in the next section to consume the service
- A template for JUnit test cases that exercise the service

The folder `build/generated/com/manning/samples/soasecimpl/example1/` contains the generated files. To implement the service, we edit the generated service implementation template, `Example1SoapBindingImpl.java`.

See `java/com/manning/samples/soasecimpl/example1/` in the examples archive for a sample implementation. The implementation class can implement the `javax.xml.rpc.server.ServiceLifecycle` interface if nontrivial initialization and cleanup are needed. For example, the service may need a database connection pool to be initialized before any requests can be served.

Note that the service implementation is completely independent of native Axis APIs; the code is portable to other JAX-RPC-compliant SOAP engines. The deployment descriptors and client-side stubs generated by `WSDL2Java` are, however, Axis specific. This is not a problem, as:

1 Every SOAP toolkit will provide tools similar to `WSDL2Java` to generate the deployment descriptors and client-side stubs.

2 The base interface provided by the generated stubs to the client applications will be the same between all JAX-RPC compliant engines.

The service implementation as well as the client application code can be moved from one JAX-RPC-compliant SOAP toolkit to another simply by regenerating the deployment descriptors and client-side stubs.

Deploying the service

To deploy the service, you will need to make the server-side classes, libraries, and deployment descriptors available to Axis as follows:

1 Start Tomcat in case it not already running.

2 Run the command `ant deploy`. The Ant script packages the classes needed as a jar file that is then copied to the `webapps/axis/WEB-INF/lib/` folder of Tomcat. In addition, the script transmits a deployment descriptor generated by `wsdl2java` to the `AdminService` of Axis.

3 Restart Tomcat.

Now that we have deployed the web service, let's see next how we can invoke it. In fact, we will see how we can invoke it from .NET as well to show the interoperability of SOAP and WSDL standards.

2.5.2 Consuming a web service

What we have done so far is to make the service available to a client. The client application can be anything: it can be a desktop application running on the desk of the traders, a web application available to the end users, or it can be invoked by other applications. Different application developers may wish to use the service in different ways. The way they invoke the service depends on the amount of knowledge they have about the service at design time.

There are three different mechanisms to make use of the service:

1   *Via the client stubs*   In this mechanism, the client application developers have access to WSDL. Using this information, integrated development environments (IDES) can provide design-time checks to make sure that the clients are invoking the service with appropriate arguments. In addition, the IDE can use the WSDL at design time to hide the details of invocation of the service.

2   *Via dynamic proxy*   If the client application developers have only access to the server-side interface when developing, it can still use it to provide client-side validation. That is, the IDE can help, at design time, to validate the arguments. However, since WSDL is only available at runtime, the code has to resolve the service details such as where it can be invoked at runtime only, via dynamic proxy.

3   *Via Dynamic Invocation Interface (DII)*   If an application does not know the interface or WSDL at design time, it can still invoke the service by getting the WSDL at runtime. In that case, the IDE cannot help in validating the arguments. The client application needs to take care of the details of getting the service information and signature of the operation and invoking the service.

Figure 2.3 provides an overview of the three mechanisms.

Pregenerated client stubs

Can we hide from a client application the fact that a service implementation may be remote? If we can, the client application can use the same code to access a remote service implementation as it would to access a local one. This is partially made possible by tools such as WSDL2Java.

Tools such as WSDL2Java generate a class that implements all the service interface methods to simply forward each method call to the real service implementation using SOAP RPC. Such generated classes are known as *client stubs*. Client applications need to do just a little more work invoking remote services than they need to invoke a local implementation if they use stubs. They need to locate a stub instance first. But once they do that, they can use the stub as if it were a local instance of the service implementation class. Listing 2.11 is an example.

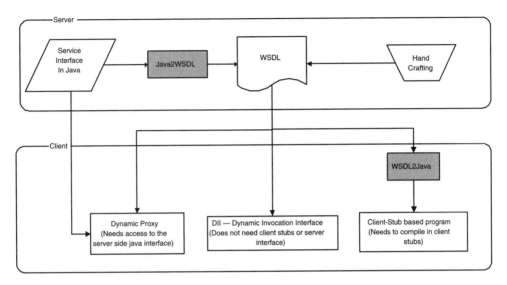

Figure 2.3   Three different ways of consuming web services using JAX-RPC: (from right to left) via stubs pregenerated from WSDL by a tool, via Dynamic Invocation Interface (DII), and via a Dynamic Proxy of the service interface

Listing 2.11   Service invocation using pregenerated stubs

```
Example1SoapBindingStub stub =
    (Example1SoapBindingStub) new BrokerageServiceLocator().getexample1();
float quote = stub.getQuote();
```

JAX-RPC mandates that stubs should also implement the `javax.xml.rpc.Stub` interface. This additional interface allows the client application to dynamically configure the stub instance with properties such as username, password, and service endpoint address.

Dynamic proxy

Can we avoid pregenerating stubs so as to make a client application completely portable between different JAX-RPC compliant SOAP toolkits? The answer is yes if the following two requirements can be met.

1   The toolkits need to generate at runtime an object that implements a given service interface.

2   The generated object should of course forward each method call to the real service implementation using SOAP RPC.

Listing 2.12 shows an example of the use of a dynamic proxy to avoid the pregeneration of toolkit-specific client-side stubs.

Listing 2.12   Service invocation using dynamic proxy

```
String wsdlLocation =
    "http://localhost:8080/axis/services/example1?WSDL";
String ourNsUri =
    "http://manning.com/xmlns/samples/soasecimpl";
javax.xml.namespace.QName serviceName =        Namespace-qualified
    new javax.xml.namespace.QName              name of the service
    (ourNsUri, "BrokerageService");

javax.xml.rpc.ServiceFactory serviceFactory =      WSDL location and service   ❶
    javax.xml.rpc.ServiceFactory.newInstance();      name identify service
javax.xml.rpc.Service service = serviceFactory.createService
    (new java.net.URL(wsdlLocation), serviceName);

Brokerage dynamicProxy = (Brokerage)         ❷ Dynamic proxy for
    service.getPort(Brokerage.class);           the service

                                            ❸  Service invocation
float quote = dynamicProxy.getQuote("MSFT");    via dynamic proxy
```

A client wishing to invoke a service using the dynamic proxy technique can identify the service to invoke by specifying ❶ the WSDL location and the namespace-qualified name of the service as declared in WSDL. The client application can then ask ❷ the JAX-RPC implementation to generate a dynamic proxy that implements the Brokerage interface (shown in listing 2.10). Once the client application gets a dynamic proxy instance, it can use it just as it would use a pregenerated stub. Invoking a service operation ❸ is as simple as calling a method on the dynamic proxy.

Dynamic invocation interface

Let's say we're creating a generic trading client that can be configured for use with any brokerage service. As the client does not have access to a Java interface describing the service, it cannot use a dynamic proxy. A DII comes in handy in such a situation. A Call object can be used to fill in the in and in/out parameters and retrieve the out and in/out parameters after invocation. Listing 2.13 is an example.

Listing 2.13   Service invocation using DII

```
String wsdlLocation =
    "http://localhost:8080/axis/services/example1?WSDL";
```

```
String ourNsUri =
    "http://manning.com/xmlns/samples/soasecimpl";
javax.xml.namespace.QName serviceName =          Namespace-qualified
    new javax.xml.namespace.QName               name of the service
    (ourNsUri, "BrokerageService");
javax.xml.namespace.QName portName =             Namespace-qualified
    new javax.xml.namespace.QName               name of the port
    (ourNsUri, "example1");
javax.xml.namespace.QName operationName =        Namespace-qualified
    new javax.xml.namespace.QName               name of the operation
    (ourNsUri, "getQuote");

javax.xml.rpc.ServiceFactory serviceFactory =
    javax.xml.rpc.ServiceFactory.newInstance();
javax.xml.rpc.Service service =              ❶ WSDL location
    serviceFactory.createService                and service name
    (new java.net.URL(wsdlLocation), serviceName);   identify service

javax.xml.rpc.Call dii =                     ❷ Port and operation
    service.createCall(portName, operationName);     identify call to make

Float quote = (Float) dii.invoke(new Object[] {"MSFT"});  ⟵❸ Making a Call
```

When using dynamic proxy (see listing 2.11), we identified the service to invoke using the WSDL location and service name. We then created a dynamic proxy implementing the service interface so that we can invoke a specific operation using a mere method call. But here, in the case of DII (listing 2.12), as we do not have access to the service interface definition in Java, we will have to identify the operation to invoke in a different way. Just as WSDL locations and service names identify a service ❶, port and operation names identify a particular operation in a service. We make use of this idea in ❷ to create a Call object that can then be used in ❸ to invoke the operation. Observe how in ❸ we are passing the arguments required by the operation as an array of objects.

We have seen three different ways to invoke the service from Java. Can we invoke the service from other platforms? Indeed, we can use .NET to invoke the service. Even though we do not want to go into details of usage of .NET for that purpose, in the next section, we will demonstrate that a service developed in Axis can be used from .NET, fulfilling the interoperability promise of web services.

2.5.3 *Using a web service from .NET*

In this section, we will consume the web service developed in Axis from .NET. Thus, we check the interoperability of the brokerage service we created in the previous section. Since desktop applications are often written on Microsoft platforms using Microsoft technologies, these kinds of clients are useful for that purpose. In .NET, you can use different mechanisms to invoke a service, depending on the language. In C#, you can use all three of the mechanisms used in Java. Since our focus is to demonstrate the interoperability, we will show the easiest mechanism: using pregenerated stubs. You will need Microsoft Visual Studio .NET 2003 installed with the Visual C#.NET option to run the example described here.

Table 2.6 describes the high-level steps involved in creating a .NET-based consumer for our brokerage service.

Table 2.6   Instructions for consuming the brokerage service with a .NET-based client

Step	Action	How to
1	Start Tomcat if it is not already running.	Run `shutdown` and `startup` scripts found in the `bin` directory of Tomcat.
2	If the TCP monitor is not already running, start it.	Use the command `ant tcpmon`.
3	Open a Microsoft Visual Studio .NET 2003 command prompt.	Use the shortcut available under Start → Programs → Microsoft Visual Studio .NET 2003 → Visual Studio .NET Tools.
4	Generate the C# client stub for our brokerage service.	See the "Generating a C# client stub" section.
5	Create a simple C# client, `Brokerage-Client.cs`, using the generated stub to retrieve a stock quote.	See the "Using a generated stub" section.
6	Compile `BrokerageClient.cs` and the generated stub (`Brokerage-Service.cs`) to produce an executable.	`csc /target:exe /out:Brokerage-Client.exe BrokerageClient.cs BrokerageService.cs`
7	Run the generated executable to see if the interoperability indeed succeeds.	

The following two subsections show you the commands and code required for steps 4 and 5 listed in table 2.6.

Generating a C# client stub

Assuming Tomcat is listening on `localhost:8080` and `tcpmon` is listening on port 8000, the command shown in listing 2.14 can be used to generate the C# client stub for our brokerage service.

Listing 2.14   Command for generating a C# client stub

```
wsdl
   /namespace:com.manning.samples.soasecimpl.example1
   /out:BrokerageService.cs
   http://localhost:8000/axis/services/example1?WSDL
```

There are other methods of generating the stubs for .NET. You can get the IDE to generate the stubs without explicitly having to use the tools like we showed. However, the principle remains the same.

Using a generated stub

The generated C# client stub can be utilized as part of a client application, as shown in listing 2.15.

Listing 2.15   Sample C# client, `BrokerageClient.cs`, using the generated stub to retrieve a stock quote

```
namespace com.manning.samples.soasecimpl.example1 {
   public class BrokerageClient {
     public static void Main(string[] args) {
       BrokerageService service = new BrokerageService();
       System.Console.WriteLine(service.getQuote("MSFT"));
     }
   }
}
```

So far we have shown how to develop, deploy, and use a service. As a developer, you must also understand what kind of services you should develop. Since there are several choices of transports and formats, as mentioned earlier, you should understand the role of standards in using services. The next section describes the choices that developers and architects face in implementing services.

2.6 Choices in service design

What we have not discussed in as much detail—so far—is service design. In this section, we will provide guidance on how you can make the right set of choices when designing services.

2.6.1 Wrap existing interfaces or design from scratch?

Several application servers and tools offer a quick way to wrap existing interfaces as services. For example, you can expose your EJBs as services. Although this allows you to quickly create "services," this may not be the right way to go about creating services.

Considerations that go into the design of a service interface are quite different from those that go into the design of APIs. As we discussed in chapter 1, a service ideally needs to possess certain characteristics in order to be consistent with the vision of SOA. In particular, a service should represent a business capability that the service provider is offering to meet the needs of service consumers. Existing APIs may or may not fit this definition of a service; there may be a mismatch in granularity. As APIs often reflect the way a system is modularized, existing APIs are likely to be defined at a finer level of granularity than the level at which you see your business capabilities. It is important that you do not look at the job of creating service definitions as merely a technical one that can be automated by tools. Doing so will mean you are simply putting old wine in new bottles and the mileage you get out of SOA will be limited.

For these reasons, it is preferable to develop services that match the needs of the applications from a business perspective.

2.6.2 *To use SOAP or not?*

SOAP-based services may not always be a viable option due to reasons beyond your control. For example, your budget may not allow the cost of hardware and/or software development needed to wrap all of your legacy applications with SOAP-based interfaces. In such cases, you can still obtain most of the benefits of SOA by reorganizing all of your applications and infrastructure with services as the fundamental elements, albeit with native protocols and data formats. You can still describe the services you offer using WSDL with appropriate extension elements describing the protocol and data format bindings. Clients of your services may benefit not only because your view of your offerings now coincides with theirs, but also because they may be able to invoke your services in the same way as they would invoke SOAP-based services, thanks to frameworks such as Apache WSIF.

> **NOTE**   *Apache WSIF*   The Apache Web Services Invocation Framework (WSIF) provides a common API to invoke any web service described using WSDL, no matter what the protocol and data format bindings are. WSIF requires a "provider" plug-in to support each type of binding. WSIF itself supplies providers needed to support invocation of web services bound to local Java classes, EJB, JMS-based applications, and Enterprise Information Systems (EIS) with J2EE Connector Architecture (JCA)-compliant adapters.

However, there are significant downsides to not using SOAP in your web services. A lot of effort has gone into the engineering of SOAP-based web services by the SOA community at large. You will not be able to take advantage of some of that work. For example, SOA security solutions are more widely developed for SOAP-based web services than for other web service implementation choices. The cost of re-engineering and adapting infrastructure developed for SOAP to your specific implementation needs to be taken into account before you can make the right choice on whether to use SOAP or not.

2.6.3 *Start with WSDL or generate it?*

The examples in this chapter clearly show the central role played by WSDL in the consumption of web services. Given that every toolkit comes with a tool to generate WSDL from interfaces specified in languages such as Java and C#, it is common to simply generate WSDL for each of the application interfaces. This leads to finely grained interfaces that are not optimal for providing services, as we discussed in section 2.6.1.

For example, a traditional brokerage application would probably have involved multiple steps before a market order is created.

```
Order marketOrder = new MarketOrder();
marketOrder.setSymbol("MSFT");
marketOrder.setBuy(true);
marketOrder.setQuantity(100);
brokerage.create(marketOrder);
```

If we had translated each of these method calls into a service invocation, a client would have been forced to make multiple round-trips to the server to create an order. Instead, our brokerage service offers a single method, `createMarketOrder` (`String symbol, boolean buy, int quantity`), to do the same.

You don't necessarily have to write WSDL by hand. You can still generate it from the code for a coarsely grained interface. However, given that WSDL is the prime contract you are signing with your service's consumers, take a look at the generated WSDL and make sure that it indeed presents the right interface. For example, when creating the brokerage service, we hand-edited WSDL generated by Axis to provide meaningful names for message parts.

2.6.4 *Should security context be part of the interface?*

Why don't our `createMarketOrder` and `createLimitOrder` methods take user ID as one of their arguments? Every order that's created should of course have an owner. However, user ID is not one of the arguments for these methods because the service should obtain it from the security context of an invocation. It is up to the security infrastructure of the service to compute and provide the security context of an invocation to the web service.

Similarly, other higher-level contexts such as a transaction context should not be a direct part of the service interface. We will discuss how these higher-level contexts can be established and used in the next chapter when we discuss SOAP extensibility via headers.

2.6.5 *RPC or document exchange?*

Choosing between RPC and document exchange requires an understanding of the usage patterns. Marshaling (encoding) schemes are the main source of incompatibility in SOAP implementations. As document exchange avoids the need for marshaling altogether, document exchange provides a higher degree of interoperability than RPC.

However, programming effort is higher for document exchange-based services than for RPC. Almost all SOAP engines support RPC with additional tools. The task of parsing the SOAP request payload and serializing the response payload is taken care of by the toolkits in case of RPC. This burden shifts to the service if it uses document exchange.

If you need to maximize interoperability, document exchange is the right choice unless the equivalent RPC interface only involves simple data types. On the other hand, if you are creating a service that is not expected to be widely exposed and if your enterprise predominantly uses a particular SOAP toolkit, RPC will make your job easier.

2.7 *Related technologies: UDDI*

In this chapter, we have seen how we can describe our web services, create them, and consume them. But how do we publicize them? How can others discover our services?

UDDI is a web services standard that seeks to answer these questions. UDDI provides standards for registries of businesses and services. Registries can be public, private, or shared between trusted partners. For example, some of the leading UDDI proponents host a Universal Business Registry (UBR) in which any business can register itself and its services.

UBR hasn't really taken off, but that is because most enterprises offer web services for use within intranets and extranets only. Private and shared registries are hence currently more useful than UBR.

Registries can even interact with each other and group together in various ways. For example, registries can work together as a hierarchical group.

What is the connection between UDDI and the other standards we have discussed in this chapter? Businesses can register in UDDI registries the WSDL for each web service they offer in UDDI registries. UDDI registries categorize and classify the registered services into searchable taxonomies. Thus, they help interested consumers locate the services they need. Once a service is discovered, its WSDL can then be retrieved from a registry. Of course, once we have the WSDL, we know very well by now how to make use of it in creating a client application.

Java APIs for XML Registries (JAXR) provides a vendor-neutral API for working with UDDI registries. JAXR is to UDDI what JAX-RPC is to SOAP RPC.

2.8 *Summary*

By now, you are familiar with the basic technologies that make up the foundation for web services: XML, SOAP, and WSDL. This chapter is not meant as an exhaustive resource on these technologies. We provided just enough background material on these topics for you to understand the rest of the book. If you are familiar with web services, you understand these technologies already. If you are not, we recommend that you refer to other XML and web services books that are dedicated solely to these topics for a more comprehensive introduction.

By now, you also have set up the environment required to run the examples in this book. In case you have not already done so, we strongly encourage you to download and execute the example we described in this chapter. This will help you in getting the most out of examples in subsequent chapters as well. The code can be found at http://www.manning.com/kanneganti.

You are also now familiar with the considerations that go into choosing the right service interface. You understand that security context should not be a direct part of the service interface. But then, how does SOAP take care of security? From what you have seen in this chapter, SOAP doesn't seem to be taking care of security at all. In the next chapter, you will see that SOAP doesn't take care of security by itself. Instead, it provides extension mechanisms to build in support for additional concerns. Security is of course one big concern and a standard extension named WS-Security addresses it. In case you are wondering if we have already shown you a hook that can be leveraged to extend SOAP, recall that we have promised to dwell a lot more on SOAP `Header` in the next chapter. Let us go there next.

Suggestions for further reading

- The Java Community Process (JCP) website is located at http://jcp.org/en/home/index.

- JAX-RPC Specifications are available at http://java.sun.com/xml/downloads/jaxrpc.html.

- JAX-RPC 1.x is evolving into JAX-WS 2.0 as described at http://weblogs.java.net/blog/kohlert/archive/2005/05/jaxrpc_20_renam.html. You can find all about JAX-WS 2.0 at https://jax-ws.dev.java.net/.

- The XML 1.1 specification, a W3C Recommendation, is available at http://www.w3.org/TR/xml11. Grammar for Document Type Definition (DTD) is also laid down by this spec.

- "Namespaces in XML," a W3C Recommendation, is available at http://www.w3.org/TR/REC-xml-names.

- The XML Schema specifications, W3C Recommendations, are available at http://www.w3.org/XML/Schema#dev.

- RELAX NG, another schema language for XML, is described at http://www.relaxng.org/.

- W3C DOM specifications are available at http://www.w3.org/DOM/DOMTR.

- The SAX website is https://sax.sourceforge.net/.

- *Processing XML with Java*, by Elliotte Rusty Harold and published by Addison-Wesley Professional in November 2002, is a good resource for learning DOM and SAX APIs. An online version is available at the author's website, http://cafeconleche.org/books/xmljava/. The book is not new, and important developments in the last few years such as StAX are not covered. Seminar notes by the same author on StAX are available at http://www.cafeconleche.org/slides/sd2004west/stax/index.html.

- The XPath 1.0 specification, a W3C Recommendation, is available at http://www.w3.org/TR/xpath. XPath 2.0 specification is a Candidate W3C Recommendation at the time of writing this book. It is available at http://www.w3.org/TR/xpath20/.

- The SOAP 1.1 specification, a W3C Note, is available at http://www.w3.org/TR/2000/NOTE-SOAP-20000508/. The SOAP 1.2 specification, a Candidate W3C Recommendation at the time of writing this book, is available at http://www.w3.org/TR/soap/.

- All deliverables published in draft/final forms by Web Services Interoperability Organization (WS-I) are available at http://www.ws-i.org/deliverables/index.aspx. In particular, "Basic Profile" 1.1 is available at http://www.ws-i.org/Profiles/Basic-Profile-1.1.html and "Simple SOAP Binding Profile" 1.0 is at http://www.ws-i.org/Profiles/SimpleSoapBindingProfile-1.0.html.

- The WSDL 1.1 specification, a W3C Note, is available at http://www.w3.org/TR/wsdl. WSDL 2.0, a Candidate W3C Recommendation at the time of writing this book, is available at http://www.w3.org/TR/wsdl20.

- The Apache Web Services Invocation Framework (WSIF) website is http://ws.apache.org/wsif/.

- Apache has recently released a rewrite of Axis named Axis2. Axis2 is based on StAX to eke out the best performance possible. Axis2 1.0 does not support JAX-RPC (or JAX-WS). Axis2 is homed at http://ws.apache.org/axis2/.

- XFire is another open-source StAX-based web services engine that is rising in popularity. XFire 1.1 does not support JAX-RPC. Support for JAX-WS is in the works. XFire is homed at http://xfire.codehaus.org/.

- The UDDI 3.0 specification, an OASIS standard, is available at http://uddi.org/pubs/uddi_v3.htm.

- The JAXR specification is available at http://java.sun.com/xml/downloads/jaxr.html.

Extending SOAP
for security

This chapter covers

- Extending SOAP with Headers
- WS-Security with JAX-RPC handlers
- SOAP intermediaries and WS-Addressing

Chapters 1 and 2 provided the background needed to start exploring SOA security. In chapter 1, you learned the basics of SOA and how it impacts security by lowering the barriers between applications. In chapter 2, you reviewed the basics of the most popular approach to realizing SOA—creating and consuming SOAP-based web services. What you have not seen yet is how SOAP can address the security concerns expressed in chapter 1.

SOAP does not address any security issues *directly*. In fact, it does not directly address other common requirements such as reliability or transactionality, either. SOAP simply provides a mechanism by which it can be extended to address additional concerns such as security, reliability, and transactionality. Is this a good idea? Shouldn't something as fundamental as security be addressed in the base SOAP specification itself? We'll answer this question first up in this chapter. Once we do that, we will describe the header-based extension mechanism SOAP provides and introduce WS-Security, a standard extension for security in SOAP.

How do SOAP-processing engines (such as Apache Axis, introduced in the previous chapter) allow for the processing of extensions such as WS-Security? This is an important question that must have popped into your mind once we mentioned that concerns such as security are addressed by SOAP extensions and not by SOAP itself. We will answer this question as well in this chapter, and show you the *handler* pattern supported by most SOAP engines to process SOAP extensions. Specifically, by continuing the example of a brokerage service introduced in chapter 2, we will show how to process SOAP extensions using Apache Axis.

Toward the end of the chapter, we will briefly introduce the idea of *intermediaries*. Intermediaries are nodes that are neither the source nor the destination endpoints for a SOAP message. They come in handy when it is desirable (for manageability and other reasons) to separate handling of extensions such as WS-Security from endpoints. For example, a centralized security service may be implemented as an intermediary that intercepts all SOAP traffic and enforces security policies.[1] We will also introduce WS-Addressing, a standard that is useful when routing messages across intermediaries. We will conclude the chapter by answering some of the frequently asked questions about the usage of SOAP extensions, headers, and handlers.

We start with a discussion on what is the right approach for addressing security in SOAP.

---

[1] Chapter 8 will elaborate on this idea in great detail.

3.1 Finding the right approach for security in SOAP

As SOAP-based web services are the most commonly found services in today's SOA implementations, can we add a security specification into SOAP itself? For good reasons, the designers of SOAP chose options other than building the security protocols into the SOAP standards. In this section, we will learn about those reasons and the choices made by designers of SOAP.

Before looking at the choices the designers faced, we will briefly discuss security in web applications. This discussion will later make it easy for you to see the reasoning behind the choices made in SOAP.

3.1.1 Lessons from web authentication schemes

A web application has multiple layers where security can be implemented (figure 3.1). For simplicity, let us focus only on authentication and how it can be implemented in each of these layers.

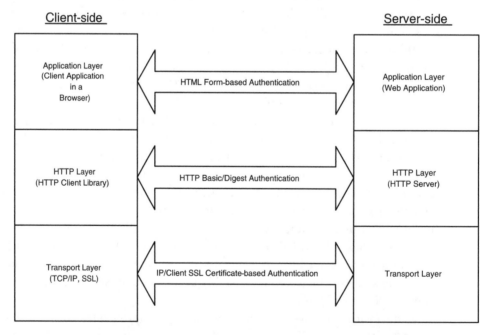

Figure 3.1   Authentication in web applications can happen at three different layers. At the transport layer, SSL certificates can be used for authentication. At the HTTP layer, the basic or digest schemes that can be implemented by the browser can be used for authentication. At the application layer, the choices are endless—we can use form-based authentication, with full control over client-side and server-side for the programmer.

There are three layers where we can implement authentication in web applications:

- Transport layer
- HTTP layer
- Application layer

Authentication in each of these three layers has advantages and drawbacks.

Authentication at the transport layer

First, we can use the information available at the transport layer. For instance, we can allow all requests coming from specific IP addresses. Or, we can restrict access to users with a verifiable SSL certificate.[2] Technically, this kind of security can be provided without the web server knowing about it. In practice, these facilities may be integrated into the web server, for ease of use.

IP address-based authentication is not good enough in most real-world web applications. Web applications generally must be accessible from everywhere. Furthermore, the threat of an attacker spoofing the IP address[3] makes IP address-based authentication ineffective for real-world use.

Authentication based on client SSL certificates is a technically superior approach to most other authentication schemes. However, it is difficult to enforce in practice, as not all end users of a web application may be equipped with an SSL certificate.

3.1.2 Authentication at the HTTP layer

At the HTTP layer, the web server can ask the client for username and password information. Almost all web servers can be configured to carry out what is known as *HTTP Basic Authentication*. In this scheme, the web server returns a 403 Authorization Required response to a client whenever it receives a request that does not have a username and password embedded as a header. The client (a browser, for example) is then supposed to prompt the user for username and password and resend the request with the typed-in credentials embedded as an additional HTTP header. HTTP can provide another—in fact, stronger—security mechanism called *Digest Authentication*, which is not widely implemented in browsers.

---

[2] Chapter 6 will introduce SSL and certificates in depth

[3] Yes, an attacker can indeed fabricate/manipulate IP packets in such a way that the server receiving the packets thinks that the sender (the attacker in this case) is at a different IP address than where he really is.

Since these authentication schemes are built into the protocol, the application does not have to bear the burden of carrying out authentications.

Although it is simple for web applications to delegate the job of client authentication to the web server, this is not too widely done because it does not provide enough flexibility and control for developers. Every web server will support a few popular credential stores such as a password file or a LDAP directory. Authentication against any other credential stores will require extensions to the web server.

Authentication at the application layer

The application can use its own custom scheme instead of or in addition to transport-layer and HTTP-layer authentication schemes. For instance, when you log in to your Yahoo! account, you are challenged to enter your username and password into a HTML form. Of course, the application could also ask your age, sex, and even your mother's maiden name. The application itself is responsible for what to ask, how to validate the answers, and how to use the results. This approach is the most general one, and is suitable in most cases. However, it is nonstandard and creates integration issues. For example, if the web application needs to be integrated into a portal, the custom authentication mechanism used by the application needs to be integrated with the portal's authentication mechanism using one of the several proprietary Single Sign-On (SSO) solutions available in the market. Still, developers often choose to implement security at the application layer because that is what they are used to. This might be fine for web applications that are not too frequently integrated into a portal, but for web services whose very reason for existence is integration, implementing authentication and other forms of security at the application layer may not be appropriate.

We have seen three different approaches that give varying degrees of control to the developer. In particular, even though authentication at the HTTP layer is very convenient, and is a part of HTTP standard, it did not become popular. Instead, developers ended up using nonstandard, unique mechanisms using form-based authentication systems.

The lesson for SOAP-based web services is clear. Naturally, they should support a standard for security mechanisms. Yet, the standard should provide the required flexibility and control to the developers. Let us take a look at how the designers of SOAP responded to this challenge.

3.1.3 *Choices for security implementation in SOAP*

Just like authentication in a web application, security in SOAP can be implemented at three different layers, as identified in figure 3.2:

- Transport layer
- SOAP layer
- Application layer

In the context of SOAP, the phrase *transport layer* refers to more than just TCP and SSL. It also refers to higher-level protocols such as HTTP, FTP, SMTP, and JMS/MQ that can be used to carry SOAP messages. The phrase *SOAP layer* refers to the engines that help expose business logic in applications as SOAP-based services. And, by *application layer*, we mean the end applications that constitute service

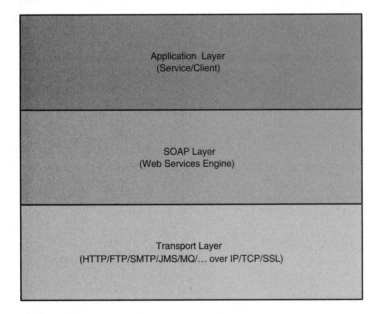

Figure 3.2   Three logical layers at which security in SOAP can be implemented. Unlike in figure 3.1, where the transport layer referred to TCP/SSL, the transport layer here represents higher-level protocols by which SOAP messages are exchanged. The SOAP layer refers to web services engines that can produce/consume standards-compliant SOAP messages. The application layer is free to interpret the SOAP messages, where the security can be implemented as a private standard between the producer and the consumer.

providers and service consumers. Let us look at the pros and cons of implementing security at each of these three layers so that you understand the choices faced by designers.

Transport-layer security

There are protocols that let the transport layer take care of security. For example, several applications such as CVS (a popular version control system) let Secure Shell (SSH) provide a secure channel. The disadvantages of implementing security in the transport layer are twofold:

1   *Transport layer security is limited to point-to-point interactions.*   We discussed this in detail in chapter 1. If a message needs to travel through several applications, of which some of the applications are only allowed to look at parts of the message, we cannot use the transport-layer security mechanisms. What we need is *message-level* security to support the multiapplication interaction found commonly in SOA implementations.

2   *Applications cannot obtain security context easily from the transport layer.*   That means they cannot easily find out information such as the authenticated user's name, role, and other details from the transport layer that authenticated and authorized the user. The problem is that there is no uniform standard to carry the security details from the transport layer to the application layer. This is because it is difficult to create a standard that is well suited for use across different kinds of transports.

The more efforts we make to provide generalized security and security context communication in the transport layers, the more we realize that it is easier to do at higher layers; that is, the SOAP layer or the application layer. Of these two, for reasons that will become obvious shortly, we will consider first the suitability of the application layer.

Application-layer security

Instead of implementing at the lower transport and SOAP layers, we could leave the security details to the application. This choice brings its own set of problems:

1   *Since each application develops its own mechanisms, integration becomes difficult.* For example, when two or more low-level services are composed to create a high-level service, the custom security mechanisms in each service will have to be integrated, possibly by implementing a custom SSO solution.

2 *Getting security right is notoriously difficult.* When application developers are charged with the task of developing a security framework, the odds are high that they will get it wrong.

In summary, while a suitable security model can be developed at the application level, it is costly, error-prone, and not suitable for web services.

SOAP-layer security

Now that we know that the other two choices are nonstarters, we are left with implementing security measures in the protocol itself. There are some lessons to learn from history here. If you recall, HTTP has authentication built-in, which is neither complete nor suitable for a large number of applications, requiring applications to implement their own security models. What prevents us from repeating the same mistake with SOAP? In other words, the primary challenge is to implement a universally acceptable security model in SOAP.

SOAP solves this problem by not building a security model into the SOAP protocol itself. Instead, the SOAP protocol is extensible meaning it supports security extensions. This strategy also happens to be the right choice for addressing other horizontal concerns such as reliability and transactions. In fact, there is precedent for these kinds of extensions. Let us study one such example from well-established standard protocols to see how we can draw lessons for SOAP.

In Simple Mail Transfer Protocol (SMTP), mail message headers such as From, To, and Reply-To are standardized. But what if an application wants to send a photograph of the sender as a header? The application may want the image only in a header, and not in the body, for a good reason: it may want to interoperate with other mail readers that do not understand how to process an image.

The solution is simple: SMTP allowed *extension headers* called "X-headers." Any vendor can make up a header that starts with "X-." For example, Emacs-based mail readers adopted a header named X-Face for sending the sender image. Web-based mailers adopted X-Originating-IP for recording the IP from where the mail is submitted.

SOAP provides a similar extension by headers mechanism that can be used for addressing security. In fact, SOAP's extension mechanism is lot more powerful than what you may expect from the analogy with SMTP. SOAP explicitly allows intermediaries—parties other than a sender and intended receiver—to act on headers, and this turns out to be quite useful when addressing security needs using headers. For instance, enterprise services can use this leeway to delegate away most if not all of the burden of security enforcement to specialized security devices in the path of SOAP messages.

As you can see, there are quite a few advantages to addressing security needs at the SOAP layer using extensions. First, SOAP makes it easy by providing a powerful extension mechanism. Second, there will never be any fear of getting locked into a particular security model that may not meet the needs of every possible scenario.

There is one downside, though. If security is left to extensions, each vendor may define a different security extension, damaging interoperability severely in the process. This possibility can be avoided by creating a standard security extension. Of course, if the security needs of a particular scenario cannot be met with the standard security extension, one is always free to create one's own security extension.

Given our conclusion that security is best addressed as an extension to SOAP, we need to first understand the details of how SOAP can be extended. We will work on that in the next section. Once we see how SOAP can be extended, we can apply our learning to start understanding WS-Security, the standard security extension for SOAP.

3.2 *Extending SOAP with headers*

SOAP allows for extensions in the form of headers. SOAP does not specify any headers by itself; instead, it provides a framework for incorporating and processing arbitrary headers. It specifies where headers can appear in a message, how they can be encoded, and what every SOAP engine or SOAP-based web service must adhere to when processing headers. The actual content of headers is governed by mutual consent of service providers and service consumers. For example, in an organization, the IT department can mandate certain header entries for the purpose of IT governance.

This situation can be chaotic, with each company defining its own SOAP extensions using custom headers. However, SOAP extensions for addressing common problems such as security are standardized by groups like OASIS. One such standard extension, WS-Security, defines a header related to security, and obviously, is of particular interest to us. In this book, we show how this standard extension can be used to develop security solutions for SOAP-based web services.

In this section, let us see what kind of support SOAP offers for headers. We will also introduce WS-Security.

3.2.1 *Anatomy of a SOAP header*

The basic structure of a SOAP message was introduced in chapter 2. As you may recall, a SOAP envelope consists of a header and a body. It is analogous to HTTP, where the body may be thought of as containing the payload—the material of interest to the application, which is typically business-level queries and results—and headers are used to negotiate application capabilities, cookies, authentication information, and other details that help the recipient make sense of the payload. The syntax, of course, varies a little bit.

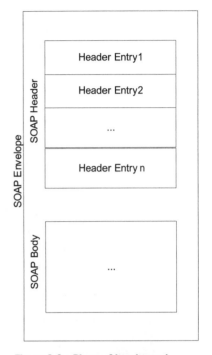

Figure 3.3 Place of header and header entries in a SOAP envelope. Within the SOAP envelope, any number of headers can be introduced prior to the body element. Any organization can make up its own header, keeping the SOAP message syntactically valid. Most useful headers are ones where there is wide industry support and tool support.

Header entries

Figure 3.3 depicts the location and composition of the `Header` element in a SOAP envelope. The header, if present, should be the first immediate child element of the SOAP envelope. All immediate child elements of the `Header` element are called *header entries*. (It is common to refer to a header entry as header in contexts where it is clear that the term refers to a header entry and not to the entirety of a SOAP message header.) A header entry is identified by its fully qualified element name, which consists of the namespace URI and the local name. All header entries must be namespace-qualified.

Let us consider an example. Say we want to add a header entry to carry the name of the company sending the message. Listing 3.1 shows how to use a header entry to indicate that Manning Publications is the message sender. To make it clear that this header is created by us, we will give it the name `MyHeader`:

Listing 3.1 Simple SOAP header entry example to add sender information

```
<soapenv:Envelope ...>
    <soapenv:Header>
        <ns:MyHeader
          xmlns:ns=
           "http://manning.com/xmlns/samples/soasecimpl">
          Manning Publications
        </ns:MyHeader>
    </soapenv:Header>
    <soapenv:Body>
    ...
    </soapenv:Body>
</soapenv:Envelope>
```

❶ Our own header entry

❷ Namespace URI

Header element

As you can see, we introduced a header entry called MyHeader ❶ in the namespace identified by a URI ❷. Of course, barring the XML syntax, these headers look very similar to the ones in SMTP headers. So, how does SOAP go farther than SMTP in extensibility? We will describe this next.

3.2.2 *Standard header entry attributes*

SOAP defines a few standard attributes that may be present on every header entry. The semantics associated with these standard attributes are fixed by the SOAP specification; it is these semantics that make SOAP extensibility lot more powerful than that of SMTP. The standard attributes defined by SOAP for header entries answer key questions that might come up in processing of the headers:

1 *Who should deal with the header entry?* Unlike in SMTP, where there is no provision for associating a target for the header data, SOAP 1.1 defines an optional actor attribute (renamed role in SOAP 1.2) to indicate who should process a header entry. How can anyone other than the recipient of a SOAP message see and process a header entry? As we very briefly pointed out in the previous section, SOAP allows intermediaries to see and process header entries. Later in this chapter, we will describe in-depth the idea of intermediaries and the significance of the actor attribute. For now, just note that it is possible to indicate who should process a header entry by providing a URI as the value for the optional actor attribute.

2 *What do we do with the header entry?* The answer to this question lies entirely within the application. However, a SOAP header entry can indicate using the mustUnderstand attribute whether the application *must*

understand the header entry. This attribute can be very effective in managing the evolution of higher-level protocols on top of SOAP. For example, it is an excellent way to introduce backward-compatible protocols.

3 *How do we parse data in the header entry?* If the data within a header entry can be encoded in multiple ways, a standard attribute named `encoding-Style` can be used to convey the encoding used. (We covered the details of encoding in chapter 2.)

Now, we can look at a more advanced example that illustrates these three attributes on a `Header` element. Let us imagine that we want to add transaction information, which contains the date and time as well as the initiator of the transaction. We want to add this information for the benefit of some party that is interested in transaction metadata. We may encode it in any way we want; we will choose SOAP encoding described in chapter 2. Listing 3.2 shows how we do this.

Listing 3.2 SOAP `Header` element attributes

```
<soapenv:Envelope ...>
  <soapenv:Header>
    <ns:transaction
      xmlns:ns=
        "http://manning.com/xmlns/samples/soasecimpl"
      soapenv:actor=                                      ❶ actor
        "http://schemas.xmlsoap.org/soap/actor/next"         specification
      soapenv:mustUnderstand="true"    ←❷ This entry must be understood
      soapenv:encodingStyle=
        "http://schemas.xmlsoap.org/soap/encoding/">       ❸ Standard SOAP
      <ns:dateAndTime>                                       encoding style
        2001-11-29T13:20:00.000-05:00
      </ns:dateAndTime>
      <ns:Initiator>John</ns:Initiator>
    </ns:transaction>
  </soapenv:Header>
  <soapenv:Body>
    ...
  </soapenv:Body>
</soapenv:Envelope>
```

In this example, we defined a new `Header` element called `transaction`. This element takes the following attributes:

■ actor: The `actor` attribute ❶ describes who the `transaction` header entry is targeted to. We will further describe this attribute in section 3.5.2. In

SOAP 1.2, this attribute is renamed `role` and is more generic than `actor`. This element specifies who is supposed to act on this entry.

- `mustUnderstand`: SOAP defines a `mustUnderstand` attribute ❷ to indicate whether a header entry must be understood by the actor at which it is targeted. By default, it is 0, which means the header entry need not be understood by the actor. That is, the actor is allowed to ignore it. On the other hand, if is set to 1, the targeted actor must act on the header entry. If it cannot, this constitutes a fault. A specially defined `MustUnderstand` fault code should be used in the generated SOAP fault.[4]

- `encodingStyle`: For the encoding style ❸ that is used to serialize the data in the `Header` element, we can use any encoding scheme that is understood by both the sender and the receiver. This understanding must be established via out-of-band communication. The details of encoding are not a part of the SOAP message.

SOAP 1.2 defines an additional standard attribute named `relay`. We will describe this later in this chapter when we introduce the significance of `actor` attribute.

Now that we understand how to extend SOAP with headers, let us turn our attention back to extending SOAP for the purpose of addressing security. From the discussion so far, it is obvious that if we want to extend SOAP for addressing security, we need to create new header entries that will carry security-related information in a SOAP message. As we saw in the previous example, anybody can extend SOAP by making up their own header entries. However, when the intent of an extension is to address a universal concern such as security, the extension needs to be standardized. This standardization will ensure interoperability and in the long run bring down the cost of using the extension, as SOAP engine vendors build in support for standard extensions. WS-Security is a good example of this process in action. It provides a standard for extending SOAP to address security concerns. The next section introduces WS-Security.

---

[4] SOAP 1.1 strictly mandates that faults generated due to problems in headers should not use the fault detail element. In fact, the standard mentions that the absence of a `detail` element in a fault can be used to conclude that the fault lies in a header entry and not in the request body. SOAP 1.2 relaxes this restriction. It also introduces a `NotUnderstood` header entry for conveying information on a mandatory header entry that could not be processed.

3.3 *WS-Security: The standard extension for security*

We saw in the previous section that SOAP can be extended by defining new header entries. While new header entries act as a vehicle for carrying additional information in a SOAP message, new header entries by themselves will not be sufficient to create a new standard. A standard should also specify how receiving parties should interpret and act on the new header entries proposed by it. In other words, a standard SOAP extension must specify the syntax as well as the semantic interpretation of new header entries. WS-Security carries out this task for addressing security in SOAP. It standardizes the names and the semantics of the entries used for security.

In this section, we will introduce WS-Security. In particular, we will describe:

- The `Security` header entry proposed by WS-Security
- How receivers should interpret and process the `Security` header
- What is not covered by WS-Security
- An example showing WS-Security in action

We will start with a discussion of the `Security` header entry proposed by WS-Security.

3.3.1 *Introduction to WS-Security*

WS-Security defines a `Security` header to make *security claims* and ensure message-level security. A security claim is any statement made regarding security. Here are some examples of security claims:

- "My name is X."
- "X is authorized to access this resource."
- "This message is signed by X."
- "This message is encrypted using X's public key."

Of course, more than one claim can be made at the same time.

Let us start off with an example showing a simple user identity claim made using username and password.

```
<soapenv:Envelope ...>
  <soapenv:Header>
    <wsse:Security ...>
      <wsse:UsernameToken wsu:Id="1">
        <wsse:Username>
          <xenc:EncryptedData>...</xenc:EncryptedData>
        </wsse:Username>
```

Security header entry ⟵┘

❶ User name token element— a part of WS-Security ⟵┘

Encrypted user name

```
      <wsse:Password>
          <xenc:EncryptedData>...</xenc:EncryptedData>
      </wsse:Password>
    </wsse:UsernameToken>
  </wsse:Security>
 </soapenv:Header>
 <soapenv:Body>
 ...
 </soapenv:Body>
</soapenv:Envelope>
```
**Encrypted
password**

We see here that the `Security` header entry is used to carry security-related information. The interesting element in this example is `UsernameToken` ❶ within the `Security` header entry. It carries an identity claim made using `Username` and `Password` elements. To keep the contents of the `Username` and `Password` elements confidential, they are encrypted.

We will see later that `UsernameToken` is one of the many kinds of *security tokens* that WS-Security uses to carry security claims. Think of a security token as simply a collection of one or more security claims. In this example, a `UsernameToken` is used to claim that the message is from a particular user.

How a token should look and how it should be used are defined by a WS-Security *token profile*. For example, the use of `UsernameToken` is standardized by the WS-Security `UsernameToken` profile. There are many other kinds of security tokens, such as X.509 certificates and Kerberos tickets. These will be discussed in chapters 4 through 8.

WS-Security defines standard security tokens that can express popular security claims. They should be sufficient for most of your needs. If you want to use your own security tokens, WS-Security allows you to do so, using custom elements and attributes within `Security` header entries. Of course, since these are not standard, the receiver may not understand them, unless there is a prior understanding between the sender and receiver about the semantics of these entities. If the receiver cannot understand a custom element or attribute, it has two choices: it can ignore them based on the local policy, or it can generate a fault.

Speaking of faults, WS-Security defines additional fault codes that can be used to communicate problems encountered when processing claims in the `Security` header entry.

WS-Security and SOAP fault codes

If a service chooses to report a fault when it finds problems with a `Security` header entry, it should always use the SOAP fault mechanism. The SOAP fault mechanism specifies a set of standard fault codes, and the syntax of the fault element, as you have seen in chapter 2. Table 3.1 lists the additional fault codes defined by WS-Security.

Table 3.1 Fault codes defined by WS-Security. These fault codes are to be used by any WS-Security implementation when it reports the problem with a security header entry.

Code	Description
UnsupportedSecurityToken	An unsupported security token was provided.
UnsupportedAlgorithm	An unsupported signature or encryption algorithm was used.
InvalidSecurity	An error was discovered while processing the security header.
InvalidSecurityToken	An invalid security token was provided.
FailedAuthentication	The security token could not be authenticated or authorized.
FailedCheck	The signature or decryption is invalid
SecurityTokenUnavailable	Referenced security token could not be retrieved.

Beyond WS-Security

So far you know this: WS-Security supports security tokens that make security claims. At this point, we should point out that there are several questions that are not answered by WS-Security:

- How does a service verify the claims made in a WS-Security header entry?
- What keys and algorithms can be used to encrypt or sign message data?
- If the claims in a request prove to be correct, how should the request be authorized, and by whom?
- How does a service advertise its security policies?
- Can a client demand a certain quality of security?

WS-Security doesn't give any particular answers to these questions. There is a reason why: WS-Security does not prescribe a single security model. WS-Security, along with other related standards such as WS-Policy, provides the syntactic and semantic support needed to implement any security model in the context of web services.

Now that you know the basics of WS-Security, it is time we showed you a working example. Here's what we will do:

1 We will start with a small example that illustrates a simple security header entry. You can run this example with the code that we provided.

2 We will subsequently describe the code used to produce such a header entry and consume a header entry using the SOAP engine that we chose in chapter 2, namely Apache Axis.

3 We will describe the details of configuration.

The ideas illustrated by this simple example will be reused time and again in subsequent chapters. We will explain the example in great detail.

3.3.2 Example: Identifying a brokerage service user

Let us consider a small example where we will write a service that understands a WS-Security Security header entry. In this example, there are two nodes: a sender (service consumer) and a receiver (service). The sender will send the username using a UsernameToken in the Security header entry. The receiver will receive the username and use it to send a response back. To make matters simple, the receiver just has to add the username to the response. Figure 3.4 illustrates this process.

> **NOTE:** Of course, all these requirements can be met without using header. We can rewrite the server and client to modify the SOAP message. However, as we described earlier, there are distinct advantages in using header entries.

In the real world, we would not send a mere username; we would send the complete credentials, encrypted, so that the service could validate them. Here, we merely want to show how to add a header entry from the sender side and process a header entry on the receiver side.

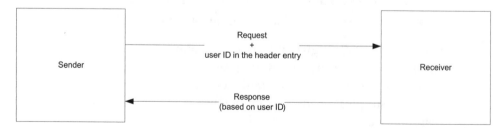

Figure 3.4   A simple request/response illustrating the use of a header entry for carrying user ID. The sender sends a user ID in the SOAP header using a WS-Security standard header. The receiver's response is based on the user ID received from the sender.

Table 3.2   Steps to add a header entry

Step	Action	How To
1	Set up your environment.	If you have not already set up the environment required to run the examples in this book, please refer to chapter 2 to do so. `ant deploy` should install all the examples.
2	Restart Tomcat server.	Run `shutdown` and `startup` scripts (`.bat` files if you are using Windows and `.sh` files if you are on Linux/Solaris/OS X) found in Tomcat's `bin` directory.
3	If it is not already running, start TCP monitor.	Run `ant tcpmon`. It should pop open a tcp monitor that shows all the traffic between the Tomcat server and our applications.
4	Run `ant demo -Dexample.id=2`.	You should be able to view the request-response pairs going through the tcpmon console.

Before we discuss the code, let's run the example. Table 3.2 lists the steps to complete.

If everything goes well, you will see the screen shown in figure 3.5.

Just as in the web service invocation example shown in chapter 2, the current example demonstrates the invocation of all the methods offered by the brokerage service. You will see that all the SOAP request messages captured by `tcpmon` now include a WS-Security `Header` element with a `UsernameToken` inside it. We changed the `createMarketOrder` and `createLimitOrder` implementations to include the username as part of the returned order ID. Observe in figure 3.5 that the user name, `chap`, sent as part of the `UsernameToken` in the `Security` header entry of the request, is returned as a part of the `orderId` element in the `createMarketOrderResponse`.

From this example, the following can be observed:

- The sender added a standard WS-Security header entry with the user ID.
- The receiver parsed and analyzed the header entry and picked out the username. And, it sent back the response with the username, illustrating that it indeed got the username.

There are several ways you can implement these tasks in the code. However, we want to be able to do these tasks without changing the client and service code. Since the header entries are extraneous to the actual task, if we can separate the implementation of header processing from the implementation of the actual client and service, we can better maintain the client and service implementations.

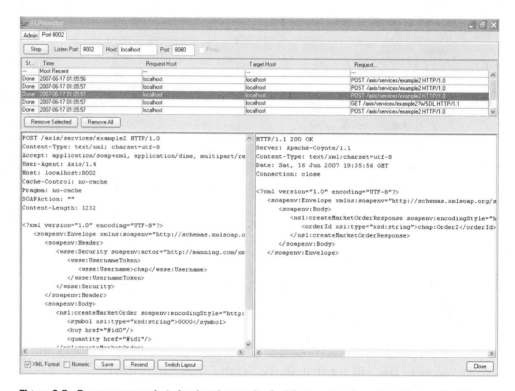

Figure 3.5 Tcpmon screenshot showing the result of adding our header entry. Observe that the request message contains a header entry with Username in it. Also observe that the orderId in the response contains the Username provided in the request.

In the next section, we will introduce the concept of *handlers*. These handlers will help us write the code that can be configured to run on both the client and service sides to add and understand the header entries. In this case, since the server's (i.e., the receiver) response depends on the header entry, we will show how the handler can communicate information it computes from the header entries to the actual service code. Figure 3.6 shows how it would all fit in.

As figure 3.6 illustrates, handlers not only can produce and consume header entries; they can also communicate the results of their work to the actual service code using a `context`.

In the next section, we will introduce handlers and show you how to put them into action in Apache Axis.

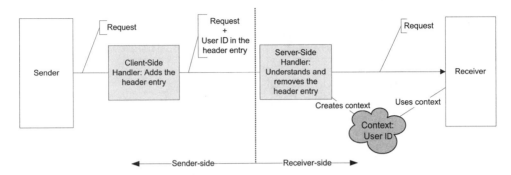

Figure 3.6 **Illustration of how handlers can produce and consume the header entries and communicate context to a service. The client-side handler adds the header entry and the server-side handler consumes the header entry. These handlers are actually part of the sender and receiver applications, respectively, and are implemented as libraries. Notice that the SOAP message passed between the applications contains the WS-Security `Header` element.**

3.4 *Processing SOAP extensions using handlers*

As we mentioned earlier, SOAP allows for any kind of extensions, including ones that are completely homegrown, as long as they are syntactically correct. But how can a SOAP engine possibly know how to deal with the extended SOAP message? Even if extensions are standardized, not all standard extensions can be supported by all engines. We need a generic mechanism to deal with extensions. Almost all SOAP engines out there provide a mechanism by which we can process SOAP extensions without having to modify the service itself. The mechanism is called a *handler* in the JAX-RPC/Axis world and a *SOAPExtension* in the .NET world.

In this section, we will show how handlers work. We will describe how they work in abstract, and then show the actual implementation, with annotations.

3.4.1 *How handlers work*

Handlers can be configured in several different ways. They can be configured on both server-side and client-side engines. Depending on the SOAP engine in use, handlers can be registered by service, by transport, or globally for all services and transports. Server-side handlers intercept requests on their way into the service and responses on their way out of the service. Client-side handlers intercept requests on their way out and responses on their way in. Figure 3.7 illustrates the sequence in which client-side and server-side handlers are invoked during request and response flows.

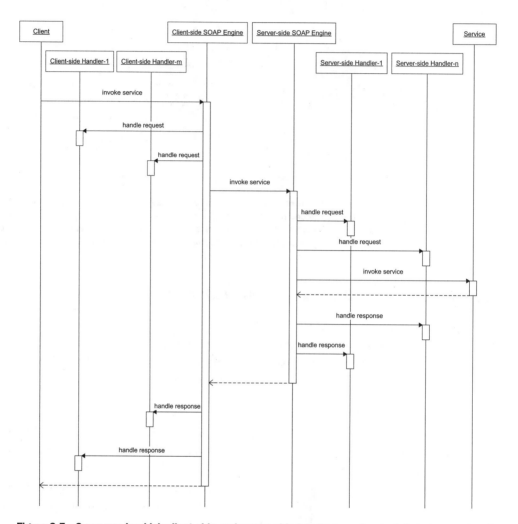

Figure 3.7 Sequence in which client-side and server-side handlers are invoked during request and response flows. Client-side handlers intercept requests on their way out to the service and responses on their way in. Server-side handlers intercept requests on their way into the service and responses on their way out.

What does a handler do with the intercepted message? Typically, handlers create or consume one or more SOAP `Header` elements in the request or response. In our example, the client-side security handler added a WS-Security element into the header. The server-side handler consumed the same header, and perhaps can use it to enforce security.

Handlers can do a lot more than merely work with headers. Some handlers may modify the message body itself. An internationalization handler may replace certain parts of the message with their equivalents in a different language. Some handlers may not change anything in the message but may simply cause a side effect. For example, an audit handler may log parts of the request and response in a database.

These handlers can be written in two different ways. We can use the APIs provided by Axis itself, or we can use the JAX-RPC handler APIs for portability reasons. To take advantage of portability, we will use JAX-RPC handler APIs in our examples.

The Java packages to understand for implementing JAX-RPC handlers are:

- `javax.xml.rpc.handler`
- `javax.xml.rpc.handler.soap`
- `javax.xml.soap`
- `javax.xml.namespace`

The first two of these packages are standardized as part of the JAX-RPC specification. The third is defined by the SAAJ specification. The last is defined by the Java API for XML Processing (JAXP) standard. You will find the javadocs for these packages in Axis documentation folders.

Now, you understand how we can use handlers to introduce and consume the header entries. We will show the actual implementation in the next section using JAX-RPC API, providing a step-by-step explanation so that you can follow the details.

3.4.2 *Outline of the solution*

We have two handlers in the package `com.manning.samples.soasecimpl.example2`:

1 We need one handler on the sender-side (client-side). It should add the user ID to the SOAP message when it intercepts the request on its way out. `ClientSideWSSecurityHandler` is the class that implements this handler.

2 We need another handler on the receiver side (server-side). It should intercept the request on its way in and parse the headers. Also, it should send the user information to the service in some fashion. In our example, we use a class named `WSSecurityUsernameHandler`.

Let us now look at the implementation of these two handlers in Axis. First, we need to understand the basic technical details of implementing a JAX-RPC handler, as explained in the next section. We will use the server-side handler to introduce JAX-RPC. That means the header entry is already there in the message—we will show how to extract it and communicate it to the service.

3.4.3 *Implementing a server-side JAX-RPC handler*

To implement a JAX-RPC handler, you need to implement the `javax.xml.rpc.handler.Handler` interface. Unless your handler is already extending some other superclass, a convenient alternative to implementing all the methods in the handler interface is extending the `javax.xml.rpc.handler.GenericHandler` abstract class. If you look at the code for the example we ran earlier, you will see that we extend `GenericHandler` and name it `com.manning.samples.soasecimpl.example2.WSSecurityUsernameHandler`.

Handler initialization

JAX-RPC requires that your handler class provides a default constructor. If you need to initialize your handler based on configuration parameters, override the `init(HandlerInfo)` method. The `javax.xml.rpc.handler.HandlerInfo` instance passed to your `init` implementation provides access to the configuration parameters as a name-value map.

For example, a client-side handler that adds a security-related header to the request might want to keep open the choice of actor at whom the header is targeted. Each client application that relies on the handler can then configure the parameter to target the header at the right actor.

```
public void init(HandlerInfo handlerInfo) {
    Map config = handlerInfo.getHandlerConfig();
    targetActorURI = (String)
      config.get(TARGET_ACTOR_PARAMETER_NAME);
}
```

Similarly, a server-side handler may look for configuration parameters such as locators for password stores and cryptography keys. These can be obtained the same way.

Handling requests, responses, and faults

A JAX-RPC handler can intercept requests by implementing the `handleRequest` method. Successful responses—responses that do not carry a SOAP fault—can be intercepted by implementing the `handleResponse` method. Responses that carry back SOAP faults can be intercepted by implementing the `handleFault` method as shown in figure 3.7.

In all cases, the `handle` methods should not save any message-related state within the handler. There is a reason for this restriction: the JAX-RPC runtime should be able to pool and reuse handler instances. Then, how do these handlers keep any information about the message? It is done through an instance of `javax.xml.rpc.handler.MessageContext`. This instance contains properties modeled as name-value pairs. Let us see how this instance can be used. When a server-side security handler authenticates the user, it may communicate that information to other handlers via user ID saved as a property in the `MessageContext`. Listing 3.3 is an extract from `WSSecurityUsernameHandler.java` demonstrating this.

> **Listing 3.3** Extract from `com.manning.samples.soasecimpl.example2.WSSecurity-UsernameHandler`: Reads a username from the WS-Security header and saves it in the `MessageContext`

```
public boolean handleRequest(MessageContext messageContext) {
    logger.debug
      ("Applying " + getClass().getName() + " to request");
    SOAPMessageContext soapContext =
        (SOAPMessageContext) messageContext;

    //...some code snipped...

    logger.debug("Locating relevant WS-Security header");
    SOAPMessage message = soapContext.getMessage();          ❶ Message
    SOAPEnvelope soapEnvelope = null;
    SOAPHeader soapHeader = null;
    SOAPHeaderElement securityElement = null;
    try {                                                    ❷ Envelope
        soapEnvelope = message.getSOAPPart().getEnvelope();  
        soapHeader = soapEnvelope.getHeader();               ❸ Header
        securityElement = Utils.getHeaderByNameAndActor
            (soapEnvelope, Constants.WS_SECURITY_SECURITY_QNAME,
             roleSet, true);                      Security entry ❹
    } catch (SOAPException e) {
        logger.error(e);
        //...some code snipped...
    }

    if (securityElement == null) {
        logger.error
          ("Did not find an applicable WS-Security header");
        //...some code snipped...
    }

    //...some code snipped...

    //locate usernametoken
    logger.debug("Locating UsernameToken");
```

```
SOAPElement usernameTokenElement = Utils.locateChildElement
    (securityElement,
     Constants.WS_SECURITY_NS_URI,
     Constants.WS_SECURITY_USERNAMETOKEN_TAG);     Username token ❺
if (usernameTokenElement == null) {
  logger.error
    ("Failed to locate UsernameToken in WS-Security header");
    //...some code snipped...
}

//locate username in the usernametoken
logger.debug
("Locating username from UsernameToken");
SOAPElement usernameElement = Utils.locateChildElement
    (usernameTokenElement,                          ❻ User name
     Constants.WS_SECURITY_NS_URI,                     element
     Constants.WS_SECURITY_USERNAME_TAG);

//check if we were successful in locating username
if (usernameElement == null) {
//...some code snipped...
}
String username = usernameElement.getValue();     Value of username
logger.debug("username: " + username);

//populate message context with username/password  ❼ Username
messageContext.setProperty                            in message
  (Constants.USERNAME_MSG_CONTEXT_PROPERTY, username);  context

//remove the processed header as soap mandates
soapHeader.removeChild(securityElement);

                                                  ❽ Header removal

//returning true to say -
//continue with the rest of the
//processing for this request
return true;
}
```

The code in this listing, despite its length, is very straightforward. We are always supplied a context to begin with as an argument to handleRequest. We get the message from the context ❶ as a first step. Next, we get the SOAP envelope ❷ from the message. Next, we get the header ❸ from the envelope and the Security element ❹, which is a WS-Security-defined header entry, from the header. (Remember that the header can contain any number of entries. We are only interested in headers that are targeted at us; that is, those with actor/role URIs matching one of the URIs in our roleSet. We will elaborate on the concept of actor/role in section 3.5.2. We are passing "true" as the last argument to getHeaderByName-AndActor to indicate that the handler is deployed as part of an endpoint. You will have to wait until section 3.5.2 to understand the need for this information.) Next we get a username token ❺ from the header entry named wsse:UserNameToken. We get the username element ❻ from the token. Finally, after seven steps, we have the username ❼ extracted from the element.

Now that we have the user ID, we must somehow communicate it to the service. We save the username in the message context for that purpose. The receiver has access to the message context and can extract the username if it requires. Finally, the handler removes ❽ the security element in the header.

Now that the handler has set the username in the MessageContext, how does the service use it? Listing 3.4 illustrates this with an extract from Example2Soap-BindingImpl.

Listing 3.4 Extract from com.manning.samples.soasecimpl.example2.Example2-SoapBindingImpl: **Reads username from** MessageContext **and uses it as part of the business logic**

```
public class Example2SoapBindingImpl
    implements Brokerage, ServiceLifecycle {

    /** MessageContext to use when looking for user id */
    private static MessageContext messageContext = null;

    public void init(java.lang.Object context)
        throws javax.xml.rpc.ServiceException {
            if (context instanceof ServletEndpointContext) {
                messageContext =
                    ((ServletEndpointContext) context).        ❶ Get the
                    getMessageContext();                             context
            } else {
                //...some code snipped...
            }
    }

    /** Places a limit order for the given symbol.
     * Info on the trader placing the order is assumed to
     * be available from MessageContext.
     * @return orderId
     */
    public String createLimitOrder
        (String symbol, boolean buy,
         int quantity, float priceLimit)
        throws java.rmi.RemoteException {
        //dummy impl - always returns userid:same value
        return
```

```
                messageContext.getProperty(Call.USERNAME_PROPERTY) +    ◁─┐
                ":Order1";                                         Get the username  ❷
        }
        //...rest of the code snipped...


    }
```

The `MessageContext` instance associated with this service instance is available at the start of the service life cycle, through the `context` ❶ object passed to `init`. Next, it gets the username from the context ❷. What the client does with the username depends on the business logic. In the example here, we are making use of it as a part of the ID we assign to the created order.

3.4.4 *Implementing a client-side JAX-RPC handler*

Now that we have seen how the server takes care of the header, we will examine how the client can insert the header into the SOAP request. The file `Client-SideWSSecurityHandler.java` contains the code for this handler.

The relevant part of the code is shown in listing 3.5:

Listing 3.5 Extract from `com.manning.samples.soasecimpl.example2.Client-SideWSSecurityHandler`: Writes username to the WS-Security header before it is sent

```
/** Adds a WS-Security header to the request
 * providing the username and password set by the
 * client endpoint in the given messageContext.
 */
public boolean handleRequest(MessageContext messageContext) {
    logger.debug
      ("Applying " + getClass().getName() + " to request");
    SOAPMessageContext soapContext =
        (SOAPMessageContext) messageContext;

    // Obtain the username from the properties file
    // Refer to the file for full details
    ...
    //now add wsse header to the soap message
    try {
      SOAPMessage message = soapContext.getMessage();
      SOAPEnvelope soapEnvelope =
          message.getSOAPPart().getEnvelope();

      Name wsseHeaderName = soapEnvelope.createName       ❶  Creation and
          (Constants.WS_SECURITY_SECURITY_TAG,               addition of
           Constants.WS_SECURITY_PREF_NS_PREFIX,             WS-Security
                                                             header entry
```

```
                  Constants.WS_SECURITY_NS_URI);        ❶  Creation and
       SOAPHeaderElement securityElement=                  addition of
           soapEnvelope.getHeader().                       WS-Security
           addHeaderElement(wsseHeaderName);               header entry

       Name userTokenElementName = soapEnvelope.createName
           (Constants.WS_SECURITY_USERNAMETOKEN_TAG,
           Constants.WS_SECURITY_PREF_NS_PREFIX,       ❷  Creation
           Constants.WS_SECURITY_NS_URI);                 and
       SOAPElement userTokenElement =                     addition of
           securityElement.addChildElement                username
           (userTokenElementName);                        token

       Name usernameElementName = soapEnvelope.createName
           (Constants.WS_SECURITY_USERNAME_TAG,
           Constants.WS_SECURITY_PREF_NS_PREFIX,       ❸  Creation
           Constants.WS_SECURITY_NS_URI);                 and
       SOAPElement usernameElement =                      addition of
           userTokenElement.addChildElement               username
           (usernameElementName);                         element
       usernameElement.addTextNode(username);   ◁──  Addition of
                                                      username value
       ...
     }
     ...
     return true;
   }
```

Just as in the server-side handler, the client-side handler gets access to the SOAP envelope through the message, which it gets from the context. Now, it will have to create the header entry and add it to the envelope. As a first step, it creates ❶ the WS-Security header entry. It immediately adds the header entry to the envelope. Then, it creates ❷ the username token and adds it to the header entry. Next it creates and adds ❸ the username element, and sets the username value at the node. We can change the order (for example, create the elements all at once and then add) and still get the same result.

These steps exactly mimic the ones on the server-side. Of course, the details of how we got the username are skipped in this illustration. For full details, please look at the source code at http://www.manning.com/kanneganti.

By now, you have learned how to write handler code. What you have not seen is how this code is added to the server or the client. Before showing how we can make handlers a part of server or the client, we will explore the concept of multiple handlers and how they can be *chained*. This concept is useful as we proceed to add more and more headers to the message. Finally, we will show the *configuration* of the handlers to the server or the client in full generality.

3.4.5 *Handler chains*

Handlers can be used for various kinds of tasks. In our example, we are using handlers to accomplish one task: separating the code that deals with the extraction of a user's identity claim from the main service code. If there are multiple tasks, we can still use one single handler to deal with all those other than the core business logic of the service. However, that is not modular, and may lead to maintainability problems. Instead, we can use handler chaining to "hook up" multiple handlers to the server or the client.

For example: On the client-side, one handler may add a WS-Security header and another might encrypt the username and password in the WS-Security header to keep them safe. The reverse may happen on the server-side: a decryption handler followed by an authentication handler to verify the username and password provided by the client. We may even want to invoke the same handler more than once when processing a message. For example, we may call an encryption handler multiple times to encrypt different parts of a message.

JAX-RPC provides for associating a chain of handlers with each service. We will show how this association happens in the next section. For now, let us see how the handler chains are invoked on the client and server-sides.

Since there are multiple handlers touching a message, there ought to be rules about how they interact. Without implying any particular order, the following rules specify how the handlers behave.

1. Any information saved in the `MessageContext` is visible to every handler in the chain as well as to the service. In example 2 (listings 3.3 and 3.4), we already saw how to set data in `MessageContext` and read it back.

2. A handler may return `true` from `handleRequest`, `handleResponse`, and `handleFault` to indicate that the next handler in the chain should be invoked. In case no more handlers are left, the message is dispatched to the endpoint. As shown in figure 3.8, handlers in a chain are called in reverse order for processing responses and faults compared to the order in which they are called for processing requests.

3. If a handler returns `false` from `handleRequest`, no more handlers in the chain are called to handle the request. The service endpoint is not called either. Instead, the handler returning `false` from `handleRequest` has the responsibility of creating the response message. The `handleResponse`

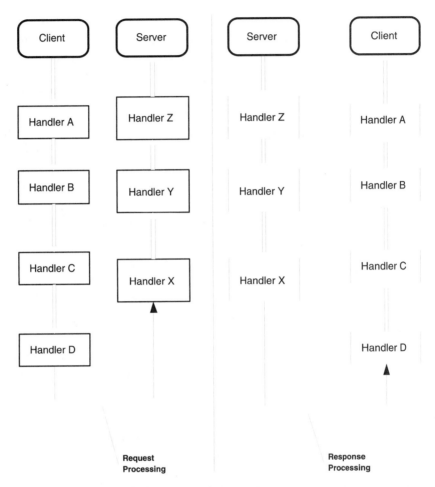

Figure 3.8 A chain of JAX-RPC handlers can be invoked on the client as well as the server-side. Handlers in a chain are called in reverse order for processing responses and faults compared to the order in which they are called for processing requests.

methods of the handlers in the chain are called in the reverse order, starting with the handler that returned `false` from `handleRequest`. For example, in the server-side handler chain shown in figure 3.8, if the `handleRequest` method of handler Y returns `false`, instead of calling the `handle-Request` method of handler Z next as part of request processing, the JAX-RPC engine switches to response processing and calls the `handleResponse` methods of handler Y and handler X, in that order.

4   If a handler returns `false` from `handleResponse`, no more handlers in the chain are called. The response message is dispatched to the endpoint. For example, in the client-side handler chain shown in figure 3.8, if the `handleResponse` method of handler C returns `false`, the JAX-RPC engine will skip the `handleResponse` methods in handles B and A and directly deliver the response to the client endpoint.

5   If a server-side handler throws a `SOAPFaultException` from `handle-Request`, the rest of the handlers in the chain and the service endpoint are not called to handle the request. Instead, the `handleFault` methods of the handlers in the chain are called in the reverse order, starting with the handler that threw `SOAPFaultException` from `handleRequest`. The handler throwing the exception has the responsibility of creating a SOAP fault in the response. (This rule is similar to rule 3.)

6   If a server-side handler throws an exception other than `SOAPFault-Exception`, the request processing is terminated. The JAX-RPC implementation generates a server SOAP fault by itself and dispatches it to the endpoint. (This rule is similar to rule 4.)

7   The JAX-RPC specification rules that a client-side handler should not throw a `SOAPFaultException`. If a client-side handler throws an exception other than `SOAPFaultException`, the exception is propagated back to the client endpoint as an instance of `java.rmi.RemoteException` or any of its subclasses.

Now, we get back to the issue of how to add handlers to the actual service. In the next section we will show the details.

3.4.6 *Configuring handlers and handler chains*

The mechanism to configure handlers and handler chains differs between the server-side and the client-side.

Server-side configuration

On the server-side, handlers and handler chains can be configured using deployment descriptors specific to the JAX-RPC implementation. For example, Axis provides the syntax for configuring handlers and handler chains in its Web Service Deployment Descriptors (WSDD). Listing 3.6 shows the Axis WSDD for a service with two handlers arranged into a chain.

Listing 3.6   Axis Web Service Deployment Descriptor (WSDD) for a service with two handlers arranged in a chain

```
<deployment
  xmlns="http://xml.apache.org/axis/wsdd/"
  xmlns:java="http://xml.apache.org/axis/wsdd/providers/java">

  <service name="example"                          ┐  Handler chain
    provider="java:RPC" style="rpc" use="encoded">    configuration for
    <handlerInfoChain>                           ◄─┘  example service

      <handlerInfo classname="x.y.DecryptionHandler">  ◄─┐ First handler
                                                          configuration

        <parameter name="symmetricAlgorithm" value="BlowFish"/>
        <parameter name="asymmetricAlgorithm" value="RSA"/>
        <parameter name="keyStoreFile" value="/jw2store.jks"/>
                                                        Config params
        <!-- Namespace qualified names of one or more     needed by
             SOAP headers consumed by this handler -->    first handler
        <header qname="wsse:Security"            ┐ Name of a header
          xmlns:wsse=".../ws/2002/07/secext"/>   │ processed by first handler
      </handlerInfo>

      <handlerInfo classname="x.y.Authenticationhandler"/>  ◄─┐ A second
                                                              handler in
      <!-- One or more actor URIs associated with the service  the chain
           and the handler chain -->
      <role soapActorName="http://y.x/cop"/>   ┐ Actors/roles associated
      <role soapActorName="http://y.x/eg"/>    │ with the chain

    </handlerInfoChain>

    <!-- service parameters and operations snipped for brevity -->
  </service>
</deployment>
```

In addition to showing a handler chain, this listing illustrates two important aspects of configuring JAX-RPC handlers. Deployment descriptors of some JAX-RPC implementations such as Axis may require declaration of:

- Namespace qualified names of one or more SOAP headers consumed by a handler
- URIs for all the SOAP actors a handler chain represents.

That's all there is to configuring server-side handlers and handler chains. Let us now shift our focus to configuring client-side handlers and handler chains.

Client-side configuration

JAX-RPC provides a programmatic API for configuring client-side handlers and handler chains. Example code in `com.manning.samples.soasecimpl.example2.` `BrokerageServiceTestCase` illustrates the API to use in client applications that employ statically generated stubs, dynamic invocation interface (DII), and dynamic proxies. Listing 3.7 is an extract that shows how to configure handlers and handler chains for a client that uses DII to invoke a web service.

Listing 3.7   Configuring handlers on the client-side for clients using DLL

```
javax.xml.rpc.ServiceFactory serviceFactory =
    javax.xml.rpc.ServiceFactory.newInstance();
javax.xml.rpc.Service service = serviceFactory.createService     ❶ Service
  (new java.net.URL(wsdlLocation), serviceName);                    instance
 //add our client side wsse handler
HandlerRegistry handlerRegistry = service.getHandlerRegistry();
java.util.List handlerChain =
    handlerRegistry.getHandlerChain(portName);        ◁┐ Get any  preexisting
 if (handlerChain == null) {                          ❷  handler chain
    handlerChain = new java.util.LinkedList();
    handlerRegistry.setHandlerChain(portName, handlerChain);
 }                                       Create a new handler
                                          chain if none exists ❸
Map handlerConfig = new HashMap();                                  ❹
handlerConfig.put
    (ClientSideWSSecurityHandler.TARGET_ACTOR_PARAMETER_NAME,  Create a new
    Constants.OUR_SECURITY_COP_URI);                           handler
handlerChain.add                                               configuration
    (new HandlerInfo(ClientSideWSSecurityHandler.class,
                  handlerConfig,
                  null));        ◁─❺ Add new handler to the chain
 //now, make the call
Call dii = service.createCall(portName, operationName);    ◁─❻ Create a call
dii.setProperty                                       Add to call, context properties
    (Constants.USERNAME_MSG_CONTEXT_PROPERTY,         needed by handlers
    "chap");
Float quote =                                         Use the call instance to
    (Float) dii.invoke(new Object[] {"MSFT"});        invoke service operation
```

JAX-RPC organizes handler chains by service instance and port name. We first need to obtain a reference to the service instance from the service factory ❶. Once we get the service instance reference, we see if there is an existing handler chain ❷ for the port we are going to use. If none exists, we add a new handler chain ❸. Then, we configure a handler by providing the parameter and value ❹. If you'll recall, in the server-side, we set these in the deployment descriptor file.

Finally, we add the handler to the chain ❺. Now, if we create a call to the service, the client-side chain we have configured is used. If there is any information, such as the username here, that we want to make available to the handlers in the chain, we add that to the call as properties ❻. The handlers will be able to access the call properties via the message context.

As explained in chapter 2, the client code can use WSDL either dynamically or statically. Listing 3.7 demonstrates how you can set up a client-side handler chain during dynamic invocation. If we are going to use static stubs, the code for setting up a client-side handler chain will be a little different. Let us see how. All the generated stubs are required by JAX-RPC to implement the `javax.xml.rpc.Stub` interface. The `Stub` interface provides a `_setProperty` method to set the username to be used. In addition, the JAX-RPC implementation will provide a custom API to get to the underlying `Service` instance and `portname`. Listing 3.8 shows the APIs provided by Axis-generated stubs.

Listing 3.8   Configuring handlers on the client-side for clients using Axis-generated stubs

```
Example2SoapBindingStub binding = (Example2SoapBindingStub)
new BrokerageServiceLocator().getexample2();
                                         ❶  Get service instance
Service service = binding._getService();   ◁┘
QName portName = binding.getPortName();    ◁┐
                                         ❷  Get portname
HandlerRegistry handlerRegistry =
  service.getHandlerRegistry();
List handlerChain =
  handlerRegistry.getHandlerChain(portName);

//configuring the handler chain is
//the same as shown before in DII      ❸  Configure chain
...

//now, make the call
binding._setProperty
  (Constants.USERNAME_MSG_CONTEXT_PROPERTY,   ❹  Set property
  "chap");
String value =
  binding.createLimitOrder("IBM", true, 100, (float)54.40);
```

The essential code to configure a client-side handler chain remains the same ❸ as the DII code in listing 3.7. The details of how we get the service and the port

❶, ❷ differ in this case. Just like in the case of DII, we can pass information from the client to the client-side handlers by setting properties on the call instance. Since all the stub implementations implement the `javax.xml.rpc.Stub` interface, we can use its `_setProperty` method to do this ❹.

Configuring handlers and handler chains for dynamic proxies is a little more involved. For an example, please look at the source code for the `testDynamic-Proxy()` method in `BrokerageServiceTestCase`.

In this section, with the help of an example, we have described how you can add handlers to a JAX-RPC SOAP engine to process SOAP extensions such as WS-Security, reducing the burden of handling SOAP extensions from the end services. As we pointed out before, this idea of processing SOAP extensions by adding handlers to the SOAP engine is not limited to JAX-RPC-based SOAP engines. For example, .NET also provides a similar mechanism named `SOAPExtension`.

It is not always possible or desirable to add handlers to a SOAP engine for processing SOAP extensions. For instance, an enterprise may use a number of SOAP engines to host a large number of services. Adding handlers to each SOAP engine may be too intrusive a solution to use in such environments. However, as WS-Security is a standard extension, almost every SOAP engine may come preconfigured with handlers to process WS-Security. Even then, there may be good reasons for processing WS-Security and some of the other SOAP extensions using intermediaries. For example, an enterprise may want to centralize security enforcement and not leave it up to every SOAP engine for enforcing appropriate levels of security.

In the next section, we will describe how this centralization can be done using intermediaries—that is, SOAP-processing nodes that are neither the source nor the destination for a SOAP message.

3.5 *Processing SOAP extensions using intermediaries*

Intercepting messages in transit and acting upon them is not without precedent. HTTP proxies are quite commonplace; they intercept HTTP requests in order to apply security policies and/or return cached responses. In fact, the SOAP specification explicitly supports the use of one or more intermediaries (such as a security service) in the message path by laying down specific rules that describe what an intermediary can and cannot do. In this section, we will introduce you to these rules.

But before we do that, we will address a question that might be bothering you at this point. Up until this point in the book, we have only showed you interactions between two endpoints. We showed you senders (or source endpoint) of SOAP messages directly connecting to the intended recipient (or the destination endpoint) for each message. How then, you may rightly wonder, does a message get routed via intermediaries? Two possibilities exist.

1   The first possibility is that a network device that understands application-level semantics intercepts each message and routes it across the right set of intermediaries. But do such network devices exist? Yes, they do, and they are commonly referred to as *Application-Oriented Networking (AON)* devices. Appendix E describes AON in more detail.

2   The second possibility is that the source endpoint connects to the first intermediary and not the destination endpoint when sending a message. The first intermediary can then do its work and pass on the message to a second intermediary. The second can then pass it to a third, the third can pass to a fourth, and so on until the last intermediary, which passes the message to the destination endpoint. How does each SOAP processing node (by node, we mean endpoint or intermediary) in the message path know what the next node should be? For very good reasons, there is no concrete answer to this question except in one special case. In general, it is up to a SOAP processing node (be it the source endpoint or an intermediary) to figure out where it will route the message next. However, as the last intermediary in a SOAP message path would almost always want to route the message to the originally intended destination endpoint, a specification named WS-Addressing provides a way to preserve the destination endpoint address as part of a message.

Next we will describe WS-Addressing. Subsequently, we will describe SOAP processing rules for intermediaries, which tell us what the intermediaries can and cannot do.

3.5.1 *Preserving the endpoint information: WS-Addressing*

Let us examine what happens at an intermediary such as a security service. The intermediary receives a message and reads the parts intended for it. It will, optionally, modify the message. For example, the intermediary may insert some new Header elements. Later, the intermediary will send the message to the next hop in the message-processing path, as shown in the figure 3.9.

As you can see, an intermediary should be able to figure out where the message should go next and route the message to that hop. In general, intermediaries are

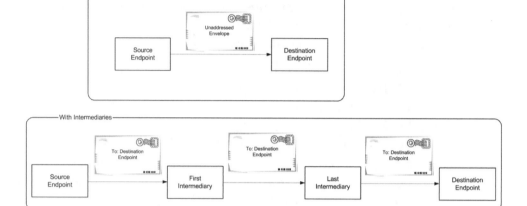

Figure 3.9   Without intermediaries in a message path, no addressing information needs to be provided in the envelope. The introduction of intermediaries will however require that the destination endpoint information be preserved so that the final intermediary can route the message to the destination endpoint.

free to determine the next hop the message should make. However, the last intermediary in a message path *usually* wants to route the message to its destination point. We say *usually* instead of *always*, as the last intermediary is free to route the message to a different destination than what the source endpoint asked for. For example, a message may get routed to a backup service instance in case the main service instance is down.

Clearly, the last intermediary needs to know the destination endpoint address. Of course, as shown in figure 3.9, this issue does not come up if there are no intermediaries. The source endpoint establishes a direct connection to the destination endpoint and the transport protocol itself handles the responsibility of routing the message to its destination. In a multihop message path, this is not the case. Responsibility of the first transport connection ends once it delivers a message to the first intermediary. Additional transport connections will have to be set up from the first intermediary to the second, second to third, and so on.

To allow the message to be routed to the final destination, we need a way of preserving the destination endpoint information for use by the last intermediary. WS-Addressing provides the needed standards here.

Listing 3.9 shows WS-Addressing in action.

Listing 3.9 WS-Addressing elements declare destination endpoint address whereas transport (HTTP) headers declare next hop address

```
POST /axis/services/proxy HTTP/1.0
Host: localhost:8000
SOAPAction: ""
Content-Type: text/xml; charset=utf-8
Content-Length: ...
Accept: application/soap+xml, ...

<?xml version="1.0" encoding="UTF-8"?>
<soapenv:Envelope ...>
  <soapenv:Header>
    <wsa:To xmlns:wsa=".../ws/2004/08/addressing">
      http://localhost:8000/axis/services/example6
    </wsa:To>
    <wsa:Action xmlns:wsa=".../ws/2004/08/addressing">
    </wsa:Action>

    <wsse:Security soapenv:actor="...">
      ...
    </wsse:Security>
  </soapenv:Header>
  <soapenv:Body>
    ...
  </soapenv:Body>
</soapenv:Envelope>
```

❶ **HTTP headers declare the next hop address**

❷ **WS-Addressing elements declare eventual destination address**

HTTP is the transport protocol in this example. The HTTP headers ❶ show that the HTTP connection is made to the next hop, `http://localhost:8000/axis/services/proxy`, with the `SOAPAction` header set to an empty string. The ultimate destination's address and `SOAPAction` parameter ❷ are different from these and preserved using `To` and `Action` headers defined by WS-Addressing.

WS-Addressing can also be used to convey the reply-to address, message ID, and correlation ID. The reply-to address is useful when using asynchronous messaging as SOAP transport. Message ID and correlation ID are also useful for replying to a particular message asynchronously.

Now that you understand WS-Addressing, we will get back, as promised, to explaining the rules SOAP lays down for message processing in intermediaries.

3.5.2 *SOAP processing rules for intermediaries*

SOAP explicitly acknowledges the possibility of intermediaries. Doing so enables a rich extension model. The fact that different nodes can take different actions on a SOAP message can help us develop horizontal services. For example, one intermediary node may take care of regulatory compliance whereas another intermediary can take care of security concerns.

In this section, we will see the message processing rules SOAP specifies to accommodate the possibility of multiple intermediaries in a SOAP message path.

Addressing a node in SOAP

SOAP makes it easy for a dynamic network of processing nodes (intermediaries + endpoint) to work together without conflicts by allowing each to clearly see what parts of a message are intended for it and what are not. As we explained earlier in this chapter, SOAP 1.1 defines an optional `actor` attribute (renamed `role` in SOAP 1.2) to indicate who should process a header entry. This facility makes it easy to partition the SOAP header entries into sets that should be processed by different nodes in the message path.

For example, an intermediary node that can take care of regulatory compliance can be explicitly fed the required data using a header that is targeted at it. All it takes is to simply set the entry's `actor` attribute to an URI that identifies the node to target it.

Typically, we set the `actor` attribute to an explicit URI when we know which specific node it is intended for. However, there are a few reserved actor URIs we can use for identifying nodes based on their position in the message path:

- `http://schemas.xmlsoap.org/soap/actor/next`, defined by SOAP 1.1, targets a header entry at the next processing node. (The equivalent in SOAP 1.2 is `http://www.w3.org/2003/05/soap-envelope/role/next`.).

- `http://www.w3.org/2003/05/soap-envelope/role/ultimateReceiver` is defined by SOAP 1.2 to explicitly target a header entry at the end recipient. Note that by default, if there is no actor, only the end recipient can act on it.

- `http://www.w3.org/2003/05/soap-envelope/role/none` is a special value defined by SOAP 1.2 to indicate that a header entry should not be processed by any node. Any node is free to look at such an entry if another entry targeted at the node refers to the contents of the former. This is an excellent way to provide information to all the nodes—for example, we can keep a timestamp for all the nodes that need that information.

- An empty string ("") as a role in SOAP 1.2 is another special case, indicating that the *base URI* should be used. The base URI is specified explicitly using the attribute `xml:base`. If that attribute is not used, the default value for the base URI depends on the protocol used to carry SOAP messages.

For HTTP, the base URI is the HTTP Request-URI or the value of the HTTP Content-Location header field.

In addition to providing a mechanism for addressing a specific node in the message path, SOAP lays down other rules that all SOAP processing nodes must comply with. We will explain these next.

Processing at a node

Once a node gets the message, it must comply with the following rules when processing the message:

1 The node should remove the header entries targeted at it before the message is transmitted to the next node. SOAP 1.2 however introduces a `relay` attribute to indicate that an unprocessed header must be relayed on to subsequent nodes in the message path.

2 As described earlier in this chapter, the node must raise a SOAP fault if it does not understand a header entry targeted at it with the `mustUnderstand` attribute set to `"1."`

3 The node can add new header entries. For example, the node can add information that needs to be communicated to subsequent nodes in the message path. There are no restrictions on what kind of header entries a node might add. For example, a node can reinsert the header it just consumed if it is needed by a subsequent node in the message path. Of course, the `actor` attribute on the reinserted node should be adjusted to match a subsequent node's URI.

4 The node can modify any part of the message itself, including header entries not targeted at it and the `Body`. However, when doing so, it is good custom to indicate to subsequent nodes how the message is transformed. For example, if a security node encrypts part of a message, it should add a header entry describing which portions of the message have been encrypted, the algorithm used, and the key used to encrypt. A subsequent node can then use this information to decrypt the encrypted parts appropriately, provided it has access to the key needed to decrypt.

You now understand how SOAP accommodates for intermediaries in message paths. What you have learned in this section should have set you thinking about questions such as: can security be truly delegated off to an intermediary, and if so, when should I do that? We will return to these questions in chapter 8, as by then you will have learned enough about WS-Security to figure out what parts can be addressed by intermediaries and what cannot.

We will conclude this chapter by answering a few frequently asked questions about SOAP extensions.

3.6 *SOAP Extensions FAQ*

As you have seen with WS-Security, SOAP provides a convenient extension mechanism for addressing concerns that SOAP doesn't take care of by itself. We can extend SOAP to take care of domain-independent concerns such as security and transactions, as well as domain-specific concerns such as metering and billing. Extending SOAP with headers is thus a powerful design pattern that needs to be mastered by practitioners of SOA.

In this section, we will answer some of the frequently asked questions about the usage of headers and handlers when extending SOAP. Note that this section is here for the sake of completeness and is not directly related to security in SOA.

3.6.1 *What should go into the headers?*

Technically, whatever you can do using the SOAP body can be done in headers. For example, the whole message body can be thought of as a header targeted at the final destination with `mustUnderstand` set to `"1."` In that case, which parts of a message should be in the headers and which parts should be in the body?

A rule of thumb is to use the SOAP message body only for information needed by the core business logic of the service. For example, if you are invoking the brokerage service to get a quote for a stock symbol, only the stock symbol belongs in the body.

What else would one want to send with a quote request anyway? You may want to send your premium account number so that the brokerage service responds faster and/or with better information. For example, the brokerage may offer premium account holders the latest quotes whereas everyone else may be provided with delayed quotes.

Typically, information in headers is utilized by some functionality that is common across a number of services. That functionality, residing perhaps in a handler (or another process as you will see in chapter 8), can access these header entries and process them. For example, a billing handler or process may meter the usage of services by customers. It may obtain the customer account number from a header and the name of the service from the body. Figure 3.10 shows this pattern of utilizing headers for enabling common services.

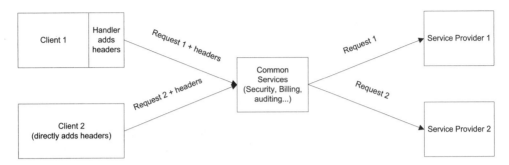

Figure 3.10 Headers are often utilized to enable common services such as security and billing.

Clients, either directly or via handlers, may add headers that common services such as security, billing, and auditing may utilize. Once the common services utilize the information available in the headers, they may remove the headers from the message and forward the request to the appropriate end service.

Several vendors provide solutions for implementing common services. For example, ESB vendors provide for centralization of common services.

3.6.2 *How do we standardize on headers?*

Since creating a namespace is easy, the temptation is to define as many headers as we require in our own namespace. However, we must remember one thing: the headers are supposed to provide a standard way of extending SOAP to implement specific functionality. If the functionality we wish to enable via an extension has already been addressed by a standard extension, we are better off sticking to the header entries defined by the standard extension.

For example, you should not create your own headers for carrying username and password, unless the meaning is drastically different from the WS-Security standard. In most cases, if the meaning is different, perhaps the purpose of the Header element and the name also is different enough to create unambiguous header names.

3.6.3 *How many handlers?*

How many handlers should we use? If we go for modularity, we should use different handlers for different tasks. That lets us mix and match the handlers via configuration mechanisms. However, performance reasons may make us put multiple tasks in one handler. Also, interdependencies between the two handlers may require us to merge them into one. You will see examples of these kinds later in the book.

3.6.4 *How do we support handlers?*

Ultimately clients have to supply the headers with requests. Since most of the information may be specific to the client, it may not be possible to write a separate process to add header entries. What this means is that the code to add header entries should be part of the client itself, since it needs access to the information only the client can provide.

Even though providing and consuming header entries is standard, it is not easy to program. Typically, in enterprises, standard libraries are provided so that the clients are spared the complexity of the coding. If you are designing custom headers for an enterprise, you should consider providing the required libraries too. The libraries may be packaged in the form of handlers if the enterprise predominantly uses JAX-RPC.

3.7 *Summary*

In this chapter, we first argued that the right approach for addressing security in SOAP is to do it via an extension to SOAP. We then described how SOAP allows itself to be extended via headers and introduced WS-Security, a standard SOAP extension to carry security tokens and ensure message-level security. We showed you how to produce and consume WS-Security-related (and other) header entries by adding handlers to a SOAP engine. Once you run the examples and study the code, you should be able to write the handlers required to process any header entries.

We also introduced the notion of SOAP intermediaries and described how SOAP messages can be routed across intermediaries using WS-Addressing. We described the rules laid down by SOAP for intermediaries and hinted at the possibility of delegating the responsibility of security enforcement to an intermediary. We will develop this idea further in chapter 8.

Toward the end, we provided guidelines for you to develop standard SOAP headers for your enterprise.

Now that you understand SOAP headers and how to process them, you can see them in action. Specifically, you will learn how to use them for authentication in chapters 4 and 5. You will also see how these headers can be used for encryption in chapter 6 and signatures in chapter 7. In all those examples, we are going to assume familiarity with handlers and will not explain that part of the code.

Suggestions for further reading

- WS-Security 1.1 Specification, an OASIS standard, is available at http://www. oasis-open.org/committees/download.php/16790/wss-v1.1-spec-os-SOAPMessage-Security.pdf. Most of the chapters in this book predate this version and are based on WS-Security 1.0. You will a find a few enhancements in WS-Security 1.1 that are not described in this book.

- Enhancements in JAX-WS 2.0, the descendent of JAX-RPC 1.x, to the JAX-RPC handler mechanism are described at https://jax-ws.dev.java.net/articles/handlers_introduction.html.

- The SOAPExtension mechanism, the equivalent of JAX-RPC handler mechanism in the .NET world, is described at http://msdn2.microsoft.com/en-us/library/esw638yk.aspx.

- The WS-Addressing specification, a W3C Recommendation, is available in two parts, at http://www.w3.org/TR/ws-addr-core and http://www.w3.org/TR/ws-addr-soap. These documents supersede the version available at the time of writing this chapter—a submission by an ad hoc industry group to W3C.

Part II

Building blocks of SOA security

Part III: SOA Security in the Enterprise					
Part II: Building Blocks of SOA Security					
WS-Security	Authentication (UsernameToken/ PasswordDigest)	Kerberos	XML Encryption	XML Signature	WS-SecureConversation
	JAX-RPC Handlers	JAAS	JGSS	Apache XML-Security	
Part I: SOA Basics					

Part II introduces the techniques you can use for addressing the following fundamental concerns of SOA security:

- Claiming and verifying identity (authentication)
  - Using passwords (chapter 4)
  - Using Kerberos (chapter 5)

- Protecting confidentiality of messages (chapter 6)
- Verifying message integrity and guarding against repudiation (chapter 7)

The techniques we will describe in this part form the basis for most of the discussion in part III, where we discuss enterprise SOA security. In this sense, we can think of the techniques described in part II as the fundamental building blocks of SOA security. Examples used in this part are deliberately kept simple and academic, as the goal here is to illustrate one building block of SOA security at a time.

You will learn about PKI, Kerberos, XML Encryption, XML Signatures, WS-Security, and WS-SecureConversation. You will use Apache Axis and JAX-RPC handlers, first introduced in part I along with Apache XML Security libraries, Java Authentication and Authorization Service (JAAS) framework, and the Java bindings of the General Security Services (JGSS) API to see each of the technologies we introduce in this part in action.

Claiming and verifying identity with passwords

This chapter covers

- Password-based authentication
- Plain-text passwords
- Digest authentication

As you saw in the previous chapter, the SOAP specification allows headers to be used for extending SOAP. WS-Security defines standard security headers for SOAP. In the first demonstration of WS-Security, we sent a username in a standard header. We also discussed the code behind that demonstration.

Sending the username along with the request is one way to claim identity. Most services require a user to establish his identity before his requests are served. This is because:

- Security restrictions require that services be provided only to authorized users. While it is not always necessary to determine user identity to figure out if a user is authorized, most often it is. For example, a low-end B2B integration service may not care who placed a purchase order as long as it is received from a trusted partner's network. Examples of services that require us to provide our identity information are of course everywhere.

- Service logic requires the knowledge of who the user is. For example, if you are checking email, the email service needs to know whose messages it needs to return.

A user *claims an identity* by sending an identifier such as a username, email address, or digital certificate. The identifier, by itself, is insufficient for a service to establish the user's identity. Only in limited situations can the service trust the user-provided identifier without any additional proof. For example, if the identifier itself is so secretive that only its legitimate owner can know it, a service can establish user identity based on the identifier. But this is usually not the case. Identifiers may be public knowledge or may be easily guessable. An identifier by itself, in general, cannot establish user identity.

In most situations, an identity claim consists of an identifier as well as proof of identity. The proof of identity can be some secret that only the identity owner and the service know. For example, a user may provide a preregistered password as proof of his identity. In this chapter, we explore the use of passwords for authentication in web services.

Several important questions come up when considering the use of passwords for authentication in web services: What kind of passwords should be supported? How does a service know what each user's password is? How do we protect the password from being stolen in transit, or simply being reused by replaying a past message as is? In this chapter, we will provide answers to all these questions. We will show two different kinds of password-based authentication in web services: clear-text password and password digest. In addition, we will study how a service validates the password. As usual, we will be illustrating all these concepts using working code that implements the standards.

Let us start with the simple case of clear-text username and password as an identity claim.

4.1 *Authentication with username and password*

In this section, we will show how WS-Security supports the use of username and password for authentication in web service invocations. This section has four parts. The first part, with the help of an example, describes how WS-Security supports the use of usernames and passwords for authentication. The second part shows the code for a sample client that uses username and password-based authentication. The third and fourth parts describe how a server can validate the information in the identity claim. The third part introduces a framework (Java Authentication and Authorization Service [JAAS]) you can use to keep the validation code generic, and the fourth part shows a sample service that uses the framework to validate username/password claims against a file-based password store.

Let's start by running an example.

4.1.1 *Example: Username and password in WS-Security*

If you recall in figure 3.5 we were sending a username along with the SOAP message. In this section, we will show an example where we will also send a password along with the SOAP message. When the username and password are correct, the server processes the request and returns the result. If not, the server returns a fault.

Running the examples

Follow the steps outlined in table 4.1 to configure the examples and execute them. These examples are used throughout the chapter. Even if you do not understand them right now, by the end of the chapter, you will understand the significance of the configuration, the layout of the code, and the choices in developing the applications.

If everything goes well, you will see the screen shown in figure 4.1.

The `tcpmon` screen will show you six SOAP calls. Of these, we will only focus on the second and third calls in this section. The first is simply a call to get the WSDL. The fourth and fifth calls are discussed later in this chapter. The sixth call is described in the next chapter.

Table 4.1 Steps that illustrate how WS-Security supports username- and password–based authentication

Step	Action	How to
1	Set up your environment.	If you have not already set up the environment required to run the examples in this book, please refer to chapter 2 to do so. `ant deploy` should install all the examples.

2	Customize your JAAS configuration file.	Go to the `conf` folder in the samples you downloaded previously when setting up the environment described in chapter 2. You will find two files: `example3-passwd.txt` and `example3-jaas.conf`. Open the latter and look for the following lines.
		
		`com.manning.samples.soasecimpl.jaas.`
		`    FileBasedAuthenticator`
		`        requisite`
		`        filePath="d:/work/eclipse/soas_code/conf/`
		`            example3-passwd.txt";`
		
		Change the `filePath` attribute in this entry to point the path to `example3-passwd.txt` on your box.

3	Configure Tomcat's JVM to pick up your JAAS configuration file.	To make the location of the conf file available to Tomcat JVM, set the `JAVA_OPTS` environment variable to `-Djava.security.auth.login.config=path-to-example3-jaas.conf-file`.
4	Restart Tomcat server.	Run `shutdown` and `startup` scripts (`.bat` files if you are using Windows and `.sh` files if you are on Linux/Solaris/OS X) found in the `bin` directory of Tomcat.
5	If it is not already running, start TCP monitor.	Run `ant tcpmon` so that you can observe the conversation. Check the "XML Format" check box to allow `tcpmon` to format shown requests and responses.
6	Run the example.	Run `ant demo -Dexample.id=3`. You should be able to view the request-response pairs going through the tcpmon console.

Examining the web service calls

Here is what the second and third calls captured by `tcpmon` do. Both of them invoke a web service—one does so with the correct password, `goodpass`, and the other does so with an incorrect password, `badpass` (shown in figure 4.1). As you would expect, the service responds with the correct answer when given the correct password and a fault when given a wrong one.

In listing 4.1, we look at the headers in the second call captured by `tcpmon`, the one where we send the correct password.

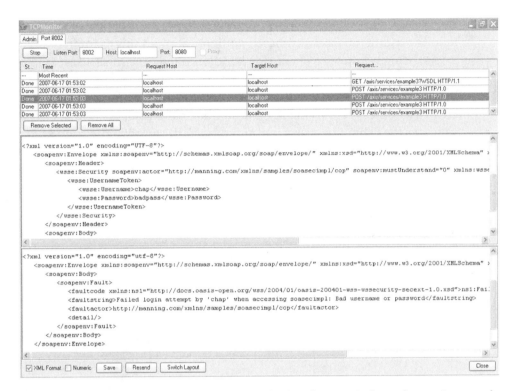

Figure 4.1 Screenshot of `tcpmon` illustrating the rejection of a request when an incorrect password is used.

Listing 4.1 Example of a security header with username and password

```
<soapenv:Header>
  <wsse:Security
    soapenv:actor="..." soapenv:mustUnderstand="0"
    xmlns:wsse=".../oasis-200401-wsswssecurity-secext-1.0.xsd">
    <wsse:UsernameToken>
        <wsse:Username>chap</wsse:Username>
        <wsse:Password>goodpass</wsse:Password>
    </wsse:UsernameToken>
  </wsse:Security>
</soapenv:Header>
```

The `Security` header entry is easy to understand. It contains the username and password in clear-text. Who adds these credentials on the client-side? How do they add them to the `Security` header entry? Who processes the entries on the server-side? How do they do it? Figure 4.2 shows an overview of the implementation of username/password-based authentication in this example.

As the figure shows, a client-side handler called `ClientSideWSSecurityHandler` adds the username and password to the `Security` header; the first server-side handler, called `WSSecurityUsernameHandler`, takes the username and password out and creates a context. Then, the second handler, called `JAASAuthenticationHandler`, validates the claim (the username and password) stored in the context. If the validation passes, information on the authenticated user (subject) is stored in the context so that the end service (`BrokerageService`) can use it.

First, let's see how the username and password are inserted by the client-side handler.

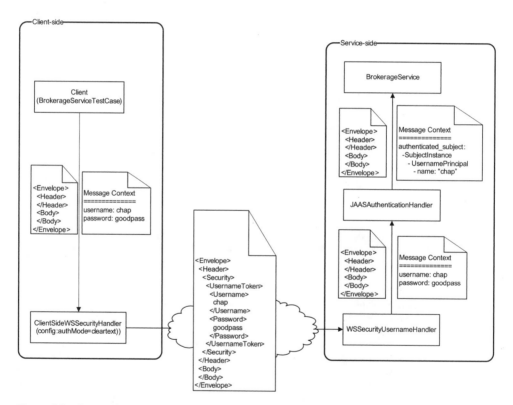

Figure 4.2 Overview of an implementation of username and clear-text password-based authentication scheme

4.1.2 *Implementing username/password scheme: client-side*

In the previous chapter, we saw how a client application can set a username in the `MessageContext` that can be used by the `ClientSideWSSecurityHandler` to create the `UsernameToken` element in the `Security` header. Exactly the same technique is used here. This time, in addition to username, the client application, `example3/BrokerageServiceTestCase.java`, also sets the password in the context, as shown in listing 4.2.

Listing 4.2 Client code adding username/password to context before invoking the service

```
Call dii = service.createCall(portName, operationName);
dii.setProperty
  (Constants.USERNAME_MSG_CONTEXT_PROPERTY, username);
dii.setProperty
  (Constants.PASSWORD_MSG_CONTEXT_PROPERTY, password);
Float quote = (Float) dii.invoke(new Object[] {"MSFT"});
```

A client-side handler, `ClientSideWSSecurityHandler`, reads the username and password now available in the context and adds them to the `Security` header entry in listing 4.1. Listing 4.3 shows a snippet of this handler's code.

Listing 4.3 Reading username/password from context and setting the Username-Token in the security header entry

```
String username = (String) messageContext.getProperty      Reads username
  (Constants.USERNAME_MSG_CONTEXT_PROPERTY);                and password from
String password = (String) messageContext.getProperty      message context
  (Constants.PASSWORD_MSG_CONTEXT_PROPERTY);

Name userTokenElementName = soapEnvelope.createName        Adds
  (Constants.WS_SECURITY_USERNAMETOKEN_TAG,                UsernameToken
  Constants.WS_SECURITY_PREF_NS_PREFIX,                    element to
  Constants.WS_SECURITY_NS_URI);                           Security header
SOAPElement userTokenElement =
  securityElement.addChildElement(userTokenElementName);

Name usernameElementName = soapEnvelope.createName         Adds a Username
  (Constants.WS_SECURITY_USERNAME_TAG,                     element to
  Constants.WS_SECURITY_PREF_NS_PREFIX,                    UsernameToken
  Constants.WS_SECURITY_NS_URI);
SOAPElement usernameElement =
  userTokenElement.addChildElement(usernameElementName);
usernameElement.addTextNode(username);
```

```
Name passwordElementName = soapEnvelope.createName
  (Constants.WS_SECURITY_PASSWORD_TAG,
   Constants.WS_SECURITY_PREF_NS_PREFIX,
   Constants.WS_SECURITY_NS_URI);
SOAPElement passwordElement =
  userTokenElement.addChildElement(passwordElementName);
passwordElement.addTextNode(password);
```

**Adds a Password
element to
UsernameToken**

The code in listing 4.3 inserts the username and password fields into the header elements of the SOAP message. As shown in figure 4.2, the client-side SOAP engine now transmits the SOAP message, with the security header in it, to the service. The server-side now has the task of reading the identity claim and validating it.

4.1.3 JAAS: A generic framework for authentication

When using a password to authenticate a user, an application needs to verify the password presented by the user. For this purpose, the application can consult a password store. Historically, there have been several locations where applications stored passwords: In Unix, passwords were traditionally stored in the file system. Database applications store passwords in the database itself. Most modern applications include support for accessing the passwords from directory using a protocol named *Lightweight Directory Access Protocol (LDAP)*.

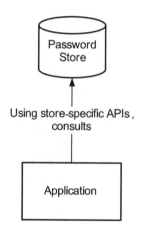

**Figure 4.3 Simplest
way to implement
authentication: the
application consults a
specific password store.**

How does the service consult a password-store? As shown in figure 4.3, the service can use a store-specific API. This approach is simple and direct. Most importantly, it works.

Still, most architects do not prefer to use a store-specific API to consult the password store because it ties the application to a specific store. For example, if we write an application today to access passwords from a file, we will need to revamp a portion of that application tomorrow when we need to access passwords from a database.

The solution is simple: We need a standardized API to access any password store. Pluggable Authentication Module (PAM) provided such API for use on UNIX. In Java, this API is specified by JAAS. JAAS lets us configure the application to use any password store as long as there is a Java class that implements the

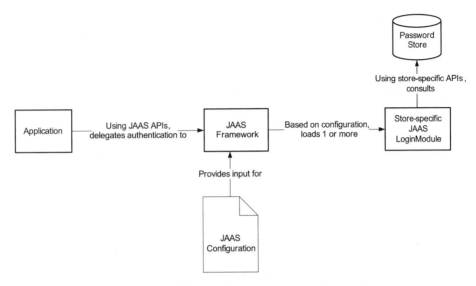

Figure 4.4   JAAS provides a standard API for applications to authenticate against any password store. Administrators can configure JAAS to use arbitrary password stores. Interaction with each password store happens through a store-specific JAAS `LoginModule` implementation.

`LoginModule` interface for that store. There are several `LoginModule` implementations available.

JAAS turns out to be the right choice to implement authentication for username/passwords in web services. Web services are often made available for use by partners; as a result our password stores may evolve over time, extending to other partners and external users. Any implementation that does not support such evolution will not work well in the integration world.

Any application using JAAS will have the following three parts:

1   Code that invokes JAAS APIs to carry out authentication, as a part of the application.

2   JAAS configuration to specify the password stores to authenticate against.

3   Store-specific implementation of JAAS `LoginModule` API for each password store specified in the configuration.

In the rest of this section, we will look at each of these parts with annotated code samples.

Application code to authenticate using JAAS

Listing 4.4 uses JAAS API to log in. This piece of code is from the file `JAASAuthen-ticationHandler.java` in the `example3` folder.

Listing 4.4 Logging in using JAAS API

```
try{
  LoginContext loginContext = new LoginContext
    (jaasAppName,                                        ❶ Initialize JAAS
     new MessageContextBackedCallbackHandler
     (messageContext));
  loginContext.login();   ←─❷ Authenticate using JAAS

  //store authenticated subject in messageContext
  messageContext.setProperty
    (Constants.AUTHENTICATED_SUBJECT_MSG_CONTEXT_PROPERTY,
     loginContext.getSubject());          Save authentication  ❸
} catch(LoginException e) {              result in MessageContext
    // Failed Login. Deal with it.
}
```

To use JAAS for authentication, we need to initialize JAAS first. This is done by creating an instance of `javax.security.auth.login.LoginContext` ❶. The constructor of `LoginContext` takes two arguments. The first is the name of the application that is invoking JAAS for authentication. JAAS uses this name to look up its configuration file and load the login modules configured for the application.

To understand the second argument, we should ask ourselves how JAAS can get the username and password submitted by the client. We are not explicitly passing them to JAAS anywhere in this code. Instead, through the second argument of the `LoginContext` constructor, we are passing an object whose methods can be called by JAAS to get the username and password. This generality is required to support a diverse set of authentication mechanisms. For example, a mechanism might want to challenge the user to present his date of birth or answer a secret question. JAAS takes care of this possibility by specifying that an implementation of the `javax.security.auth.callback.CallbackHandler` interface be provided when constructing a `LoginContext` instance. JAAS will call back this implementation to get hold of user credentials as part of the login process.

Once JAAS is initialized by constructing a `LoginContext` instance, the application can call the `login` method of `LoginContext` to carry out the authentication ❷. At this time, JAAS uses the callback handler we supplied in ❶ to get the username and password. If the login fails, JAAS throws an exception.

If the login succeeds, JAAS authentication module provides a `Subject` ❸ that encapsulates all the information about the user who just logged in. See the callout for more information on what a `Subject` instance contains. In this case, we are saving the `Subject` instance in the message context so that subsequent handlers and the service itself can use it to determine who called the service.

NOTE   *What is in a `javax.security.auth.Subject` instance?* Think of `Subject` as a collection of all the information about a user or an entity. For example, a `Subject` may have a username, a password, and a list of groups to which the named user belongs. A `Subject` can have one or more identities, each known as a security principal. Principals are implemented in Java as instances of classes implementing the `java.security.Principal` instance. Think of a `Principal` as a name associated with the `Subject`. For example, a `UsernamePrincipal` may specify the name of the user, whereas a `MemberOfGroupPrincipal` may specify the name of a group to which the user belongs. A `Subject` can also have one or more security credentials, some that can be shared publicly and some that need to be private. For example, a password is a private credential.

There is one missing piece in the preceding code: the callback handler that JAAS needs to extract the username and password submitted by the user. In interactive applications, these handlers might pop up dialog boxes to ask the user for the name and password. In the example illustrated in figure 4.2, the username and password submitted by the client as part of the `Security` header entry are extracted and saved in `MessageContext` by a handler named `WSSecurityUsername-Handler`. The `JAASAuthenticationHandler` that is subsequently invoked can use a callback handler that will read the username and password from `MessageContext` instead of asking any external agent. Listing 4.5 shows the code that implements such a callback handler.

Listing 4.5   JAAS CallbackHandler implementation to read username and password from MessageContext

```
protected class MessageContextBackedCallbackHandler
   implements CallbackHandler {
     private MessageContext messageContext;
     public MessageContextBackedCallbackHandler
        (MessageContext messageContext) {
        this.messageContext = messageContext;
     }
}
```

❶ **Constructor saves a reference to MessageContext**

```
public void handle(Callback[] callbacks)
  throws java.io.IOException,
     UnsupportedCallbackException {
  for (int i = 0; i < callbacks.length; i++) {          ❷ Iterates over
    Callback ithCallback = callbacks[i];                   each callback
    if (ithCallback instanceof NameCallback) {
      NameCallback nameCallback =                         ❸ Answers Name-
        (NameCallback) ithCallback;                          Callback with
      String username = (String)                             username from
        messageContext.getProperty                           MessageContext
        (Constants.USERNAME_MSG_CONTEXT_PROPERTY);
      nameCallback.setName(username);
    } else if (ithCallback
      instanceof PasswordCallback) {
      PasswordCallback passwordCallback =
        (PasswordCallback) ithCallback;
      String password = (String)                          ❹ Answers
        messageContext.getProperty                           PasswordCallback
        (Constants.PASSWORD_MSG_CONTEXT_PROPERTY);           with password from
      passwordCallback.setPassword                           MessageContext
        (password.toCharArray());
    } else {
      // ... Unknown callback
    } //end if
  } //end for
} //end handle(...)
}//end class
```

The constructor of MessageContextBackedCallbackHandler ❶ is given a Message-Context instance that can be looked up for username and password values when asked by JAAS framework. During authentication, the handle method ❷ is called by JAAS with a list of callbacks to be answered. If the callback is NameCallback ❸— that is, if JAAS asks for the username—the callback handler will submit the username available from the message context. Similarly, if the callback is Password-Callback ❹, the callback hander will submit the password available from the message context.

Now you know how an application can invoke JAAS for authentication. Where exactly does the application specify what JAAS should do as part of the authentication process? For example, what password store(s) should JAAS consult during authentication? Should JAAS do any additional checks such as making sure that the request originated from a trusted network? All this information is specified by the JAAS configuration file. Let us see next how JAAS can be configured to authenticate against one or more stores for an application.

Configuring JAAS

JAAS needs to be provided with the location of a configuration file. Revisit table 4.1, where we have given the instructions to run the examples in this chapter. You will see that in step 3, we set the `java.security.auth.login.config` system property of Tomcat's JVM to the path of our JAAS configuration file. A part of the configuration file for this example, `conf/example3-jaas.conf` is shown in listing 4.6.

Listing 4.6   Extract from a JAAS configuration file

```
soasecimpl {      ◁—❶

   ... /* login modules skipped here are explained later */

   com.manning.samples.soasecimpl.jaas.FileBasedAuthenticator   ◁—❷
      requisite   ◁—❸
      filePath="d:/work/eclipse/soas_code/conf/example3-passwd.txt";   ◁—❹
};
```

Here is how to read this configuration snippet. For the application named in ❶, JAAS must use the login modules whose class names are listed as shown in ❷. For each login module listed for the application, a flag ❸ indicates how JAAS should combine the module's result with the results of other login modules that are also listed as part of the application's JAAS configuration. Possible values of this flag and their meanings are:

- `required`   This module must succeed if a login has to succeed. Regardless of whether this module succeeds or fails, subsequent modules will be tried anyway. This is useful if we have subsequent modules that should always be called, such as audit modules that record all login attempts.

- `requisite`   Same as `required`, except that subsequent login modules will not be tried if this login module fails.

- `sufficient`   Login is considered successful if this module succeeds; modules subsequent to this one are not tried if this one succeeds.

- `optional`   Regardless of the result of this login module, subsequent modules will be tried.

Figure 4.5 summarizes the behavior you would see for each these flags.

Each login module listed for authentication in an application may need its own customizations. JAAS facilitates this by allowing for each login module an

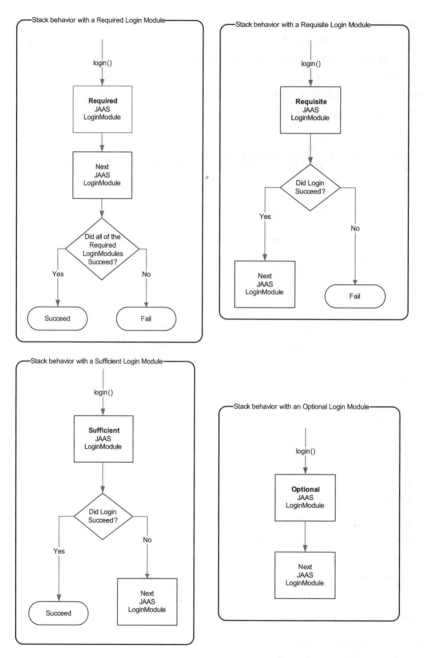

Figure 4.5 Flow charts depicting how the result of a JAAS login module can be combined with the results of the rest of the modules configured for an application.

arbitrary number of options in the form of name=value pairs. For example, in ❹ in listing 4.6, the path to the password file is set for the FileBasedAuthenticator login module.

Now you know what JAAS configuration files look like. For each application, you specify one or more login module classes, specify whether each of the modules is required, requisite, sufficient, or optional, and set any options required by the module.

We will next see how to implement a JAAS login module.

Implementing JAAS login module

The way we've explained it so far, any server can load a LoginModule to authenticate against any store as long as the module implements a specific API assumed by JAAS. LoginModule implementations already exist for most password stores in use; we do not have to code them in general. Sun's Java Development Kit (JDK) provides frequently required modules such as the ones for checking against an LDAP store and using native authentication mechanisms in UNIX/NT. See the javadocs for the com.sun.security.auth.module package for more details.

In our example introduced in 4.1.1, we could have used such readily available implementations. Some of the authentication mechanisms proposed by WS-Security use special techniques that are not supported by the JAAS module implementations in Sun's JDK. We will show you in this section how to implement a simple JAAS LoginModule. We will enhance it as our requirements grow.

Figure 4.6 shows the sequence of interactions between the application and login modules via JAAS APIs. We saw previously that an application starts off the login process by constructing a LoginContext with the application name and a callback handler instance as arguments. Initially, JAAS loads the login module classes configured for the named application, instantiates them using default constructors, and calls initialize on each of them. As a part of the initialization, JAAS supplies the login module instance with the Subject to populate, the callback handler to use during login, configured options, and a container for sharing login state with other modules.

The application uses the constructed LoginContext to login. Since more than one module might be configured, the login in each module is a two-step process. As a first step, the JAAS framework calls the login() function of each login module configured. The net result of these calls will be a success or a failure to login. If the result is successful the commit() function is called on each module. If it is a failure, the abort() function is called on each. Login modules should not fill in the principal/credential information into Subject until the commit() function is called.

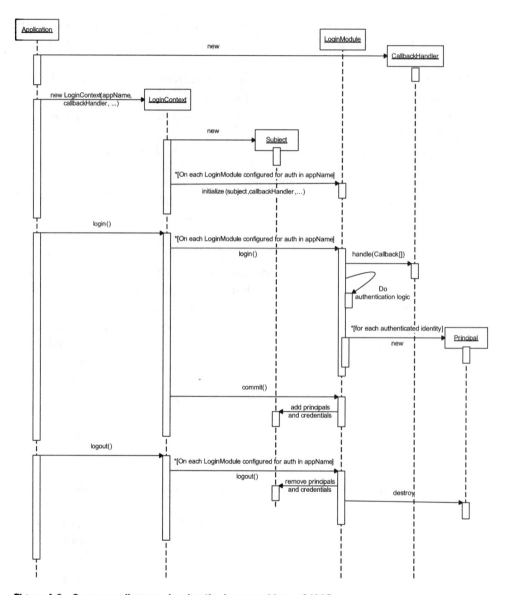

Figure 4.6 Sequence diagram showing the inner workings of JAAS.

Whatever principals or credentials are added to the Subject by the module should be cleaned up when logout() is called.

Listing 4.7 is the relevant snippet of the code that handles the login portion, from the file FileBasedAuthenticator.java in the folder named jaas. The reader is encouraged to look at the file to understand how to set the subject in `commit()` and clean it up in `logout()`.

Listing 4.7 Code extract from a JAAS login module

```
Callback[] callbacks = new Callback[2];      ←❶
callbacks[0] = new NameCallback("Username: ");        ❷
callbacks[1] = new PasswordCallback("Password: ", false);
try {
    callbackHandler.handle(callbacks);       ←❸
} catch (UnsupportedCallbackException uce) {
    logger.error("Error: "                               ❹
        + uce.getCallback().getClass().getName()
        + " not supported by authenticating app", uce);
    throw new LoginException
    ("Internal error in authentication");
}

username = ((NameCallback) callbacks[0]).getName();      ❺
if (username == null) {
    throw new LoginException("No username specified");
}

char[] passwordChars = null;                             ❻
try {
    passwordChars =
    ((PasswordCallback) callbacks[1]).getPassword();
}

// Verify the password in a file .. skipped
return true;
```

Upon a call to `login()`, the login module creates an array of callbacks ❶ and populates it with one call back per credential it requires for authentication. In this example, the login module creates two callbacks, one for username and one for password ❷.

The callbacks are implementations of the interface `javax.security.auth.callback.Callback`. The first argument is the prompt to the user. In our application, we do not need it. But, as we explained, JAAS is a general-purpose framework, to be used even in GUI applications, which is where this prompt is used. The `PasswordCallback` takes additional argument whether to echo responses to the screen.

If we want the application to ask for additional information, all we need to do is provide additional callbacks. For example, we implemented `NonceCallback` in our example for later use. Of course, the callback handler should understand what is required. For most username and password schemes, these simple callbacks would suffice.

The callbacks are passed to the application's `CallbackHandler` ❸ so that it can provide the credentials required for authentication. You have already seen a sample implementation of `CallbackHandler` in listing 4.5. If the application's `CallbackHandler` cannot provide a value for one of the callbacks, it will throw an `UnsupportedCallbackException` ❹. When that happens, the login module throws a `LoginException` in turn to indicate that login has failed. Otherwise, the login module reads the credentials ❺ and ❻ provided by the application's `Callback-Handler` and verifies them to see whether the identity claim is genuine or fake.

Congratulations! If you followed along so far, you not only know how to use JAAS in an application, you also can write a JAAS login module implementation for your own password scheme. To summarize what we learned in this section: we can use JAAS to work with any password store. We can even change the choice of password store with a simple configuration change without affecting the rest of the system. For most popular store choices such as LDAP, we can use readily available login modules. For other stores, we can create our login module implementations. In the next section, we will see how server-side handler can use JAAS to verify the username and password.

4.1.4 *Implementing username/password scheme: server-side validation*

In this section, we will see how we can use JAAS to validate user credentials. Since we have covered JAAS already, we are going to provide only the web service-specific APIs here.

In the examples here, we will use JAX-RPC handlers to process the username and password, just as in the previous chapter. Recall that the username and password come as a part of the `UsernameToken` element in the `Security` header. We have the option of writing a single handler that extracts these credentials and verifies them using a password store. Since we already demonstrated in the previous chapter a handler that saves credentials from `UsernameToken` in the message context, we will use that handler here, too. We will write a second handler that takes the username and password from the context and authenticates. This strategy will allow us to replace the logic we use to fetch identity claims and the logic needed to verify the claims independently of each other. Figure 4.7 provides an overview of the solution.

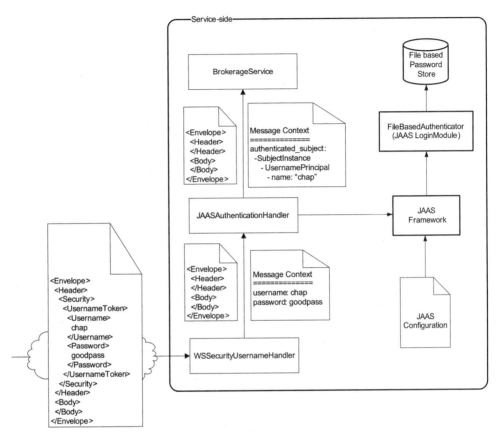

Figure 4.7 Overview of the server-side implementation

Let's look at the first handler, `WSSecurityUsernameHandler`. It is exactly the same as listing 3.3 except in listing 4.8 the following lines have been added. As before, we removed the exception logic to make the code simpler.

Listing 4.8 Extract from `WSSecurityUsernameHandler`: Reads username and password from the WS-Security header and saves them in the `MessageContext`

```
public class WSSecurityUsernameHandler
        extends ExtendedGenericHandler {

    public boolean handleRequest(MessageContext messageContext) {
        //... [Same as the example in the previous chapter]
        SOAPElement passwordElement =
```

```
    Utils.locateChildElement (usernameTokenElement,      ❶
        Constants.WS_SECURITY_NS_URI,
        Constants.WS_SECURITY_PASSWORD_TAG);

//...code to check passwordElement != null snipped...
String password = passwordElement.getValue();

//populate message context with username/password
messageContext.setProperty                             ❷
    (Constants.USERNAME_MSG_CONTEXT_PROPERTY, username);
messageContext.setProperty
    (Constants.PASSWORD_MSG_CONTEXT_PROPERTY, password);

//remove the processed header as soap mandates
soapHeader.removeChild(securityElement);    ◁─❸
    return true;
    }
}
```

We first get the password from the `Password` element in the `UsernameToken` header entry ❶. As we need to somehow communicate the username and password to the downstream handlers and service, we use the message context to do that, by setting properties ❷. Finally, we remove the header, since we are done processing it ❸.

The next handler, `JAASAuthenticationHandler`, is entirely new. It needs to take the username and password and verify them. As explained earlier, we can verify them in multiple ways. Ultimately, the server needs to convince itself that the message could have come only from the person identified by the username in the header. To make the code independent of password store and its APIs, we will use the JAAS that accesses any password store with JAAS `LoginModules`, as follows:

```
public class JAASAuthenticationHandler
    extends ExtendedGenericHandler {
  //...
  }
```

Just like `WSSecurityUsernameHandler`, this class extends `ExtendedGenericHandler`. At initialization time, it needs to read in the application name to use when using JAAS for authentication. As we saw in the last chapter, JAX-RPC provides handlers with the opportunity to read in handler configuration info in the `init` method.

```
    public void init(HandlerInfo handlerInfo) {
      Map config = handlerInfo.getHandlerConfig();
      jaasAppName = (String) config.get(JAAS_APP_CONFIG_PARAM);    ◁─❶
      //... code to verify jaasAppName!= null snipped...
    }
```

All we're doing here is accessing the handler configuration ❶ and reading the application name to use when initializing JAAS.

The next method in the handler is `handleRequest`. It takes the username and password from the message context and validates via JAAS, as explained in detail in the previous subsection on JAAS.

So far, we have seen how to do authentication with username and password. There is one crucial property of the mechanism we have studied so far that should catch the attention of security practitioners: *we exchanged the username and password in clear-text*. We all know that it is a bad idea to transmit user credentials in clear-text. Anybody who is snooping on the network can get usernames and passwords and reuse them with the same service or different services. In the next section, we'll look alternatives to transmitting passwords in clear-text.

4.2 *Using password digest for authentication*

Although there is a simple *sledgehammer* solution to the clear-text password problem, it is not the right kind of solution for SOA for the reasons discussed in chapter 1. The sledgehammer approach is to use transport-level security by routing every SOAP message through SSL/TLS. That would result in encryption of the entirety of messages exchanged, thus protecting the password from a man-in-the-middle (MIM) attack. As we discussed in chapter 1, transport-level security is not good enough when there are more than two parties involved in a message exchange and when different parts of a message should be encrypted differently. SOA is often used for integrating multiple applications in the context of a single high-level business process. In such cases, blanket encryption using SSL/TLS is not a feasible solution.

So, it is natural to ask if there is a way to hide the password without encrypting the entirety of a message as in SSL/TLS. This scheme must not only foil any attempt to extract the password, but also disallow simple replay of the whole message. Password digest-based authentication accomplishes these goals.

In this section, first we will introduce the theory behind the password digest-based authentication. Next, we will show how to implement that scheme, first on the client-side then on the server-side. We will use JAAS to implement the validation on the server-side and reuse the code from the previous section.

4.2.1 *How password digest authentication works*

The problem with sending the password in plain text is that the MIM can grab it. What if we do not send the password? What if we send something else instead of a password to prove that we have the password? For example, instead of the password p, we can send f(p), where f is a function that transforms password p. The receiver can recompute f(p) using its knowledge of the user's password[1] and match the result with the value submitted by the user. In this scheme, we've eliminated sending the password, but the MIM may still steal the password if he can compute p from f(p). That is, from the proof of the password, the attacker may get the password itself.

We can solve this problem by using *one-way functions*. One-way functions safeguard the password from intruders. These functions do not have easily computable *inverse functions*. That is, given f(p), for all practical purposes, the attacker cannot compute p. Secure Hash Algorithm-1 (SHA-1) is an example of such a function.

Still, the scheme is not completely secure. The MIM need not compute p from f(p) to send a fake message. He can simply use f(p) as is. So, we need to somehow change f every time we use it so that f(p) cannot be replayed. So, what we really need is a way to change the one-way function each time we send the password.

We can get such a function by taking in another argument. That is, instead of sending f(p), we send f(p,n), where n is called *nonce*. It is a number that is never repeated—a number that is only used once—nonce.

The use of nonce introduces complexity on the receiver side. A simple function can be agreed upon a priori by the sender and the receiver. How can they agree upon the nonce, given that it must change every time? One obvious solution is to send the nonce (n) along with f(p,n).

Surely, a MIM can also see the nonce n when it's sent along with f(p,n). That means he too can send the same nonce n and f(n,p). The situation is no better than sending f(p), unless the receiver accepts a nonce only once. Any attempts by the MIM to replay the same nonce n and f(p,n) will fail.

---

[1] Later we will account for the fact that password stores on the server-side seldom store the user's password as is. Instead, they store each password p in a transformed form p' from which it is not easy to recover the original password. The receiver can never compute f(p). It can only compute f(p'). For this reason, assume that we mean p' wherever we use p in this section.

Can a receiver endlessly remember all the nonce values it has seen? Any such design imposes an undue burden on the receivers. We can make the scheme easier for receivers if we add the current date to the nonce. That is, we send f(p,n,d) instead of f(p,n).

Let's examine why this design works. The receiver can remember all the nonce values it has seen that day. If a MIM attempts a replay attack the same day, the receiver will detect it, as there is a repetition of the nonce. If MIM attempts a replay attack on a different day, f(p,n,d) will not match, as the date d is a part of the digest computation.

In practice, a day may also be too long a timeframe to remember all nonce values used within that time so a timestamp t is used instead of date d. Requests older than a short while (say, five minutes) are rejected by the receiver. The value f(p,n,t) is commonly referred to as a *password digest*.

The password digest authentication process is shown in figure 4.8.

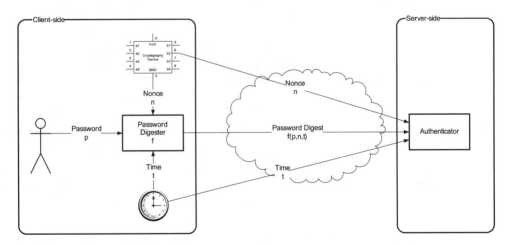

Figure 4.8 Authentication with password digests

As you'll learn next, WS-Security combines all these ideas in password digest-based authentication.

4.2.2 *Password digest authentication in action*

A password digest is computed as a function of the nonce, timestamp, and the password. As long as the time disparity between clocks on the server and client-sides is not too much, this scheme works well. Look back at the example you ran when reading section 4.1.1; if you look at the fourth and fifth calls (the first was a WSDL GET; the second and third relied on clear-text passwords) captured by `tcpmon`, you will see how a WS-Security `UsernameToken` can be used to carry a password digest.

> **Listing 4.9 Example of a security header with a username and password digest**

```
<soapenv:Header>
  <wsse:Security ...>
    <wsse:UsernameToken>
      <wsse:Username>chap</wsse:Username>
      <wsse:Password Type="...#PasswordDigest">...</wsse:Password>      ←—❶
      <wsse:Nonce EncodingType="...#Base64Binary">...</wsse:Nonce>      ←—❷
      <wsu:Created xmlns:wsu="...">2005-06-27T10:41:15.463Z
      </wsu:Created>                                                         ❸
    </wsse:UsernameToken>
  </wsse:Security>
</soapenv:Header>
```

In listing 4.9 the `Password` element in `UsernameToken` ❶ is identified to be a `PasswordDigest` by its `Type` attribute. WS-Security's `UsernameToken` profile specifies the password digest function `f` as follows.

```
f(p,n,t) = Base64(SHA-1(n.t.p))
```

where `.` is the concatenation operator, `p` is the UTF-8 representation of the password, `n` is the nonce (raw bytes, not the base64-encoded representation you see in ❷), and `t` is the UTF-8 representation of the timestamp (in UTC) in the format shown in ❸. SHA-1 is a popular one-way hash function. UTF-8 and base64 are the names of encodings; see the corresponding callouts for more.

> **NOTE** *What is UTF-8 encoding?* How are characters represented digitally? Digital computers look at all data as 0s and 1s. To represent characters in digital form, we need to convert them into numbers. Character set standards such as ASCII and Unicode standardize the bits used to represent characters. For example, in ASCII, character A is represented using 65, B is represented using 66, and so on. A password such as "ABC" is really 01000001 01000010 01000011 when stored digitally. The number assigned to each character in a character set standard is called its *code position*. Some character set standards only define the positions for a small number of characters, whereas others define the positions for a large set of characters. For example, ASCII defines 128 code positions, whereas Unicode defines the code positions for thousands of characters.

Both of them are identical if we limit ourselves to the first 128 code positions defined in Unicode.

Large character sets will result in bloated file sizes if used naively. For example, as Unicode has a large number of characters, if we use 4 bytes to represent each character in a text file, a file consisting of characters from just the first 128 code positions will use four times the bytes required to store equivalent ASCII data. This problem can be solved by using variable-length encoding schemes, where the number of bytes used to represent a code position is not fixed. UTF-8 is one such encoding scheme. It uses 1 to 4 bytes to represent each Unicode code position, based on the code position. It is designed such that a UTF-8 encoded file consisting of simply ASCII characters is identical to an ASCII-encoded file consisting of the same characters.

What is base64 encoding?   Base64 can take any data and convert it into printable ASCII. It is an easily computable function that is easy to reverse, too. If we want to send binary data in XML, the preferred choice is to convert it into base64. When we encrypt or compute digests, typically, we produce binary data, even though we start from printable ASCII. In most of the code examples in this chapter, you will see that we use base64 to encode such binary data before putting it into XML.

When computing password digests, it is important to be clear about the encoding used to represent the characters in the password. WS-Security mandates the use of UTF-8 when adding a password to the digest computation.

Let us now take a look at how we can implement the password digest scheme; that is, send the password digest as a header entry from the client-side and understand it and validate it on the server-side. Figure 4.9 provides an overview of our implementation strategy.

The left side of figure 4.9 shows how the client-side produces the header entry for the password digest using a handler. The handler inserts the header entry into the message as shown in the middle of the figure. The right side of the figure shows how the server takes the digest and passes that information via `MessageContext` to the `JAASAuthenticationHandler`. The `JAASAuthenticationHandler`, as the name suggests, uses JAAS to validate the password digest.

We will elaborate on each of the components in the figure in the following subsections: first the client-side then the server-side.

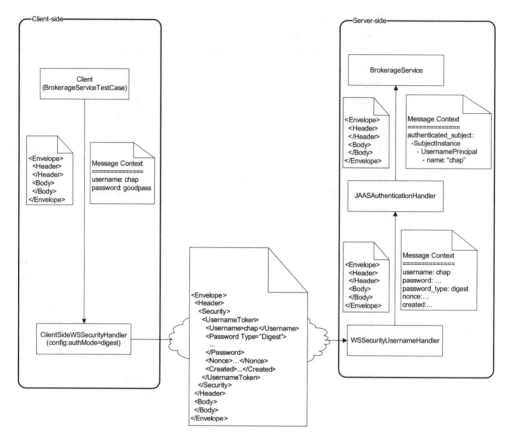

Figure 4.9 Overview of a username/password digest-based authentication scheme.

4.2.3 *Implementing password digests: client-side*

In this section, we'll see how password digest–based authentication is implemented in ClientSideWSSecurityHandler.java, a client-side handler. The handler code we describe here extends the code you have seen before for clear-text password-based authentication. Table 4.2 shows the implementation logic broken down into steps.

Table 4.2 Client-side implementation logic for password digest based-authentication

Step	Action	Implementation strategy
1	Initialize.	Create a nonce generator using `java.security.SecureRandom`. Read configuration to figure out how many bytes we want to use in nonce. Create an instance of `java.security.MessageDigest`. Create a `javax.xml.datatype.DatatypeFactory` instance needed to instantiate a `javax.xml.datatype.XMLGregorianCalendar` instance for the timestamp portion.
2	Generate a nonce.	Use the nonce generator created during initialization to generate a nonce.
3	Take the current time as the timestamp.	Use the `XMLGregorianCalendar` instance available from XML `DatatypeFactory` to format current time in UTC as required by the WS-Security specification.
4	Convert password to the form stored on the server-side.	Assuming that the password on the server-side is stored in SHA-1 hashed form, use the `MessageDigest` instance created in step 1 to do the same hash on the client-side as well.
5	Use the nonce, time-stamp, and the password to generate a digest.	Use `MessageDigest` instance to create a digest of password (in the form stored on the server-side), nonce, and timestamp.
6	Add the password digest using a `Username-Token` element in the `Security` header entry.	Use DOM and SAAJ APIs to add the required elements in the `Security` header entry

Let us now discuss each of these steps in detail.

Step 1: Initializing the handler

In the `init()` method of `ClientSideWSSecurityHandler`, we initialize the objects needed when handling messages. The objects initialized include a nonce generator, a message digester, and a date formatter (listing 4.10).

Listing 4.10 Initialization code in `ClientSideWSSecurityHandler`

```
try {
    nonceGenerator = SecureRandom.getInstance("SHA1PRNG");    ←—❶
    digester = MessageDigest.getInstance("SHA-1");    ←—❷
} catch (NoSuchAlgorithmException e) {
    logger.error(e);
    throw new RuntimeException(e);
}
```

```
try {
    xmlDatatypeFactory = DatatypeFactory.newInstance();    ◁─❸
} catch (DatatypeConfigurationException e) {
    logger.error(e);
    throw new RuntimeException(e);
}
String numBytesInNonceStr = (String)
    config.get(NUM_BYTES_IN_NONCE_PARAMETER_NAME);    ◁─❹
if (numBytesInNonceStr != null) {
    numBytesInNonce = Integer.parseInt(numBytesInNonceStr);
}
```

Here's what we do in this code. We create a random number generator, an instance of `java.security.SecureRandom` ❶, which we will use later for generating nonce values. The algorithm we use for random number generation is SHA1PRNG, a SHA-1 based pseudo-random number generation algorithm.

We create a `digester` object that can compute SHA-1 ❷. In Java, such a facility is built into the class `java.security.MessageDigest`.

We create an `xmlDatatypeFactory` ❸ that will be needed later to format time-stamps in the form that WS-Security mandates.

Since the nonce can be any number of bytes, we read it in as a configuration parameter ❹.

Step 2: Generating the nonce

Listing 4.11 illustrates how we generate the nonce. We create a byte array of the size read from client configuration in step 1 and use the `nonceGenerator` that was also initialized in step 1 to generate a nonce of the configured size.

Listing 4.11   Generating nonce

```
byte[] nonce = new byte[numBytesInNonce];
nonceGenerator.nextBytes(nonce);
```

The nonce to use in password digest is now available as a byte array.

Step 3: Generating the timestamp

Next we need to generate the timestamp in a neutral time zone so that the digest scheme can work across time zones. Listing 4.12 shows the code that generates a UTC timestamp in the format specified by WS-Security.

Listing 4.12   Generating the timestamp

```
XMLGregorianCalendar now =
      xmlDatatypeFactory.newXMLGregorianCalendar
      (new GregorianCalendar
            (TimeZone.getTimeZone("UTC")));
String created = now.toXMLFormat();
```

The timestamp to embed in the password digest is now available in the right format.

Step 4: Getting and transforming the password

To compute the digest, we need three pieces of information: the nonce, the timestamp, and the password. The first two are taken care of in steps 2 and 3, respectively. Let us now focus on the password.

Recall that the client sets the username and password in the message context in order to make them available to handlers. Our handler can get the password from the message context. Since this code is virtually same as listing 4.3, we are not repeating it here.

There is one catch that we need to address here. On the server-side, passwords are not stored in their original form to reduce the risk of unauthorized access. They get stored in a cryptic format that cannot be decrypted easily. The exact format depends on the store the server-side uses. Therefore, the digest computation code on the server-side cannot get the original password from the store. It can only get what is stored in the password store. If password digests are to work in practice, the client also has to use the same type of password for digest computation as the sender.

In our example, we are going to assume that the password is stored on the server-side as a base64-encoded SHA-1 hash of the password. So, our client code also has to obtain a base64 encoded SHA-1 hash of the password before computing the digest.

The code in listing 4.13 takes the bytes that the password would consist of in UTF-8 encoding, creates a SHA-1 hash of that, and encodes the result in base64. The final result is used in place of the password for computing the digest.

Listing 4.13   Generating the transformed password

```
//as the service only has a hashed version of the
//password, we need to hash it before including it
//in the digest
byte[] utf8Password = password.getBytes("UTF-8");
```

```
byte[] sha1Password = digester.digest(utf8Password);
byte[] base64EncodedSHA1Password =
        Base64.encodeBase64(sha1Password);
```

The password is now available in the form it should be in when computing the digest.

Step 5: Generating the digest

Finally, we have all the components for computing a digest: nonce, timestamp, and the right form of the password. We compute the digest using the code in listing 4.14.

Listing 4.14   Generating the digest

```
digester.update(nonce);
digester.update(created.getBytes("UTF-8"));
digester.update(base64EncodedSHA1Password);
byte[] digest =
        Base64.encodeBase64(digester.digest());
```

In these statements, we add the nonce, timestamp, and password to the digester. In the final statement of the code, we generate the digest and encoding it in base64.

Step 6: Attaching the headers and sending the message

The last step in the client-side handler is to attach the headers to the message. We showed in listing 4.3 how to add elements to the headers. The only trick here is to add the attributes to the elements, too, signifying the encodings. For example, the following snippet sets the encoding type to be base64 for nonce:

```
nonceElement.addAttribute
  (encodingTypeAttrName,
   Constants.WS_SECURITY_BASE64_ENCODING_TYPE);
```

Please read through the file `example3/ClientSideWSSecurityHandler.java` for a full working example. As you may recall, chapter 3 showed you the code to insert header entries into the SOAP message. This file will show you how to write client-side handlers that insert the right headers to claim identity.

In this section, you have seen how the client inserts the password digest as the header entry. As illustrated in figure 4.9, we need to take this header entry to the server-side and validate the digest. In the next section, we will see how we can do that.

4.2.4 Implementing password digests: server-side validation

The server-side handler essentially has to repeat the calculations made by the client. In addition, it needs to take care that the nonce is not repeated, as we discussed earlier. In this section, first we will show the algorithm for the server-side handler. Next, we will discuss the code that implements the tricky portions of the algorithm. We will also present cues to understand the complete implementation. Look at figure 4.9 to get an overview of our implementation approach.

Table 4.3 shows the implementation logic broken down into steps.

Table 4.3 Server-side implementation logic for password digest-based authentication

Step	Action	Implementation Strategy
1	Gather the digest information in security header entry.	We use a JAX-RPC handler, `WSSecurityUsernameHandler`, to gather all the required data from the security header and put it in the message context for use by the downstream handlers.
2	Invoke JAAS APIs for authentication.	We use a JAX-RPC handler, `JAASAuthenticationHandler`, to invoke JAAS APIs for authentication. Callbacks of JAAS modules for information such as the username, password digest, nonce, and timestamp are answered by `MessageContextBacked-CallbackHandler` using the information stored in the message context during step 1.
3	Use custom JAAS login modules to do digest-based authentication.	We configure JAAS with custom login modules that verify the password digest and check on nonce/timestamp to prevent replay attacks.

Let us now discuss each of these steps in detail.

Step 1: Gathering digest info in the security header entry

First, in the `WSSecurityUsernameHandler` class, we extract the username and password elements from the `Security` header just as in listing 4.8. The only additional code needed here is to get the nonce and the creation timestamp. Listing 4.15 shows the additional code used for reading the nonce. The creation timestamp is simply read in as a string and stored in message context, just like a username. That code is not shown here.

Listing 4.15 Reading the nonce from the security header

```
SOAPElement nonceElement = Utils.locateChildSOAPElement
    (usernameTokenElement,
     Constants.WS_SECURITY_NS_URI,
     Constants.WS_SECURITY_NONCE_TAG);
```

```
String encodingType = nonceElement.getAttribute          ❶
    (Constants.WS_SECURITY_ENCODING_TYPE_ATTR);
if ((encodingType == null) ||
    (encodingType.length() == 0) ||
    (encodingType.equals
      (Constants.WS_SECURITY_BASE64_ENCODING_TYPE))) {
    try {
        nonce = Base64.decodeBase64                       ❷
            (nonceElement.getValue().getBytes("UTF-8"));
    } catch (UnsupportedEncodingException e) {
        throw new RuntimeException(e);
    }
} else {
    //...code snipped to keep the discussion simple...
}
soapContext.setProperty                                   ❸
    (Constants.NONCE_MSG_CONTEXT_PROPERTY, nonce);
```

We first examine the EncodingType attribute ❶ on the Nonce element to check whether the nonce is base64-encoded. If so, we decode ❷ the base64 encoding of the nonce and store it in message context ❸.

Step 2: Invoking JAAS for digest-based authentication

After we get the credentials (username, nonce, timestamp, and password digest), how do we validate them? There is an easy approach: we simply repeat the calculation done on the client-side and compare the digests. Since we already introduced a JAAS module (FileBasedAuthenticator, shown in listing 4.7) for password verification, we are going to extend it to validate the digest as well. A JAX-RPC handler named JAASAuthenticationHandler will invoke this login module and others described in the next section via JAAS.

The JAAS login modules for digest-based authentication will need to get the nonce and timestamp along with the username and digest. So, as shown in listing 4.16, we extend the MessageContextBackedCallbackHandler to supply those values as well.

Listing 4.16 Handling the callbacks for digest authentication

```
// ...code common to this listing and listing 4.5 snipped...
} else if (ithCallback instanceof PasswordTypeCallback) {
    PasswordTypeCallback passwordTypeCallback =
        (PasswordTypeCallback) ithCallback;
    String passwordType = (String)                        ❶
        messageContext.getProperty
        (Constants.PASSWORD_TYPE_MSG_CONTEXT_PROPERTY);
```

```
        passwordTypeCallback.
            setPasswordType(passwordType);           1

    } else if (ithCallback instanceof NonceCallback) {
        NonceCallback nonceCallback =
            (NonceCallback) ithCallback;
        byte[] nonce = (byte[])
            messageContext.getProperty                    2
            (Constants.NONCE_MSG_CONTEXT_PROPERTY);
        nonceCallback.setNonce(nonce);

    } else if (ithCallback instanceof TimestampCallback) {
        TimestampCallback timestampCallback =
            (TimestampCallback) ithCallback;
        String timestampAsString = (String)
            messageContext.getProperty
            (Constants.                                    3
                CREATION_TIME_STR_MSG_CONTEXT_PROPERTY);
        timestampCallback.setTimestampAsString
            (timestampAsString);
    }
//...Rest of the code common to this listing and listing 4.5 snipped ...
```

Since we use the same custom JAAS module for both clear-text passwords and digest-based authentications, one of the callbacks our custom JAAS module makes is for the password type ❶. In the case of digest authentication, our JAAS module would of course need to know the nonce and timestamp. It asks for these using `nonceCallback` ❷ and `timestampCallback` ❸. These callback classes are standard classes bundled with JDK. You can take a look at the implementation of these classes in the `jaas` folder.

The actual verification of the credentials happens in the JAAS module. It is more involved than verifying the password, as we have to deal with nonce time-outs and so on. We will take a look at it next.

Step 3: Custom JAAS modules implementation for digest authentication

Let's see what we need to do to validate the credentials. All this code is implemented in the `jaas` folder:

1 *Make sure that the timestamp is within tolerance limits; reject otherwise* This code is implemented in the file `TimeCheckJAASModule.java`.

2 *Make sure that the digest matches; reject otherwise* This code is very similar to the computation on the client-side and is available in the file `File-BasedAuthenticator.java`.

3 *Make sure that the nonce is new; store if it is or reject otherwise* This code is available in the file `NonceCheckJAASModule.java`.

Each of these three different functions is implemented as a separate login module under JAAS so that we can use each of these login handlers in other situations as well. For example, we can imagine a scenario where we allow a user to log in only if the timestamp is within the limits. Such a scheme may be useful in some time-sensitive web requests.

In the configuration file, we specify that in order to log in, the user will have to pass all the login requirements—that is, all the JAAS modules will have to allow the user in.

The configuration file looks like listing 4.17.

Listing 4.17 JAAS configuration for digest mechanism

```
soasecimpl {
  com.manning.samples.soasecimpl.jaas.TimeCheckJAASModule          ❶
    requisite
    timestampMandatory="false"
    timeoutInSeconds="30";

  com.manning.samples.soasecimpl.jaas.FileBasedAuthenticator       ❷
    requisite
    filePath=". . ./conf/example3-passwd.txt";

  com.manning.samples.soasecimpl.jaas.NonceCheckJAASModule         ❸
    required
    cacheName="soasecimpl"
    nonceMandatory="false"
    nonceTTLInSeconds="30";
};
```

First, we configured `TimeCheckJAASModule` to check the timestamp ❶. Since this is a requisite module, if it fails, the whole login process fails and the user's credentials are rejected. Notice that we can send the required options to that module via the arguments.

Next, we configured the `FileBasedAuthenticator` module ❷ to compute and verify the digest. As with ❶, this is a requisite module.

Finally, we configured `NonceCheckJAASModule` ❸. If this module succeeds we do not have to check any further.

A word of caution: in practice, it may be expensive to have so many login modules. Business scenarios may make such login modules necessary. For example, when two businesses merge, you may want to use the existing JAAS modules and configure them to allow employees of both organizations access to certain resources. We merely want to illustrate the technology so that you can use it in appropriate business scenarios, instead of suggesting it as a best practice.

Now, we will see how these modules are implemented. Since all these modules are quite similar, we will examine only one: `NonceCheckJAASModule`.

Implementing NonceCheckJAASModule

This module needs to store nonces so that it can detect reuse of nonce values. In practice, we would want this store to be persistent so that even if the server is restarted, the application is still secure. If the server restart takes longer than the tolerance limit, we do not need to persist the nonce values; they would have expired anyway. In our illustration, we are only going to store them in memory using `NonceCache`, an implementation of `HashMap`.

Before using this module, JAAS framework initializes it by calling the `initialize` method, as shown in listing 4.18. In this method, we read in the options provided for this module in the JAAS configuration. We also create a cache for nonce values.

Listing 4.18 `NonceCheckJAASModule` **initialization**

```
public void initialize
      (Subject subject, CallbackHandler callbackHandler,
        Map sharedState, Map options) {

    this.callbackHandler = callbackHandler;

    nonceMandatory = Boolean.parseBoolean                      ❶
        ((String)options.get(NONCE_MANDATORY_OPTION));

    cacheName = (String) options.get(NONCE_CACHE_NAME_OPTION); ❷
    if (cacheName == null) {
        cacheName = "global";
    }

    synchronized(nonceCaches) {
        cache = (Map) nonceCaches.get(cacheName);
        if (cache == null) {
          String nonceTTLAsString = (String)
              options.get(NONCE_EXPIRY_DURATION_OPTION);
          long nonceTTL;
          if (nonceTTLAsString != null) {                      ❸
              nonceTTL = Long.parseLong(nonceTTLAsString);
          } else {
              nonceTTL = TimeCheckJAASModule.
                    DEFAULT_TOKEN_EXPIRY_DURATION;
          }
```

```
        cache = Collections.synchronizedMap
                (new NonceCache(nonceTTL));
        nonceCaches.put(cacheName, cache);
    }
  }
}
```
❹

We read three configuration options in this intialization code.

We first check whether the configuration mandates the availability of a nonce in every authentication request ❶.

We read the name of the cache to use for storing nonce values ❷. By default, if a name is not provided, the cache name is assumed to be `global`. This option allows concurrent use of this login module by different services in the same JVM. Each service can set up its JAAS configuration to use a different cache name.

Finally, we read the time to live (TTL) value for each nonce value in the named cache ❸. If a TTL option is not set, a default is assumed.

If the cache is not there under the required name, a new cache is created ❹ with the right expiry period.

The code for login follows these guidelines: first get the required information from the calling party; then make the decision based on the obtained information. The code in listing 4.19 gets the information via callbacks.

Listing 4.19 Getting the nonce information from the user

```
Callback[] callbacks =
    new Callback[] {new NonceCallback()};
try {
    callbackHandler.handle(callbacks);
} catch (java.io.IOException ioe) {
    logger.error(ioe);
    throw new LoginException
    ("Internal error in authentication");
} catch (UnsupportedCallbackException uce) {
    logger.error("Error: "
            + uce.getCallback().getClass().getName()
            + " not supported by authenticating app", uce);
    throw new LoginException
        ("Internal error in authentication");
}
```
❶

❷

Here, we create the required callback ❶ that is used to communicate with the calling party. The class `NonceCallback` is an implementation of the interface `Callback` and is available in the folder `jaas`.

If the calling party cannot handle the nonce callback function we generate a login exception ❷. As explained earlier in the section on JAAS, the client for the JAAS module should implement the callback handler such that it understands and handles all the callbacks required by the JAAS module.

Next, we need to extract the information from nonce callback and verify that it is not a repeat, as shown in listing 4.20.

Listing 4.20 Verification that nonce is not repeated

```
byte[] nonce =                                          ❶
    ((NonceCallback) callbacks[0]).
    getNonce();
//...[Code to fail, if nonce is not there]

String base64Nonce = new String                         ❷
    (Base64.encodeBase64(nonce), "US-ASCII");

synchronized(cache) {
    if (cache.containsKey(base64Nonce)) {
        logger.warn                                      ❸
            ("Repeated nonce: Replay attack?");
            throw new LoginException("Nonce repeated");
    }
    cache.put                                            ❹
        (base64Nonce,
        new Long(System.currentTimeMillis()));
}
return true;
```

In this code, we first get the nonce from the callback ❶. The callback function stores it when the callback handler provides it with the nonce.

We look up the nonce cache for repetition of a nonce ❸. As byte arrays are not good hash keys, we are using a base64 version of nonce as the key ❷.

If the nonce is not a repeat, we store it in the cache ❹ and return success.

The other two modules are very similar to this one. For example, the time check, JAAS module gets different initialization options such as tolerance limit and uses a different callback handler and different logic to decide if it should let the user in.

4.3 Is password authentication the right solution for you?

In this chapter, we studied password-based authentication claims. That is, the user supplies the password as proof of his identity. We also studied a variation of the password—a password digest scheme. Can you use these authentication mechanisms for your solutions?

First let us understand why password-based authentication schemes are good. Using a password to access a system is very common. In fact, most of the web uses password-based schemes to allow users access to web resources. As such, users find it natural to use a password for access.

Moreover, passwords are easy to implement. After all, we have been using password-based schemes in computer systems long enough to acquire libraries, processes, and expertise to manage the systems. Many companies have processes to deal with lost passwords and so on.

Plain-text passwords are applicable in limited situations. For example, in an intranet, where there is no chance of snooping on the network, plain-text passwords pose no harm. Or, if the traffic itself is encrypted, for example via a VPN, there is no need to look beyond plain-text passwords for simple authentication. Or, some older systems may be integrated with only plain-text passwords.

If our situation does not qualify for plain-text passwords, we can still use digest authentication. In the next subsection, we examine why digest passwords are secure.

4.3.1 Why is the digest scheme secure?

Now that we have seen the digest scheme in action, let us see why it is secure. To understand why, let's look at the actions of the potential attacker. He is listening on the wire and grabs the nonce, timestamp, and the digest. Here are the possibilities:

- He sends those three exactly as they are within the tolerance. The server, since it remembers the nonce, will consider it as a replay attack and reject the credentials.

- He sends these three pieces after the tolerance limit has expired. The server will not remember this nonce. Since the timestamp is outside the tolerance limit, the message is rejected as a possible replay.

- He modifies the timestamp so that it falls within the hour. The server will compute the digest and match against this digest. Since the timestamp differs, the digests also will differ, causing the message to be rejected.

All these scenarios work if only the digest function has some nice properties:

- It should be fast to compute. Every message needs to carry the password digest—it needs to be cheaply computed.

- It should be difficult to compute the inverse for. While it is possible to compute the password by the brute-force method of trying every password, such a method should not succeed in a reasonable amount of time.

- It should not map different inputs to same output; that is, the digest for two different passwords should not be the same. While this property is not a real requirement for password digests, we will see the need for this property in later chapters where we use digests for ensuring message integrity.

One of the standard functions used in digest computation is SHA-1. This function produces a digest of 160 bits from the input. Since the input is really three terms—nonce, timestamp, and password—we create the combined input as a concatenation of nonce, timestamp, and password in that order. The order allows for varying the length of the password without any padding.

Does SHA-1 stand up to our requirements? It is fast to compute and the inverse is difficult to compute. As with any function, since it coerces large inputs to small outputs, it will map several different inputs to the same digest. It is computationally difficult to figure out which inputs map to the same digest. So, for our purposes, SHA-1 will suffice.

4.3.2 *Problems with digest authentication*

One interesting aspect of digest authentication is that it is not as popular as it ought to be. The recommendation strongly endorses it; the language comes with ready-made libraries; it is simple enough to implement. What is the issue?

If you look at how we solved the issue of dependency on the store, you will remember that we used JAAS. The server never even has to know the password. In digest authentication, the server needs access to the password to compute the digest. There are two problems with this. One is that JAAS does not define a way to get the password unless the authentication already succeeded. The second issue is that most JAAS modules do not support digest-based authentication. So, unless we are ready to write a JAAS module for our store that supports digest-based authentication, we cannot use digest-based authentication.

Even if we are prepared to write our own JAAS module, there's still a problem with digest-based authentication. It turns out that most password stores really do not store passwords at all for security reasons. They store only a transformed password. When they need to verify a password match for a given candidate, they apply the same transformation and verify for an exact match. The transformation function, just like the digest, is usually made to be difficult to invert. Therefore, the JAAS module cannot get the original password from the store. It means that the client—i.e., the sender—also has to use the same transformed password when computing the digest. How does it know which store uses which transformation algorithm? In general, there is no clear answer to this question.

So, in the final analysis, if digest mechanism has to work, the following problems need to be solved:

- Clients need to know the transformation function applied to the passwords when they are stored in the password store.
- Server needs to have a JAAS module that supports digest based authentication.

Ultimately, all these requirements make the implementation considerably more complicated than the clean implementation of simple username and password scheme. Therefore, password digest is not as popular as it could be.

4.3.3 *Limitations of password-based schemes*

We have seen where password-based schemes are applicable and how password digest schemes improve security for a password-based scheme. Despite all the advantages of familiarity and availability of good implementations, password-based schemes (both plain text and digest) have some limitations.

The overall security of any system is only as strong as its weakest link. In password-based authentication, the password is the weakest link. Password-based authentication is based on the assumption that only a legitimate user can know his correct password. All of us know the fallacy in this assumption.

Most users choose predictable passwords. For example, *password* is probably the most popular password. Most people use the names of their significant others or pets as passwords. Even if a password is not predictable, it is still susceptible to brute-force dictionary attacks. A hacker can use a program to try out all the words in a dictionary along with minor variations on them such as adding a number as a prefix or a suffix to each word. The hacker's dictionary might even be customized per organization, to try terms frequently used in that organization.

IT administrators are very aware of this problem and seek to redress it by setting up a password policy and enforcing it using tools. For example, a password quality meter can stop users from registering predictable passwords. They can even force people to retire old passwords after a time period.

Sadly, even all those measures do not help us in securing passwords. Passwords can be "repurposed" by unethical administrators. It is quite common for people to reuse username and password combinations for several systems. Any administrator of a service can reuse that knowledge to gain unauthorized access to a different service.

Two popular technologies that form the basis for solutions without these drawbacks are Kerberos and digital certificates. We'll discuss the first of these, Kerberos, in the next chapter. Digital certificates are introduced in chapters 6 and 7, where we will discuss them in conjunction with encryption and/or signatures.

4.4 *Summary*

Let's consider the big picture: In SOA, a user can be an individual or an application. In either case, an identity claim needs to be authenticated. Password schemes are the simplest mechanisms for such authentication.

In this chapter, we covered two different password schemes for user authentication.

First we discussed plain-text passwords, which most of you may be familiar with. If you followed that part of the chapter, you learned how to use Username-Token in WS-Security to claim identity. You also learned how to use JAAS to validate the claims made in these tokens against a store and scheme of your choice. You also saw how we can stack up JAAS modules to create complex authentication mechanisms that can serve many useful business scenarios.

Even though JAAS is not a part of the WS-* standard, you will find it useful in most situations. It is especially helpful when you want to protect against changing password stores. In fact, we will reuse it in subsequent chapters where we use authentication schemes other than the ones presented here.

Next, we discussed the digest authentication scheme. We showed how it effectively prevents MIM attacks by using nonces and timestamps. We implemented the digest scheme by extending the earlier example with one more login module in the JAAS handler.

This chapter focused on using passwords to claim and verify identity. The schemes described here paid much attention to replay attacks, preventing a MIM (or a malicious service provider) from taking your credentials and repeating them to claim your identity.

You also may have observed several best practices: separation of code into different modules so that we can make use of them in different situations and use of configuration files to make the application flexible.

Finally, we described the suitability of the password-based schemes. They are appropriate for several different situations; however, they have serious limitations conceptually. That is, the use of a password as proof itself is a weakness in the system.

In the next three chapters, we will describe two technologies—Kerberos and public key infrastructure (PKI)—that will help you overcome the limitations of passwords in claiming and verifying identity.

Through most of this chapter, we have assumed that authentication can happen at a single point. We assumed that a single system has access to all the password/credential stores in order to authenticate any identity claim submitted to it. This assumption often proves false when businesses cooperate to offer their customers each other's services without the need for additional authentication. We also have not seen how we can go on to determine whether a caller has sufficient privileges to make a request once we verify his identity. These topics will be discussed in part III of this book.

Suggestions for further reading

- WS-Security UsernameToken Profile 1.1, an OASIS Standard, is available at http://www.oasis-open.org/committees/download.php/16782/wss-v1.1-spec-os-UsernameTokenProfile.pdf. This chapter was written based on version 1.0 of the profile.

- The JAAS Reference Guide is available at http://java.sun.com/j2se/1.5.0/docs/guide/security/jaas/JAASRefGuide.html.

- The SHA-1 Specification is available at http://www.itl.nist.gov/fipspubs/fip180-1.htm.

- RFC 3548 describes base16, base32, and base64 encodings. The RFC is available at http://tools.ietf.org/html/3548.

- RFC 3629 describes the UTF-8 encoding scheme. The RFC is available at http://tools.ietf.org/html/3629.

5

Secure authentication
with Kerberos

This chapter covers

- Alternatives to password-based authentication
- Kerberos and Java GSS API
- WS-Security with Kerberos

In the previous chapter, we showed you how to claim your identity using passwords. We discussed two schemes: one that requires you to submit your password in clear text and another that helps you guard your password from snoopers—people who intend to steal it while it is on the wire. Both schemes required you to first register a username and password with your service providers. Like most users, you probably reuse the same username and password when registering with several services. This makes you susceptible to *repurposing* attacks. Administrators of a service you are registered with can steal your username and password and spoof your identity on other services. Is there a way out of this mess without burdening yourself with the inhuman task of creating and remembering unique username and password combinations for each service? Kerberos is the security technology that first provided an answer to this question.

In fact, Kerberos answers several other significant questions related to SOA security. How do we ensure the confidentiality of messages while they are in transit? Can we detect tampering of messages by a man in the middle? Kerberos answers these questions as well.

In this chapter, we will introduce Kerberos and describe how it can be used for secure authentication in SOA. We will not delve into how Kerberos can be used for addressing other SOA security concerns such as protecting message confidentiality and detecting message tampering. Later chapters will describe how you can address these issues using PKI, a more scalable solution to the problems Kerberos was designed to address.

Given our reference to PKI as a superior technology compared to Kerberos, you might be wondering if you still need to learn about Kerberos. In our opinion, Kerberos is still a technology you will want to understand for a couple of reasons.

First, Kerberos was the first full-fledged security framework that tackled most of the security requirements we discuss in this book. In fact, several ideas in SOA security standards can be traced to Kerberos. A good understanding of Kerberos will help you better appreciate the more recent SOA security technologies we will introduce in the rest of the book.

The second reason why Kerberos is important is a practical one. Microsoft uses Kerberos (with its own extensions) for security in its server offerings. Therefore, if you are working with any enterprise solutions, it is likely that you will have to deal with Kerberos. This chapter will help you understand and develop the right solution in those cases.

In this chapter, we will first establish Kerberos as a viable security solution for SOA. We do that by identifying the requirements of an authentication system. Next, we will show how to put Kerberos into practice through an example. This example will show you how to use Java Generic Security Service (JGSS), a standard Java API for authentication with Kerberos. By the end of this chapter, you will see how WS-Security supports Kerberos and how you can implement this support in your web services and clients.

5.1 Authentication requirements in SOA

We concluded the previous chapter with a rant about how password-based authentication is inherently insecure. In particular, we pointed out that:

- The weakest link in a password-based authentication mechanism is the password itself. A password is just too easy to steal and use.

- Enterprises can go to great lengths to protect passwords by enforcing password policies, but these are not good solutions because they make the lives of users difficult in the name of security. Worse still, there is no policy that can make people guard their passwords well.

- No password policy can effectively deal with one menace: misuse of passwords by service providers themselves. Users tend to reuse their easy-to-remember passwords for multiple services, many of which cannot be trusted not to steal the password.

These are just the tip of the iceberg. In fact, we can describe several other ways that a password-based system fails to meet the requirements of an authentication system for SOA. Now may be the time to describe these requirements so that we can see how other alternatives fare. Table 5.1 shows these requirements.

Table 5.1 Requirements an authentication system should satisfy if it is to be appropriate for use in SOA

Requirement	Description
Multifactor authentication	The authentication system must allow users to claim identity in multiple ways. For example, it must be possible to authenticate based on what the user has or what the user is in addition to, or instead of, what the user knows. What the user knows is his password. He may also have a smart card that can prove his identity. What the user is can be proven with a biometric device such as a digital fingerprint or a retina scan. All these are valid forms of identification and should be supported by themselves or in combination with the rest.

continued on next page

Table 5.1 Requirements an authentication system should satisfy if it is to be appropriate for use in SOA *(continued)*

Requirement	Description
Protection against service-provider abuse	The authentication system must not require the user to send a shared secret such as a password or its variation (such as a digest) to a service in order to prove his identity. For example, the authentication system can challenge the caller with a question that can only be answered correctly by someone who has access to the caller's password. This will better protect the caller's secret in case the same secret is being used to contact multiple services, not all of which are administered by trusted parties.
SSO to multiple services	The authentication system must allow the possibility of using a single set of user credentials to authenticate with a variety of services including legacy services that demand custom passwords.
Delegatable authentication	If the user wants to authorize somebody else to invoke a service on his behalf, he should be able to do that without revealing the secret credentials he uses to prove his identity to the authentication system. For example, when visiting a hospital, you may digitally grant your consent to let the hospital's applications contact applications from other hospitals to obtain your medical history.
Mutual authentication	It is not just the servers that are interested in knowing who exactly they are talking to; clients are often as interested knowing for sure that the server they are talking to is indeed a genuine one. For example, when submitting your credentials to a bank, you would like to know for sure that you are indeed communicating with the bank's application. The authentication system must support mutual authentication of parties involved in a transaction.
Protection against replay attacks	Whatever the authentication strategy, it should be possible to protect against the possibility of someone else capturing our requests and simply replaying them.

As you can see, SOA imposes a long list of onerous requirements on authentication systems. For those who are not very familiar with modern security technologies, these requirements might even seem far too ambitious. Fortunately, we live in an age when most of these requirements can be met by not one, but two popular technologies: Kerberos and PKI. Throughout the rest of this chapter, we'll discuss Kerberos. PKI is introduced in the next two chapters, where we will discuss it in conjunction with encryption and/or signatures.

In the next section, we will introduce the basic set of ideas behind Kerberos and how they all can come together to meet the requirements listed in table 5.1. We will begin our discussion by describing the specific security problem Kerberos was originally meant to address.

5.2 Introduction to Kerberos

Kerberos was invented in the '80s to solve a security issue for a university campus network. In a typical university, students themselves administer most of the lab machines. According to the Kerberos legend, some of the students found it interesting and funny to capture each other's passwords by abusing the administrative privileges. The university was forced to come up with a solution to this menace without withdrawing the administrative functions available to the students. Thus, the Kerberos authentication scheme was born. The main problem that Kerberos solved was authentication in multiple applications that did not trust each other. It also tackled the problems of SSO and delegatable authentication described in the previous section.

The modern-day Internet is not too different from the university campus network for which Kerberos was designed. As shown in figure 5.1, there are just too many unknown service providers we rely on without knowing if we can really trust them.

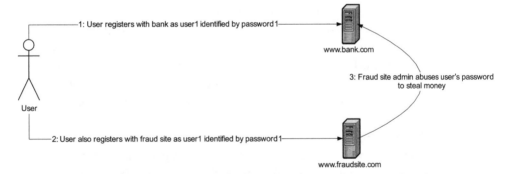

Figure 5.1 **Example of service provider abuse Kerberos was designed to eliminate. Users often tend to reuse passwords across services. A malicious service provider can easily abuse the passwords registered by users to spoof user identity on a different service.**

In other words, the core problem of protecting one's identity credentials such as passwords from abuse by malicious service providers is still a relevant one. In the rest of this section, we will describe how Kerberos solves this problem. In particular, we will describe:

- The basics of encryption that underlie Kerberos
- How encryption can be leveraged to do authentication

- Basic concepts in Kerberos such as Key Distribution Center (KDC), long-term key, session key, and ticket
- The sequence of steps in authenticating a client to a service
- How Kerberos supports mutual authentication and delegatable authentication

5.2.1 *Basic ideas behind Kerberos*

Kerberos solves the problem of service provider abuse with a basic set of ideas that are all clever but simple refinements of the ideas that underlie encryption. To understand Kerberos, you need to understand some principles of encryption. Even though we are going to discuss encryption in depth in the next chapter, we will provide here just enough background to understand Kerberos.

First, a quick introduction to encryption.

Encryption protects the secrecy or confidentiality of data passing over the wire by transforming it in such a way that only the intended receiver can recover and read the original data. You have already seen in action the idea of transforming data before sending it on the wire, albeit with a slightly different goal.

Recall the password digest mechanism we discussed in chapter 4. The goal behind the password digest is to enable a client to protect its password from a man in the middle and still prove to a server that it indeed is in possession of the password. A client using a password digest mechanism uses a transformation function (a digest function, to be more specific) f to transform its password p[1] into f(p) before sending it over the wire.

The challenge in digest computation is to pick a specially designed transformation function f that will make it extremely difficult, if not impossible, to do the inverse transformation. As what is passed over the wire is f(p) and not p, a man in the middle cannot steal the password unless he can compute the inverse of f. This means that the intended recipient cannot compute the inverse either. The intended recipient is assumed to already be in possession of the original password p so that it can simply recompute f(p) and match the result against the value transmitted by the sender.

The needs of encryption are clearly different. In encryption, we want the intended recipient (and the intended recipient alone) to recover and read the original data.

---

[1] Password digest functions transform not just the password p, but also a nonce n and timestamp t to thwart replay attacks, but we will ignore that detail here to keep the discussion simple.

In other words, the intended recipient must be able to compute the inverse of the transformation function.

So, each encryption function must come with a decryption function also. The encryption function encrypts a secret and the decryption function can decrypt the encrypted secret. To put it mathematically: if f is the encryption function, and g is the decryption function, then g(f(s))= s. Figure 5.2 shows how this works:

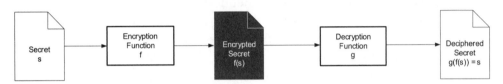

Figure 5.2   Relationship between encryption and decryption functions: the decryption function can recover a secret encrypted by the encryption function.

So, if two computer programs want to exchange confidential information, one of them needs to know the encryption function and the other needs to know the decryption function. This is easy enough until we start having multiple senders and receivers. Since no receiver should be in a position to compromise the information being sent to the other, we will need as many encryption functions as there are receivers.

Coming up with a different encryption function for every receiver is not an easy task. A common trick is to simply parameterize a well-known encryption function f with a key k in such a way that only the receiver who knows the key value used can decrypt the message. The sender sends f(s,k) and only the designated receiver who knows the key value k can get back s. Figure 5.3 shows this in action:

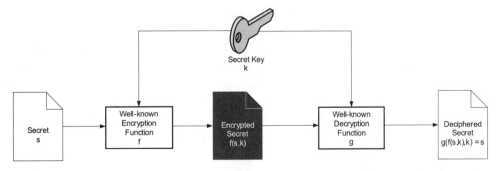

Figure 5.3   To protect a secret even when using a well-known encryption function, the sender can use a secret key k that is only known to the intended receiver. The intended recipient uses its knowledge of the secret key to match the modification of the encryption function in the decryption function.

Now that you understand the basics of encryption, the next few subsections describe how Kerberos employs encryption to create an authentication mechanism that does not expose user identity to service provider abuse.

Leveraging encryption to do authentication

Let us take a look again at figure 5.3 and see if we can spot a simple way to leverage encryption to accomplish authentication.

Let's say each user is assigned a distinctive key that he can use for encryption. Each user can authenticate himself to a server by sending his identity claim (which may, for example, consist simply of a username) both in plain text as well as in an encrypted form. As a server knows the key for each user, it can authenticate users by decrypting the encrypted claim and comparing it with the claim in plain text. Thus, we can use encryption as a way for authentication.

Is this mechanism less susceptible to service provider abuse? The answer is no. Just as with password-based authentication, a user will have to register a secret (which in this case is the decryption key) with every server in order for the servers to authenticate the client. Just as with the password, the server can abuse this knowledge by pretending to be the user.

Yet, there is a way to make sure that the service provider does not need to know the key, thereby eliminating the risk of password or key misuse. Kerberos offers some clever mechanisms to do that, which we will describe in the next subsection.

Basic concepts in Kerberos

To solve the problem of service provider abuse, the designers of Kerberos needed to eliminate the need for users to register a secret with every server. They met this requirement by saying that clients only need to register a secret with a central authority called the KDC and not with every server they wish to interact with.

Under the Kerberos scheme, every user registers a *long-term key* that can be computed from the user's password using a well-known function. The KDC holds the long-term keys for all the users. The only two parties that know a user's long-term key are the user and the KDC itself. Note that the KDC has no knowledge of the user's password. It only knows the user's long-term key.

Servers register long-term keys, too. Each server registers a long-term key with the KDC, and that key is once again known only to two parties: the server and the KDC.

Armed with the knowledge of long-term keys for every user and server, the KDC can facilitate secure authentication (and communication) in the following

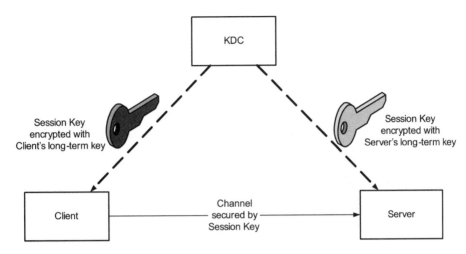

Figure 5.4 A KDC can act as a "broker" that supplies a session key.

way. When a user wants to authenticate and communicate with a server, she simply requests what is known as a *session key*. Figure 5.4 shows how a KDC responds to such a request.

The KDC dynamically generates a session key and sends two copies of it—one to the user (the client) and one to the server. Each copy of the session key is encrypted using a well-known encryption function that is parameterized by the long-term key of the intended recipient. This protects the session key from all users other than the user and server involved. Each party can use its long-term key to decrypt the session key copy provided by KDC. Subsequently, the client and the server use the session key to encrypt all communication between them.

There is one subtle issue here. For any client and server to establish secure communication, the KDC needs to send a copy of the session key to both of them. But, this scheme imposes an undue burden on the KDC and makes it the bottleneck. An easy way out would be to have the KDC send both copies of the session key to the client. The client can then send the server's copy of the session key along with the first message.

Figure 5.5 shows this idea pictorially.

This picture is not complete because we have not yet addressed one important aspect. Looking at the session key, there is no way to ascertain which client it is coming from. In other words, we can see how a session key can be used to encrypt all communication between the client and the sender, but we cannot yet see how

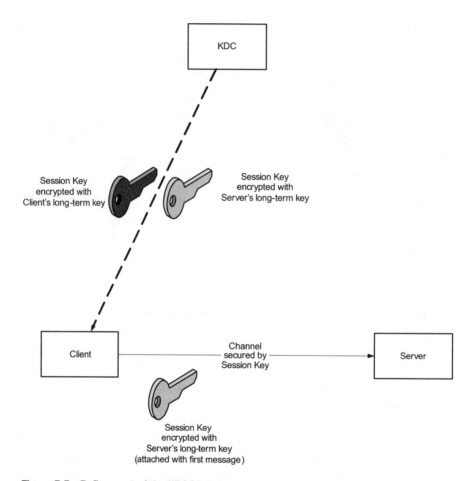

Figure 5.5   Refinement of the KDC idea.

the session key can be used to do authentication. Kerberos addresses this problem by introducing the concept of a *ticket*.

A ticket consists of the client's identity information and the session key granted to the client by the KDC for a particular service, and is encrypted using the service's long-term key. As the service's long-term key is not known to anyone except the KDC and the service itself, a ticket cannot be forged. That is, when the server decrypts the ticket, it knows that it can only come from the KDC.

The use of ticket for authentication is shown in figure 5.6. The only difference between figure 5.5 and figure 5.6 is that the server's copy of the session

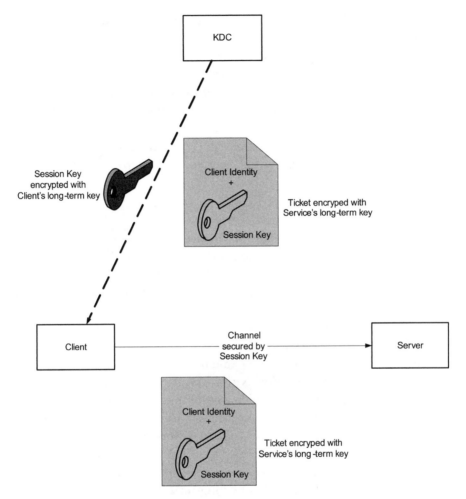

Figure 5.6 Further refinements to combine client identity details and session key as part of a ticket.

key is enclosed in a ticket so that the server can determine the identity of the client.

Finally, this is what we have: We have a ticket that cannot be made up by any one other than the KDC because only the KDC has knowledge of the target service's long-term key. The ticket cannot be captured and used by any MIM, as he has no way to decipher the session key needed to communicate with the service. Plus, the ticket can be used for authenticating the client as well as securing the communications between the client and the target service.

You are now familiar with all the basic ideas that Kerberos introduced to eliminate the possibility of service providers abusing knowledge of users' credentials. A user no longer needs to give out the password that forms the basis for his identity claim; instead, KDC gives out a session key that can only be used by a genuine user who is in possession of his secret. Remember the user's password never needs to be transmitted—not to service providers and not even to the KDC.

Now that you have an informal understanding of how Kerberos works, we will next describe the formal sequence of steps involved in Kerberos-based authentication.

5.2.2 Authentication sequence

Figure 5.7 shows the sequence of steps involved in Kerberos-based authentication.

In this figure, the KDC is divided into two parts: Authentication Service and Ticket Granting Service. We will describe the functionality of these two parts next. Once you understand the functionality of both parts, you will see that this division helps make Kerberos more efficient.

Authentication Service (AS)

The Authentication Service, as the name indicates, authenticates the clients. The end result of this authentication is that the client gets credentials to talk to a Ticket Granting Service (TGS), which we will describe later.

Staying true to the idea of never asking a user to transmit his password over the network, AS does not demand the password from the client. Instead, AS takes the client's authentication request at its face value and supplies the credentials the client can in turn use to contact the TGS. The credentials supplied by AS are encrypted with the client's long-term key; only the real only the real client can make use of the credentials.

Kerberos treats TGS like any other service. To talk to TGS, the client needs a ticket and a session key, and these are exactly what AS provides. Since these are used by the client to contact the TGS that is part of the KDC, these credentials are specially referred to as the *Ticket Granting Ticket (TGT)* and *Logon Session Key*, respectively.

Ticket Granting Service (TGS)

The purpose of TGS is to grant a ticket so that a secure session between a client and server can be established. Once the client has a TGT and the Logon Session

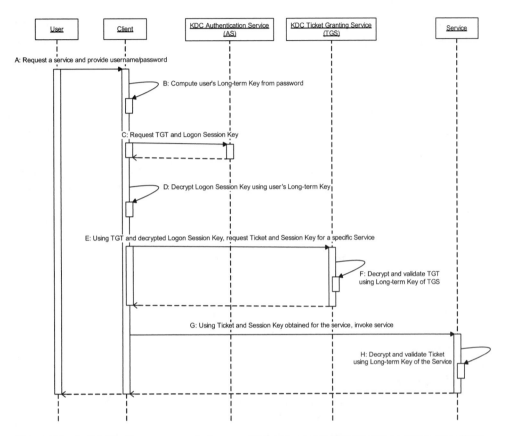

Figure 5.7 **Authentication sequence between a Kerberos-enabled client and a service. The client application authenticates to the service without revealing the user's password to the service. The user password is not submitted to the KDC either. Logon Session Key returned by KDC AS can only be used by the client if it is in possession of the user's long-term key, computable from the user's password.**

Key, it can contact the TGS and request a ticket and a session key to talk to the target service. The TGS uses its own long-term key to verify the TGT and, if successful, provides the client with a ticket and session key to use with the target service.

The client contacts the service and just like the TGS, the service can verify the ticket presented using its own long-term key. These steps complete the authentication of the client by the service.

At the start of this chapter, we identified various requirements an authentication mechanism must support in order to satisfy the security needs of SOA. We argued at the time that an authentication mechanism must provide more than just client authentication. For example, we pointed out that mutual authentication and delegatable authentication are also required. In the next section, we will see how Kerberos supports these additional requirements.

5.2.3 *Beyond client authentication*

Kerberos is designed to do a lot more than authenticate clients. It can provide mutual authentication, delegatable authentication, message confidentiality and integrity guarantees, message sequencing, and replay detection. Of these, we will restrict the discussion here to a very brief introduction of mutual authentication and delegatable authentication, as the rest of the topics will be covered in later chapters.

Mutual authentication

Just as clients authenticate themselves to a service, the service can in turn authenticate itself to the clients. For example, the service can extract a part of the client information embedded in the service ticket and send it back encrypted using the session key. This information proves the service's identity to the client, as client information and session key can only be extracted from the service ticket by those who have access to the service's long term key.

Delegatable authentication

A client can ask the KDC to provide it with a ticket that it can then share with a third party to use on its behalf. This request can be made in two ways. If the client is willing to let the third party use all the services on its behalf, the client can ask the AS for a TGT that can be used by the third party in turn to get service tickets from the TGS. If, on the other hand, the client only wishes to grant the third party its privileges to invoke a particular service, it can ask the TGS for a *proxy ticket* that can be used by the third party to invoke a particular service.

So far, we have seen how Kerberos operates, and what it can do. The rest of the chapter focuses on how to use Kerberos to secure web services, in particular to authenticate users. Here, we get into a lot of the nitty-gritty details of Kerberos, and the material can be difficult to navigate. In the next subsection, we will provide you with a roadmap to the rest of the chapter so that you will know where you are headed and how each of the remaining sections ties into the big picture.

5.2.4 *Roadmap for the rest of the chapter*

There are two top-level sections in the rest of the chapter. The scope for each of these two sections is:

- Section 5.3 illustrates through an annotated example how to use Kerberos in a generic client server application. Here, we are not going to deal with any WS-Security–specific details. Instead, we will show how we can communicate with AS and TGS to get a ticket and session key. As such, this part is independent of web services.

- Section 5.4 covers the WS-Security–specific details we omit in Section 5.3. In particular, it describes the mechanism specified in the WS-Security Kerberos Token Profile to communicate the service ticket from a SOAP client to a SOAP service.

Together, these two sections will show you how to implement Kerberos-based authentication in a web service invocation. Table 5.2 maps each of the steps in the authentication process (shown in figure 5.7) to the subsections where they are discussed. This table also briefly describes the implementation strategy used in each step so that you know what APIs, libraries, and specifications you will learn about in different subsections.

Table 5.2 Implementation roadmap for Kerberos-based authentication of a web service client

Step (as shown in Figure 5.7)	Action	Section describing the implementation	Implementation strategy
Step A to Step D	Client obtains TGT and Logon Session Key from KDC AS. Obtains password from the user, computes his long-term key, and uses it to decrypt the Logon Session Key.	5.3.1	Use the JAAS login module for Kerberos available in Sun's JDK.
Steps E and F	Client uses the TGT and Logon Session Key to obtain a service ticket and session key from the KDC TGS.	5.3.1	Use Java GSS API.

continued on next page

Table 5.2   Implementation roadmap for Kerberos-based authentication of a web service client *(continued)*

Step (as shown in Figure 5.7)	Action	Section describing the implementation	Implementation strategy
Step G	Client invokes the Service using service ticket and session key.	5.4.2–5.4.4	Use a JAX-RPC handler to add Service Ticket to WS-Security headers as described in the Kerberos Token Profile for WS-Security.
		In a full implementation, the session key should be used for protecting the confidentiality and integrity of messages, as described by WS-Security and Kerberos Token Profile for WS-Security. This step is not demonstrated by the examples in this book. If you follow the examples in chapters 6 and 7 that show how to accomplish the same goals using PKI instead of Kerberos, you will be able to read the Kerberos Token Profile for WS-Security and teach yourself how to implement this step.	N/A.
Step H	Server reads the service ticket submitted by the client, decrypts it using its own long-term key, and validates it.	5.4.5	Extract service ticket from WS-Security header.
		5.3.2	Decrypt and validate the service ticket using Java GSS API.

To summarize the details presented in the table 5.2, section 5.3 will demonstrate the use of JAAS and GSS APIs for obtaining TGT, Logon Session Key, service ticket, and session key on the client-side and validating the service ticket on the server-side. We leave the details of adding a service ticket to a web services call for a later section (section 5.4). As we mentioned earlier, you will not see in this chapter how to use the session keys to protect confidentiality and integrity of messages. You will have to wait until chapters 6 and 7 to see how to take care of those concerns.

5.3 *Implementing Kerberos with JAAS and GSS APIs*

In this section, we are going to illustrate how a generic client and a server communicate with KDC. In the client part, we will show how a client gets a session key and a ticket. In the server part, we will show how a server understands the ticket. For these purposes, we will use the JAAS API, introduced in the previous chapter, with a JAAS login module that is Kerberos-specific. In addition, we will introduce a new API (GSS) that is used to contact KDC.

5.3.1 *Client-side implementation*

As shown in figure 5.7, a client needs to do the following to use Kerberos-based authentication:

1 Get a TGT and a Logon Session Key from KDC AS, and decrypt Logon Session Key using the long-term key computed from the password.

2 Get a service ticket from KDC TGS.

3 Use the service ticket to authenticate when contacting the service.

In this section, we are not going to show how to do the third step, as that is the subject of the next section. Because of interdependencies, first we will show the code for step 2, and where it requires the TGT and Logon Session Key, we will show the code for step 1.

Introduction to GSS

To perform step 2—that is, to get a service token once we have the TGT and Logon Session Key—we use the General Security Services (GSS) API defined in the `org.ietf.jgss` standard Java package. GSS provides a generic API to use mechanisms such as Kerberos and digital certificates for authentication, guarding message confidentiality and integrity, sequencing messages, and guarding against replay attacks. In this chapter, we are only interested in using GSS to get a service ticket from TGS on the client-side and verify service tickets presented by clients on the service-side. Figure 5.8 shows how GSS can be used for this purpose.

Client-side activities B and C in figure 5.8 are the subject of this subsection. Steps A and E are server-side activities and are described in the next subsection (5.3.2). Step D varies based on the client-server protocol, and its implementation in the context of web services is described in section 5.4.

Identifying the target service to GSS

Let's now look at the code needed to implement steps B and C in figure 5.8. In step B, we should provide two arguments to a method named `createContext`: The name of the service we wish to get a ticket for and our credentials (TGT). Let's first see how we can provide the first of these two arguments.

GSS provides a special data structure, `GSSName`, to identify clients or services. Listing 5.1 shows how we can create an instance of this data structure to identify our target service.

Listing 5.1   Identifying the target service

```
GSSManager gssManager =                    ❶ Gets a handle to
       GSSManager.getInstance();             GSSManager
GSSName serviceName = gssManager.createName    Identifies the
       ("service1@host1", GSSName.NT_HOSTBASED_SERVICE);   target service
```

We start off by getting hold of `GSSManager` ❶, a factory for creating all other GSS-related objects. We use the retrieved `GSSManager` instance to identify the target

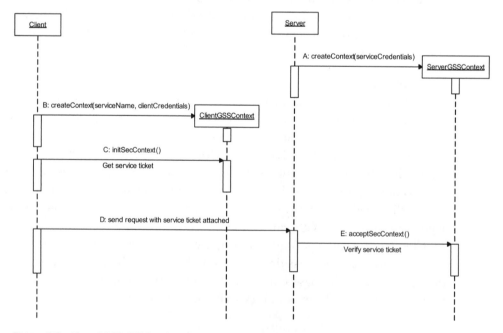

Figure 5.8   Use of GSS API for the limited purpose of obtaining a Kerberos service ticket on the client-side and verifying it on the server-side.

service. As you can see, this is done using the `createName` method in `GSSManager`. This method takes two parameters: a name string and a namespace identifier. The namespace identifier has to be specified using an OID. (See the callout regarding the definition of an OID.) In this example, we are using a predefined OID to identify the namespace for host-based services.

> **NOTE** *What is an OID?* Object Identifiers (OIDs) are identifiers assigned by IANA, a standards organization, in compliance with the guidelines laid down by a standard named ASN.1. OIDs are defined in hierarchical namespaces. For example, Kerberos V5 mechanism is identified by the OID 1.2.840.113554.1.2.2, which corresponds to `iso.member-body.United States.mit.infosys. gssapi.krb5`. GSS uses OIDs to identify security mechanisms and name formats.

Providing the client credentials(TGT) to GSS

You have seen how to identify the target service. Now, let's shift our attention to providing the second argument to the `createContext` method shown in step B of figure 5.8. Listing 5.2 shows the code required to provide client credentials to GSS.

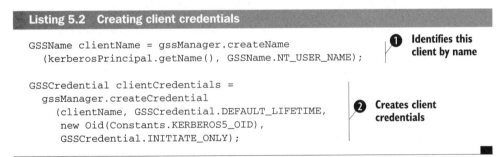

Listing 5.2   Creating client credentials

```
GSSName clientName = gssManager.createName
   (kerberosPrincipal.getName(), GSSName.NT_USER_NAME);
```
❶ **Identifies this client by name**

```
GSSCredential clientCredentials =
   gssManager.createCredential
      (clientName, GSSCredential.DEFAULT_LIFETIME,
       new Oid(Constants.KERBEROS5_OID),
       GSSCredential.INITIATE_ONLY);
```
❷ **Creates client credentials**

In this listing, we first create a `GSSName` ❶ to identify the client name just like we identified the service in the previous example. Notice the predefined OID we use to indicate the namespace. We then create the client credentials ❷ we want to provide to GSS. What we really want to do here is encapsulate the TGT in a GSS data structure that can be later used when getting the service token using GSS. Instead, what do we see here? We are simply providing the client name and specifying that we want to create a Kerberos ticket that can be used to initiate a service invocation. How does GSS get to the TGT required to obtain a service ticket from the TGS? The answer is that GSS obtains the TGT automatically from the `Subject` in the current access control context.

NOTE *What is current access control context in Java?* The Java security model controls access to resources based on (a) what code is requesting access to a resource and (b) the user executing that code.

> The first of these checks is required because an application may sometimes attempt to run code that it downloaded at runtime from untrusted sources. For example, a browser may run an applet downloaded from a web site. Clearly, such code should have restricted permissions.

> The second check is required because an application may need to utilize the privileges granted to a user if it has to act on the user's request. For example, in our case, we need to utilize the privileges granted to a user in order to request a service ticket using his TGT.

> The combination of the results of these two checks constitutes an *access control context*. The access control context that is in effect when executing a piece of code is said to be *current access control context*. Applications can switch the current access control context when needed. One way of doing so is provided by the doAs static method in `javax.security.auth.Subject`.

If GSS is to get the TGT by looking up the `Subject` in the current access control context, we need to do the following activities first:

1 Create a `Subject` instance that represents the user's identity.

2 Obtain a TGT and Logon Session Key from the KDC and store them as private credentials of the `Subject` instance created in step 1.

3 Associate the `Subject` instance with current access control context in the Java application.

The first two steps can be carried out using `Krb5LoginModule`, a JAAS login module for Kerberos that is shipped as part of Sun's implementation of JDK. The last step is carried out using the doAs static method in `javax.security.auth.Subject`.

Listing 5.3 Obtaining TGT via JAAS login and passing it via current access control context to `ServiceTicketGrabber`

```
//assuming that JAAS is set up talk to KDC
LoginContext loginContext =
  new LoginContext(appName, callbackHandler);   ❶ Login using JAAS
loginContext.login();                              gets us TGT

Subject kerberosSubject = loginContext.getSubject();   ❷ Retrieves logged-
                                                          in Subject
```

```
byte[] serviceToken = (byte[]) Subject.doAs
   (kerberosSubject,
   new ServiceTicketGrabber
   (kerberosSubject, messageContext));
```

❸ **Executes ServiceTicketGrabber as logged-in Subject**

In this code listing, we first do the JAAS-based login ❶ that we are so familiar with by now. We assume here that JAAS has been configured to use the Krb5LoginModule for the named application. The Krb5LoginModule contacts the KDC on the host given by the java.security.krb5.kdc system property and obtains a TGT and a Logon Session Key from the KDC AS. It adds the obtained TGT and Logon Session Key to the private credentials of the Subject associated with the LoginContext.

In order to make GSS use the TGT we obtained using Krb5LoginModule, we need to set the Subject associated with the current access control context when executing the GSS calls. So, we get the logged-in Subject ❷ from the JAAS Login-Context and use the doAs static method in javax.security.auth.Subject ❸ to switch the Subject in the current access control context when executing Service-TicketGrabber. The doAs method takes two arguments: the subject to set in the current access control context and an instance of a class that implements the java.security.PrivilegedAction interface. To implement the Privileged-Action interface, all a class needs to do is implement a run() method that returns any Object. We will next look at how our ServiceTicketGrabber class implements this method.

Obtaining the service ticket

What should be in the run() method of ServiceTicketGrabber? As the name suggests, we would like to grab a service ticket from the KDC using GSS APIs. So, as shown in steps B and C of figure 5.8, the run() method must make createContext and initSecContext calls. These calls require the gssManager, serviceName, and clientCredentials created in listings 5.1 and 5.2. Listing 5.4 shows selected parts of the run() method.

Listing 5.4 `ServiceTicketGrabber` **implementation**

```
public Object run() {
   //skipping code to initialize gssManager, serviceName and
   //clientCredentials that was shown previously

   GSSContext gssContext = gssManager.createContext
      (serviceName, kerberos5Oid,
       clientCredentials, GSSContext.DEFAULT_LIFETIME);
```

❶ **Passes serviceName and TGT to GSS**

```
byte[] serviceTicket =
  gssContext.initSecContext(new byte[0],0,0);
return serviceTicket;
}
```

❷ **Obtains service ticket**

We first identify the target service and provide GSS with the client credentials ❶. This step provides us with a `GSSContext` instance upon which we can call the `initSecContext(...)` method to obtain a service ticket ❷. The `initSecContext` method takes three arguments: a byte array representing the token generated by the peer (service), the offset into the byte array where the token begins, and the length of the token. All three arguments are given dummy values here, as there is no token that the service provides to the client before the client asks KDC for a service ticket.

Strictly speaking, the byte array returned by `gssContext.initSecContext` is a little more than a Kerberos service ticket in two ways. First, Kerberos itself specifies that the client should wrap the service ticket in a data structure named `KRB_AP_REQ` when sending the ticket to the server. In addition to a service ticket, a `KRB_AP_REQ` structure consists of a protocol version number, message type, application options, and what is called an *authenticator* to defend against replay-of-service tickets. Second, GSS wraps `KRB_AP_REQ` into another data structure that also contains a mechanism identifier. The mechanism identifier is required because GSS is not restricted to Kerberos and can be used with many other security mechanisms. What is returned by `gssContext.initSecContext` is a `KRB_AP_REQ` wrapped by GSS.

Phew! We finally have a service ticket we can use. Observe that GSS stays independent of the client-server protocol by leaving it to the client to figure out how the service token should be sent to the service. We will soon see how we can add a Kerberos service ticket to the WS-Security header, but first, let us complete the task we set for ourselves in this section: understanding how we can implement Kerberos-based authentication in generic client-server interaction. We still have to understand how we verify a service ticket submitted by a client on the service side.

5.3.2 *Service-side implementation*

Figure 5.7 tells us that we need the service's long-term key in order to verify a service ticket (step H). If we do a JAAS login using the `Krb5LoginModule`, in the process of decrypting the Logon Session Key provided by the AS, it will automatically compute the long-term key and store it in the Subject associated with the Login-Context. So, just like on the client-side, the first thing to do on the server-side is a JAAS login using the Krb5LoginModule. We will not show the code for doing this, as you should be well-versed with it by now.

Once we have the service's long-term key, we can verify the service ticket using the createContext and acceptSecContext methods shown in steps A and E of figure 5.8, respectively. Listing 5.5 shows these calls in action.

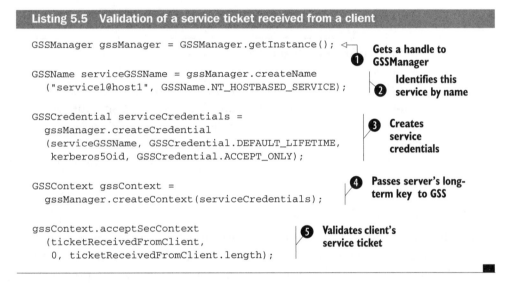

Listing 5.5   Validation of a service ticket received from a client

```
GSSManager gssManager = GSSManager.getInstance();          ← ① Gets a handle to
                                                               GSSManager
GSSName serviceGSSName = gssManager.createName              ② Identifies this
  ("service1@host1", GSSName.NT_HOSTBASED_SERVICE);            service by name

GSSCredential serviceCredentials =                         ③ Creates
  gssManager.createCredential                                 service
  (serviceGSSName, GSSCredential.DEFAULT_LIFETIME,            credentials
   kerberos5Oid, GSSCredential.ACCEPT_ONLY);

GSSContext gssContext =                                    ④ Passes server's long-
  gssManager.createContext(serviceCredentials);               term key to GSS

gssContext.acceptSecContext                                ⑤ Validates client's
  (ticketReceivedFromClient,                                  service ticket
   0, ticketReceivedFromClient.length);
```

Just as on the client-side, in this listing, we first get a handle to the GSSManager instance ① and use it to identify the service ② and create its credentials ③. The credentials mention that the service will simply accept calls instead of initiating calls like the client.

We create a GSSContext ④ next and it is at this time that GSS looks up the server's long-term key from the Subject associated with the current access control context. For this reason, this listing must be executed as the Subject that logged in using JAAS Krb5LoginModule. For brevity, we have not shown that here, but you have already seen in listing 5.3 how to do it.

Finally, we verify the ticket received from the client ⑤.

If we want to do mutual authentication, we should capture the bytes returned by acceptSecContext and return them to the client along with the service response. GSS even allows for security mechanisms that require multiple round-trips to initialize and accept security context. Kerberos of course does not require multiple round-trips, as we saw here. See the javadocs for GSS APIs for more such advanced details.

In this section, you have seen how a generic client and a server communicate with the KDC in order to use Kerberos-based authentication. What you have not seen yet is how a client presents its service ticket when invoking a SOAP-based web service (step D in figure 5.8). This is the topic of the next section.

5.4 *Using Kerberos with WS-Security*

The Kerberos token profile for WS-Security standardizes the usage of Kerberos in SOAP-based message exchanges. In this section, we will illustrate the use of this standard through an example. We will first tell you how you can set up the environment required for running the example and run it. Using the request message you see in the example, we will explain how WS-Security allows Kerberos tickets to be included in the `Security` header entry of a SOAP message. Then we will show you the code required on the client- and server-sides to construct and parse a `Security` header with a Kerberos ticket.

5.4.1 *Running the Kerberos example*

To run the Kerberos example, you will need a KDC instance. The instructions given here assume a KDC instance available with Active Directory in Microsoft Windows Server 2003. It is outside the scope of this book to provide instructions on installing an Active Directory instance. Table 5.3 provides the instructions to run the example.

Table 5.3 Steps to run the example that illustrates how WS-Security supports Kerberos-based authentication

Step	Action	How To
1	Set up your environment.	If you have not already set up the environment required to run the examples in this book, please refer to chapter 2 to do so. `ant deploy` should install all the examples.
2	Create two user accounts—one for client and one for server—in Active Directory.	Use the Active Directory Users and Computers utility available under Administrative Tools in the Windows Control Panel to create the required user accounts.

continued on next page

Table 5.3 Steps to run the example that illustrates how WS-Security supports Kerberos-based authentication *(continued)*

Step	Action	How To
3	Export the server's account (also called the service principal) information into a file (called the keytab file). The info in this file can be used by the server to validate service tickets submitted by clients.	Install the tools available under the `\Support\Tools` folder of your Windows CD. This gets you a tool named `ktpass` that you can use to generate the keytab file. The command to generate the keytab file is: `ktpass -princ soasecimpl/myhost.myorg.com @REALM -mapuser username@REALM -pass mypass -out c:\temp\soasecimpl.keytab` In this command, replace `myhost.myorg.com` with the name of the host you have deployed the example web services on, REALM with your KDC realm name, `username` with the name of the user account you created in Active Directory for use by the server, `mypass` with the password you wish to assign to the service, and `c:\temp\soasecimpl.keytab` with the path to the file in which you want the service principal information to be stored. Note that the REALM name is always an uppercase version of the windows domain name (for example `MYORG.COM`)
4	Customize the JAAS configuration file to match the set up you have done in previous steps.	The JAAS configuration file, `example3-jaas.conf`, can be found in the `conf/` directory of the example archive you downloaded in Step 1. You will see that this file lists JAAS modules for three applications: `soasecimpl`: The server-side uses the JAAS modules listed for this app to authenticate client requests. `GSSContextAcceptanceJAASModule`, the second module listed for this app, uses GSS API to validate service ticket shown in listing 5.5. You will need to set the `serviceGSSName` option for this module to `soasecimpl@myhost.myorg.com`, where `myhost.myorg.com` is the name of the host you have deployed the example web services on. `soasecimplclient`: The client-side uses the `Krb5LoginModule` listed here to obtain the TGT and service ticket as shown in listings 5.3 and 5.4. `soasecimplserver`: The server-side uses the `Krb5LoginModule` to read the keytab file generated in step 3 and compute the long-term key needed to validate the service tickets submitted by the clients. You will need to customize the `keyTab` and `principal` options of `Krb5LoginModule`. Set the former to the path to the keyTab file produced in step 3 and the latter to `soasecimpl/myhost.myorg.com`, where `myhost.myorg.com` is the name of the host you have deployed the example web services on.

continued on next page

Table 5.3 Steps to run the example that illustrates how WS-Security supports Kerberos-based authentication *(continued)*

Step	Action	How To
5	Customize JVM system properties required by the client-side to match the setup you have done in previous steps.	As we will be using JAAS to obtain the TGT and service tickets, we need to set a system property in the client's JVM to point to the JAAS configuration file we set up in step 4. The `Krb5LoginModule` invoked by JAAS in turn looks up KDC information from JVM system properties. Our example client code also looks up JVM system properties for information such as the client user name, client user password, and service name. All these system properties needed by the client-side are set up by the Ant script we use to run the example client. This script gets the values required for these system properties from a file named `build.properties`. Hence, you need to customize a few values in `build.properties` as described next. `kerberos.kdc`: Active Directory hostname `kerberos.realm`: Active Directory realm name `kerberos.testclient.user`: Username of the client-side user you have created in step 2 `kerberos.testclient.password`: Password of the client-side user you have created in step 2 `kerberos.testservice.gssname`: `soasecimpl@ myhost.myorg.com`, where `myhost.myorg.com` is the name of the host you have deployed the example web services on. `jaas.config`: Absolute path of the JAAS configuration file you have customized in step 3.
6	Customize JVM system properties on the server-side to match the setup you have done in previous steps.	Set the `JAVA_OPTS` environment variable to `-Djava.security.auth.login.config=path-to-jaas.conf-file -Djava.security.krb5.realm=active-directory-realm-name -Djava.security.krb5.kdc=active-directory-realm-name`.
7	Restart Tomcat server.	Run `shutdown` and `startup` scripts (`.bat` files if you are using Windows and `.sh` files if you are on Linux/Solaris/OS X) found in Tomcat's `bin` directory.
8	If it is not already running, start TCP monitor	Run `ant tcpmon` so that you can observe the conversation. Check the XML Format check box to allow `tcpmon` to format shown requests and responses.
9	Run the example.	Run `ant demo -Dexample.id=3`. You should be able to view the request-response pairs going through the tcpmon console.

After these steps, you should be seeing the execution of a number of web service calls, as shown in figure 4.1. The last of these calls is the one that relies on Kerberos for authentication. Take a look at how the request looks in this call to understand how Kerberos can be used with WS-Security.

In the next section, we will describe how to add a Kerberos ticket to the WS-Security header.

5.4.2 *Adding a Kerberos ticket to a WS-Security header*

In section 5.3, you saw how a generic client can get a service ticket from a KDC. The client needs to submit the service ticket to the server, along with its requests. In this section, we will describe how this can be done in the case of SOAP-based web services using standard elements, attributes, and attribute values defined by WS-Security and the Kerberos Token Profile for WS-Security.

WS-Security defines a `BinarySecurityToken` element that can be included in the `Security` header to carry binary tokens such as Kerberos tickets and digital certificates. Listing 5.6 shows an example request to see how this looks in practice.

Listing 5.6   Use of BinarySecurityToken to carry a Kerberos service ticket

```
<soapenv:Envelope ...>
  <soapenv:Header>
    <wsse:Security ...>                          WS-Security              Identifies token
      <wsse:BinarySecurityToken  <─┘            BinarySecurityToken       as a GSS wrapped
          ValueType="...#GSS_Kerberosv5_AP_REQ"              <─┘          KRB_AP_REQ
          EncodingType="...#Base64Binary">          <─
          ...                                <─       Base64 encoded      Indicates that
      </wsse:BinarySecurityToken>                     GSS-wrapped         base64 encoding
    </wsse:Security>                                  KRB_AP_REQ          is in use
  </soapenv:Header>
  <soapenv:Body>
    ...
  </soapenv:Body>
</soapenv:Envelope>
```

As you can see, to use Kerberos-based authentication, a SOAP client takes the GSS-wrapped `KRB_AP_REQ` token (computed using the code in listing 5.4), encodes it in base64, and sends it as a `BinarySecurityToken` in the `Security` header. On the server-side, the server needs to extract the service ticket from the `BinarySecurityToken` in the `Security` header and validate it as shown in listing 5.5 to complete authentication. Quite simple, isn't it?

5.4.3 *Using a Kerberos ticket for authentication*

Let us now look at sample implementations of a SOAP client and service that use Kerberos-based authentication. Figure 5.9 provides an overview of the approach we take.

The client-side and server-side components you see in figure 5.9 are exactly the ones you saw in figure 4.2. Of course, the components have a little more code in them now to support Kerberos-based authentication. The ClientSide-WSSecurityHandler on the client adds a BinarySecurityToken to the Security header. The first handler on the server-side, WSSecurityUsernameHandler, parses the Security header, extracts the Kerberos token and saves it in the message context. The second handler, JAASAuthenticationHandler, validates this token and populates the authenticated subject information in the message context. The end service makes use of the authenticated subject information in carrying out its business logic.

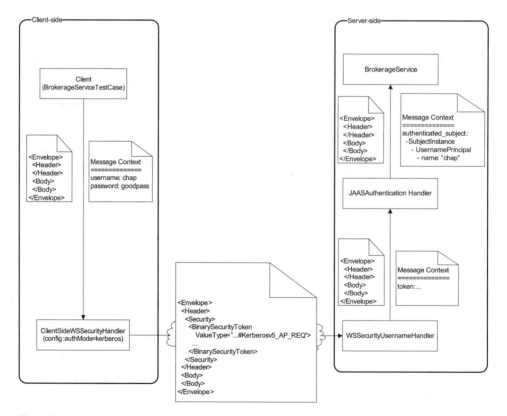

Figure 5.9 Overview of the implementation of a Kerberos-based authentication scheme

In the next two subsections, we walk you through the additional code that goes into client-side and server-side components to support Kerberos-based authentication. Let's start with the client-side.

5.4.4 Adding a Kerberos ticket on the client-side

We extend the `ClientSideWSSecurityHandler` initialization code you have seen in previous chapter to take an additional configuration parameter, `authMode`, to choose between clear-text/digest passwords and Kerberos.

Listing 5.7 Extract from `init` method of `ClientSideWSSecurityHandler`

```
public void init(HandlerInfo handlerInfo) {
  Map config = handlerInfo.getHandlerConfig();

  //figure out if we should do auth and if so, in what way
  String authModeString = (String)
    config.get(AUTH_MODE_PARAMETER_NAME);       Reads configured
  if (authModeString != null) {                 authentication mode
    authMode = Integer.parseInt(authModeString);
  }

  //do necessary initialization in each auth mode
  switch (authMode) {
    //...other cases snipped...
    case KERBEROS5_AUTH_MODE: {
      jaasAppName = (String)                     Reads application name
        config.get(JAAS_APP_CONFIG_PARAM);       to use in JAAS login
    }
  }
}
```

In case Kerberos is configured as the authentication mode, we use JAAS and GSS APIs as shown earlier to get a service ticket. Once we get the service ticket, adding it as a `BinarySecurityToken` in the WS-Security header is easy, as shown in listing 5.8.

Listing 5.8 Adding a Kerberos service ticket as a `BinarySecurityToken` in the `Security` header

```
protected void addKerberosToken
  (SOAPEnvelope soapEnvelope, SOAPHeaderElement securityElement,
   MessageContext messageContext, byte[] serviceTicket)
   throws SOAPException {
```

```
          Name tokenElementName = soapEnvelope.createName
             (Constants.WS_SECURITY_BINARY_TOKEN_TAG,
              Constants.WS_SECURITY_PREF_NS_PREFIX,
              Constants.WS_SECURITY_NS_URI);
          SOAPElement tokenElement =
             securityElement.addChildElement(tokenElementName);

          Name valueTypeAttrName = soapEnvelope.createName
             (Constants.WS_SECURITY_VALUE_TYPE_ATTR);
          tokenElement.addAttribute
             (valueTypeAttrName,
              Constants.WS_SECURITY_GSS_KERBEROS5_AP_REQ_TYPE);

          Name encodingTypeAttrName = soapEnvelope.createName
             (Constants.WS_SECURITY_ENCODING_TYPE_ATTR);
          tokenElement.addAttribute
             (encodingTypeAttrName,
              Constants.WS_SECURITY_BASE64_ENCODING_TYPE);

          tokenElement.addTextNode
             (new String
              (Base64.encodeBase64(serviceTicket), "US-ASCII"));
      }
```

	Adds BinarySecurityToken to Security header
	Identifies BinarySecurityToken as a GSS-wrapped KRB_AP_REQ
	Indicates use of base64 encoding
	Adds base64 encoded ticket data

That is all there is to it on the client-side. Let us now look at the code on the server-side that extracts the BinarySecurityToken from the Security header and validates it.

5.4.5 Processing a Kerberos ticket on the service-side

Just as we did with usernames and passwords, we extract a Kerberos ticket from the WS-Security header in WSSecurityUsernameHandler, store it in MessageContext, and validate it in JAASAuthenticationHandler. Figure 5.9 illustrates our approach. Use it as your guide to understanding the overall flow as you read through the code presented in this section.

Copying a Kerberos ticket from Security header to message context

Listing 5.9 shows the code in WSSecurityUsernameHandler to copy the Kerberos service ticket from the Security header to message context.

> **Listing 5.9   Code to copy a Kerberos service ticket in Security header to message context**

```
SOAPElement tokenElement = Utils.locateChildElement
   (securityElement,
    Constants.WS_SECURITY_NS_URI,
    Constants.WS_SECURITY_BINARY_TOKEN_TAG);
if (tokenElement == null) { return false; }
```

❶ **Locates a BinarySecurityToken in Security header**

```
byte[] token = null;
String encodingType = tokenElement.getAttribute
  (Constants.WS_SECURITY_ENCODING_TYPE_ATTR);
if ((encodingType == null) ||
    (encodingType.length() == 0) ||
    (encodingType.equals
      (Constants.WS_SECURITY_BASE64_ENCODING_TYPE))) {
  token = Base64.decodeBase64
    (tokenElement.getValue().getBytes("US-ASCII"));
} else {
  //...create Fault saying
  //"BinarySecurityToken EncodingType not understood"
}

String tokenType = tokenElement.getAttribute
  (Constants.WS_SECURITY_VALUE_TYPE_ATTR);
if (Constants.WS_SECURITY_GSS_KERBEROS5_AP_REQ_TYPE.
    equals(tokenType)) {
  soapContext.setProperty
    (Constants.GSS_TOKEN_MSG_CONTEXT_PROPERTY,
      token);
} else {
  // ... Unknown binary token type
}
```

2 Decodes if token is base64-encoded

3 Copies token to message context

In this code, we first locate a `BinarySecurityToken` element in the `Security` header **1**. We assume here that the Kerberos token is in the first `Binary-SecurityToken` element. This is only a simplifying assumption on our part. There is no restriction that a Kerberos token should be the first `BinarySecurityToken` in a WS-Security header.

Once we locate a `BinarySecurityToken` element, we look up whether it has an attribute named `EncodingType` **2**. If there is none, then, as specified by WS-Security, we assume that the token is base64-encoded and decode it. Of course, if the `encodingType` attribute does indeed exist, we inspect its value and apply base64 decoding only if appropriate.

We inspect the `ValueType` attribute of the `BinarySecurityToken` element to see if the value of the token is a GSS-wrapped `KRB_AP_REQ` **3**. If it is, we copy the decoded token to `MessageContext` and make it available to the downstream handlers and the service.

Validating a Kerberos ticket available in message context

To complete the authentication, we need to modify the `JAASAuthentication-Handler` you saw in chapter 4 to validate the Kerberos ticket available in message context. To do this, we will enhance `MessageContextBackedCallbakHandler` to handle a `GSSTokenCallback` and simply code a new JAAS module, `GSSContextAcceptance-JAASModule`, that `JAASAuthenticationHandler` can use to validate the ticket.

In listing 5.5, you saw the code needed to verify service tickets on the service-side. You also saw in the previous chapter how to write a JAAS `LoginModule`. So, the only new ground we are breaking in `GSSContextAcceptanceJAASModule` is in the `commit()` and `logout()`/`abort()` methods. Let's first describe the `commit()` method, where we need to save the authenticated client's information in the subject of the login context. Listing 5.10 shows how we do this.

Listing 5.10   Code to populate subject information post-login in `GSSContextAcceptanceJAASModule`

```
public boolean commit() throws LoginException {
  try {
    GSSName clientGSSName = gssContext.getSrcName();          ❶ Reads client's name,
    String username = clientGSSName.toString();                  available from GSS
    subject.getPrincipals().                                     post-validation
      add(new UsernamePrincipal(username));                   ❷ Adds a UsernamePrincipal
  } catch (GSSException e) {                                     to authenticated subject
    logger.warn(e);
    throw new LoginException
      ("Failed to commit client info");
  }

  return true;
}
```

In this code, we create a `UsernamePrincipal` from the client name available through `GSSContext` ❶ and add it to the subject ❷.

The `GSSContext` established during login should be disposed of at the time of `logout()` or if the login process is aborted.

Listing 5.11   Code to dispose of `GSSContext` during logout

```
public boolean logout() throws LoginException {
    try {
        gssContext.dispose();
    } catch (GSSException e) {
        logger.warn(e);
    }
    logger.debug("aborted login process");
    return true;
}
```

You now know how to implement Kerberos-based authentication in SOAP-based web services and clients. In the previous chapter, you saw how to implement two variants of password-based authentication. In chapter 7, you will see how to use digital signatures for authentication. Which of these methods should you use for any given web service call? We will discuss this question in the next section.

5.5 *What authentication scheme to use?*

In these first five chapters, we have seen three different kinds of authentication systems. We are sure to see more in the coming chapters. There is no one solution that is suitable for all business situations; which is why we are covering so many different schemes.

For example, consider the case of our running example, the brokerage firm. How does the brokerage firm authenticate trade requests coming in from end users? Users may be submitting trades using a web page or a desktop application. The web page can use HTTPS and desktop applications can use SSL to encrypt all traffic exchanged, including the username and password submitted along with the request.

In such a scenario, a simple username and password scheme works well. It is fully protected by transport-level security in SSL. Besides, the data transmitted is small enough not to impose a performance penalty. Also, we can design it in such a way that username and password are only seen by one trusted application on the server-side. That is, these applications have only point-to-point communication.

Brokerage user profiles may be stored in a single database or LDAP directory. In either case, we can directly program without using JAAS.

Let us consider the employees of the brokerage firm. They too can use applications over HTTPS. These applications tend to be complex. Communication may not be point-to-point like in the previous case. In such a case, transport-level security is not sufficient. The right way would be to secure the communication using a password digest. Since it is likely that all the employee profiles are stored in a single source such as LDAP, our applications understand what kind of transformation to apply to the password before generating the digest.

Even in this scenario, one can make a case for not using JAAS and directly validating the credentials within the application code. If another brokerage company merges with our brokerage firm, suddenly we need to grant permission to a whole new set of employees. We can make profiles for the other firm's employees also be part of the same LDAP server, but there may be reasons why this is not desirable. If we use JAAS, it is easy to set up a stack of login modules in the configuration without too much of a code change.

Now, suppose the brokerage firm already standardized on Active Directory. In that case, using Kerberos for web services authentication deserves strong consideration. For one thing, there will be in-house expertise in dealing with Kerberos. It is likely that will be other applications that are "Kerberized." So, it would not be too much to set up and configure the web services to use Kerberos.

On the other hand, consider the case of a brokerage firm that does not already have Kerberos set up in any form. In such a case, it may not make sense to introduce Kerberos just because the firm wants to adopt SOA. It is important to recognize that the power of Kerberos comes at the cost of substantial complexity. We have seen in this chapter that developing client-server applications that rely on Kerberos for authentication is a far more complex task than username/password authentication. When deploying Kerberos in a large enterprise, getting all the network applications to work with Kerberos is an expensive proposition due to its complexity.

Of course, in organizations that need a very high level of security, the expense is well worth it, as Kerberos provides a security mechanism far superior to traditional username/password authentication. For instance, traditional password mechanisms cannot support delegatable authentication and mutual authentication, but Kerberos can.

But even in cases where complexity is not a concern, Kerberos may not be the best choice. Kerberos does not scale outside an enterprise, as it depends on a central KDC or a chain of KDCs with established trust relationships. For example, it is unlikely that a brokerage will be able to secure its communications with exchanges using Kerberos. PKI, introduced in the next chapter, provides a better option most of the time. PKI is more widely deployed and understood than Kerberos. With commercial vendors marketing digital certificates, there is much more momentum behind PKI than behind Kerberos. For example, while the Kerberos token profile for WS-Security took a long while to come out of draft stage, the X.509 Certificate token profile was fairly quickly adopted as a standard.

Still, there are several legitimate uses for Kerberos, the most important reason being, of course, that it is used in Microsoft server software. There is another reason—it can be the basis for a full-fledged security solution. Indeed, we can use the lessons from Kerberos in SOA security frameworks. You will learn about these frameworks in chapter 8.

5.6 *Summary*

We started this chapter by going one step ahead of what we did at the end of the last chapter. While the previous chapter ended by simply identifying what's wrong with password-based authentication in SOA, we started this chapter by drawing up all the requirements we can think of for an ideal authentication mechanism. Once we identified all the requirements, we claimed that the requirements we drew up are not as unattainable as they may first seem. We are sure you agree with us now that you have learned about Kerberos.

Kerberos was primarily designed to prevent abuse of user credentials by malicious service providers. Kerberos accomplishes this goal by cleverly leveraging the ideas behind encryption to eliminate the need for transmitting a password over the network. Anyone can ask the KDC, a central authority, for a ticket to contact a service, but only a genuine client will be able to use the ticket provided by KDC to establish its identity to the service.

The Kerberos Token Profile for WS-Security specifies how to use Kerberos for authentication in web services. You have learned the details of this specification in this chapter. You also learned how to implement Kerberos-based authentication in web services using the Kerberos JAAS module available with Sun's JDK and Java GSS APIs.

Kerberos is a complex topic. Whole books have been written about it. In this chapter, we limited ourselves to explaining how Kerberos can be used for authentication in web service implementations.

Kerberos can also be used for protecting the confidentiality and verifying the integrity of messages. The next two chapters discuss these aspects of security in depth. Although we will not be showing any Kerberos-related examples in the next two chapters, interested readers will not find it difficult to construct such examples on their own by combining the material presented in this book with Kerberos Token Profile for WS-Security.

Suggestions for further reading

- RFC 4120 is the authoritative specification for Kerberos. It is available at http://tools.ietf.org/html/4120.

- RFC 2743 standardizes GSS API. It is available at http://tools.ietf.org/html/2743.

- RFC 2853 describes Java bindings for GSS API.

- Sun JDK 1.5.0 and 1.4.x ship with a guide for using Kerberos in Java. The guide is titled "Single Sign-on Using Kerberos in Java" and is written by Mayank

Upadhyay and Ram Marti. You can find the guide at http://java.sun.com/j2se/1.5.0/docs/guide/security/jgss/single-signon.html.

- The JAAS login module for Kerberos included in Sun JDK is documented at http://java.sun.com/j2se/1.5.0/docs/guide/security/jaas/spec/com/sun/security/auth/module/Krb5LoginModule.html.

- WS-Security Kerberos Token Profile 1.1 is available at http://www.oasis-open.org/committees/download.php/16788/wss-v1.1-spec-os-KerberosTokenProfile.pdf.

- Microsoft's "Step-by-Step Guide to Kerberos 5 (krb5 1.0) Interoperability" provides a lot of useful information needed to work with Microsoft's implementation of Kerberos. The guide is available at http://www.microsoft.com/technet/prodtechnol/windows2000serv/howto/kerbstep.mspx.

- An overview of the `ktpass` tool used in Section 5.5.1 is available at http://www.microsoft.com/technet/prodtechnol/windowsserver2003/library/TechRef/64042138-9a5a-4981-84e9-d576a8db0d05.mspx.

Protecting confidentiality of messages using encryption

This chapter covers

- Public key infrastructure
- JCE and Apache XML security
- Certificate authorities

In the preceding chapters, we've seen how to extend SOAP via headers. In particular, we saw how to add user credentials so that the application can determine whether the request came from a genuine user. We introduced various techniques to secure credentials so that they cannot be misused by any party listening over the wire or by the service providers themselves.

There is more to security than mere authentication. Imagine that you are requesting a brokerage firm to buy some shares using the funds you have in a bank account. The firm requires you to authenticate with username and password. Suppose you use the digest mechanism so that password is not available to the eavesdropper. Is that enough? Wouldn't you also want to safeguard the bank account information you are providing?

What this scenario points out is that we need a way to encrypt the message so that only the intended recipient can understand it. Traditionally, this task is accomplished by encrypting the whole message. As we mentioned in chapter 1, straightforward encryption of the whole message is not good enough to meet the requirements of SOA. Instead, a mechanism is needed to encrypt different parts of a message differently.

There are other advantages to being able to encrypt parts of a message. Encryption and decryption are computationally intensive operations. By encrypting only the confidential parts of a message, we can enhance the performance of a solution without compromising on security. Selective encryption also helps if parts of a message need to be kept in plain text for reasons beyond our control. For example, a critical legacy application may depend on a part of the message and we may not be allowed to modify the application in any way.

In this chapter, we will describe how the web services standards support selective encryption of messages. Encryption in web services is built on the solid foundations of encryption technology that is widely used on the web. The technology is well understood, with good implementations and support structure. To understand how encryption can be used in SOAP messages, we need to understand the basics of encryption technology first. In the first three sections of this chapter (6.1-6.3), we will cover these in detail. In particular:

- The first section will introduce a tool that helps you snoop on the network to see messages in transit. This tool will help you see the need for encryption.

- The second section will introduce you to symmetric key encryption, asymmetric or public key encryption, and hybrid encryption. You will also learn about how PKI and digital certificates help in the adoption of encryption on a large scale.

- The third section will show you how to program with digital certificates. We will show you how to create a digital certificate and how to use it for point-to-point encryption with SSL/TLS. We will introduce Java Cryptographic Extension (JCE) and other Java APIs you can use for implementing encryption with Java.

If you are familiar with encryption, particularly PKI and SSL, feel free to jump to the start of section 6.4. This section will describe the standards for encryption in web services, specifically how WS-Security supports the XML Encryption standard and how you can implement the same using the Apache XML Security library. Section 6.5 will discuss a few practical issues you are likely to face when using encryption in the real world.

We will start our discussion by showing you how you can snoop on the network to intercept messages without the consent of the sender or the receiver. We will show you how encryption protects the confidentiality of a message even when it is intercepted by a man in the middle. This example will help you see the need for encryption before we get into the nitty gritty of encryption.

6.1 Encryption in action: an example

Recall how we depicted the message exchanges in the preceding chapters using `tcpmon`. We set up a proxy, over which we sent our requests. This proxy prints the request and response so that we can understand the messages between the client and the server. We employed `tcpmon` as simply a pedagogical tool, which required active consent from the sender and receiver, in terms of configuration.

Now we are going to introduce you to a different tool called `ethereal`, which allows us to watch what is really happening over the wire. As it happens, this tool lets us examine the flow of messages *without the consent of the participants*. In this section, we will use this tool to intercept HTTP and HTTPS traffic.

Table 6.1 shows how to run this example:

Table 6.1 Steps to use `ethereal` for intercepting HTTP and HTTPS traffic. Watch steps 5 and 9 to understand what kind of traffic is really going over the wire.

Step	Action	How To
1	Install ethereal.	Download WinPcap (assuming you are on Windows) and ethereal installers from http://www.ethereal.com/. Install WinPcap followed by ethereal.

continued on next page

Table 6.1   Steps to use `ethereal` for intercepting HTTP and HTTPS traffic. Watch steps 5 and 9 to understand what kind of traffic is really going over the wire. *(continued)*

Step	Action	How To
2	Open a web page that contains a login form but does not use HTTPS.	Go to http://www.manning-sandbox.com/login!withRedirect.jspa but do not log in just yet. Leave the browser window open.
3	Set up ethereal to capture HTTP traffic.	Start `ethereal`. Go to "Capture -> Interfaces..." and "Prepare" the interface over which you are connecting to the Internet.
		In the resulting Capture Options dialog, enter `tcp port 80` as the capture filter. This is to instruct ethereal that all TCP packets originating from port 80 or destined to port 80 on any network node should be captured.
		In addition, uncheck the "Capture packets in promiscuous mode" check box, as we are only interested in snooping on packets originating from/destined to our box. Select the "Update list of packets in real time" option.
		Click OK to start capturing. This will bring up a dialog showing the number of packets captured. You may not find any packets captured at this time, as you have yet to do any HTTP activity.
4	Carry out HTTP activity using the login form opened in step 2.	Go back to the browser window you used to reach the login page, type in your username and password, and click the Login button
5	Stop packet capture and analyze captured traffic.	Once your login succeeds or fails, stop the capture process in ethereal. You should now see a list of packets captured as shown in figure 6.1.
		Right-click the first HTTP packet and choose to "Follow tcp stream." You can now see the HTTP conversation that took place between your browser and the login server.
		In particular, look at the first line after the end of the HTTP headers in the POST request. You will notice that your username and password are visible in clear-text.
6	Open a web page that contains a login form and uses HTTPS.	Log out of manning sandbox in case your login was successful. Now go to http://www.manning-sandbox.com/login!withRedirect.jspa but do not log in just yet. Leave the browser window open.
7	Set up ethereal to capture HTTPS traffic this time.	Use step 2's instructions but replace port 80 with port 443.
8	Carry out HTTPS activity using the login form opened in Step 7.	Go back to the browser window, type in your username and password, and login.
9	Stop packet capture and analyze captured traffic.	Once your login succeeds or fails, stop the capture process in ethereal. You should once again see a list of packets captured.
		Right-click the first TLS packet and choose to "Follow tcp stream." You will see that you can no longer decipher the conversation that took place between your browser and the login server.

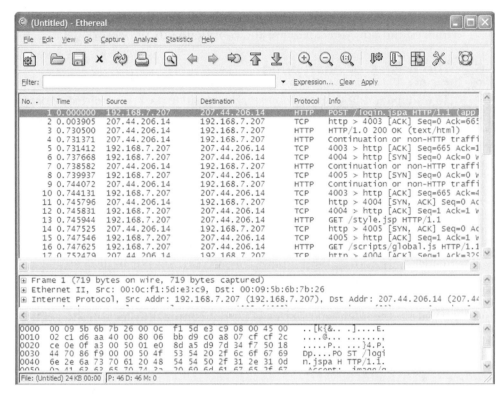

Figure 6.1 Screen shot of `ethereal` illustrating the capture of network data without the consent or cooperation of the participants.

Figure 6.1 shows a screenshot of ethereal after step 5, which shows us the packet details that are going over the wire. In fact, you can see the protocol and understand the actual contents of each packet. After step 9, the same application will show that packet contents are not in the clear; i.e., they appear as gibberish.

We can learn the following from this example:

1 When using HTTP, the message is transmitted in a clear-text protocol. We can easily see the username and password.

2 When using HTTPS, the message is transmitted in encrypted form. There is no way a man in the middle can understand any part of the message, including the username and password. Of course, we have yet to discuss the details of encryption technology behind HTTPS, so, it is premature to say if the encryption we see here is good enough.

We will now describe the technology behind encryption in order for you to better understand how you can guard the confidentiality of network data.

6.2 *The basics of encryption*

To understand how encryption works, consider the case where one party sends a message to another party. How can the sender make sure that only the intended receiver can read the message? If he sends the data as is, as you saw earlier, anybody who happens to be in the path can read the message. To make sure that it cannot be read, he needs to send it in a form that nobody (including perhaps even the sender) other than the receiver can understand. That is, the sender transforms the data in the message into *cipher* data, and the receiver undoes the transformation so that he can get back the original data from the cipher data.

These transformations are called *encryption* and *decryption* respectively. Mathematically speaking, these operations are carried out by two functions E and D, where E is the encryption function and D is the decryption function. To encrypt a message m, you apply the function E to m, thereby producing the cipher data E(m). If you are the intended receiver, you would apply the function D to get the original message back. To state in mathematical terms: D(E(m)) = m.

Why is such a scheme secure? Actually, the security does not lie in the scheme—it lies in the algorithms. If it is computationally difficult to guess m from E(m) then we can say that only the party that possesses D can decrypt the message. There are several other features that are required of these algorithms if they have to be used repeatedly. In the rest of this section, we will examine different kinds of encryption algorithms and describe the situations in which they are appropriate. In particular, we will describe two kinds of encryption algorithms: symmetric key and asymmetric key (or public key) algorithms, which are required for you to understand PKI. We will also see why and how these two kinds of algorithms are often combined to create what is known as *hybrid encryption*.

6.2.1 *Types of encryption algorithms*

As we mentioned previously, the effectiveness of encryption in protecting the confidentiality of a message depends on the encryption algorithm used. Let's examine a sample encryption algorithm so that you can see what we mean.

One of the earliest known encryption algorithms is Caesar shift. It shifts each letter by certain positions to create the cipher text. For example, with a shift of 1, "a" becomes "b" and "b" becomes "c." If the sender encrypts a message using such a shift, the receiver can decrypt by applying the reverse shift to the received cipher data. The shift amount is a required parameter, or the *key* to the encryption and decryption functions.

It is easy to see that a Caesar shift algorithm is weak. All we need to do is try all 25 shifts (assuming we only use the English alphabet in a message) to forcefully crack the encryption. If we want to refine Caesar shift to make decryption more challenging, we can apply arbitrary substitutions, where each letter may get transformed into a different letter. Decryption now requires the knowledge of a whole substitution table, not just a mere numeric key indicating the magnitude of shift. Such an algorithm is not strong either; all we need to do is to look at the patterns in the text. If we know that the word "the" occurs frequently, we can easily look for such frequent words in the cipher text too.

If you are beginning to get the feeling that devising secure encryption functions is difficult, you are right. Consider some of the popular technical attacks you have to guard against:

- *Brute force method*   Under this method, the attacker tries all the possible keys. If the number of possible keys is small, this method is easy to apply. In fact, with advanced computing power these days, even large numbers of keys, up to billions, can be tried in hours. Thus, we need to make the possible key universe as large as possible.

- *Frequency analysis*   In this method, the attacker takes a look at several cipher texts and attempts to break the cipher by comparing the frequency distribution of letters/words/phrases in the cipher text with the frequency distribution he may know of letters/words/phrases in the domain. Note that not all algorithms are susceptible to this attack. For example, if the encryption scrambles the message randomly then frequency analysis does not work.

- *Known text attack*   Some messages always contain the same information in known places. For example, every legal letter may end with a standard disclaimer. Using such knowledge, it may be possible to understand the algorithm. That is, the attacker knows the E(m,k) for some specific messages and may try to deduce k from it.

- *Chosen plain text attack*   Under this model, the attacker tricks the sender into encrypting known messages. That is, he gets E(m,k) for any message he desires. Depending on the algorithm, it may be possible to deduce k from the pairs (m, E(m,k)).

Unfortunately, given a function, it is difficult to prove that it is cryptographically strong. It takes a lot of theoretical analysis, peer review, and public usage before we can develop confidence in the cryptographic strength of any algorithm. The actual development of algorithms should be left to professionals. Fortunately, there are several standard algorithms both in public and private domains for us to choose from. In fact, several of these algorithms have been coded, tested, and incorporated into standards for us to use.

Now, we will look at some standard algorithms. We will first describe a class of algorithms known as *symmetric-key algorithms*.

Symmetric-key encryption algorithms

Caesar shift is a simple but good example of a class of encryption algorithms known as symmetric-key algorithms. A symmetric key algorithm is one in which the encryption and decryption functions are parameterized by the same key.[1] To understand this definition, let's re-examine how text that is encrypted using Caesar shift is decrypted. To decrypt, we apply the reverse shift to the cipher text. If decryption is to succeed, the amount of reverse shift during decryption has to match the amount of shift carried out during encryption. If we call the amount of shift and reverse shift the *key* for encryption and decryption functions then Caesar shift is a symmetric-key algorithm because we use the same key during encryption and decryption.

To explain it mathematically, if we denote the message with m, the key with k, the encryption function with E, and the decryption function with D, the following is true for symmetric-key encryption: D(E(m,k),k) = m.

Symmetric-key algorithms have been widely investigated and are well understood. Some are block-oriented algorithms, which take a block of text and encrypt it (think of a transformation that reverses the text in each block); some are stream-oriented algorithms, where each byte is encoded as it comes out using a varying encryption scheme (think of the earlier shifting algorithm modified to increment the shift by 1 after every letter). Here is a list of some popular symmetric-key algorithms. Most algorithms have public-domain implementations ready to be used in our applications.

DES: This is a block-oriented algorithm that uses 56-bit keys. Given the computational power available to hackers these days, 56-bit keys are considered easy to crack; DES is no longer recommended.

Triple DES (3DES): In this scheme, DES is applied three times to the message, with three different keys, thus increasing the key length to 168 bits. Most

---

[1] Even if the encryption and decryption keys are different, as long as the keys can be inferred from one another, the algorithm can be considered a symmetric-key algorithm.

implementations do decryption as the second step rather than encryption. That is, the cipher text is computed as `E(D(E(m,k1),k2),k3)`.[2] 3DES is quite slow compared to other symmetric encryption algorithms, such as AES.

RC2 and RC4: This algorithm can theoretically use up to 2048 bits.

RC5: This algorithm is more recent than RC2. It also features a variable key length of up to 2040, with a block length of 32, 64, or 128 bits.

AES: This algorithm is a recent standard from NIST (National Institute of Science and Technology). It is a fast and compact algorithm, suitable for implementation in hardware or software with a key length of 128, 192, or 256 bits. Encryption standards in web services often recognize AES as an algorithm that all compliant implementations must support.

Symmetric-key algorithms suffer from one drawback. To understand what this is, let us look at an end-to-end scenario. The sender and receiver need to establish an algorithm and the key for the algorithm before they can start communicating securely. Negotiating which algorithm to use is easy; the sender can send a list of algorithms it is capable of using, in the order of preference, and the receiver can pick one out of them. Next, they need to pick a key. How do they decide on a key *securely*?

The two parties can negotiate the algorithm using messages in clear-text, but they cannot communicate a key to each other in clear-text. There is no danger if a snooper knows the algorithm—after all, only a handful of algorithms are used in practice—but if he knows the key, the secrecy of the messages is compromised.

A key can be agreed upon out-of-band. For example, one party can call up the other party on the phone and agree upon a key to use. But that would restrict the number of parties one can work with. One cannot possibly call everyone else on Earth to agree upon a key with each person. One may want to use dynamically generated keys, but now there is a bootstrapping problem. To secure a message exchange, one needs a key, but the key itself needs to be securely communicated first.

Is there a possibility of establishing keys up front in a central store? That is, for every pair of communicating parties, can we create a central key store that contains a key for encryption? The answer is no, because that would be a logistical nightmare! First of all, it means we would need around n² keys for *n* parties,

---

[2] There is a good reason for using decryption instead of encryption in the second pass of 3DES implementation. EDE—that is encryption, decryption, followed by encryption—provides backward compatibility with simple DES, when all three keys are chosen to be the same; that is, when k1=k2=k3.

making the key store scale poorly. Second, if we want to add a new party, we will need to set up n additional keys.

A symmetric-key algorithm is of limited use unless we find a way to securely share the key between the sender and receiver. This chicken-and-egg problem can be solved using an alternative class of encryption algorithms known as asymmetric-key or public-key encryption algorithms. Let us study them next.

Public-key encryption algorithms

If the need to share the same key between the sender and receiver is what limits the applicability of symmetric-key algorithms, can't we use different keys for encryption and decryption? Yes, we can. When the sender wants to send a message securely, he can encrypt it using `k1` and the receiver can decrypt it using `k2`. This is the basic idea behind public-key encryption. The equation that makes it all work is `D(E(m,k1),k2) = m`.

At first glace, the situation does not seem to have improved; we are simply using two keys instead of one, where each application gets two keys. The difference is that one of the keys (`k1`) is published publicly so that everyone is able to see it, and the other (`k2`) is kept private so that only the key's owner knows it. In the end, for each application, there is only one private key that needs to be guarded.

Here is how the keys are used: if an application wants to send a confidential message `m` to another application, it will send the cipher text `E(m,k1)`, which can only be decrypted by an application that knows the corresponding key `k2`, which means only the intended recipient can decrypt it.

What if the receiver wants to send a response message back to the sender? It needs to follow the same mechanism of using the other application's public key. Figure 6.2 shows how public-key encryption happens in either direction.

For public-key encryption to work, every party needs to publish its public key someplace. Unlike in the symmetric-key situation, where the number of keys needed by n parties is n^2, in public-key encryption, we only need to keep track of the same number of keys as the parties; that is n. In fact, in section 6.2.2 where we describe PKI, you can see how we can optimize the public-key distribution mechanism even further.

The most popular public-key encryption algorithm used today is RSA. It can be implemented with any key length. In later sections, we will show how to use RSA in Java. For now, we will discuss a few important properties of public-key encryption algorithms in general that are useful for PKI.

Because public-key encryption algorithms are computationally more expensive than symmetric-key algorithms, they are never used in practice to encrypt

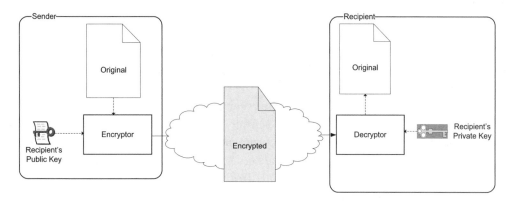

Figure 6.2 Public-key encryption in action: The original message encrypted using the recipient's public key can be decrypted using the recipient's private key.

arbitrarily large messages. Instead, they are limited to encryption of small messages. Still, public-key encryption algorithms are very useful for two purposes: digital signatures and hybrid encryption. We will first describe digital signatures and take up the topic of hybrid encryption after that.

We have previously defined public-key encryption algorithms as those that satisfy the equation $D(E(m,k1),k2) = m$. There is a second equation that public-key encryption algorithms satisfy: $D(E(m,k2),k1) = m$. Comparing the two equations, we see that encryption and decryption keys can be swapped. *A message encrypted using one of the two keys can always be decrypted using the other key.*

We used the property expressed in the first equation as follows: A party X can openly distribute its public key to anyone who wishes to communicate with it. Any messages encrypted with that public key can only be decrypted by the associated private key that is only known to X. Now, here's what the second equation means: If X encrypts a message with its private key everyone who knows its public key can decrypt it. How is this second property of public key encryption useful?

In practice, this is useful to solve a problem that is different than what we are focusing on in this chapter, but related. We have been looking only at how we can use encryption to keep sensitive parts of a message confidential, but we haven't yet thought of how we can guarantee message integrity. That is, if a man in the middle modifies a part of the message, we would not be able to detect it. We can use the second property of public-key encryption that we just presented to tackle this problem. Although preserving message integrity is the topic of the next chapter, we need to briefly discuss it here, as some of the lessons involved are necessary to understand the rest of this chapter.

How can a recipient possibly check that the received message has not been tampered with en route? The sender can help the recipient in this process by providing a value computed from the message along with the message. The receiver can recompute the same value and check whether the result matches the value provided by the sender. For example, the sender can provide a checksum,[3] the sum of all the bytes in the message. The receiver can also sum up all the bytes and check whether the result matches the sender-provided checksum. Unfortunately, checksums do not offer good enough protection against data tampering. An attacker can simply swap the bytes in the message without damaging the checksum. For example, if you asked to transfer $1001 from a bank account, an attacker might be able to change the amount to $1100 without changing the checksum. So, we need a function that makes it difficult to produce an input that produces the given output. Cryptographic hash functions such as SHA-1 (introduced in chapter 4 when we discussed password digests) fulfill this requirement.

Suppose that the sender attaches SHA1(m) to message m when communicating it to the receiver. Does this digest suffice for guaranteeing message integrity? What if the attacker replaces the whole of the message m with m' and attaches SHA1(m')? To rule out this possibility, we need a way of making sure that SHA1 value was computed by none other than the sender.

If the sender encrypts SHA1(m) as E(SHA1(m)) using his private key and attaches it to the message, the receiver can verify that the message has not been tampered with along the way by decrypting E(SHA1(m)) using the sender's public key and comparing it with SHA1(m), which the receiver computed independently. As we know that public-key encryption is expensive, we also have to make sure that the computed value, SHA1(m) in this example, is short enough no matter how long m is. Otherwise, the cost of computing E(SHA1(m)) may be too high, making this technique impractical for use. Fortunately, cryptographic hash functions such as SHA-1 produce short fixed-length output no matter how long the input is. That is why they are often referred to as *message digest algorithms* and the values they compute are referred to as *message digests*.

The act of computing the message digest and encrypting the result with the sender's private key is known as *signing*. That is, the sender digitally affixes a signature to a message to prove that he is indeed the sender of the message and that

---

[3] A checksum is the result obtained by "adding" all the bits in a message. The algorithm used for computing checksum is irrelevant for our discussion here. Think of it as addition of bits in some manner to create a number that can be represented in a fixed number of bits.

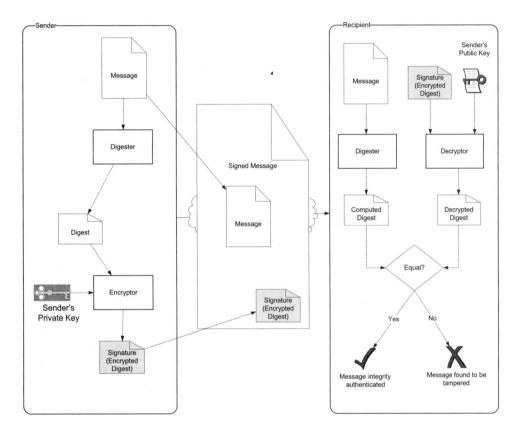

Figure 6.3 How signatures work: The sender attaches a message digest that is encrypted using his private key. The recipient uses the sender's public key to decrypt the encrypted message digest. If the result of this decryption matches the digest value independently computed by the recipient, the message is proven to be intact; otherwise, a man in the middle must have tampered with the message en route.

the message is genuine. Figure 6.3 illustrates this idea. We'll focus more on signatures in the next chapter. For now, you've learned enough to understand PKI.

Let's recap what you have learned so far about encryption algorithms. Let's say you want to receive confidential messages from your partners. You can do so using symmetric-key encryption algorithms if each of your partners can securely share with you the secret key he will use for encryption. But you have a bootstrapping problem. To secure your message exchange, you need a key, but the key itself needs to be securely communicated first. If you use public-key encryption algorithms instead of symmetric-key algorithms, you do not have this problem. You can publish your public key openly. Anyone who needs to securely communicate with you can use your public key to encrypt his messages, and only you can decrypt those messages, as you are the only one in possession of your private key. But public-key encryption algorithms are too expensive computationally, and can only be used for small messages. In other words, neither symmetric-key algorithms nor public-key algorithms provide a perfect solution for all encryption needs.

Fortunately, there is a way to take care of these problems by combining the best of both worlds using a hybrid encryption scheme. We will describe this in the next subsection.

Hybrid encryption

Hybrid encryption combines the efficiency of symmetric-key encryption with the relative ease of setting up public-key encryption. Recall the big hurdle in using symmetric-key encryption: difficulty establishing the initial key securely. If we use public-key encryption to securely communicate a randomly chosen symmetric key at the start of a conversation, we can cross that hurdle. For all the subsequent communications, we can use that symmetric key. Figure 6.4 illustrates how this can happen.

There are two benefits to this hybrid scheme. First, since it uses symmetric-key encryption except for the initial key establishment, it is simple and fast. Second, we do not need to distribute keys to all parties. We only need to publish public keys for server applications. Since clients initiate the contact, they only need to generate a random key for symmetric encryption and communicate it using public key of the server application.

Now you know how different types of encryption algorithms work in theory. We can take for granted that all these algorithms work well in theory. From now on, we will turn to practical aspects. For example, how are public keys distributed? How do applications negotiate the algorithms to use? The answer to all these questions is PKI.

6.2.2 PKI: A framework for encryption

While introducing you to the basics of encryption, we have described various types of encryption algorithms. We discussed symmetric-key encryption algorithms, public-key encryption algorithms, and a hybrid scheme that combines the two. All through this discussion, we have repeatedly hinted that one also needs to look into an algorithm's key distribution requirements before deciding whether it is appropriate for use. PKI provides a cost-effective and proven framework that addresses the key distribution requirements in public-key encryption. Of course, hybrid encryption can also use this framework, as its key distribution requirements are the same as those of public-key encryption.

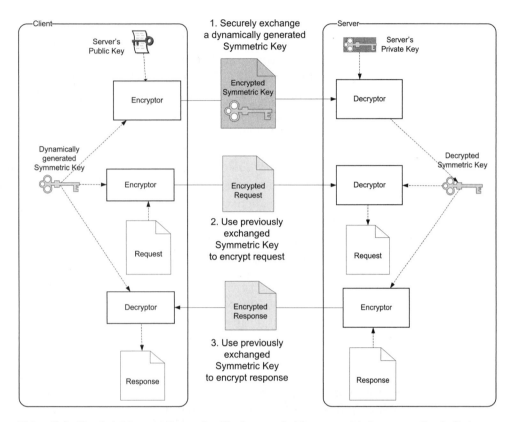

Figure 6.4 **How hybrid encryption works: The key needed for symmetric-key encryption is first exchanged securely using public-key encryption. All subsequent message exchanges use symmetric-key encryption.**

Consider the issue of publishing keys. One easy choice for publishing these keys would be some central stores. Say application A wants to send a message to B. A can get the public key for B from a central store S. But what guarantee is there that this is the key for B? A man in the middle can easily pose as S and give A his public key instead. Such an attack is easily detected if S adds B's "name" (we put the name in the quotes here because a name can be any general-purpose name—more details in the next section) along with its key and signs using its own private key. A can verify S's signature to make sure that the message came untampered from S. Of course, we are assuming that everyone knows the central store's public key in order to verify its signatures.

This scheme will work; however, every application needs to communicate with the central store for any public key. As such, the central store will become the bottleneck in any implementation. But, there is no need to get this information from a central store. The same information, *signed by the central store S*, can be obtained from any source, and the confidence in that information does not change. Just as a photo ID with a government seal can be presented by the person to whom the ID was issued, the owner of a public key (B in our example) can itself present a copy of its public key that is signed by the central store S. In a sense, B is acting as a proxy for its own public key information.

It's time we call all these entities by their proper names. A central store trusted by the application is called a *Certificate Authority* or *CA*. The information signed by a central store—a public key, the name of the entity who owns the key, and other details such as expiry date—is called a *(digital) certificate*. In other words, a certificate not only provides the public key of the certified party, but also provides the certified party's identification information.

Now put it all together as in figure 6.5.

Let us see what the terms used in this figure mean:

- *Subject info*   This information specifies who the certificate is issued to in X.500 DN format. It contains the name, organization, organizational unit, and a serial number. The serial number allows for more than one certificate in the same name. (Note: X.500 is a set of directory services standards. A directory [think of your corporate LDAP directory] is a collection of entries. Each directory entry is a collection of multivalued named attributes and is uniquely identified by what is known as a distinguished name (DN). A DN is structured in a way that allows the directory to be viewed as a tree of entries. For example, an entry with DN CN=Prasad Chodavarapu, OU=Authors, O=Manning, L=Bangalore, ST=Karnataka, C=IN can be seen as a node named CN=Prasad Chodavarapu with OU=Authors as its parent, O=Manning as its grandparent, and so on. Public-key certificates were first standardized by the X.509 specification, which belongs to the X.500 family of standards. X.509 adopted X.500 DNs when it needed a way of identifying who a certificate belongs to.)

- *CA info*   Since the client needs to know whose public key can be used to verify the certificate, the name of the issuer is also kept in the certificate. Clients normally accept only the CAs that they trust. If you recall, the CA signs a certificate by encrypting a digest of the information in the certificate with its private key. The CA information should also contain the encryption algorithm and the digest algorithm used by the CA.

- *Validity dates*   These dates specify the period in which the certificate is valid.
- *Public key*   This is the key provided to the subject. This field also needs to provide which algorithm is to be used with this key.

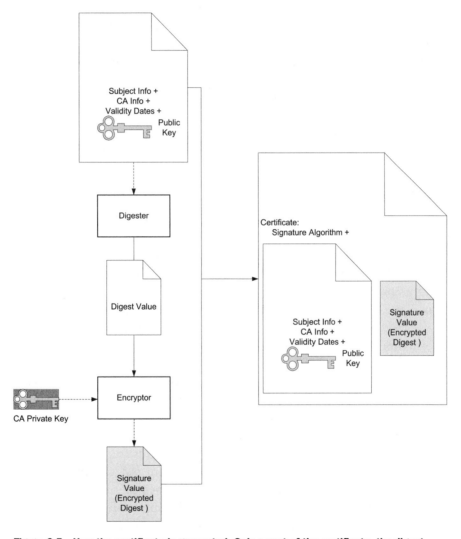

Figure 6.5 How the certificate is generated. Only a part of the certificate, the digest, needs to be encrypted (as a signature) by the CA. The certificate which contains the public key of the application is guaranteed by the CA. This signing is a one-time activity— the application can use a signed certificate as long as the contents of the certificate do not change.

■ *Signature value* This signature is produced by taking the digest of the entire certificate, sans the digest and the digest algorithm, and encrypting it. This means that the digest algorithm name is repeated here as well.

Certificates also allow extensions that can be used to carry additional information. For example, the Certificate Revocation List (CRL) Distributions Points extension specifies the parties one can contact to acquire the list of certificates revoked by the issuing authority. The Certificate Key Usage extension can be used to restrict the uses a certificate may be put to. For example, one may specify that the certificate must be used for signing-only or to identify a CA itself.

The last use we'll mention for certificates is interesting. In the discussion so far, we have assumed that all parties trust a single CA. That assumption is not really required, and can be easily relaxed using the concept of *certificate chain*s. We will discuss this concept next.

Certificate chains

Let's recap what we've described about PKI so far. PKI is a framework that addresses public key distribution. Central to PKI are the concepts of certificate and CA. CAs issue certificates. A certificate is a digital document that ties a public key to a particular identity. Every certificate is digitally signed by the issuing CA using its public key. This eliminates the possibility of fake certificates, unless, of course, the CA makes the mistake of issuing a certificate to an impostor.[4]

For PKI to work, applications need to trust a CA. Furthermore, the CA's identity information and public key should be known a priori to all applications. But what if not every application trusts the same CA? In fact, this is a very common occurrence. If you compare a certificate to a passport and a CA to a national government, it is obvious that a single CA cannot hope to issue certificates for everyone, just as a single national government cannot possibly be the passport-issuing authority for the entire world. PKI accommodates multiple CAs by introducing a concept known as *certificate chaining*. Let's discuss this concept using an example.

Let's say the ACME brokerage company (from our running example introduced in chapter 1) sets up its own CA to avoid the cost of paying an external CA every time it requires a certificate for one of its applications or employees. Now, what if ACME's trade execution application needs to present its certificate to an external application, such as a stock exchange application? The stock exchange application is of course not going to accept certificates issued by ACME's CA.

---

[4] How CAs guard against granting certificates to imposters is beyond the scope of discussion here.

The stock exchange application may only accept certificates issued by a well-known CA such as, say, VeriSign. There are two options to make ACME's trade execution application work with the stock exchange application. The ACME trade execution application can get a second certificate from VeriSign and present it instead. Or, the ACME trade execution application can present along with its certificate (issued by ACME CA) another certificate issued by VeriSign that documents the identity and public key of the ACME CA. In other words, a certificate issued by ACME CA can be made more credible by chaining it to the certificate issued by VeriSign to ACME CA.

In fact, a certificate chain can consist of more than two certificates. Each certificate in the chain is issued by a CA that can in turn be certified by another CA. Given a certificate chain, an application can validate it by traversing through the chain and checking if there is at least one certificate issued by a CA that the application trusts.

This completes the journey through the basics of encryption. You now know about symmetric encryption, public-key encryption, hybrid encryption, and PKI, perhaps more than you need to know for SOA security.

Returning to SOA security, we will devote the next section to using PKI to secure messages in SOA. To start we will show you how you can create a digital certificate for point-to-point encryption with SSL/TLS. Next we will show how to encrypt in Java using JCE and other APIs. See the callout for other uses of PKI such as authentication.

NOTE *PKI-based authentication* PKI certificates, when combined with digital signatures, provide an alternative to the authentication mechanisms we have discussed in the previous two chapters, namely password-based schemes and Kerberos. Using PKI, each party can prove its identity to the other by signing the message with its private key and attaching its certificate to the message. The other party can:

1 Validate the sender's public key and identity information by checking the CA's signature in the certificate.

2 Verify that the request indeed came from the party identified in the certificate by checking the signature provided.

Notice that this method can be used for mutual authentication as well. Clients can authenticate services and services can authenticate clients. This mechanism is also much more secure than username and password-based authentication, given the problems with passwords we detailed in the previous two chapters. Because managing the certificates is difficult this scheme is not widely used.

6.3 Programming with digital certificates

So far you saw the theoretical side of encryption. You now know what symmetric encryption is and how to exchange a symmetric key using public-key encryption. You also know how PKI provides a cost-effective framework for public key distribution using digital certificate chains.

Before proceeding to encryption in SOA, let us understand how to create and use digital certificates. This knowledge is required for implementing encryption in SOA. The first step in working with certificates is to create one. In the next section, we will create a *self-signed certificate*—that is, a certificate signed by ourselves acting as our own CA.

6.3.1 Creating digital certificates

JDK supports use of digital certificates through its tools and APIs. We depend on these in our examples throughout the book. This subsection describes these tools and APIs.

A tool named `keytool` is packaged with the JDK to let us manage a key store. A *key store* may contain the certificates for the entities that we're dealing with and our own key pairs with associated certificate chains, if any. Each entry in a key store, be it a certificate or a key pair, is identified by a unique *alias*. Passwords can be used to protect the whole store and each of the private keys we save in the store.

Listing 6.1 shows how to create a key pair and store it in a key store using `keytool`.

Listing 6.1 Creating a key pair and storing it in a key store using Java `keytool`

```
$keytool -keystore example4.keystore -genkey -alias \
   http://manning.com/xmlns/samples/soasecimpl/cop -keyalg RSA \
   -keypass goodpass
Enter keystore password:  goodpass
What is your first and last name?
  [Unknown]:  Prasad Chodavarapu
What is the name of your organizational unit?
  [Unknown]:  Authors
What is the name of your organization?
  [Unknown]:  Manning
What is the name of your City or Locality?
  [Unknown]:  Bangalore
What is the name of your State or Province?
  [Unknown]:  Karnataka
```

```
What is the two-letter country code for this unit?
  [Unknown]:  IN
Is CN=Prasad Chodavarapu, OU=Authors, O=Manning, L=Bangalore,
ST=Karnataka, C=IN  correct?
[no]:  yes
```

Let us examine each of the options shown in listing 6.1.

- -keystore is used to set the path to the key store file. If a file does not already exist at the given path, keytool creates it.

- -genkey indicates to keytool that we wish to generate a key pair.

- -alias indicates the identifier we wish to assign to the generated key pair. Any string can be used as an alias. In this example, we are using a URI as an alias for reasons we will mention later.

- -keyalg is used to choose the key-generation algorithm. In this example, we are generating an RSA key pair.

- -keypass is used to specify the password with which we want to protect the generated private key. No one will be able to retrieve the generated private key from the key store unless they have both the store password and the key password.

The keytool will prompt us for the store password. If the key store is being created as a result of this command, the given password is set as the store's password. If not, the given password is checked against the store's password.

The keytool also generates a self-signed certificate after generating a key pair. A self-signed certificate is one in which the public key and the identity of its owner are signed using the owner's private key instead of a CA's private key. In other words, the certificate owner and the signing CA are one and the same. To create the certificate, keytool needs to know who the certificate belongs to. For this reason, it prompts you for the information needed to create a "name" (an X.500 distinguished name to be precise).

Once the certificate is generated, you can inspect and confirm the contents of key store using keytool itself, as shown in listing 6.2.

Listing 6.2 Inspecting the contents of a key store using Java `keytool`

```
$ keytool -keystore example4.keystore -list -v
Enter keystore password:  goodpass

Keystore type: jks
Keystore provider: SUN
```

```
Your keystore contains 1 entry

Alias name: http://manning.com/xmlns/samples/soasecimpl/cop
Creation date: Jul 10, 2005
Entry type: keyEntry
Certificate chain length: 1
Certificate[1]:
Owner: CN=Prasad Chodavarapu, OU=Authors, O=Manning, L=Bangalore,
ST=Karnataka,C=IN
Issuer: CN=Prasad Chodavarapu, OU=Authors, O=Manning, L=Bangalore,
ST=Karnataka,
 C=IN
Serial number: 42d04632
Valid from: Sun Jul 10 03:18:34 IST 2005 until: Sat Oct 08 03:18:34
IST 2005
Certificate fingerprints:
  MD5:  2C:11:43:C0:25:FB:02:3B:72:5C:71:79:1F:B7:05:F0
  SHA1: 2B:64:85:3A:35:28:FA:B3:E9:0B:BC:9E:64:F3:8C:DE:C7:7D:01:61
```

Notice that the "names" of the owner and issuer are the same here because this is a self-signed certificate. Now, if you want to get our public key certified by a CA such as VeriSign, you need to prepare what is known as a Certificate Signing Request (CSR). `keytool`'s -certreq option comes in handy for generating a CSR, as shown in listing 6.3.

Listing 6.3   Generating a CSR with Java `keytool`

```
$keytool -keystore example4.keystore -certreq –alias \ http://manning.com/
    xmlns/samples/soasecimpl/cop
Enter keystore password:  goodpass
-----BEGIN NEW CERTIFICATE REQUEST-----
MIIBtjCCAR8CAQAwdjELMAkGA... [7 lines deleted]
-----END NEW CERTIFICATE REQUEST-----
```

If you send your CSR to a CA, the CA will return a signed certificate after verifying, often through physical documentation, that the identity you claim in the CSR is genuine. Once the CA returns a signed certificate (or certificate chain in case the CA includes its own certificate signed by some other CA), you can import it into the key store to replace your self-signed certificate. See the official Sun JDK documentation for `keytool`'s -import option to understand how you can import the certificate.

6.3.2 *Point to point encryption with digital certificates (SSL/TLS)*

We saw how to create certificates and store them in a key store. The next task is to use these certificates to encrypt messages. We will start by encrypting username and password, for which there are two choices:

1. We can use HTTPS instead of HTTP as the transport for SOAP. This has the benefit of keeping changes to our application code, both on the client and service side, minimal. We will end up encrypting every bit that is passed on the wire—not just the username and password. Such blanket encryption may or may not be appropriate, as explained the beginning of the chapter.

2. We can change our client and server to only use encryption for username and password.

In this subsection, we will implement the first of these two possibilities. We will implement the second in section 6.4.

HTTPS uses SSL or TLS to encrypt all data transmission over the wire. Both SSL and TLS use hybrid encryption and/or similar techniques to safeguard data confidentiality. As a bonus, we also get free server authentication, as both SSL and TLS require servers to identify themselves using digital certificates.

To use HTTPS transport with SOAP, we need to follow these steps:

1. Create a self-signed certificate to identify the host on which Tomcat is running.

2. Configure Tomcat to use the certificate.

3. Configure the client to trust the certificate.

4. Invoke the web service from the client code via HTTPS.

You have already seen how you can create a self-signed certificate, which is the first step. When creating a certificate for a machine as opposed to a user, you need to provide the machine's fully qualified domain name (FQDN) when `keytool` prompts you for first and last name. Tomcat assumes that its key pair is always stored in the key store using `tomcat` as the alias; so don't forget to use that as the alias when you create the self-signed certificate for the Tomcat host.

The second step of the process is to configure the HTTPS connector in Tomcat to make use of the certificate you created. Tomcat comes with its SSL/TLS connector commented by default. Edit `conf/server.xml` in your Tomcat server's home directory, and uncomment the SSL/TLS connector configuration and set it up as shown in listing 6.4. You will need to replace the values shown here for `keystore-File` and `keystorePass` with values that are appropriate for your key store.

Listing 6.4 SSL/TLS connector configuration in Tomcat

```
<Connector port="8443"
  keystoreFile="d:/work/eclipse/soas_code/conf/example4.keystore"
  keystorePass="goodpass"
  ...
  scheme="https" secure="true"
  clientAuth="false" sslProtocol="TLS" />
```

Restart Tomcat. You should now be able to reach the Tomcat homepage on port 8443 of your Tomcat host.

As the third step, we now need to set up our test client to trust Tomcat's certificate. This step is analogous to the step in browsers where we are asked to accept a certificate certified by an unknown CA. In case of browsers, we have GUI wizards to import the certificate. Let us do the same manually, as in listing 6.5, for our test client.

Listing 6.5 Exporting Tomcat's digital certificate from its keystore and importing it into a client keystore

```
$ keytool -keystore example4.keystore -export -alias tomcat \
  -file tomcat.cer
Enter keystore password:  goodpass
Certificate stored in file <tomcat.cer>

$ keytool -keystore client.keystore -import -alias tomcat\
  -file tomcat.cer
Enter keystore password:  goodpass
Owner: CN=localhost, OU=Authors, O=Manning, L=Bangalore,
ST=Karnataka, C=India
Issuer: CN=localhost, OU=Authors, O=Manning, L=Bangalore,
ST=Karnataka, C=India
Serial number: 42dc0c56
Valid from: Tue Jul 19 01:38:54 IST 2005 until: Mon Oct 17 01:38:54
IST 2005
Certificate fingerprints:
   MD5:  C0:AE:CE:9E:A7:1A:51:34:32:72:E6:49:F9:02:6C:7C
   SHA1: CA:43:5E:1E:64:27:CF:66:0B:D5:99:E6:94:71:BE:9E:37:BC:7C:0F
Trust this certificate? [no]:  yes
Certificate was added to keystore
```

Now that we have the client's key store set up to trust Tomcat's certificate, we tell the client to use this key store by setting the `javax.net.ssl.trustStore` system property to the path of the client's key store. In the samples you downloaded in chapter 2, you can do this simply by changing the value for `ssl.truststore` in `build.properties`.

As the final step, we have to modify the client code to use HTTPS. The exact mechanism of these modifications depends on whether our client uses a pregenerated stub. Since we generate the stubs from WSDL, we need to modify WSDL with the right service address to invoke the service via HTTPS. Of course, we have to regenerate the stubs for our client code again. This is the line in WSDL that you have to modify:

Before:

```
<wsdlsoap:address
  location="http://localhost:8080/axis/services/example4"/>
```

After:

```
<wsdlsoap:address
  location="https://localhost:8443/axis/services/example4"/>
```

If we're using a dynamic proxy or DII, we need to make sure that the WSDL fetched by the client at runtime provides the right service address. When serving WSDL for currently deployed services, Axis dynamically sets the protocol and host/port information in the service address based on the address used by the client to fetch WSDL. For example, if the client uses HTTPS to fetch WSDL, Axis provides an HTTPS URI as the service address. So, if we are using dynamic proxy or DII, all we need to do is change the location from which we fetch WSDL at runtime. Here is the relevant code from `example4/BrokerageServiceTestCase.java`.

```
if (sslOrEncryption == USE_SSL) {
    wsdlLocation = "https://" +
        System.getProperty("axis.host","localhost") + ":" +
        System.getProperty("axis.ssl.port", "8443") +
        "/axis/services/example4?WSDL";
} else {
    wsdlLocation = "http://" +
        System.getProperty("axis.host","localhost") + ":" +
        System.getProperty("proxy.port", "8080") +
        "/axis/services/example4?WSDL";
}
```

As you can see, the only difference is the protocol (HTTP vs. HTTPS) and the port number (8080 vs. 8443). Our code has a conditional to test which port we are using, as we use the same code for HTTP and HTTPS. The rest of the code remains unchanged. In fact, if you examine the code generated by WSDL, you will find it similar to this code—there you will find the service address is hard-coded from WSDL.

We are now ready to run the test (assuming that you have done an `ant deploy` when running previous examples in this book; if not, refer to chapter 2). Edit `build.properties` once again on the client-side and make sure that `axis.host`, `axis.ssl.port`, and `ssl.truststore` are all set to the right values. Run `ant demo -example.id=4`. It results in two test runs. We are only interested in the first one here. The second will error out, as we don't have the setup needed to run that one successfully. We will run it again in section 6.4.

Unlike the earlier cases, we cannot demonstrate what transpires over the net using `tcpmon`. Since the data is encrypted, `tcpmon` cannot act as the proxy. If you would like to look at the traffic, you can use `ethereal`, which we showed earlier. Even `ethereal`, for a purely unrelated technical reason, does not work if the client and the server are on the same machine, if you are using Windows. If you run the client and server on different machines, and capture the packets going to and from the port 8443 on either machine, you will see the traffic going over in HTTPS. Of course, you cannot make sense of it, since it is encrypted.

Limiting SSL/TLS to point-to-point exchanges

The steps we described work—they let the client and server communicate over a secure channel. Is it really safe? Consider the case of a commerce site where you submit your credit card information over SSL. The browser shows you a lock icon, giving you the confidence that nobody in the middle can view your information.

Notice that you have no control over how the data is handled after it reaches the commerce site. The site may in turn submit your confidential data to another agency, without putting in enough safeguards to protect your data. The site's server may also have been compromised by a Trojan that captures the information submitted by clients to send it to rogue machines.

In June 2005, the data from 40 million credit cards was compromised in a similar situation. The data was flowing through a company that verifies cardholder credit for merchants. Even though the company was not supposed to retain the data, the company held it in a database for future analysis. That system was cracked, and consequently all the data was compromised.

The lesson here is that if there are multiple parties in an exchange, SSL/TLS does not provide the end-to-end security that the user needs.

There is one more reason why transport-level encryption is inadequate for web services. HTTPS forces blanket encryption of the complete package, which is unnecessary in some cases. Services routinely exchange large amounts of data. Encrypting all of that data is costly.

For these reasons, we like to encrypt messages selectively, targeted toward the final intended recipients. We will look into selective encryption in section 6.4. To get to selective encryption, we need to understand how to encrypt using certificates in Java, which is the topic of the next section.

6.3.3 *Java APIs for encryption*

As we argued, selective encryption is important for SOA security. In this subsection, you will learn how you to use Java APIs to encrypt (and decrypt) arbitrary data. In the next section, you will learn more about selective encryption of SOAP messages, in particular.

The first API you need to get familiar with is the `java.security.KeyStore` class. Given that each security tool vendor may choose a different format for a key store, the `KeyStore` API focuses on presenting a uniform API that can be used with any underlying store. Here is an example showing how you can load a key store.

```
KeyStore keyStore =                                        ❶
  KeyStore.getInstance(KeyStore.getDefaultType());
keyStore.load                                              ❷
  (keyStoreInputStream, keyStorePassword.toCharArray());
```

As shown in the code, you first need to create a `KeyStore` instance using the `get-Instance` factory method ❶. You need to specify the type of store you will be loading into the instance as an argument. The type name will be provided by your key store vendor. Sun JDK 1.5 ships with the capability to handle two types of stores: JKS and JCEKS. Previous versions of Sun JDK supported only JKS stores. In any case, you can defer this choice by using the value returned by `KeyStore.get-DefaultType()`. The default type is JKS on Sun JRE unless you override it using the `keystore.type` property in `<JRE_HOME>/lib/security/java.security`.

Once you have a `KeyStore` instance, loading the contents of a key store into the instance is simple. Provide the password for the key store and an input stream from which the contents can be read to `KeyStore`'s `load` method ❷.

Once you have loaded a `KeyStore` instance, you can retrieve a key from it, be it your own private key or the other party's public key, and use it for encryption or decryption. The java APIs that support you in this are defined by JCE in the `javax.crypto` package. This package provides a uniform API for encryption, key generation, and other cryptographic activities, abstracting away the differences between different algorithms. Listing 6.6 illustrates the use of some of the main classes in this API. This listing shows the first step in the hybrid encryption scheme illustrated by figure 6.4. A key needed for using a symmetric-key encryption algorithm is dynamically generated by the sender and secured for transmission to the receiver using a public-key encryption scheme that relies on the receiver's public key. A certificate stating the receiver's public key is assumed to be available with the sender in its key store.

Listing 6.6   Dynamically generating a symmetric key and encrypting it using intended recipient's public key

```
SecretKey symmetricKey =                                      ❶  Generates symmetric key
   KeyGenerator.getInstance("DESede").generateKey();             usable with Triple DES

X509Certificate recipientCert = (X509Certificate)            ❷  Looks up recipient's
   keyStore.getCertificate(recipientCertAlias);                  certificate in key store

Cipher keyTransportCipher =                   ❸  Creates a cipher based
   Cipher.getInstance("RSA");                     on RSA algorithm
keyTransportCipher.init                                      ❹  Sets up cipher to use
   (Cipher.ENCRYPT_MODE, recipientCert);                         recipient's public key
byte[] encryptedKeyBytes =   keyTransportCipher.doFinal      ❺  Cipher encrypts
   (symmetricKey.getEncoded());                                  symmetric key
```

In this example, we first generate a symmetric key ❶ for use with the Triple DES algorithm. The `ede` suffix in the algorithm name, `DESede`, is used to indicate that the cipher text is to be computed as $E(D(E(m,k1),k2),k3)$, where E is DES encryption algorithm, D is DES decryption algorithm, and `k1`, `k2`, and `k3` are three keys.

Next, we retrieve the intended recipient's certificate from a key store ❷. How we figure out the recipient certificate alias is an interesting issue we have to deal with. The easiest way to answer this riddle is to assume that all certificate aliases in our key store are identical to the recipient URIs.

To secure the symmetric key generated in ❶, we instantiate a `javax.crypto.Cipher` object ❸. The `Cipher` class provides an algorithm-independent API to encrypt and decrypt data. You create a `Cipher` instance by calling the `getInstance` factory method with an argument that describes how you want your data to be encrypted. This argument can simply be the name of an algorithm, but if you understand encryption techniques really well, you can also specify advanced options. For example, when using block encryption, you can specify how data should be split up into blocks and how data should be padded if is shorter than a block. In the listing here, we simply create a cipher that uses the RSA algorithm.

A `Cipher` instance can work in two modes: encrypt and decrypt. It also needs the key required by the encryption/decryption algorithm. We set up either of these in ❹.

The final step is to use the `Cipher` instance to encrypt our symmetric key's bytes. If you want to encrypt something other than a symmetric key, the code is exactly the same. Simply pass the bytes you wish to encrypt to the `doFinal` method ❺.

You now know how to encrypt arbitrary data using Java APIs. To use it to encrypt SOAP messages, we need to understand how the client can select only portions of a SOAP message for encryption and how the server can decrypt it. We will go into those details next.

6.4 *Encrypting SOAP messages*

Until now, we have discussed encryption in a generic setting. Almost all of the encryption technology we saw can be applied to any data exchanged over the wire. Of course, that means it applies to SOAP messages as well. Encrypting SOAP messages poses additional challenges:

- *Need for selective encryption*   SOAP messages can pass through multiple SOAP processing nodes, as we will see in part III of this book. For example, almost all purchases on the web will involve the purchaser, merchant, and at least one financial institution that channels funds for the purchase. Typically, that means different parts of the message may be encrypted for different clients.

- *Need for syntax respecting encryption*   SOAP envelopes have to be well-formed XML documents even after we apply selective encryption.

- *Need for including metadata along with encryption*   As we may not be encrypting the whole message, we need a standard way to communicate what parts have been encrypted and how.

In fact, some of these challenges are applicable to all XML-based messaging protocols, not just SOAP. A standard named *XML Encryption* provides solutions to these challenges. WS-Security makes extensive use of XML Encryption in specifying how SOAP messages can be encrypted. Now, we will show an example to understand the use of XML Encryption in WS-Security.

6.4.1 Example: Sending user credentials with selective encryption

We will use the same example that we considered earlier when demonstrating point-to-point encryption with SSL/TLS. We want to safeguard the secrecy of username and clear-text password as they are passed over the network as part of a SOAP request. In chapter 4, you saw how username and password are exchanged as part of a WS-Security header. See listing 6.7 to refresh your memory.

> **Listing 6.7   Header of a sample SOAP message using username/password–based authentication**

```
<soapenv:Header>
    <wsse:Security ...>
        <wsse:UsernameToken>
            <wsse:Username>chap</wsse:Username>
            <wsse:Password>goodpass</wsse:Password>
        </wsse:UsernameToken>
    </wsse:Security>
</soapenv:Header>
```

To understand what a selectively encrypted message looks like, let's run an example. Table 6.2 provides instructions for running the example.[5]

Table 6.2   Steps to run the example that illustrates how WS-Security supports selective encryption

Step	Action	How To
1	Set up your environment.	If you have not already set up the environment required to run the examples in this book, please refer to chapter 2 to do so. `ant deploy` installs all the examples.
2	If it is not already running, start TCP monitor.	Run `ant tcpmon` so that you can observe the conversation. Check the "XML Format" check box to allow `tcpmon` to format shown requests and responses.
3	Run the example.	Run `ant demo -Dexample.id=4`. You should be able to view the request-response pairs going through the tcpmon console.

After running the example, examine the web service requests and responses captured by `tcpmon`. Observe how username and password are encrypted in the request:

---

[5] One or more known issues in Apache Axis 1.x prevent this example from running successfully. See appendix A for a description of these issues.

Listing 6.8 Overview of SOAP header contents after encrypting the `UsernameToken` element shown in listing 6.7

```
<soapenv:Header>
  <wsse:Security ...>
    <xenc:EncryptedKey ...>...</xenc:EncryptedKey>
    <xenc:EncryptedData ...>...</xenc:EncryptedData>
  </wsse:Security>
</soapenv:Header>
```

Compare the header in listing 6.8 with that in listing 6.7. You can see that the `User-nameToken` element is now gone, and instead, two different elements, `EncryptedKey` and `EncryptedData`, appear.

Overview of the EncryptedData element

Take a look at listing 6.9, which shows the simpler of these two: `EncryptedData`. This element is used to replace whatever XML fragment we are encrypting with its encrypted form. In our case, we are replacing the entirety of `UsernameToken` element.

Listing 6.9 A sample `EncryptedData` element

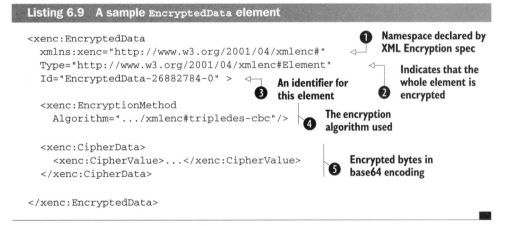

```
<xenc:EncryptedData
  xmlns:xenc="http://www.w3.org/2001/04/xmlenc#"          ❶ Namespace declared by
  Type="http://www.w3.org/2001/04/xmlenc#Element"            XML Encryption spec
  Id="EncryptedData-26882784-0" >                         ❷ Indicates that the
                                 ❸ An identifier for          whole element is
                                    this element              encrypted

  <xenc:EncryptionMethod
    Algorithm=".../xmlenc#tripledes-cbc"/>                ❹ The encryption
                                                             algorithm used

  <xenc:CipherData>
    <xenc:CipherValue>...</xenc:CipherValue>              ❺ Encrypted bytes in
  </xenc:CipherData>                                         base64 encoding

</xenc:EncryptedData>
```

The `xenc` namespace prefix used in this example is bound to a URI defined by the XML Encryption standard ❶. Elements such as `EncryptedData` and `EncryptedKey` that are defined by the XML Encryption standard belong to the namespace identified by this URI.

The `Type` attribute specifies what this `EncryptedData` element is substituting for. The XML Encryption spec defines standard values for two of the frequently replaced items: whole element or content within an element. Here (in ❷), we indicate that the whole element has been encrypted. If we had encrypted only the content within an element, we would have indicated that using `http://www.w3.org/2001/04/xmlenc#Content` as the value of the `Type` attribute.

We defined an identifier for this `EncryptedData` element using an attribute named `Id` (in ❸). The identifier is needed later to associate this element with the key that was used for this encryption.

The `EncryptionMethod` element ❹ specifies the algorithm used for encryption. The XML Encryption spec defines standard URIs to use for popular algorithms such as 3DES, AES, and RSA v1.5. In this example, we are using the standard URI defined for 3DES.

The `CipherData` element ❺ provides the encrypted bytes in one of two ways. As shown here, you can use a `CipherValue` element to provide the encrypted bytes as base64-encoded text. Or, you can use a `CipherReference` element to refer to an external location where the encrypted bytes are available. We will discuss how references work in the next chapter, as XML Signatures make use of them a lot more than XML Encryption does in practice.

Next, we will look into the second new element introduced in listing 6.8, `EncryptedKey`.

Overview of the EncryptedKey element

To understand what goes into `EncryptedKey`, we need to ask ourselves one question: *How can we help the intended recipient locate and decrypt the encrypted parts?* This question is answered by WS-Security as follows: *Prepend* a header entry to a WS-Security header giving out all the information required to help the intended recipient in decryption.

Why prepend? If a particular fragment is encrypted more than once for whatever reason (it is not difficult to imagine situations where a fragment we submit to one of the involved parties is in turn submitted to another as part of a larger encrypted block) then decryptions have to happen in the right order. If all the encryptors prepend header entries describing what has been encrypted then the decryptors can simply process each of these header entries sequentially and do decryption in the right order.

What information should be in the header entries in order to help the decryptor?

- The decryptor needs to know which encrypted nodes it should decrypt. Why is this necessary? For example, can't the decryptor look for all `EncryptedData` elements in the envelope and decrypt them? Think about it—not all encrypted elements in the message may be intended for a single recipient. Each recipient needs to somehow know which of the encrypted elements are for its consumption and which are not. So, what we need is a `ReferenceList` of encrypted elements.

- Each `EncryptedData` element is already giving out the algorithm used. What it is not giving out is the key used. If the key used is somehow shared a priori between the two parties we really don't need to give it out. For example, if the key can be computed from a password, we don't need to add the key information (except when we are encrypting the username and password themselves, as in our example). Instead, if we are using a dynamically generated key like in hybrid encryption, we need to attach an `EncryptedKey`. In addition, if more than one key has been used in encrypting different parts of the document, we need to specify which encrypted elements can be decrypted by each key. That is, we also need a `ReferenceList` of elements encrypted by the key as part of an `EncryptedKey` element.

To summarize, we need to prepend to the WS-Security header:

- A `ReferenceList` if the encryption key is some how agreed upon a priori.
- One or more `EncryptedKey` entries if the key used for data encryption itself needs to be transported to the other party. Each `EncryptedKey` element should in turn consist of a `ReferenceList` of elements encrypted by that key.

As a `ReferenceList` is also needed as part of `EncryptedKey` elements, we can take a look at what is in an `EncryptedKey` element, and, in the process, learn about `ReferenceList` as well. Listing 6.10 shows a sample `EncryptedKey` element.

Listing 6.10 A sample `EncryptedKey` element

```
<xenc:EncryptedKey
  xmlns:wsse="...wssecurity-secext-1.0.xsd"
  xmlns:xenc="http://www.w3.org/2001/04/xmlenc#"
  xmlns:ds="http://www.w3.org/2000/09/xmldsig#">

  <xenc:EncryptionMethod
    Algorithm=
    "http://www.w3.org/2001/04/xmlenc#rsa-1_5"/>

  <ds:KeyInfo>
    <wsse:SecurityTokenReference>
      <ds:X509IssuerSerial>
        <ds:X509IssuerName>
          CN=Prasad Chodavarapu,OU=Authors,O=Manning,...
        </ds:X509IssuerName>
```

❶ Binds namespace prefixes to URIs

Identifies algorithm used for encrypting the key

❷ Identifies a different key used for encrypting the key

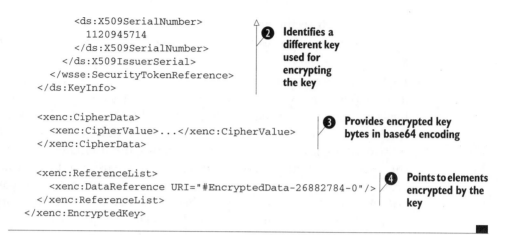

```
        <ds:X509SerialNumber>
            1120945714
        </ds:X509SerialNumber>
      </ds:X509IssuerSerial>
    </wsse:SecurityTokenReference>
  </ds:KeyInfo>

  <xenc:CipherData>
    <xenc:CipherValue>...</xenc:CipherValue>
  </xenc:CipherData>

  <xenc:ReferenceList>
    <xenc:DataReference URI="#EncryptedData-26882784-0"/>
  </xenc:ReferenceList>
</xenc:EncryptedKey>
```

❷ Identifies a different key used for encrypting the key

❸ Provides encrypted key bytes in base64 encoding

❹ Points to elements encrypted by the key

You have previously seen the xenc and wsse prefixes being bound to namespaces defined by the XML Encryption and WS-Security specs, respectively. The new one you see in ❶, ds, is bound to the namespace URI defined by the XML Signature spec that we will discuss in the next chapter.

The EncryptionMethod element identifies the algorithm used for encrypting the key. Here, we are using RSA v1.5 to do hybrid encryption. That is, we are using public-key encryption to encrypt the key that is used for symmetric encryption.

We said we are using RSA v1.5, but how do we say which of the recipient's public keys (if it possesses more than one) is used for symmetric-key encryption? The KeyInfo element is used to convey this information ❷. In this particular case, we are using the recipient certificate's issuer name and serial number to identify the public key used. There are quite a few other ways we could have done this. We could have embedded the entirety of the certificate as base64-encoded data in a <wsse:BinarySecurityToken> element (just like we embedded a Kerberos service ticket in the previous chapter) with the ValueType attribute set to wsse:X509v3. To keep the discussion simple, we will not list all the possible ways of specifying Key-Info. You can refer to the WS-Security X.509 Certificate Token Profile spec for a discussion of all the possibilities.

Just as we did in EncryptedData (see listing 6.9), the CipherData element provides encrypted bytes using a CipherValue ❸ element. This time, of course, what we are encrypting is the dynamically generated key that needs to be transmitted securely.

As discussed previously, we need to identify exactly which EncryptedData elements can be decrypted with the key described by the EncryptedKey element. This identification is done using a `ReferenceList` element ❹. How can we identify a particular `EncryptedData` element in a document? If an `Id` is set on the element (see callout for more details on identifiers), we can refer to it using the `#Id` syntax defined in the URI spec to identify fragments of a resource. That is exactly what we do here in the `DataReference` element.

NOTE *All you need to know about identifiers in XML* In this chapter and the next, we often need to identify elements that are encrypted, digested, or signed. How can we unambiguously identify an element in an XML document? A specification named *XPointer* answers this question for elements as well as other information items in a XML document. Without going into too much detail on the XPointer specification, we can simply say that the two most obvious methods to identify elements are XPath expressions and identifiers. Identifiers are often preferred over XPath for reasons of simplicity and performance. Because of historical reasons, there is considerable confusion over what constitutes an identifier in XML.

The XML 1.0 specification does talk of identifiers, but leaves the choice of the attribute that will hold the identifier value to the DTD or schema. An attribute declared to be of type ID in the DTD/schema provides the identifier value for the element it is defined on. Of course, an identifier value cannot appear more than once in a document, even if different elements use differently named attributes of type ID.

The problem with schema-determined identifiers is that an application needs to be in possession of the DTD/schema to know which attribute values constitute the identifiers. SOAP handlers often do not have the DTD/schema for the XML they are acting on. For this reason, WS-Security defined a special attribute named `wsu:Id` (where `wsu` is a namespace prefix that is bound to the WS-Security–Utility namespace) for holding the identifier value, except in elements defined by the XML Encryption and XML Signature specifications that already have an `Id` (in no namespace) attribute defined on them. In this book, we stick to this definition of an identifier.

At the time of this writing, a special attribute named `xml:id` is being proposed along the same lines as `wsu:Id` for use in all XML-based applications. The example code provided with this book does not understand `xml:id`-based identifiers.

Let's recap what you have learned in this section so far.

- WS-Security supports selective encryption of elements in a SOAP message.
- Each encrypted element (or its content, depending on what is encrypted) is replaced by an `EncrytedData` element that specifies the encryption algorithm and the encrypted bytes.
- If the key used for encryption has been prearranged, a `ReferenceList` element can be used in the `Security` header entry to identify which elements in the message are encrypted.
- If the encryption key is a dynamically generated one that needs to be securely shared with the other party, an `EncryptedKey` element can be used in the `Security` header entry to transport the generated key securely. In this case, the list of the message elements encrypted by the dynamically generated key is identified using a `ReferenceList` element nested inside the `EncryptedKey` element.

Now that you understand how WS-Security supports selective encryption in SOAP messages, you are ready to look into the code that implements all these details. Figure 6.6 provides an overview of the implementation strategy we adopted in this example.

Assuming that you have read at least one the past three chapters, figure 6.6 should look very similar to what you have seen before. On the client-side, we have an `EncryptionHandler` that is responsible for encryption, and on the server-side, we have a `DecryptionHandler` that is responsible for decryption. In this example implementation, the subject of encryption and decryption happens to be the `UsernameToken` element created on the client-side by the `ClientSideWSSecurity-Handler` and consumed on the server-side by the `WSSecurityUsernameHandler`.

Just as in the previous chapters, we will dig into the details of the client- and server-sides separately. To emphasize that `EncryptionHandler` and `Decryption-Handler` will switch sides if we discuss encryption of response messages (messages originating from the server-side and addressed to the client-side), we will use the terms *encrypting side* and *decrypting side* instead of client-side and server-side. Let's start with the encrypting side.

6.4.2 *Encrypting-side implementation*

In this subsection, we will show how to implement the encrypting side.

In figure 6.6, we can see that we have two handlers on the client-side. The first one is `ClientsideWSSecurityHandler`, which we discussed in the previous chapter.

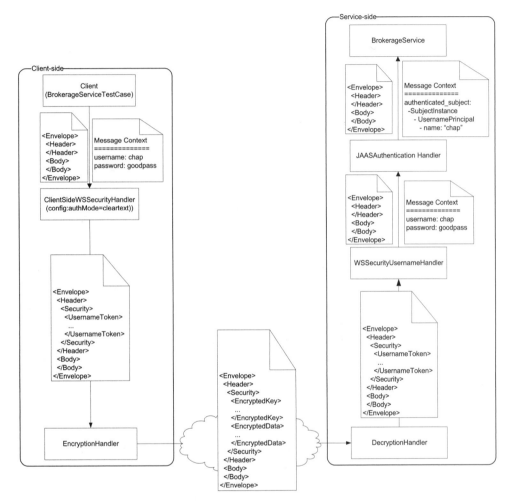

Figure 6.6 Sample implementation of SOAP encryption and decryption. In this example, UsernameToken is encrypted by a client-side EncryptionHandler and recovered by DecryptionHandler on the service-side.

It is responsible for inserting the username and password in the headers. The second handler, called EncryptionHandler, implements encryption using the hybrid encryption scheme shown in figure 6.4.

To selectively encrypt parts of a message, the EncryptionHandler needs to carry out the steps identified in table 6.3.

Table 6.3   Steps to selectively encrypt parts of a message

Step	Action
1	Identify the portions of the message to encrypt.
2	Pick an algorithm and a key to encrypt the parts of the message.
3	Extract portions of the message identified in step 1 and replace them with encrypted data.
4	Add information on the encryption carried out to the `Security` header. As we will be using a hybrid encryption scheme in this example, this task is again divided into two. First, encrypt the key used in step 2 and add it to the `Security` header along with list of nodes encrypted by the key. Next, add to the `Security` header information (such as the public key used) on how the key is encrypted.

All the code for these steps is in the file `EncryptionHandler.java`. This class heavily depends on the functionality of `org.apache.xml.security.encryption.XMLCipher` from Apache's XML Security library. `XMLCipher` provides a higher-level API than `javax.crypto.Cipher` (introduced in section 6.3.3) for encrypting XML. It subsumes the functionality of `Cipher` and provides facilities to parse/serialize and replace encrypted/decrypted elements in a DOM.

Before we explain the implementation of steps in table 6.3, we need to tell you how `EncryptionHandler` is initialized. We will do that next.

Initial setup

There is some setup that needs to be done before `EncryptionHandler` can do the four steps in table 6.3. We need to initialize Apache's XML Security library. Since this needs to be done only once, we implement this as a static call in the `EncryptionHandler` class:

```
org.apache.xml.security.Init.init();
```

In addition, when the `EncryptionHandler` is initialized (that is, when its `init()` method is called), we need to configure it with answers to the following questions:

1   *In which direction is this handler being used: request or response?*   The answer to this question is needed to determine which of the two methods—`handleRequest` or `handleResponse`—should do encryption.

2   *Which of the message elements needs to be encrypted?*   We need to specify the XPath for these elements.

3   *Should we encrypt entire elements or just their content?*   By default, entire elements are encrypted.

4   *Which symmetric-key encryption algorithm should we use?*   By default, the handler uses 3DES. Of course, we can configure the handler to use any symmetric-key algorithm.

5   *Which public key encryption algorithm should we use?*   By default, the handler uses RSA v1.5.

6   *Where is the key store?*   Here is where the handler looks for the certificate of the intended receiver.

7   *Which certificate in the key store belongs to the intended receiver?*   The handler needs to know the certificate's alias in the key store, in order to retrieve the certificate.

By the end of the initialization, the code knows answers to all these questions from the configuration file. Most of the initialization code is straightforward except for the code that compiles XPath expressions. The `javax.xml.xpath` package in Sun JDK 1.5 is very well documented. Take a look at the javadocs for that package (reference 5 in the "Suggestions for further reading" section at the end of this chapter) to understand how to compile and evaluate XPaths in java.

Now that you know how `EncryptionHandler` is initialized, let's look at how it carries out each of the four steps we identified in table 6.3.

Step 1: Identifying the nodes to encrypt

This is the first step that needs to be done when the handler is called. In our example, the `soapenv:Header/wsse:Security/wsse:UsernameToken` element that needs to be encrypted. It is possible to encrypt any element in the complete envelope, including already-encrypted data. Here is how we get the list of the nodes[6] to encrypt:

```
NodeList nodesToEncrypt = (NodeList)
                  xpathToEncrypt.evaluate
                  (soapEnvelope, XPathConstants.NODESET);
```

The second argument to the function makes it return all the nodes that match the XPath, which is exactly what we want. Later on, we will encrypt these nodes and replace the originals with the encrypted nodes. For now, let's look at how `EncryptionHandler` implements step 2.

---

[6] Although we use the word "node" here, what we really mean is an *element*. The XML Encryption spec supports encryption at three granularities: document, element, and element content. In all three cases, what needs to be encrypted can be identified by an element.

Step 2: Picking an algorithm and the key for encryption

Once the `EncryptionHandler` identifies the list of nodes to encrypt, it needs to pick an algorithm and the key for encryption. It already knows which algorithm it should use; the handler got that information during initialization. Now, it needs to generate a symmetric key.

In section 6.3.3, we introduced you to the JCE APIs, which are useful when implementing encryption. Listing 6.6 showed you to how to use the JCE `Key-Generator` API to generate a key. We use the exact same code in `Encryption-Handler`, but we need to do some additional work here.

`KeyGenerator` needs a JCE-given name for the algorithm to generate a key. Apache XML Security library, on the other hand, needs the name of the algorithm as a URI standardized by the XML Encryption spec. We use the URI form when configuring the handler. So, we need to convert the algorithm name from URI form to JCE-given name as shown in the following code.

```
String algorithmJCEName= JCEMapper.
               getJCEKeyAlgorithmFromURI(dataEncryptionAlgo);
KeyGenerator keyGenerator = KeyGenerator.getInstance
               (algorithmJCEName);
SecretKey symmetricKey =
               keyGenerator.generateKey();
```

So, we know the nodes to encrypt and the encryption algorithm. Let's replace the original ones with the encrypted nodes—that is, selectively encrypt the part of the message.

Step 3: Replacing original nodes with encrypted nodes

Now that the `EncryptionHandler` has generated a key, it can extract the nodes identified in step 1 and replace each of them with an `EncryptedData` element, like the one shown in listing 6.9. When doing this step, the `EncryptionHandler` also needs to assign a unique identifier to each of the `EncryptedData` elements it creates. These identifiers will come in handy in step 4, when the `EncryptionHandler` adds a `ReferenceList` of encrypted elements to the `Security` header. Listing 6.11 shows the code for implementing this logic.

Listing 6.11   Replacing nodes to encrypt with `EncryptedData` elements

```
String prefixForEncryptedNodeIds =            ❶ Generates a prefix for
    "EncryptedData-" + hashCode();               EncryptedData identifiers
for (int i = 0; i < numNodesToEncrypt; ++i) {
    Node ithNodeToEncrypt = nodesToEncrypt.item(i);
    . . .
```

```
XMLCipher xmlDataCipher =                         ❷  Instantiates
    XMLCipher.getInstance(dataEncryptionAlgo);        XMLCipher
xmlDataCipher.init                                    Sets XMLCipher to
    (XMLCipher.ENCRYPT_MODE, symmetricKey);       ❸  encrypt using given key
xmlDataCipher.getEncryptedData().setId
    (prefixForEncryptedNodeIds + "-" + i);        ❹  Sets identifier of the
xmlDataCipher.doFinal                                 EncryptedData element
    (soapDoc,                                     ❺  Replaces original node
    (Element) ithNodeToEncrypt,                       with EncryptedData
    onlyEncryptElementContent);                       element
}
```

The primary goal of this listing is to show you how to use the XMLCipher API for encrypting elements in a SOAP message.

You can instantiate the XMLCipher class using the getInstance factory method ❷. This method takes as an argument the algorithm you intend to use for encryption. The algorithm must be in the form of a URI. For all the available URIs, you can refer to the class org.xml.security.utils.EncryptionConstants.

Just like a JCE Cipher instance, XMLCipher can work in two modes: encrypt and decrypt. As this listing is part of EncryptionHandler, the XMLCipher instance is set to work in the encrypt mode using the init method ❸. The init method also takes as an argument the key to use for encryption.

Post initialization, an XMLCipher instance knows what algorithm and key to use for encryption. The only thing it does not know yet is what to encrypt. XMLCipher's doFinal method ❺ gets this information through its arguments and replaces the identified element in an XML document with an EncryptedData element. The arguments to doFinal are the document to which the node to encrypt belongs, the node to encrypt, and a Boolean value to specify whether to encrypt the entirety of the given node or just its content.

There is one important detail in listing 6.11 that we have yet to describe. As we noted earlier, the EncryptionHandler needs to assign a unique identifier ❹ to each of the EncryptedData elements it creates so that it can refer to them later when creating a ReferenceList of EncryptedData elements. The EncryptionHandler can use "EncryptedData-*i*" as the unique identifier for the *i*-th EncryptedData element it generates. The uniqueness of these identifiers may be violated if more than one instance of an EncryptionHandler is used on the encrypting side (possibly to encrypt different parts of the same message differently). The strategy used here incorporates the hashcode of the EncryptionHandler instance ❶ in the unique identifiers generated for EncryptedData elements.

We are done looking at how `EncryptionHandler` implements three of the four steps we identified earlier. The only step that's left now is to add encryption information to the `Security` header entry. Let's see how to implement that next.

Step 4: Adding info on encryption to the Security header

In step 2, the `EncryptionHandler` generated a key and used it in step 3 for encryption. As the decrypting-side will need the same key for decryption, the `Encryption-Handler` needs to communicate this key securely to the decrypting-side. As shown in listing 6.10, WS-Security provides an `EncryptedKey` element for this purpose. In this section, we will show you the code for creating an `EncryptedKey` element and adding it to the `Security` header. We will also show you how to add information on the public key used for generating the `EncryptedKey` element.

To produce the `EncryptedKey` element, we turn once again to the Apache XML Security library. This library provides us with classes such as `EncryptedKey` and `ReferenceList`. We fill in instances of these classes with data, and at the end use their serialization facilities to convert the data into XML form.

The activity in this step can be subdivided into the parts shown in table 6.4.

Table 6.4   Steps to selectively encrypt parts of a message

Step	Action
4a	Look up the decrypting side's certificate in the key store specified by the handler's configuration.
4b	Encrypt the symmetric key used for encryption in step 3. For this encryption, use the public-key algorithm specified by the handler's configuration and the certificate retrieved in step 4a.
4c	Construct an instance of the `EncryptedKey` class using the result of step 4b.
4d	Construct an instance of the `ReferenceList` class, populate it with the identifiers of `EncryptedData` elements generated in step 3, and add it to the `EncryptedKey` instance constructed in step 4c.
4e	Add, a `SecurityTokenReference` to `EncryptedKey` to refer to the recipient's certificate used in step 4b.
4f	Serialize the `EncryptedKey` instance as XML and add it to `Security` header entry.

We will walk you through the code for each of these steps next, starting with step 4a, which is shown in listing 6.12.

Listing 6.12   (Step 4a) Looking up the decrypting side's certificate in the key store

```
X509Certificate recipientCert = (X509Certificate)
    keyStore.getCertificate(recipientCertAlias);
```

```
if (recipientCert == null) {
    throw new RuntimeException(
        "Did not find a certificate in the keystore for: "
            + recipientCertAlias);
}
```

In this listing, we simply use the Java KeyStore API introduced in section 6.3.3 to retrieve the decrypting side's certificate from a key store. The location of the key store and the recipient certificate's alias come from the handler configuration, as we described earlier.

Next we need to encrypt the symmetric key generated in step 2 with the public key in the recipient's certificate. The XMLCipher class we used in step 3 for encryption does not support public-key encryption. Since we need to encrypt the key with public-key encryption, we fall back to JCE APIs, as shown in listing 6.13.

Listing 6.13 (Step 4b) Encrypting the symmetric key used for encryption in step 3

```
Cipher keyTransportCipher = Cipher.getInstance
    (JCEMapper.translateURItoJCEID(keyEncryptionAlgo));
keyTransportCipher.init(Cipher.ENCRYPT_MODE, recipientCert);
byte[] encryptedKeyBytes =
    keyTransportCipher.doFinal(symmetricKey.getEncoded());
```

Listing 6.13 is very similar to listing 6.6 but for one minor detail. As JCE does not recognize the URIs used in EncryptionHandler configuration to identify encryption algorithms, we first have to convert the key encryption algorithm URI into a name that JCE recognizes. Once we do that, the rest of the code is the same as in listing 6.6. By the end of this snippet of the code, we get the encrypted bytes. Now we need to put these bytes in XMLCipher as shown in listing 6.14.

Listing 6.14 (Step 4c) Instantiating the EncryptedKey class using the result of step 4b

```
XMLCipher xmlKeyCipher =
    XMLCipher.getInstance(keyEncryptionAlgo);
EncryptedKey encryptedKey =
    xmlKeyCipher.createEncryptedKey
        (CipherData.VALUE_TYPE,
         new String
         (Base64.encodeBase64(encryptedKeyBytes),
          "US-ASCII"));
```

To construct an `EncryptedKey`, we first need to create an `XMLCipher` instance. Once we do that, we can use the `createEncryptedKey` method in `XMLCipher` to construct an `EncryptedKey`. The first argument we pass to this method, `CipherData.VALUE_TYPE`, indicates that the `CipherData` element in the `EncryptedKey` will contain a `CipherValue` (the encrypted key bytes) as opposed to a `CipherReference` (a reference to another element). The second argument provides the base64-encoded bytes in the encrypted key.

The next step is to add a `ReferenceList` containing the identifiers of the `EncryptedData` elements generated in step 3 to the `EncryptedKey` instance.

Listing 6.15   (Step 4d) Adding `ReferenceList` to `EncryptedKey`

```
ReferenceList encryptedDataRefList =
    xmlKeyCipher.createReferenceList
    (ReferenceList.DATA_REFERENCE);
for (int i=0; i < numNodesToEncrypt; ++i) {
    encryptedDataRefList.add
        (encryptedDataRefList.newDataReference
        ("#" + prefixForEncryptedNodeIds + "-" + i));
}
encryptedKey.setReferenceList(encryptedDataRefList);
```

We construct a `ReferenceList` instance using a method in `XMLCipher` named `createReferenceList`. The argument we pass to this method, `ReferenceList.DATA_REFERENCE`, indicates that the constructed `ReferenceList` will refer to `EncryptedData` elements (as opposed to `EncryptedKey` elements). Once we have a `ReferenceList` instance, we add to it references to each `EncryptedData` element created in step 2. Observe that we are computing the identifiers for `EncryptedData` elements the same way we computed earlier, thus making sure that the references work.

We also need to add information about the recipient's certificate that was used to encrypt the key to `EncryptedKey`. As shown in listing 6.10, this is done using a `KeyInfo` element that wraps a `SecurityTokenReference`. Listing 6.16 shows the code for this step.

Listing 6.16   (Step 4e) Adding a reference to the recipient's certificate to `EncryptedKey`

```
Element securityTokenReference = soapDoc.createElementNS
    (Constants.WS_SECURITY_NS_URI,
    Constants.WS_SECURITY_TOKEN_REF_TAG);
```

```
securityTokenReference.appendChild                           ❷
    (new XMLX509IssuerSerial(soapDoc, recipientCert).
        getElement());
KeyInfo keyTransportKeyInfo = new KeyInfo(soapDoc);          ❸
keyTransportKeyInfo.addUnknownElement
    (securityTokenReference);
encryptedKey.setKeyInfo(keyTransportKeyInfo);        ◄─❹
```

The `KeyInfo` ❸ class in the Apache XML Security library does not know what a `SecurityTokenReference` element is. Fortunately, the class allows addition of an unknown DOM `Element` to `KeyInfo` ❹. We fall back on this facility here. We first create a `SecurityTokenReference` element ❶ and add to it the information on the recipient's certificate used in key encryption. The certificate information is added as an instance of `XMLX509IssuerSerial` ❷, another class defined by the Apache XML Security library.

Now that we have filled out all the information required in an `EncryptedKey` instance, we can serialize it as an XML element and prepend it to the `Security` header entry, as shown in listing 6.17.

Listing 6.17   (Step 4f) Serializing the `EncryptedKey` instance as XML and prepending it to the `Security` header

```
Element encryptedKeyElement = xmlKeyCipher.martial
                (soapDoc, encryptedKey);
securityElement.insertBefore
    (encryptedKeyElement, securityElement.getFirstChild());
```

This completes the encryption logic on the encrypting side. Let us now look at the decryption logic on the decrypting-side.

6.4.3   *Decrypting-side implementation*

Since we already studied the encrypting-side code carefully, the decrypting-side code is easier to understand.

In the example illustrated by figure 6.6, we see three handlers on the server-side. Of these, you have already seen the `WSSecurityUsernameHandler` and `JAAS-AuthenticationHandler` in previous chapters. We will restrict our description here to the only new handler on the server-side, `DecryptionHandler`.

The logic in `DecryptionHandler` can be divided into the steps shown in table 6.5.

Table 6.5 Steps to decrypt parts of a SOAP message that are encrypted using a hybrid encryption scheme

Step	Action
1	Identify the `Security` header entry that is applicable to the decryptor. You will see in chapter 8 that there may be multiple `Security` header entries in a SOAP message. The decryptor has to identify the `Security` header entry that it should look into, based on the `actor` attribute we will be describing in chapter 8.
2	Look for `EncryptedKey` elements in the `Security` header entry identified by step 1. For each element found, carry out the rest of the steps.
3	Identify the certificate used to encrypt the encryption key. Information on the certificate will be available in the `KeyInfo` child of the `EncryptedKey` element retrieved in step 2.
4	Look up the key store to find the private key corresponding to the public key in the certificate identified by step 3.
5	Decrypt the encryption key using the private key identified in step 4.
6	Using the encryption key retrieved in step 5, decrypt each of the `EncryptedData` elements referred to in the `ReferenceList` child of `EncryptedKey`. Replace each of the `EncryptedData` elements with the decrypted data.
7	Remove the processed `EncryptedKey` element from the `Security` header entry.

Before any of these steps are done, the `DecryptionHandler` is to be initialized of course. Because the initialization code for `DecryptionHandler` is similar to that of `EncryptionHandler`, we will not be showing it here.

We will also not show you the full code for all of the steps listed in table 6.5. We will only describe the structure and flow of control in the `DecryptionHandler`. You can look up the rest of the source code from the `DecryptionHandler.java` file under the `java/com/manning/samples/soasecimpl/example4` folder in the examples archive you downloaded in chapter 2.

The code for step 1 is in the function `getSecurityElementForThisTarget`, an extract of which is shown in listing 6.18.

Listing 6.18 (Step 1) Locating the relevant `security` header entry

```
soapEnvelope = message.getSOAPPart().getEnvelope();
soapHeader = soapEnvelope.getHeader();
securityElement = Utils.getHeaderByNameAndActor
  (soapEnvelope, Constants.WS_SECURITY_SECURITY_QNAME,
   roleSet, true);
```

In step 2, we take the Security element located by code in listing 6.18, iterate through its children and look for EncryptedKey elements in it. For each Encrypt-edKey element found, we need to do steps 3-7, shown in listing 6.19. The high-level code for these tasks is in the function processEncryptedKey:

Listing 6.19   (Steps 3-7) Code for processing an EncryptedKey element

```
XMLCipher xmlKeyCipher = XMLCipher.getInstance();        ❶
xmlKeyCipher.init(XMLCipher.DECRYPT_MODE, null);

EncryptedKey encryptedKey = xmlKeyCipher.loadEncryptedKey    ❷
    (soapDoc, encryptedKeyElement);
String keyEncryptionAlgo =                      ❸
    getKeyTransportAlgorithm(encryptedKey);
byte[] decryptedKeyBytes = getDecryptedKey(encryptedKey,    ❹
                          keyEncryptionAlgo);

ReferenceList refsToEncryptedData =        ❺
    encryptedKey.getReferenceList();
decryptData                                         ❻
    (soapEnvelope, refsToEncryptedData, decryptedKeyBytes);
```

In this code, we first initialize an XMLCipher instance to work in decrypt mode ❶. We pass to it the EncryptedKey element so that it can parse the element and create an object form of it ❷. The getKeyTransportAlgorithm method ❸ of Decryption-Handler looks up the EncryptionMethod child in the EncryptedKey element to find the public-key encryption algorithm used for key encryption. If the Encryption-Method child is not found, the algorithm is assumed to be RSA v1.5. The get-DecryptedKey method ❹ of DecryptionHandler uses JCE APIs to decrypt the key using the algorithm identified in ❸.

Once the decrypted key is available, the decryptData method of Decryption-Handler iterates through the EncryptedData elements identified by ReferenceList ❺ and replaces them with the decrypted data ❻.

This completes the high-level walk-through of code on the decrypting side. We have not explained much of the decryption code here, as you can easily follow from our discussion of the code on the encrypting side. As we said before, you can read the entire source code in DecryptionHandler.java.

You probably now know all that you need to know about encryption of SOAP messages. We will conclude this chapter with a discussion of the practical issues in encryption.

6.5 *Practical issues with encryption*

If encryption is so good, why not use it everywhere? Are there any guidelines on where to use it? Are there any drawbacks in using it? Encryption poses interesting choices and questions such as what to encrypt, how to encrypt, and what kind of tools we should use.

Ideally you would like to encrypt every bit of information, but that certainly has drawbacks. For example, if we encrypt all the credit card transactions, including the total amount to be paid, we may not able to write applications that can audit or generate alerts based on the amount. Moreover, sometimes it may be legally necessary for us to leave some of the information in clear text.

When evaluating encryption strategies, we need to look at the infrastructure requirements for each strategy. For example, if we choose PKI and run our own CA, the life cycle processes for a certificate—allocation, management, renewal, and revocation—can get costly and may require special-purpose software.

Coming to the actual implementation of encryption, there are two issues: one is interoperability with existing encryption schemes and the other is inadequacy of implementations. Interoperability is an issue when picking an encryption algorithm, for instance. For example, if an existing application or platform cannot deal with AES, we may have to use a different algorithm.

> **NOTE** *Addressing interoperability problems that may arise out of encryption* SOA places strong emphasis on interoperability, so it is important to design generic solutions to the interoperability problems that may arise from the different capabilities and requirements of different parties. For example, if a client implementation knows how to use 3DES as well as AES, and a service implementation only supports 3DES, how does the client figure out that it should stick to 3DES when talking with that service? We will address this question in chapter 9, where we introduce the ideas of security policy declaration and intersection.

One shortcoming we notice in most implementations, despite the use of mature tools and libraries, is that they do not handle certification revocation well. They may not verify the revocation lists often enough to identify technically valid, yet canceled, certificates.

Even with a good implementation, we are not ensured of the confidentiality of the message. Ultimately, the security system can only be as good as its weakest link. The human element often turns out to be the weakest link in security. We should have comprehensive logging, auditing, and password management policies in place when designing a secure application.

The question of the right choice of encryption toolkits to use does not have a single answer. As you can guess, there is no single toolkit that can solve all needs. For example, we presented a highly useful toolkit from Apache in this chapter. The XMLCipher class, which provides so much support for encrypting XML, does not support PKI when it comes to key transport. Since the APIs[7] are not yet standard, we may get locked into an inferior toolkit. Until good solutions emerge, we may have to build our own toolkits on top of existing ones to fill in the missing functionality.

When proposing a security solution, one always has to watch out for the impact of security enforcement on the overall performance of the system. Encryption and decryption add a lot of computational overhead. This is the primary reason behind the popularity of hybrid encryption, in which we get the convenience of PKI without losing out on the efficiency offered by symmetric-key encryption. In addition, these days hardware-based PKI systems offer an efficient solution for managing security. Even without special hardware, there is one particular optimization we can make in the way we use hybrid encryption schemes in SOAP message exchanges (see callout).

NOTE *More efficient use of the hybrid encryption scheme with WS-SecureConversation* Take a look back at figure 6.4, which pictorially describes the concept of hybrid encryption. In this picture, a symmetric key is established up front using public-key encryption and used for encryption in all further exchanges. If you look at the way we implemented encryption of SOAP messages using WS-Security header entries, you will see that there is no reuse of previously established symmetric keys. The EncryptionHandler is generating a new symmetric key for every message and adding it to the WS-Security header as an EncryptedKey. This kind of implementation will mean additional per-message CPU cost for key generation, key encryption, and key decryption, as well as network costs for transmitting the encrypted key every time. If we can somehow reuse the symmetric key established in the first message for all subsequent exchanges, we will eliminate the per-message cost and simply pay a fixed cost up front for key establishment. WS-SecureConversation makes this possible. WS-SecureConversation is described in appendix B.

---

[7] JSR-106 is charged with standardizing these APIs.

In summary, one needs to consider a range of issues when implementing encryption in real-world enterprises. In this section, we sought to provide you with a sampling of issues you are likely to see in practice.

6.6 *Summary*

In this chapter, we studied the ways we can protect the confidentiality of messages. We started out by looking at the theory behind encryption. Despite the complex mathematics of the actual encryption algorithms, the basics of encryption are simple. We hope you understood the various concepts such as symmetric and asymmetric algorithms and how they come together to solve the needs of encryption in real-world applications.

We also told you about the infrastructure needed for using encryption in practice. In particular, we explained the need for PKI. We introduced you to the ideas behind PKI —digital certificates, digital signatures, CAs, and certificate chaining. Finally, we also showed you the actual details in a certificate.

Even though all this material is not directly related to SOA security, we needed to cover this ground for two reasons. We believe that the practitioners of SOA security should understand the mechanisms of encryption that are used everywhere. We also believe that you may have to build on top of inadequate toolkits or vendor offerings which require you to understand this material.

Once we understood the theory, we looked at the JCE classes that are useful for implementing encryption schemes in Java. We showed how to create and examine digital certificates. Through an example, we showed how to use Java APIs for encrypting point-to-point communications using digital certificates.

There are special requirements for using encryption with SOAP. In particular, for selective encryption of SOAP messages, we need to understand how to use XML Encryption. As usual, WS-Security standards help us communicate the details in the header elements so that the receiving party can understand how to decrypt the elements in SOAP message. We walked through the code for two JAX-RPC handlers that use the Apache XML Security library and JCE for encrypting and decrypting SOAP messages.

If you followed the examples provided in this chapter, you gained enough knowledge to send and receive encrypted SOAP messages. Even though we illustrated encryption in header elements, you can use the same code to encrypt any element in the message.

As we briefly described in the section on signatures, encryption does not protect against data tampering. To protect against such threats, we will use digital signatures. You have seen the basics of signatures in this chapter. However, using them in conjunction with SOAP and WS standards poses additional challenges. These challenges and the corresponding solutions are the subject of the next chapter.

Suggestions for further reading

- For a quick but more-detailed explanation of cryptography basics and SSL/TLS, see *Web Security, Privacy and Commerce, 2nd Edition*, written by Simson Garfinkel and published by O'Reilly Media Inc. in January 2002. (ISBN is 0596000456.)

- The reference manual for `keytool` is available at http://java.sun.com/j2se/1.5.0/ docs/tooldocs/windows/keytool.html.

- "XML Encryption Syntax and Processing," a W3C Recommendation, is available at http://www.w3.org/TR/xmlenc-core/.

- Apache XML Security libraries can be downloaded from http://xml.apache.org/ security/Java/index.html.

- Javadocs for `javax.xml.xpath` package in Sun JDK 1.5 can be found at http:// java.sun.com/j2se/1.5.0/docs/api/javax/xml/xpath/package-summary.html.

- JSR-106, Java Specification Request for the standardization of APIs for XML Encryption, can be found at http://www.jcp.org/en/jsr/detail?id=106. A draft of the API is available for public review at http://jcp.org/aboutJava/communityprocess/pr/jsr106/.

Using digital signatures 7

This chapter covers

- XML canonicalization
- XML signature
- Signing SOAP messages

In the previous chapter, we learned how to apply encryption to safeguard the confidentiality of messages. When studying the basics of encryption and PKI, we also briefly looked at digital signatures and how they aid in the detection of message tampering. In this chapter, we will study signatures in detail, particularly to verify the integrity of SOAP messages received over an unsafe network.

The theory behind digital signatures is easy—in fact, we learned most of it in the previous chapter. Just like with encryption, the structure of the data, namely XML and SOAP, makes signing of a SOAP message complex. Before going into these details, let's first recap the basics of signatures.

The goal of signing a message is to detect message tampering. If the sender can create a checksum and communicate it securely to the receiver, the receiver can recompute the checksum and compare it with that provided by the sender. Instead of using a simple checksum, we prefer to compute a message digest using a cryptographic hash algorithm (such as SHA-1) for the following reasons:

- Even a small change in the message produces a substantially different digest value. This means that flipping a single bit in a 1MB document produces a digest value that is clearly different from the original one.

- It is very difficult to find two messages that produce the same digest. That is, if an attacker wants to change the message without breaking the digest, he cannot do so.

The message digest itself can be tampered with in transit. To take care of such a problem, the sender can send a Message Authentication Code (MAC) that is computed using the digest and a shared secret key. If a man in the middle tampers with the message, he cannot possibly fix the MAC value as well, since he does not have possession of the secret key. Figure 7.1 shows this technique pictorially.

Clearly, a MAC provides us with the ability to check whether the message has been tampered with in transit. A MAC-based message integrity check suffers from two drawbacks:

1 *Dependency on a shared secret*   A shared secret needs to be established between the sender and the recipient. From the discussions in the previous chapter, we know how difficult it is to manage a shared secret.

2 *Inability to counter repudiation*   As the key is shared, the sender can always claim that the recipient is making up a message exchange that never happened. The recipient will not be able to conclusively prove that the sender indeed sent the message in question. Thus, MAC cannot establish repudiation.

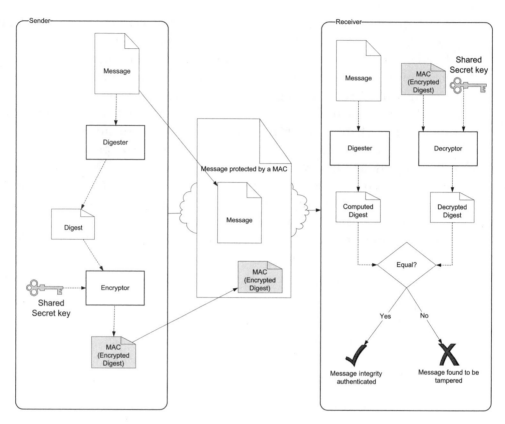

Figure 7.1 A MAC is a message digest encrypted using a shared secret key. The receiver can use a MAC as shown to detect whether the message has been tampered with along the way by a man in the middle.

PKI and digital signatures provide a better solution than MAC. The sender can digitally sign a message—that is, encrypt the message digest using his private key—before sending it to the recipient. The sender can also attach his digital certificate to provide the recipient with his identity information and public key. The recipient can verify the sender's certificate using PKI and then use the public key available in the certificate to verify the signature—that is, decrypt the digest and compare it with a recomputed digest.

In summary, this mechanism establishes two facts: the identity of the sender and the proof that the message is from that sender. Nonrepudiation is ensured since only someone with the sender's private key could have signed the message.

Figure 7.2 illustrates the use of PKI in verifying the integrity of messages.

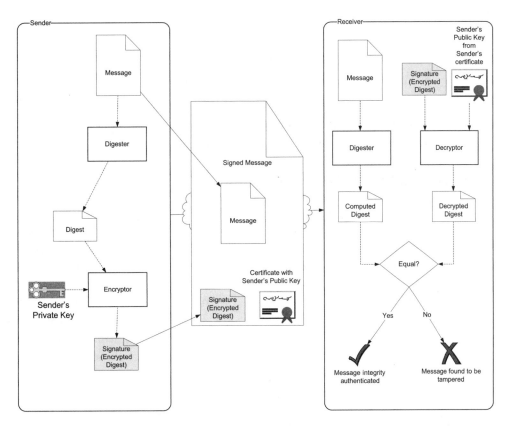

Figure 7.2   PKI and digital signatures provide another way to verify message integrity. Unlike with MACs, PKI does not require a shared secret. The sender signs a message by using his private key to encrypt a digest of the message. The receiver can use the sender's public key, available from the sender's digital certificate, to decrypt the signature and verify the message digest.

A man in the middle tampering with the message cannot fix the encrypted digest in the digital signature because he doesn't have the sender's private key. In addition, the recipient can conclusively prove that the message could only have come from the sender because the digest has been encrypted with the sender's private key.

That is all you need to know about the theory of digital signatures. In the rest of the chapter, we will go into the details that make this theory work. In particular, we will describe:

- The basics of XML signatures, the challenges in signing XML and how to overcome them using canonicalization.

- Signing SOAP messages in compliance with the XML Signature and WS-Security specifications, and a sample implementation in Java for signing SOAP messages and verifying signatures on SOAP messages.

- Practical issues with signatures when adopting them for securing message integrity in the real world.

We will start with a discussion of the challenges in signing XML and how to overcome them. These lessons are directly applicable to SOAP messages.

7.1 *The basics of XML signatures*

We told you in the previous chapter and in the introduction to this chapter that you can detect tampered messages using digital signatures. In these previous discussions, we never specified any constraints on the types of messages you can protect with digital signatures. The basic idea of using an encrypted message digest as a signature that can be verified to detect tampered messages is applicable to any kind of message. Signatures on XML messages need to tackle additional challenges that are unique to XML. Since the same challenges apply to SOAP message signatures, we will describe a technique named canonicalization that helps us tackle the toughest and most critical of these issues. Solutions to the rest of the challenges will be self-evident in section 7.2 where we show you examples of signatures on SOAP messages.

7.1.1 *Challenges in signing XML*

When applying a signature-based solution to ensure integrity of XML-based messages, additional challenges need to be tackled.

Syntactically equivalent XML documents may produce different signatures

The toughest and most fundamental challenge in signing XML comes from the fact that digest algorithms used to produce signatures do not understand XML syntax. The algorithms simply work on a specific sequence of input bytes. Consequently, two syntactically equivalent XML messages may get two different signatures. For example, attribute values may be quoted using a single quote (') or a double quote ("). Line endings may be represented in a platform-specific way. All these insignificant differences will cause two syntactically equivalent XML messages to produce two different signatures.

There are practical consequences to this problem, as shown in figure 7.3.

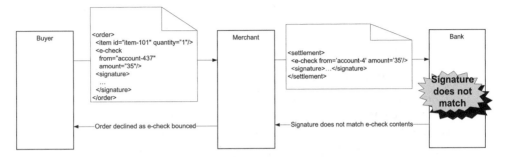

Figure 7.3 **Superficial differences in how XML is serialized can result in signature mismatch. In the example shown here, the merchant's application extracts an e-check from an order and submits it as part of a settlement request to the bank. The bank finds a signature mismatch, as the merchant's application serializes the e-check in a slightly different fashion than the buyer's application.**

If an XML message travels through multiple parties before it reaches the ultimate destination, there is a good possibility that the byte sequence received will not be the same as the byte sequence sent by the sender, even though none of the intermediate parties intended to modify the message. For example, as shown in figure 7.3, if you create the electronic equivalent of a check (let's refer to it as an *e-check*) using your digital signature and submit it to a merchant for buying goods/ services over the web, your merchant's application may inadvertently modify the byte sequence in the e-check when it parses your request XML, extracts the e-check, and serializes it back into bytes for submission to the bank. In figure 7.3, observe that the e-check element lost line breaks and whitespace characters after the merchant's application reserialized it. This transformation happens because XML syntax allows quite a few variations when serializing a document. So, in order to make sure that these variations do not result in failure to veriy signatures, we need to lay down one standard way of serializing an XML document when signing and verifying signatures. The XML canonicalization specifications fulfill this need. We will describe them in section 7.1.2. For now, let's move on to the next challenge in signing XML.

The need for signing selected elements in an XML document

We often need to sign selected elements in a given XML document as opposed to signing the whole document. There are several reasons for signing only a part of an XML message. Figure 7.3 illustrates one of these reasons. When multiple parties are involved in a message exchange, different parts of a message may be intended for different parties. For example the buyer needs to sign the e-check separately, as the bank gets to see only the e-check and not the rest of the message. Another reason for signing only a part of message is performance. In some situations, we may not want to incur the cost of signing the complete message.

The need for communicating metadata on signatures

When signing XML messages such as SOAP requests, we need to communicate metainformation about signatures, preferably in the very XML message that was signed. For example, we would like to let the recipient know which portions of the message are signed and with what keys. It is helpful if this information can be represented as an XML fragment that can be added to the original document to create a signed document.

The need for representing signatures using XML

If what is being signed is XML, as is often the case in web services, it makes sense to represent the signature as well using XML. Further, we might want to represent a signature as XML even if what is being signed is not XML. For example, if a SOAP message involves attachments (yes, SOAP messages can have attachments besides the XML Envelope we have seen so far; we will discuss attachments in appendix C), we may want to sign the contents of some of the attachments and represent the signature value in XML.

Observe that none of these additional challenges are related to the principles of signing a message; these challenges are all unique to signing XML. We will explicitly describe here how the first of these challenges can be addressed; you will see for yourself how the rest can be easily addressed when we introduce the XML Signature standard in section 7.2. We will focus now on the solution for the first and toughest of these challenges: standardizing (or canonicalizing) how XML is serialized so that two syntactically equivalent XML documents produce the same signature.

7.1.2 XML canonicalization

As we just discussed, XML syntax allows a few variations when serializing a document, and this poses a fundamental challenge in the use of signatures to detect tampering of XML messages. The solution to this challenge comes from the XML canonicalization specification, which discusses each possible variation in XML syntax and proposes a transformation that will convert any well-formed XML document into one "standard" serialized representation. This transformation is known as canonicalization or *c14n* (there are 14 letters between the first letter and the last).

Mathematically speaking, you can think of canonicalization as a transformation of an XML document. It takes a well-formed XML document and produces a syntactically equivalent XML document that is standard in the sense that any further canonicalization results in the same document. As shown in figure 7.4, if we were

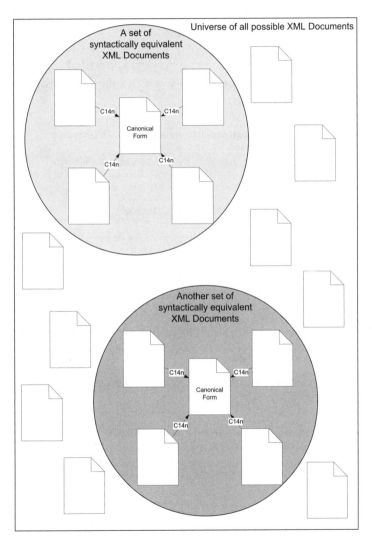

Figure 7.4 XML canonicalization (c14n) process divides the universe of all possible XML documents into sets of syntactically equivalent documents. Each such set can be represented by a canonical form to which every member of that set can be reduced using the canonicalization process.

to take all possible XML documents, the canonicalization process would divide them into equivalent sets, each of which can be represented by the canonical forms or standard representations.

There are several ways to describe how a canonical XML document is obtained from an XML document. Here, we are going to show a set of rewrite rules that produce a canonical form when you keep applying them to an XML document until you cannot produce any further changes. These rewrite rules also have some special properties. You can apply them in any order; you will always end up with the same canonical form. And, the process always terminates in a finite number of steps. Table 7.1 presents these rewrite rules.

Table 7.1   Canonicalization scheme for each possible variation in an XML document

Possible variations	Canonicalization
Character encoding	Convert to UTF-8 if any other encoding is used.
Character sequence used for line breaks	Standardize to #xA (line feed).
Optional XML declaration	Remove.
Optional DTD declaration	Remove.
Character references	Expand character references. For example, replace A with A, B with B, etc.
Use of CDATA sections rather than escaping special characters	Replace all CDATA sections with the equivalent character content, replacing special characters with character references.
Use of empty element tags (such as `<a/>`) rather than a start/end tag pair (such as `<a></a>`)	Replace all empty element tags with a start/end tag pair.
Whitespace within tags (for example, `< a >` or `< /a >`)	Remove.
Whitespace before the root element and after the end of the document	Remove.
Whitespace in element content	Retain.
Choice of quotation marks (' or ") to delimit attribute values	Use double quotes to delimit all attribute values.

continued on next page

Table 7.1 **Canonicalization scheme for each possible variation in an XML document** *(continued)*

Possible variations	Canonicalization
Attribute values	Use attribute value normalization defined in XML specification. Specifically: Expand character references. Replace each tab, line feed, and carriage return with a space. Expand entity references and repeat steps 1, 2, and 3 on the replacement text. If the attribute value is declared by a DTD to be anything other than CDATA (character data), remove leading and trailing spaces and replace sequences of whitespace characters with a single space. If a DTD is not available (as in SOAP messages), attribute values are assumed to be CDATA. Replace all special characters (such as &, <, and ") with character references (such as `&amp;`, `&lt;`, and `&quot;` respectively).
Default attributes	Add all missing attributes for which default values are available.
Attribute order	Sort attributes by their namespace URI (not prefixes) and local names in lexicographically ascending order. Attributes in no namespace come first. Namespace nodes (of the form `xmlns:...=...`) come before other attributes, and the default namespace node (`xmlns=...`) comes first.
Namespace declarations	See subsection "Inclusive and exclusive canonicalization" for a detailed description, as canonicalization of namespace declarations is quite an involved task.

The rewrite rules in table 7.1 are all simple. They may be tedious to apply, but they are straightforward. There is one remaining variation for which we haven't yet described a rewrite rule: variation in namespace declarations (the last row in table 7.1). For reasons we will describe shortly, there is no perfect way to rewrite namespace declarations when canonicalizing an XML document. In fact, there are two different possibilities for rewriting namespaces, as described next.

Inclusive and exclusive canonicalization

Canonicalization of XML documents without namespaces is easy as the rewrite rules can attest. Let us now examine how namespaces complicate canonicalization.

Consider the task of canonicalizing namespace declarations in the *entirety of an XML document*. What are the possible variations in namespace declarations that canonicalization should address? Prefixes bound to namespaces may vary, there may be superfluous namespace declarations, and namespace declarations on each element may appear in any order.

We can take the following simple approach to these issues.

1   We do not change the prefix names at all. If this means that we treat two identical documents using different namespace prefixes as different, so be it. There are very good reasons why this is the right approach. If one part of the document refers to another using an XPath expression, it is very likely that we will break the reference when rewriting prefixes.

2   We eliminate all superfluous namespace declarations. We remove a namespace prefix binding on an element if the same binding (that is, a binding with same prefix and same namespace URI) is in scope for its immediate parent element.

3   We order namespace declarations using the same rules that we described in table 7.1 for ordering attributes.

These rewrite rules for namespace declarations, combined with the rules in table 7.1, produce a unique canonical form for any XML document, regardless of the order in which they are applied.

Signing the entirety of an XML document may not be what we need in some applications. For example, if we are sending a SOAP message that contains an e-check, we may want to sign only the e-check element. In that case, we need to sign a single element of an XML document. Therefore, we need to define how to canonicalize a single element.

Let us take a look at an example from chapter 2.

```
<soapenv:Envelope
 xmlns:soapenv="http://schemas.xmlsoap.org/soap/envelope/"
 xmlns:xsd="http://www.w3.org/2001/XMLSchema"
 xmlns:xsi="http://www.w3.org/2001/XMLSchema-instance">
 <soapenv:Body>
  <ns1:getQuoteResponse
     soapenv:encodingStyle="http://schemas.xmlsoap.org/soap/encoding/"
     xmlns:ns1="http://manning.com/xmlns/samples/soasecimpl">
     <quote xsi:type="xsd:float">103.25</quote>
  </ns1:getQuoteResponse>
 </soapenv:Body>
</soapenv:Envelope>
```

In this document, say we want to canonicalize the namespace declarations for the quote element. The simplest choice is to canonicalize the whole document and just pick out the quote element. As there are no superfluous namespace declarations in this example and as namespaces declarations for each element are already in the right order, this process would yield:

```
<quote xsi:type="xsd:float">103.25</quote>
```

This simple mechanism is not suitable for our purpose. If the `quote` element is signed in this form, a man in the middle can change the namespace URIs bound to `xsi` and `xsd` prefixes without getting detected. But that is a clear violation of the `quote` element's integrity, as the element derives some of its semantics from the namespace bindings for `xsi` and `xsd` prefixes. Ideally, the canonical form for the namespace declarations on the `quote` element should look like this:

```
<quote
  xmlns:xsd="http://www.w3.org/2001/XMLSchema"
  xmlns:xsi="http://www.w3.org/2001/XMLSchemainstance"
  xsi:type="xsd:float">
  103.25
</quote>
```

How do we get to this canonical form of namespace declarations? As we have shown, we cannot get this with simple selection from a canonical XML document. Since namespace declarations for `xsi` and `xsd` prefixes are inherited, we somehow should get the right declarations from the ancestor elements. It turns out that this is not easy. Instead, we have two imperfect solutions for this problem, shown in figure 7.5.

In the first solution, we blindly include all the name space declarations that are in scope, whether or not they are used. This scheme is known as *inclusive canonicalization* or simply XML canonicalization. It is identified by the URI `http://www.w3.org/TR/2001/REC-xml-c14n-20010315`. For example, the previous `quote` element, under this canonicalization, will appear as follows:

```
<quote
  xmlns:ns1="http://manning.com/xmlns/samples/soasecimpl"
  xmlns:soapenv="http://schemas.xmlsoap.org/soap/envelope/"
  xmlns:xsd="http://www.w3.org/2001/XMLSchema"
  xmlns:xsi="http://www.w3.org/2001/XMLSchema-instance"
  xsi:type="xsd:float">103.25</quote>
```

In the other solution, *exclusive canonicalization* (identified by the URI `http://www.w3.org/2001/10/xml-exc-c14n#`), only those namespace prefixes that are used on elements and attributes in the document subset being canonicalized are included, along with any nonempty default namespace declaration in scope on the root of the document subset. So, in our example, exclusive canonicalization of namespace declarations would yield the following:

```
<quote
  xmlns:xsi="http://www.w3.org/2001/XMLSchema-instance"
  xsi:type="xsd:float">
  103.25
</quote>
```

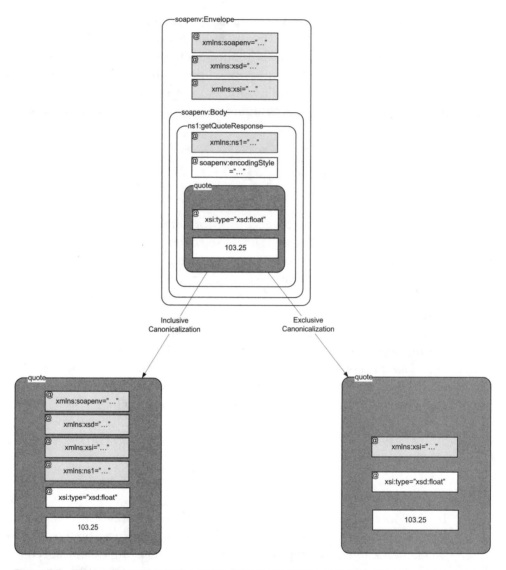

Figure 7.5 Two possible schemes for canonicalizing namespace declarations on the quote element. In the first scheme, called inclusive canonicalization, all namespace declarations in scope for the quote element are included. In the second scheme, exclusive canonicalization, only those namespace prefixes that are used on quote and its descendant nodes (such as `xsi:type attribute` in this example) are included.

Both canonicalization schemes clearly have drawbacks. The drawback in exclusive canonicalization is apparent in our example; we will describe that first. We lost track of the URI bound to the xsd prefix. An attacker can redefine the namespace URI bound to the xsd prefix without getting caught. The solution people have adopted is to provide the exclusive canonicalization algorithm with an additional list of prefixes to be included using the <exclc14n:InclusiveNamespaces Prefix-List="prefix1 prefix2 ... prefixn"/> parameter. This solution will result in the inclusion of listed prefixes even if they are not used as element/attribute prefixes in the canonicalized document subset. The problem with this is that you cannot compute all the required namespaces dynamically.

What is wrong with inclusive canonicalization? It suffers from a different drawback: It is very fragile. If we add a namespace declaration to any ancestor, it changes the canonical form of the element, too. Let's say we create a digest of the quote element in its inclusive canonical form. The digest value thus computed is very fragile, as any change (even a harmless addition) in the namespace declarations of the quote element's ancestors (such as the SOAP Envelope or Body elements) will also mean a change in the inclusive canonical form of quote. For example, if we add a wsu:Id to the Body element carrying the quote, the namespace binding of the wsu prefix will get added to the inclusive canonical form of quote, as shown in figure 7.6.

This excessive dependence on context is undesirable for canonicalization of elements in a SOAP message. We will see in part III that a SOAP message may pass through multiple applications, each of which may modify different parts of the envelope. We will also see that there is a frequent need to extract some elements (SAML assertions, in particular) and their digest values from one message and embed them in another. All these requirements mean that digest values keep changing, invalidating the signatures.

NOTE *The xml:id specification breaks inclusive canonicalization further* Inclusive canonicalization is broken in one other way. A few standard attributes such as xml:lang and xml:space have been defined over the years in the reserved xml namespace. The xml:lang attribute can be used to identify the human language used in contents and attribute values of any element in a document. The xml:space attribute can be used to indicate how whitespace in the element's content should be handled. Both of these attributes are inherited by descendents of the element on which they are set unless explicitly overridden. As all standard attributes defined in the xml namespace behaved similarly at the time inclusive

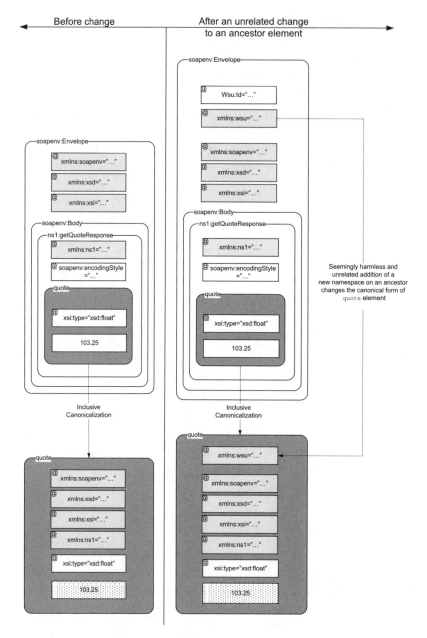

Figure 7.6   A demonstration of how fragile inclusive canonicalization can be.
A seemingly innocuous and unrelated change—addition of a `wsu:id` attribute to
the `Envelope` element, an ancestor of `quote`—changes the canonical form of the
`quote` element.

canonicalization was being standardized, it was wrongly assumed that all attributes in the `xml` namespace would be scoped the same way. The spec for inclusive canonicalization declares that the nearest occurrences of attributes in the `xml` namespace must be included on the root of the canonicalized document subset, unless they are already present. This assumption is being broken by the recent `xml:id` specification.

The `xml:id` attribute can be used to set an identifier on any XML element without the need for a DTD or schema (just like `wsu:Id` defined by WS-Security). Obviously, it would be wrong to propagate the nearest identifier onto the canonicalized document subset root.

This is less of an issue in WS-Security–based applications, as `wsu:Id` is used as an identifier rather than `xml:id`.

As you may have realized, neither inclusive nor exclusive canonicalization come anywhere near solving the problem of variation in namespace declarations. In any given situation, one needs to pick the better scheme, based on the knowledge one has about the situation. We will visit the question of which canonicalization algorithm to prefer under what circumstances later in section 7.3 when we discuss practical issues in signatures.

We started this section by identifying the challenges in signing XML. Of the challenges we identified, the most fundamental is in producing the same signature when two syntactically equivalent XML documents are signed. You now know how to use XML canonicalization to overcome this challenge (modulo the difficulty in canonicalizing namespace declarations). We will now move on to addressing the rest of the challenges we identified earlier by explaining how the XML Signature and WS-Security specifications standardize the way we sign SOAP messages.

7.2 *Signing SOAP messages*

Let's get back to the focus of this chapter: the use of digital signatures to verify the integrity of messages. As we discussed in the previous section, signing XML documents such as SOAP messages is more complicated than signing an arbitrary message. In addition to using XML canonicalization to cancel variations in XML syntax, we need to worry about:

- How we can represent the signature and its metadata within the signed XML document itself
- How we can sign selected parts of an XML document as opposed to signing its entirety.

In this section, we will address these two issues. In particular, we will discuss:

- The elements defined by the XML Signature and WS-Security specifications for standardizing the use of signatures in SOAP

- The usage of Apache XML Security Library and JAX-RPC handlers to sign SOAP messages and verify the integrity of signed SOAP messages

Let's start with an example that shows how SOAP messages are signed.

7.2.1 *Example: Signing order creation request*

In this example, a brokerage customer digitally signs his request to create a market order. Table 6.2 provides instructions for running the example.[1]

Once you run the example, inspect the SOAP request message captured by `tcpmon` to understand how the sender is signing his market order. You will see the message structure shown in figure 7.7.

The structure of the signed message is a little too complex to understand at first sight. We drill down into the signed request so that you can understand its structure.

Table 7.2   Steps to run the example that illustrates selective signing of SOAP message elements

Step	Action	How to
1	Set up your environment.	If you have not already set up the environment required to run the examples in this book, please refer to chapter 2 to do so. `ant deploy` installs all the examples.
2	If it is not already running, start TCP monitor.	Run `ant tcpmon` so that you can observe the conversation. Check the "XML Format" check box to allow `tcpmon` to format shown requests and responses.
3	Run the example.	Run `ant demo -Dexample.id=5`. You should be able to view the request-response messages as they are captured in the `tcpmon` console.

---

[1] One or more known issues in Apache Axis 1.x prevent this example from running successfully. See appendix A for a description of these issues.

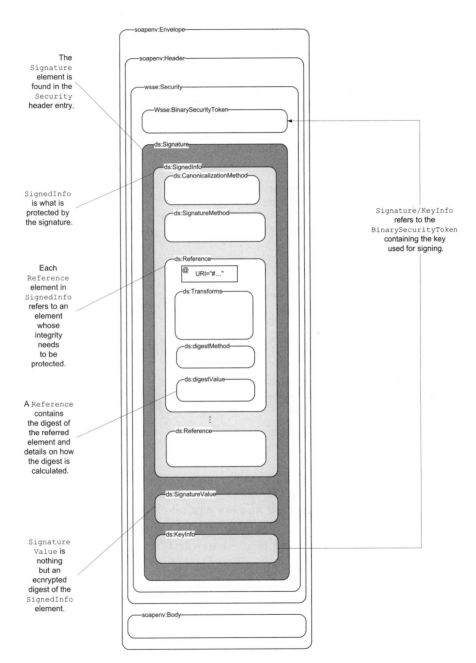

The
`Signature`
element is
found in the
`Security`
header entry.

`SignedInfo`
is what is
protected by
the signature.

Each
`Reference`
element in
`SignedInfo`
refers to an
element
whose
integrity
needs
to be
protected.

A `Reference`
contains
the digest of
the referred
element and
details on how
the digest is
calculated.

`Signature`
`Value` is
nothing
but an
ecnrypted
digest of the
`SignedInfo`
element.

`Signature/KeyInfo`
refers to the
`BinarySecurityToken`
containing the key
used for signing.

soapenv:Envelope

soapenv:Header

wsse:Security

Wsse:BinarySecurityToken

ds:Signature

ds:SignedInfo
ds:CanonicalizationMethod

ds:SignatureMethod

ds:Reference

@ URI="#..."

ds:Transforms

ds:digestMethod

ds:digestValue

ds:Reference

ds:SignatureValue

ds:KeyInfo

soapenv:Body

Figure 7.7 **High-level overview of an XML signature used to protect the integrity of a SOAP message.**

Structure of a signed SOAP message

In listing 7.1 we start by examining the signed message at a high level, without going into details of the `Signature` element.

Listing 7.1   Example of a signed SOAP message

```
<soapenv:Envelope ...>

  <soapenv:Header>
    <wsse:Security ...>

      <wsse:BinarySecurityToken
        ValueType="...#X509PKIPathv1"
        EncodingType="...#Base64Binary"
        wsu:Id="SignatureKey-2478770"
        xmlns:wsu="...utility-1.0.xsd">
        ...
      </wsse:BinarySecurityToken>

      <ds:Signature xmlns:ds=".../xmldsig#">
        ...
      </ds:Signature>

    </wsse:Security>
  </soapenv:Header>
  <soapenv:Body wsu:Id="Signed-2478770-0"
    xmlns:wsu="...utility-1.0.xsd">
    <ns1:createMarketOrder ...>
      ...
    </ns1:createMarketOrder>
  </soapenv:Body>
</soapenv:Envelope>
```

❶ WS-Security header

❷ Sender's certificate chain

❸ Signature

❹ Signed SOAP body with order creation request

Just as we did for authentication and encryption elements, a WS-Security header ❶ is used as the container for signature related information.

A `BinarySecurityToken` ❷ is used to carry the sender's certificate chain (explained in section 6.2.2). This certificate chain securely provides the sender's public key to anyone who wishes to verify the signature made by the sender. We have used a `BinarySecurityToken` once before; we used it in chapter 5 to carry a Kerberos service ticket. To indicate that the enclosed token is an X.509 certificate chain (packaged in the `PKIPath` format), the `ValueType` attribute is set here to a URI defined by WS-Security's X.509 Certificate Token Profile. The `Encoding-Type` attribute is set to indicate that the embedded (binary) certificate chain is base64-encoded. In addition, an identifier is set using the `wsu:Id` attribute so that we can refer to this token from within the `Signature` element.

The `Signature` element ❸ carries all the information on what is signed, how it is signed, and what the signature value is. It is defined in a namespace standardized by the XML Signature specification. We will look at what goes into this element later.

The SOAP body ❹ containing the order creation request is what we sign in this example. A `wsu:Id` attribute is set on the SOAP body so we can refer to it from within the `Signature` element.

Now let's look at what goes into the `Signature` element.

Structure of a Signature element

The `Signature` element consists of three child elements, as shown in listing 7.2.

Listing 7.2   Outline of a `signature` entry in the WS-Security header

```
<ds:Signature>
  <ds:SignedInfo>              ❶ This is what
    ...                           is signed
  </ds:SignedInfo>

  <ds:SignatureValue>          ❷ Signature value: encrypted
    ...                           digest of SignedInfo
  </ds:SignatureValue>

  <ds:KeyInfo>                 ❸ Info on key
    ...                           used to sign
  </ds:KeyInfo>
</ds:Signature>
```

The `SignedInfo` element ❶ is actually what is signed. But didn't we say we were going to sign the SOAP body containing the order creation request? Yes, we did, but what happens in reality is we sign the `SignedInfo` element and that in turn contains the digest values for all the elements we really want to protect using the signature. In this case, we want to protect the integrity of the entire SOAP `Body` element, and the `SignedInfo` element contains the digest value of the `Body` element. We will show you the contents of `SignedInfo` shortly.

The `SignatureValue` element ❷, as the name suggests, is where the value of the signature is. As you should understand by now, a signature is nothing but an encrypted digest of what is signed (the `SignedInfo` element, as we just said). Because the encrypted digest is binary data that cannot be embedded in XML as is, the encrypted digest is included in the `SignatureValue` element using base64 encoding.

The `KeyInfo` element ❸ provides information on the key that can be used to verify the signature. We will return to a discussion of `KeyInfo` shortly. We will first look at the contents of the `SignedInfo` element ❶.

Structure of a SignedInfo element

When we dig deeper into the contents of `SignedInfo` element, we see something like listing 7.3.

Listing 7.3 Example of `SignedInfo` element in a signature

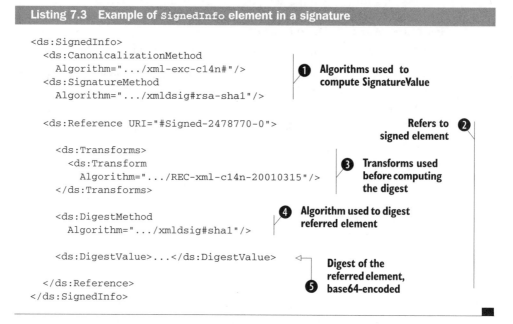

```
<ds:SignedInfo>
  <ds:CanonicalizationMethod
    Algorithm=".../xml-exc-c14n#"/>            ❶ Algorithms used to
  <ds:SignatureMethod                             compute SignatureValue
    Algorithm=".../xmldsig#rsa-sha1"/>

  <ds:Reference URI="#Signed-2478770-0">              Refers to ❷
                                                   signed element
    <ds:Transforms>
      <ds:Transform                            ❸ Transforms used
        Algorithm=".../REC-xml-c14n-20010315"/>    before computing
    </ds:Transforms>                               the digest

    <ds:DigestMethod                           ❹ Algorithm used to digest
      Algorithm=".../xmldsig#sha1"/>              referred element

    <ds:DigestValue>...</ds:DigestValue>        Digest of the
                                                referred element,
  </ds:Reference>                             ❺ base64-encoded
</ds:SignedInfo>
```

`SignedInfo` essentially answers the questions: What is protected by the signature, and how?

In listing 7.3, you can see that the "how" question is answered first. The first two child elements of `SignedInfo`, `CanonicalizationMethod` and `SignatureMethod` ❶, define the processing used to arrive at the `SignatureValue`. It is important to include these as part of `SignedInfo`; otherwise, an attacker can deceive the recipient into using weaker algorithms than the ones used by the sender.

The rest of `SignedInfo` is simply a collection of one or more `Reference` elements ❷ that are used to specify "what" is secured against tampering. The URI attribute on a Reference element is used to indicate what is being secured. In this example, we are using the #Id (fragment identifier) syntax to refer to an element in the current document using its ID. Refer to listing 7.1 and you will see that the ID Signed-2478770-0 identifies the Body element in the SOAP message. It is perfectly possible to refer to external resources using absolute URIs, but that would usually not be the case when we are using signatures to check tampering of SOAP messages.

How are elements identified by Reference elements protected by the signature? Every Reference element contains the digest ❹, ❺ of the referred element. Because all Reference elements are part of the SignedInfo that is protected by the signature, the contents of elements identified by Reference elements are indirectly protected.

When computing the digest of an element referred to by a Reference element, some amount of preprocessing may be necessary before the digest is computed. For example, canonicalization needs to happen if the referred resource is an XML fragment. (Note that we are talking about canonicalization of the resource being digested, as opposed to the canonicalization of SignedInfo. The latter is what we discussed in ❶). The Transforms element ❸ in Reference allows one or more transformations to be applied to the resource's content before it is digested. The transformations happen in a pipeline, with the output of a transform feeding the input for the next transform. The first transform is fed the content retrieved by resolving the referred URI. The output of the last transform is fed to the digester to compute the digest value.

Now that you understand the structure of SignedInfo element, let's take a look at KeyInfo, the other element in Signature that we promised to discuss in depth.

Structure of a KeyInfo element

Before we take a look at a sample KeyInfo element, let's recall why it is needed by looking it at the steps a receiver needs to take in order to validate a signature.

1 Verify that the information in SignedInfo is consistent with the rest of the message. Recall that SignedInfo contains the digests of the elements the signature is intended to protect. The receiver of a message needs to verify that these elements have not been tampered with. This can be done by taking each Reference in SignedInfo and going through the same computations as the sender did: applying the same series of transformations on the referred element and using the same digest algorithm to

produce the digest. Since all the information needed to verify the digests is already in the `Reference` element, the receiver can verify without any a priori arrangement with the sender.

2   Verify that `SignedInfo` itself has not been tampered with. For this, the signature on the entirety of `SignedInfo` needs to be verified using the canonicalization and signature algorithms specified in `SignedInfo`. It is easy to do the canonicalization given the algorithm, which is specified in the `SignedInfo` element. But, how does a receiver verify the signature? If you recall, a signature is nothing but an encrypted digest of what was signed. The receiver can recompute the digest of `SignedInfo` and compare the result with the digest provided by the sender. Before he can do that, he needs to decrypt the digest in the signature. For this, the receiver needs a key to use for this purpose. The `KeyInfo` child element under `Signature` provides information on the key (certificate for PKI-based signatures; shared secret for MACs) that can be used to verify the signature.

Now, take a look at listing 7.4 and what the `KeyInfo` element contains in our example.

Listing 7.4   Example of `KeyInfo` element in a signature

```
<ds:KeyInfo>
  <wsse:SecurityTokenReference>
    <wsse:Reference URI="#SignatureKey-2478770"/>      Reference to a
  </wsse:SecurityTokenReference>                    ❶ security token
</ds:KeyInfo>
```

Let's look at the use of `SecurityTokenReference` in `KeyInfo`. We have already seen one kind of `SecurityTokenReference` in the previous chapter. There, we needed to unambiguously refer to the *receiver's* certificate, from which the sender took the public key to encrypt a message. Since a receiver can have any number of certificates, that reference tells the receiver which private key to use to decrypt. The need here is different. In this case, the sender needs to:

1   Provide a mechanism for the receiver to verify that the message has not been tampered with.

2   Provide his identity to the receiver in a verifiable way.

Both goals can be achieved if the sender somehow provides a certificate that proves the identity of the sender as well as provides a public key for use in signature verification. That means the certificate referred to is the *sender's*. That is the essential difference from the previous chapter.

If the receiver already has access to the sender's certificate, possibly in a key store, the sender can use the same mechanism as in the encryption example—simply refer to the certificate using the issuer name and serial number. Generally, where a prior trust relationship may not exist between the sender and the receiver, the sender has to send a certificate issued by a CA that is trusted by the receiver. Alternately, the sender can also attach a chain of certificates that ends in a certificate signed by a CA trusted by the receiver.

In listing 7.4 we see that a `wsse:Reference` ❶ (not to be confused with the `ds:Reference` we saw under `SignedInfo`) is used to refer to a security token embedded in the same message with the given ID, `SignatureKey-2478770`. If you revisit the message outline shown in listing 7.1, you will notice that this ID belongs to a `BinarySecurityToken` containing the sender's certificate chain. (Other ways of referring to the sender's certificate chain are possible. See the WS-Security X.509 Certificate Token Profile specification for a detailed list.)

You now know all the elements that go into a `Signature` in a SOAP message. This is a good time to take a look back at figure 7.6 and compare what's shown in that figure with what you have learned in this section.

We will now look at the code that went into this example. Figure 7.8 shows an overview of the implementation.

Figure 7.8 should look very similar to what you have seen in previous chapters. On the client-side we have a `SigningHandler` that is responsible for signing, and on the server-side we have a `ServerSideWSSecurityHandler`[2] that is responsible for verifying the signature.

Just as in previous chapters, we will dig into the details on the client- and server-sides separately. To emphasize that the signing and signature verification logic in the handlers shown here will switch sides when we discuss signing of response messages (messages originating from the server-side and addressed to the client-side), we will use the terms *sender-side* and *receiver-side* instead of client-side and server-side. We will discuss the sender-side first.

---

[2] You might be wondering why we didn't name the server-side handler `SignatureVerification-Handler`. We will clarify this when we discuss the implementation of this handler.

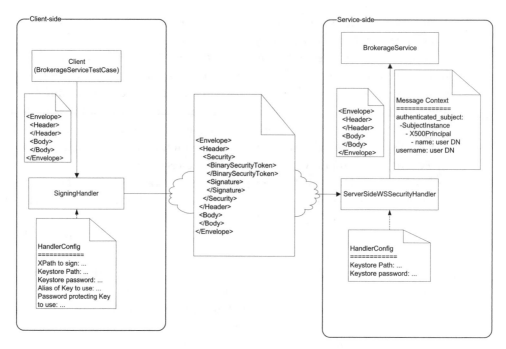

Figure 7.8 **Overview of the example implementation of signatures to guard the integrity of a SOAP request.**

7.2.2 Sender-side implementation

So far in this chapter, you have seen how SOAP messages can be signed. Now, let's see the Java code that can be used on the sender's side to create a signature. As shown in figure 7.8, the job of signing a message is taken up by the `Signing-Handler`, which we will discuss now. The code for this handler can be found in `example5/SigningHandler.java` at http://www.manning.com/kanneganti.

Handler intialization

The `SigningHandler` is initialized with information on which direction to sign in (request/response), what to sign, and what keys to use. Just as we did in `Encryption-Handler`, the message elements to protect with a signature are specified using an XPath expression. Key information needed for signing is retrieved from a key store. This information includes the private key used in signing and the certificate chain carrying the associated public key.

When initializing the handler, the XPath of elements to protect the parameters needed to retrieve the key information—the alias of the key pair and the password protecting the private key—are obtained as configuration parameters.[3] In previous chapters, you saw the code to initialize a handler using configuration information, so we will not be showing it here. Look up the init method in the source if you would like understand it in detail.

There is one additional step that we did not do before. Once we retrieve the certificate chain carrying the public key of the sender, we need to encode it in bytes that we can embed in a WS-Security BinarySecurityToken element. The Java Certification Path API defined in the java.security.cert package comes in handy here, as shown in listing 7.5.

Listing 7.5   Encoding a certification path for use in a signature element

```
Certificate[] ourCertificateChain =                           ❶
    keyStore.getCertificateChain(ourKeyAlias);
CertPath ourCertificationPath = CertificateFactory.getInstance  ❷
    (Constants.X509_CERTIFICATE_TYPE).
    generateCertPath(Arrays.asList(ourCertificateChain));

byte[] ourCertPathBytes =                                      ❸
    ourCertificationPath.getEncoded ("PkiPath");
ourBase64EncodedCertPath = new String                         ❹
    (Base64.encodeBase64(ourCertPathBytes), "US-ASCII");
```

Facilities for encoding a certificate chain are provided by the CertPath class. So, we will first create a CertPath instance ❷ using the chain of certificates we retrieve from a key store ❶. As CertPath is an abstract base class, it does not provide a public constructor. Each implementation of Java Cryptography Architecture (JCA), called the cryptographic service provider, will provide its own implementation of the CertPath. We can use the services provided by a CertificateFactory to locate and construct the appropriate instance of the class implementing CertPath.

With a CertPath instance in hand, we can encode the certificate chain. We use the PKIPath encoding scheme here ❸ as recommended by the WS-Security X.509 Certificate Token Profile. As PKIPath is a binary encoding scheme, we need to further encode the bytes produced in the previous step using base64 encoding ❹.

---

[3] If the SigningHandler is intended for use in an interactive client application, it helps to use a JAAS KeyStoreLoginModule to prompt the user for key pair alias and password. See chapter 4 for details on JAAS.

Signing a message

Just like EncryptionHandler and DecryptionHandler, SigningHandler can work in both directions. That is, it can sign parts of a request or parts of a response. So, the first thing to do in the handleRequest or handleResponse method is determine if the SigningHandler is configured to sign in the current direction (request/response) or not. We saw that code in the previous chapter.

Once the handler determines that it should sign parts of the message in the current direction, it needs to complete the steps in table 7.3 in order to get the envelope to the signed form shown in listing 7.1.

Table 7.3 Steps to sign select parts of a message

Step	Action
1	Determine the elements to sign.
2	Make sure that all elements to sign have an Id attribute set so that we can refer to them using fragment URIs in SignedInfo References.
3	Insert a Security header targeted at the target actor unless it is already present in the envelope.
4	Prepend a Signature element to the Security header.
5	Prepend a BinarySecurityToken to the Security header and embed the certificate path we have encoded in the init method (listing 7.5) for use here.
6	Add KeyInfo to the Signature element.
7	Add a Reference to each of the elements to sign in SignedInfo. Compute and fill in the digest values for each of the elements.
8	Compute the signature value on the prepared SignedInfo element and fill in the SignatureValue element under Signature.

Note that the order in which we execute these activities is very important considering the following:

- Any changes we make to the envelope should happen before we start computing the digest and signature values. Otherwise, we may ourselves be invalidating the digests and the signature.

- Prepending BinarySecurityToken after prepending Signature to the Security element allows for better performance during signature verification. By the time the receiver looks at KeyInfo/Reference in Signature, it would already have seen the BinarySecurityToken, and hence it would not need to search the entire envelope for the token to resolve the reference.

- SignedInfo should be completely filled in before SignatureValue can be computed.

Some of the steps shown here, such as figuring out the elements to sign by evaluating an XPath expression (step 1) and inserting a Security header entry for the target actor (step 3) are very similar to steps shown in EncryptionHandler and elsewhere. We will skip describing those steps here and focus on the rest of the procedure (steps 4-8). We'll also skip the simple task of iterating over all elements to sign, checking if an ID is available on each, and setting one in case there isn't one (step 2). We will start with step 4, in which we prepend a Signature element to the Security header.

Creating a signature element (step 4)

We have seen the utility of XMLCipher and related classes provided by the Apache XML Security library in the previous chapter. In this chapter, we will rely on XMLSignature and related classes defined in the same library. Just as XMLCipher did for encryption, XMLSignature provides Java APIs to create, parse, and manipulate the contents of the XML elements required to implement signatures.

The Apache XML Security library requires that its initialization method, org.apache.xml.security.Init.init(), be called before any of its classes can be used. Just as we did in EncryptionHandler, we use a static initializer block in SigningHandler to accomplish this.

The code snippet in listing 7.6 creates a Signature element and prepends it to the WS-Security header entry.

Listing 7.6 Creating a signature element and prepending it to the WS-Security header. The signature is not fully filled in.

```
XMLSignature xmlSignature = new XMLSignature
   (soapPart,
    "",                                                    ❶
    signatureAlgo,
    Canonicalizer. ALGO_ID_C14N_EXCL_OMIT_COMMENTS);

securityElement.insertBefore                               ❷
(xmlSignature.getElement(), securityElement.getFirstChild());
```

In this code, we first construct an XMLSignature instance ❶ using the following arguments:

1 The first argument to the constructor is the DOM `Document` instance we will be creating the signature elements in.

2 The second argument is the base URI to prepend to all relative URIs. In our case, we do not need any of the relative URIs such as fragment identifiers to be interpreted relative to any external URI, so we will simply pass the empty string as base URI.

3 The third argument is the signature algorithm to use. The `signatureAlgo` value is set at initialization time to the configured value; if none is set, it defaults to `XMLSignature.ALGO_ID_SIGNATURE_RSA_SHA1`.

4 The fourth and final argument is the canonicalization algorithm to use when signing `SignedInfo`. We use exclusive c14n, as it will make the `SignatureValue` more robust to changes (such as additional namespace bindings on the SOAP envelope) that should not break the signature. As we are generating `SignedInfo` programmatically, there aren't going to be any comments in it. So we let the c14n algorithm omit comments.

Once the `XMLSignature` instance is available, we obtain the DOM element underlying the instance and add it as the first element in the WS-Security header ❷.

Why prepend instead of appending the `Signature` element to the `Security` header entry? Say we are signing a message that is partially encrypted. The receiver needs to know that the signature should be verified before decryption is attempted. By prepending the `Signature` element, we let the receiver see the `Signature` element before the currently existing elements (such as an `Encrypted-Key`) in the security header entry.[4]

Let us now look at the code for next step (step 5 in table 7.3) in the sender-side implementation. In this step, we will be prepending the sender's certification path to the `Security` header entry as a `BinarySecurityToken` element.

Adding the certification path as a BinarySecurityToken (step 5)

Looking back at listing 7.1, we see that we need to prepend our certification path to the `Security` header entry using a `BinarySecurityToken` element. We repeat here, for convenience, the structure of the `BinarySecurityToken` we need to create and prepend to the `Security` header entry.

---

[4] We can communicate the order of operations to the receiver using other conventions as well, but the standards suggest this one, as it allows efficient implementations.

```
<wsse:BinarySecurityToken
  ValueType="...#X509PKIPathv1"
  EncodingType="...#Base64Binary"
  wsu:Id="SignatureKey-2478770"
  xmlns:wsu="...utility-1.0.xsd">
  ...
</wsse:BinarySecurityToken>
```

We have already seen in listing 7.5 how to encode the sender's certification path using PkiPath and base64 encodings. All that's left is to see how we can embed the encoded bytes as the content of the BinarySecurityToken element. Listing 7.7 shows this.

> **Listing 7.7 Creating and adding a `BinarySecurityToken` that contains the sender's certification path to the `Security` header entry**

```
private Element buildCertPathBST                           ❶ Creates a BST with
    (SOAPPart soapPart, String wsuIdForCertificateBST) {     sender's cert path
    Element certificatePathAsBST = soapPart.createElementNS
        (Constants.WS_SECURITY_NS_URI,                       Creates BST
        Constants.WS_SECURITY_PREF_NS_PREFIX + ':' +         element
        Constants.WS_SECURITY_BINARY_TOKEN_TAG);
    certificatePathAsBST.setAttributeNS                      Sets ValueType
        (null, Constants.WS_SECURITY_VALUE_TYPE_ATTR,        attribute on
        Constants.WS_SECURITY_X509V3_CERT_CHAIN_TOKEN_TYPE); BST
    certificatePathAsBST.setAttributeNS
        (null, Constants.WS_SECURITY_ENCODING_TYPE_ATTR,     Sets EncodingType
        Constants.WS_SECURITY_BASE64_ENCODING_TYPE);         attribute on BST
    certificatePathAsBST.setAttributeNS
        (Constants.WS_UTIL_NS_URI,
        Constants.WS_UTIL_PREF_NS_PREFIX + ':' +             Sets wsu:Id
        Constants.WS_UTIL_ID_ATTR_NAME,                      attribute on BST
        wsuIdForCertificateBST);
    certificatePathAsBST.appendChild                         Sets BST
        (soapPart.createTextNode(ourBase64EncodedCertPath)); content
    return certificatePathAsBST;
}

String wsuIdForCertificateBST =                   ❷ Generates a value
    "SignatureKey-" + hashCode();                   for Wsu:Id
Element certificatePathAsBST =                      Calls the method
    buildCertPathBST(soapPart, wsuIdForCertificateBST); defined in ❶
securityElement.insertBefore
    (certificatePathAsBST,                          Prepends BST to
    securityElement.getFirstChild());               Security header entry
```

This code shows very straightforward use of DOM APIs. The only part that really needs an explanation is how we compute the Id to set on the BinarySecurityToken.

It is dynamically computed using the handler's hash code ❷ so that `Binary-SecurityToken` elements added by more than one handler instance do not end up with the same ID.

Let's now move on to the code for the next step (step 6 in table 7.3) in sender-side implementation. In this step, we will create and add a `KeyInfo` element to the `Signature` element created in step 4.

Adding KeyInfo to the signature (step 6)

We now have the Signature and `BinarySecurityToken` elements prepended to the `Security` header, as shown in listing 7.1. Now, we are ready to start filling in the content of the `Signature` element shown in listing 7.2. Let us first deal with the `KeyInfo` element. Listing 7.4 showed what we want in the `Signature`'s `KeyInfo` element. Here it is once again.

```
<ds:KeyInfo>
  <wsse:SecurityTokenReference>
    <wsse:Reference URI="#SignatureKey-2478770"/>
  </wsse:SecurityTokenReference>
</ds:KeyInfo>
```

As we have set a `wsu:Id` on the `BinarySecurityToken` we just created, we can create a `KeyInfo` element, add to it a `SecurityTokenReference` element and add to that a `wsse:Reference` pointing to the `BinarySecurityToken` using its `wsu:Id`. Listing 7.8 shows how to do this.

Listing 7.8 Populating `KeyInfo` in the `Signature` element

```
private void populateKeyInfoInXMLSignature
    (XMLSignature xmlSignature,
     String wsuIdForCertificateBST, SOAPPart soapPart) {      KeyInfo that
    KeyInfo keyInfo = xmlSignature.getKeyInfo();              should be filled in
    Element securityTokenReference =
        soapPart.createElementNS                              Creates an STR
        (Constants.WS_SECURITY_NS_URI,                        element
         Constants.WS_SECURITY_TOKEN_REF_TAG);
    Element wsseReference =
        soapPart.createElementNS                              Creates a wsse:Reference
        (Constants.WS_SECURITY_NS_URI,                        element
         Constants.WS_SECURITY_REF_TAG);
    wsseReference.setAttributeNS                  Sets Reference    Adds the
        (null, Constants.WS_SECURITY_REF_URI_ATTR,  URI to point    Reference
         "#" + wsuIdForCertificateBST);             to BST          element
    securityTokenReference.appendChild(wsseReference);                to STR
    keyInfo.addUnknownElement(securityTokenReference);      Adds STR to
}                                                            KeyInfo
```

The code in this snippet, once again, involves simple DOM API calls, as the XMLSignature instance constructed in step 4 exposes a KeyInfo element for direct manipulation. Let's now move on to the next step (step 7 in table 7.3), where we add a Reference to each of the elements that need to be protected using signatures.

Adding a reference to SignedInfo (step 7)

We now have KeyInfo, one of three children of the Signature element shown in listing 7.2, in place. We still have to fill in SignedInfo and SignatureValue. We cannot compute SignatureValue until SignedInfo is filled in. So, we will focus on SignedInfo next.

Listing 7.3 showed what goes into a SignedInfo. Of what is shown there, we already have set CanonicalizationMethod and SignatureMethod when we constructed the XMLSignature instance in listing 7.6. We just need to add a Reference element for each of the elements we want to secure using the signature, as shown in listing 7.9.

Listing 7.9 Adding a reference to each of the elements that need to be protected using signatures

```
private void addReferencesToSign
    (XMLSignature xmlSignature, NodeList nodesToSign,
    SOAPPart soapDoc) throws SOAPException,
    TransformationException, XMLSignatureException {
    int numNodes = nodesToSign.getLength();
    Element rootElement = soapDoc.getEnvelope();
    for (int i = 0; i < numNodes; ++i) {              ◄─❶
        Element ithElement = (Element) nodesToSign.item(i);
        Transforms transforms = new Transforms(soapDoc);
        if (Utils.isDescendantOf
            (xmlSignature.getElement(), ithElement)) {
            transforms.addTransform                               ❷
                (Transforms.TRANSFORM_ENVELOPED_SIGNATURE);
        }
        transforms.addTransform(c14nAlgo);

        if (rootElement.equals(ithElement)) {
            xmlSignature.addDocument("", transforms);
        } else {                                                  ❸
            xmlSignature.addDocument
                ("#"+Utils.getElementId(ithElement),
                transforms);
        }
    }
}
```

```
xmlSignature.addResourceResolver(new WsuIdResolver(soapPart));    ←—④
addReferencesToSign(xmlSignature, nodesToSign, soapPart);
```

In this listing, we define a method named `addReferencesToSign` that takes all the responsibility of populating `SignedInfo` with `References` to elements that should be protected by the signature. This method loops ❶ over the elements to protect and adds a `Reference` for each of those elements using the `addDocument` method ❸ provided by the `XMLSignature` class in Apache XML Security library.

The `addDocument` method of the `XMLSignature` class takes the identifier (URI) of a document and adds a `Reference` to it in `SignedInfo`. When adding a `Reference`, the `addDocument` method computes the digest of the referred element. We can optionally specify the transforms ❷ to apply before computing its digest. In general, we only need to apply the canonicalization algorithm the handler is configured to use. In the special case where the `Signature` element is part of the element being signed, we need to add an *enveloped signature transform*. This transform removes the signature element from the digest calculation. Why is this necessary? The mere act of setting the computed digest will invalidate the digest when the `Signature` element is part of the element being signed. It is necessary to discard the `Signature` element during digest computation. Also, notice that we set the enveloped signature transform before we set the canonicalization transform. This ordering is important. We want to canonicalize the element being signed only after we remove the `Signature` element from it. If we do it in the reverse order, it is possible that the canonical form degrades into a noncanonical form when we remove the `Signature` element.

How does `XMLSignature`'s `addDocument` method resolve the URI provided to it? We help do that with a resource resolver ❹. Apache XML Security defines a resolution service provider interface, `ResourceResolverSpi`, to implement for different URI schemes. Any number of resolvers can be set to allow different kinds of URIs to be resolved. As we are only signing elements within the signed SOAP envelope, we exclusively use fragment identifiers as URIs. We only need to set one resource resolver. The sample `ResolverFragment` class in the `org.apache.xml.security.utils.resolver.implementations` package fits our needs except for one small hitch. This resolver does not understand WS-Security–defined `wsu:Id` as an identifier. We extend it as `WsuIdResolver` and set it ❹ for use in our `XMLSignature` instance. The code for `WsuIdResolver` can be found in listing 7.10.

Listing 7.10 Extension of Apache XML Security Library's `ResolverFragment` class to resolve a `wsu:Id` identifier to an element bearing that identifier

```
public class WsuIdResolver extends ResolverFragment {
    private Document doc;

    /** Doc we will be resolving Ids in. */
    public WsuIdResolver(Document doc) {
        this.doc = doc;
    }

    public XMLSignatureInput engineResolve
        (Attr uri, String baseURI)
        throws ResourceResolverException {
        assert("".equals(baseURI));              ◁──❶

        String uriNodeValue = uri.getNodeValue();    ◁──❷
        Node selectedElem = null;
        if (uriNodeValue.equals("")) {           ❸
            selectedElem = doc;
        } else {
            String id = uriNodeValue.substring(1);   ◁──❹
            selectedElem = Utils.lookupElementById
                (doc.getDocumentElement(), id);      ❺
            if (selectedElem==null) {
                Object exArgs[] = { id };
                throw new ResourceResolverException
                    ("signature.Verification.MissingID", exArgs,
                     uri, baseURI);
            }
        }

        XMLSignatureInput result =
            new XMLSignatureInput(selectedElem);
        result.setExcludeComments(true);         ❻
        result.setMIMEType("text/xml");
        result.setSourceURI(uriNodeValue);
        return result;
    }
}
```

Here's what we do in this code. We first verify that `baseURI` is an empty string ❶, as our implementation does not support the use of base URIs. We read the URI to resolve from the given URI attribute (DOM `Node`) ❷. If the URI is an empty string, we should resolve it to the entirety of the document ❸. Otherwise, we can assume that the URI will be of the form `"#Id"` ❹. This is guaranteed, as the `engineCanResolve` method (not shown here) in the base class returns false unless the URI is an empty string (`""`) or of the `#Id` form. Now that we know the ID of the element we wish to find, we simply have to walk through the DOM tree and find the element bearing this ID ❺. We have seen this code in `DecryptionHandler` as well (when resolving `ReferenceList` in `EncryptedKey`). So, we will skip describing it in detail.

The result of ID resolution is returned in the form an `XMLSignatureInput` instance. This class encapsulates a node set or byte sequence that can be acted upon by signature transforms. Here, we construct an instance of `XMLSignature-Input` and initialize it with the element we resolved the given URI to ❻. The XML Signature specification states that comments should not be included when resolving URIs of the form `#Id` (also called *barename XPointers*).[5] So, we indicate the same in the returned `XMLSignatureInput` instance, along with the MIME type of the result and the source URI that was resolved.

We are now almost done discussing the code for `SigningHandler`. The only step we have yet to discuss from table 7.3 is step 8, where we compute the signature.

Creating the SignatureValue (step 8)

Now that `SigendInfo` is filled in, all we have to do is sign. The code for this can't be simpler!

```
xmlSignature.sign(ourKey);
```

This completes the sender-side of implementation. Let's now look at the receiver-side implementation.

7.2.3 Receiver-side implementation

For the receiver-side implementation, we enhance `DecryptionHandler`, which you saw in the last chapter, to also handle verification of signatures and rename it `ServerSideWSSecurityHandler`. Why not write a different handler as we have been doing all along? Now, we have come to a stage where the ordering of different activities on the receiving side is dependent on the contents of the received message. For example, if a sender encrypts a message after signing it, we should first decrypt and then verify the signature. We modify `DecryptionHandler` to process elements of a `Security` header entry in the order they appear. Listing 7.11 shows the part of the code in `ServerSideWSSecurityHandler` that invokes appropriate methods to process each of the elements of a `Security` header entry.

---

[5] If comments are to be retained, it suggests the use of XPointer syntax: `#xpointer(/)` instead of `""` and `#xpointer(id('Id'))` instead of `#Id`.

Listing 7.11 Code in `ServerSideWSSecurityHandler` to handle elements of a `Security` header entry in the order they appear

```
Map securityTokenCache = new HashMap();
Iterator headerEntriesIter =
    securityElement.getChildElements();
while (headerEntriesIter.hasNext()) {
    Object child = headerEntriesIter.next();
    if (!(child instanceof SOAPElement)) {         ❶
        //SOAPElement can also have TEXT children
        continue;
    }
    SOAPElement childElement = (SOAPElement) child;
    String childNamespaceURI = childElement.getNamespaceURI();
    if (EncryptionConstants.EncryptionSpecNS.
            equals(childNamespaceURI)) {           ❷
        processEncryptionEntry
            (childElement, soapContext, faultActor);
    } else if (org.apache.xml.security.utils.Constants.
            SignatureSpecNS.equals(childNamespaceURI)) {   ❸
        processSignatureEntry
            (childElement, soapContext,
             faultActor, securityTokenCache);
    } else if
        (Constants.WS_SECURITY_NS_URI.
            equals(childNamespaceURI) &&
         Constants.WS_SECURITY_BINARY_TOKEN_TAG.      ❹
            equals(childElement.getLocalName())) {
        processBST
            (childElement, soapContext,
             faultActor, securityTokenCache);
    } else {
        logger.warn("Not directly processing " +
            childElement.getLocalName());
    }
}
```

In this code, we iterate over each child element of the `Security` header entry ❶. Observe that we are careful enough to skip over TEXT children (if there are any). If the child element is from the namespace reserved by the XML Encryption specification, we delegate the responsibility of processing the element to a method named `processEncryptionEntry` ❷. If the child element is from the namespace reserved by the XML Signature specification, we delegate the responsibility of processing the element to a method named `processSignatureEntry` ❸. If the child element is a `BinarySecurityToken`, we delegate the responsibility of processing the element to a method named `processBST` ❹.

As we have already seen the code to handle encryption-related elements in the previous chapter, let's focus on the code required to process signature-related elements. This code needs to process `BinarySecurityToken` and `Signature` elements, using the `processSignatureEntry` and `processBST` methods respectively. Before going into the details, let's look at the process of signature verification so that you will have high-level understanding of the functionality needed:

1   We first need to locate a key that can be used to verify the signature. To get the key, we need to extract `KeyInfo` (shown in listing 7.4) from the `Signature` element and resolve the `SecurityTokenReference` to obtain the key that can be used to verify the signature. Locating the token using the ID found in the `Reference` URI can be costly if we scan a long message looking for an element with the given ID. In our example, the sender has tried to help us out by making sure that the `BinarySecurity-Token` containing the sender's certification path comes before the `Signature` element. We can take advantage of such assistance by caching the security tokens if and when we find them as we walk down the list of elements in the `Security` header entry. If the `BinarySecurityToken` is not found and cached by the time the `Signature` element is encountered, we can scan through the message looking for the ID referenced in the `KeyInfo`. In either case, if the token happens to be a certificate or a certification path, we need to validate it. This validation requires the sender's certification chain to consist of at least one CA whose public key is known to us beforehand.

2   We need to verify the digest values of each of the `References` in `SignedInfo`. If these values tally up correctly, we then need to verify the `SignatureValue` using the key found and validated in the previous step.

3   Together, these activities establish that signed parts of the message have not been tampered with. They also establish that the message originated from the subject identified in the certification path, as no one else other than the subject could have signed the message. This is equivalent to authentication of the sender's claimed identity. Just as we did in the handlers shown in chapter 4, we will save the authenticated subject information in `MessageContext` so that downstream handlers and service can make use of the information if needed.

Let us now look at the code that goes into each of these steps.

Processing certificates and certification paths

We saw previously that a method `processBST` is called when we encounter a Binary-
SecurityToken element in the `Security` header entry. Listing 7.12 shows how to
process a `BinarySecurityToken` when it happens to contain an X.509 certificate or
certificate chain. The certificate or certificate chain in the `BinarySecurityToken` is
validated, and if validation succeeds, the process certificate/chain is saved in a
security token cache that can be looked up later when verifying signatures.

> **Listing 7.12 Code to process `BinarySecurityToken` elements containing an X.509
> certificate or certificate chain**

```
private Object processBST
    (Element bstElement, SOAPMessageContext soapContext,
     String faultActor, Map securityTokenCache) {
    try {
        String tokenId = Utils.getElementId(bstElement);
        logger.debug("Processing BST with id: " + tokenId);

        Object token = securityTokenCache.get(tokenId);
        if (token != null) {
            logger.debug
                ("We already have a cached security token with id: "       ❶
                + tokenId + ". We won't process it again!");
            return token;
        }

        //Process the BST, based on its type.
        String bstType = bstElement.getAttributeNS                         ❷
            (null, Constants.WS_SECURITY_VALUE_TYPE_ATTR);

        if (Constants.WS_SECURITY_X509V3_CERT_TOKEN_TYPE.
                equals(bstType)) {
            //it's a Certificate
            byte[] certBytes = decodeBST(bstElement);
            Certificate cert =
                CertificateFactory.getInstance                             ❸
                (Constants.X509_CERTIFICATE_TYPE).
                generateCertificate
                (new ByteArrayInputStream(certBytes));
            Utils.validateCertificateChain(cert, keyStore);
            securityTokenCache.put(tokenId, cert);
            return cert;
        } else if
            (Constants.WS_SECURITY_X509V3_CERT_CHAIN_TOKEN_TYPE.
                equals(bstType)) {
            byte[] certPathBytes = decodeBST(bstElement);                  ❹
            CertPath certPath =
                CertificateFactory.getInstance
```

```
                        (Constants.X509_CERTIFICATE_TYPE).
                        generateCertPath
                        (new ByteArrayInputStream(certPathBytes));        ❹
                    Utils.validateCertificationChain(certPath, keyStore);
                    securityTokenCache.put(tokenId, certPath);
                    return certPath;
                } else {
                    logger.debug("Unrecognized BST ValueType: " + bstType);
                    //for unrecognized token types, we will just
                    //leave the bstElement in cache as is.
                    securityTokenCache.put(tokenId, bstElement);
                    return bstElement;
                }
            } catch (Exception e) {
                createFaultInContextAndThrow
                (soapContext,
                 Constants.SOAP_CLIENT_FAULT_CODE,
                 "Error processing Binary Security Token: ",
                 faultActor, e);
                return null; //never reached
            }
        }
```

In this code, we first check to see if the given BinarySecurityToken has already been processed and cached. If so, we simply return the cached token ❶. This happens if the BinarySecurityToken element follows the Signature element that uses it rather than preceding it. In such a case, we scan and locate the Binary-SecurityToken, process it, and cache it when we encounter the Signature that refers to it.

We next determine the type of BinarySecurityToken by looking at its Value-Type attribute ❷. The way we process a BinarySecurityToken will depend on the type of the token it holds.

If the BinarySecurityToken happens to be holding a certificate ❸, we first do base64 decoding of its content and then generate a java.security.cert.Certificate instance using the CertificateFactory API we introduced in section 7.2.2 (see listing 7.5). The certificate can be validated if we know the public key of the CA that signed it or if we have a trusted copy of the certificate itself. We use the Utils.validateCertificateChain method for this purpose. We will look at that method in a short while. Once the certificate is validated, it is stored in the cache.

If the BinarySecurityToken happens to be holding a certification path ❹ instead of simply a single certificate, we do similar processing. After doing base64 decoding, we generate an instance of java.security.cert.CertPath using the CertificateFactory API. To validate the sender's certification path, we need to know in advance the public key of at least one of the CAs in the sender's certification chain, or we need to have a trusted copy of the subject's certificate. Once again, we use the Utils.validateCertificateChain method to validate the sender's certification path and save the validated certification path in the cache.

Listing 7.13 shows the code in the Utils.validateCertificateChain method to validate the sender's certification path.

Listing 7.13   Code to validate a certificate or a certificate chain

```
public static PKIXCertPathValidatorResult validateCertificateChain
    (Certificate cert, KeyStore keyStore)
    throws ... {
    List certList = new LinkedList();
    certList.add(cert);                                            ❶
    CertPath certPath = CertificateFactory.getInstance
        (Constants.X509_CERTIFICATE_TYPE).
        generateCertPath(certList);
    return validateCertificationChain(certPath, keyStore);
}

public static PKIXCertPathValidatorResult validateCertificationChain
    (CertPath certPath, KeyStore keyStore)
    throws ... {
    CertPathValidator validator =                          ❷
        CertPathValidator.getInstance("PKIX");
    PKIXParameters validationParams =
        new PKIXParameters(keyStore);                          ❸
    //Turn off CRL checking as we do not have a CRL distro
    validationParams.setRevocationEnabled(false);
    return (PKIXCertPathValidatorResult)                   ❹
        validator.validate(certPath, validationParams);
}
```

When asked to validate a Certificate ❶, we wrap it as a CertPath with a length of one so that we can use the same method to validate both certificates and certificate chains.

To validate a CertPath, we get hold of a CertPathValidator instance that can validate certification paths encoded using the PkiPath scheme ❷. A CertPath-Validator using the PKIX algorithm can do this validation. PKIX is name of the Internet Engineering Task Force (IETF—a standards body) working group that defines PKI-related standards such as the PkiPath encoding scheme for certification paths.

To validate a certification path, the validator needs the public keys of trusted subjects and CAs. In addition, we may want to specify what the validator should or should not do. For example, we may not want the validator to check with any CRL distribution points if we do not have access to one. These settings and choices can be communicated to the validator using a PKIXParameters instance. Here, we initialize a PKIXParameters instance ❸ with the trusted certificates from a key store and turn off CRL lookup. (Note that real applications should not be turning off CRLs, as they provide an important protection mechanism against certificate abuse.)

Finally, to validate, we simply call the validator's validate method ❹ and provide it with the CertPath instance to validate and the validation parameters.

Now that we know how to validate the certificate or certification path presented by the sender as a BinarySecurityToken in the Security header entry, let's look at how we can use the validated certificate or certification path to verify a signature.

Verifying signatures

The XML Signature API you have seen in the sender-side implementation can also be used on the receiver-side to verify signatures. Listing 7.14 shows how you can do this.

Listing 7.14 Code to validate a signature element

```
//Parse the signatureRelatedElement into a
//XMLSignature instance
XMLSignature xmlSignature =
    new XMLSignature(signatureRelatedElement,"");         ❶

//Get the certificate used in the signature
Object signingToken = readAndValidateSigningToken        ❷
    (xmlSignature, soapContext,
     faultActor, securityTokenCache);
X509Certificate signingCert;
if (signingToken instanceof CertPath) {
    signingCert = (X509Certificate)
        ((CertPath) signingToken).getCertificates().get(0);  ❸
} else if (signingToken instanceof Certificate) {
    signingCert = (X509Certificate) signingToken;
} else {
    throw new UnsupportedOperationException(...);
}

//Validate the signature. We need to set the
//resolver in order to let the validator resolve references
SOAPMessage message = soapContext.getMessage();
SOAPPart soapPart = message.getSOAPPart();               ❹
logger.debug(soapPart.getEnvelope().toString());
xmlSignature.addResourceResolver
    (new WsuIdResolver(soapPart));
```

```
if (xmlSignature.checkSignatureValue(signingCert)) {
    //Now that we found the signature to be
    //valid, we know for sure who sent the request
    //let's fill in the authenticated subject information
    //into message context
    Subject authenticatedSubject = new Subject();
    authenticatedSubject.getPrincipals().
        add(signingCert.getSubjectX500Principal());
    soapContext.setProperty
        (Constants.AUTHENTICATED_SUBJECT_MSG_CONTEXT_PROPERTY,    ❺
         authenticatedSubject);
    soapContext.setProperty
        (Constants.USERNAME_MSG_CONTEXT_PROPERTY,
         signingCert.getSubjectX500Principal().getName());
} else {
    throw new RuntimeException
        ("Signature did not validate");
}
```

We first parse the `Signature` element into an `XMLSignature` instance ❶. Using `Key-Info` in `Signature`, we locate and validate the key needed to verify the signature ❷. The `readAndValidateSigningToken` method (not shown here; you can look it up in the example source code archive) extracts the `wsu:Id` of the `BinarySecurityToken` holding the required key from `KeyInfo/SecurityTokenReference/Reference` and looks up the `securityTokenCache` to see if the corresponding `BinarySecurityToken` has already been processed and cached. If not, it scans through the envelope to locate and process the `BinarySecurityToken` with the given ID. In either case, we end up with a security token we can use to verify the signature.

What we need for validating a signature is a certificate holding the public key of the sender. If the security token obtained in the previous step is a certification path instead, the first certificate in the path is the sender's certificate ❸.

When validating a `Signature`, we also need to verify the `DigestValues` of each of the elements referred by `SignedInfo/References`. As we use `wsu:Ids` to identify signed elements, we need a `WsuIdResolver` (introduced previously) to locate the referred elements. We construct a `WsuIdResolver` here and provide it with the document (`soapPart`) it needs to scan when resolving `wsu:Ids`. The constructed resolver instance is provided to `XMLSignature` so that it can use the resolver when verifying the signature ❹.

Finally, we rely on `xmlSignature.checkSignatureValue(signingCert)` to verify the digest values and signature value. Now that the signature has been verified using a certificate that has been found to be valid, we can say for sure that the message originated from the user (subject) identified by the signing certificate. We set the authenticated subject information and the username in message context for the benefit of downstream handlers and the endpoint itself ❺.

This concludes our discussion of the code that goes into verifying signatures on SOAP messages. As you now know the theory as well as the APIs needed to implement signatures, it is time to look into any practical issues you may face when adopting signatures. The next section will help you do this.

7.3 Practical issues with signatures

Signatures provide a very important piece of the security puzzle. As you have seen in this chapter, signatures provide the ability to detect tampering of data transmitted over an unsafe network. Signatures also come in handy for addressing another important security concern in enterprises: nonrepudiation. Enterprises need to guard against customers, partners, or other parties disowning messages they previously communicated. In theory, this is simple. All that is needed are records of digitally signed messages received from customers. In practice, it will require a very careful application of digital signatures to conclusively prove that the apparent sender of the message did indeed send it.

Quite a few choices need to be made when applying signatures, and it is easy to get them wrong. This section focuses on the choices you are often faced with and gives you high-level advice that will help you avoid the traps when adopting signatures.

7.3.1 Three rules of signatures

The XML Signature specification provides three useful guidelines for deciding what should be signed and what should be construed as secure based on signatures.

1 *Only what is signed is secure*   A signature does not guarantee the integrity of everything in the envelope it belongs to. It only guards those parts of the message that are signed. Furthermore, not all the information in the signed parts is guarded. Data discarded by transforms applied before signing cannot be guarded by the signature. External resources (such as images and style sheets) referred to from signed parts are not secure unless the content of those resources is also signed.

2 *Only what is seen should be signed*   In the case of UI applications, signatures should only be used to sign the data presented to the user. Any data that is not shown to the user should not be included in the signature. Equally, it is preferable to include in the signed info as much as possible

of the transforms (such as style sheets) applied to the data for visual presentation. If somebody signs a document, it is assumed that they see everything in the document. If we add anything that they do not see, it may invalidate the signature legally.

3 *See what is signed* Applications receiving signed messages should only "see" and act on transformed and signed data instead of the raw or pre-transformed data. The application can only trust the transformed data, since that is what is guaranteed by the signature.

Next, we will look at the design choices that we encounter when using signatures. The first choice involves mixing signatures with encryption.

7.3.2 *Mixing encryption and signatures*

We have to be careful when combining encryption and signatures. The goals of one can be compromised by the other if not correctly mixed. For example, if we encrypt signed data without encrypting the signature as well, we leave the door open for guessing attacks. It is always a good idea to also encrypt the signature (or the digest) associated with the encrypted data.

The order of encryption and signature can be deciphered from the order in which the respective entries appear under the WS-Security header.

Next, we will see how we can sign a message that has different syntactically valid forms. That is, when there are different ways the message can be written, which one do we sign?

7.3.3 *Which canonicalization scheme?*

By far, the trickiest decision when applying signatures is what to sign. Even the applications that are not supposed to touch a message may really touch the message, but leave it in a form that is syntactically equivalent. To allow for such situations, we must sign a canonical form. As you may recall, there are two canonical forms—inclusive and exclusive. Which one do we prefer?

The short answer is that there is no one preferred form. Obviously, there are drawbacks to both inclusive and exclusive canonicalization. Inclusive canonicalization makes signatures liable to break even on unrelated changes, whereas exclusive canonicalization may leave out a few namespace bindings, leaving the door open to a security attack that tampers with the omitted bindings without being detected.

The choice of the canonicalization schemes should really be made on a case by case basis, based on the following principles:

- Use inclusive canonicalization as much as possible, since it does not suffer from the security problems that exclusive canonicalization does.

- When using inclusive canonicalization, make sure that the namespace context of the signed element is stable. For example, when signing the whole of a SOAP `Body`, make sure that no more namespace bindings get added to the `Envelope` element. In general, namespace bindings should not be defined in a larger scope than necessary, to reduce the possibility of breaking signatures that use inclusive canonicalization.

- If you cannot be sure that the namespace context of the signed element remains stable, use exclusive canonicalization, but make sure that none of the attribute values and element content depends on qualified names in their content. For example, use exclusive canonicalization if you know beforehand that the signed element needs to be imported into a different XML document (such as another SOAP envelope).

- When using exclusive canonicalization, if you cannot make sure that attribute values and element content do not depend on qualified names in their content, restrict the list of allowed prefixes to a known set that is passed in to the canonicalization transform using the `<exclc14n:Inclu-siveNamespaces PrefixList="prefix1 prefix2 ... prefixn"/>` parameter.

This completes our discussion of the practical issues involved with signatures. There is one additional issue that we have not addressed here, as described in the callout.

> **NOTE** *Signing binary data attached to SOAP messages* In this chapter, we have applied the techniques standardized by the XML Signatures specification to sign selected or all parts of SOAP messages. This assumes that all parts of a SOAP message qualify as XML. This is true for all of the examples you have seen in this chapter. Because XML does not allow binary data, SOAP allows binary data to be attached to SOAP messages in multiple ways. In such cases, we will need to figure out how to apply the XML Signature standards you learned in this chapter. We discuss this topic separately in appendix C.

7.4 Summary

In this chapter, you have seen how digital signatures can be applied to guard the integrity of SOAP messages.

We started off describing why digital signatures are such an important security mechanism, and contrasted them with MACs to demonstrate their power and ease of use. We then talked about the challenges in applying signatures to XML. In particular, we discussed the need for XML canonicalization and showed you how canonicalization eliminates superficial differences between multiple representations of the same XML document. We described the need for two different XML canonicalization algorithms—inclusive and exclusive—and showed how neither is perfect.

We used an example to show you how signature information can be carried in a WS-Security header entry. We then presented the code to sign a SOAP message on the sender's side and verify the signature on the receiver's side.

Finally, we discussed the use of signatures in the real world and explained how poor choices can reduce the efficacy of signatures in practice.

This chapter concludes part II, which is devoted to showing you the nuts and bolts of SOA security. In this part, you have learned to apply WS-Security to authenticate identities, protect data confidentiality, and verify data integrity. In part III, we will take full advantage of these capabilities to build enterprise-class SOA security architectures.

Suggestions for further reading

- The specification for inclusive XML canonicalization is available at http://www.w3.org/TR/xml-c14n.

- The specification for exclusive XML canonicalization is available at http://www.w3.org/TR/xml-exc-c14n/.

- Constraints on the use of XML as a namespace prefix are described in the XML Namespaces specification at http://www.w3.org/TR/xml-names11/#xmlReserved.

- The specification for xml:id is available at http://www.w3.org/TR/xml-id/.

- "XML-Signature Syntax and Processing," a W3C Recommendation, is available at http://www.w3.org/TR/xmldsig-core/.

- JSR-105, a Java Specification Request for the standardization of APIs for XML signatures, can be found at http://www.jcp.org/en/jsr/detail?id=105. The API is available at http://jcp.org/aboutJava/communityprocess/final/jsr105/index.html.

Part III

Enterprise SOA security

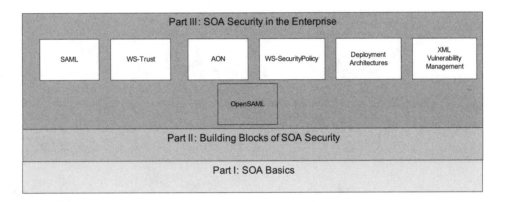

In the final part of this book, we discuss how you can combine the building blocks you learned in part II to construct SOA security services in an enterprise.

Part III consists of chapters 8, 9, and 10.

In chapter 8, we show how you can offer SOA security as a service in an enterprise. You will learn about Security Assertion Markup Language (SAML), WS-Trust, WS-Addressing, and Application-Oriented Networking (AON). These are technologies that are evolving to help you offer security as a horizontal service. We will also show you an example security service in action using Apache Axis and OpenSAML, an open source library.

In chapter 9, we will show you how to codify security policies to enable declarative security and enhance interoperability. WS-Policy and WS-Security-Policy will be introduced in this chapter.

In chapter 10 we will discuss all the real-world issues you need to tackle when implementing SOA security in an enterprise. As with any other real-world design problem, there is no "one size fits all" SOA security architecture. In chapter 10 we discuss the issues you will need to tackle and the choices you have to address for each issue. Deployment architectures and XML vulnerability management are two of the important topics discussed in this chapter.

Implementing security as a service

In part II, you saw some of the technological building blocks needed to implement security for web services: authentication, encryption, and signatures. If you are going to secure only a few simple services, what you have learned up to this point should hold you in good stead. For example, if you are an application developer simply seeking to secure the services offered by your back-end modules to your front-end modules, you already know enough to get your work done.

If you are developing or implementing an enterprise-class SOA security solution, there are a few more fundamental pieces that are needed to develop full-fledged frameworks, strategies, and architectures.[1] In particular, we must address the security management issues that we described in the first chapter. To recap, enterprise SOA security solutions need to address the following concerns:

- *Ease of development*   Are there ways we can reduce or eliminate the burden of security enforcement from developers of services and service consumers? If we can find such ways, the cost of developing a new service or service consumer can be brought down.

- *Manageability*   How can we ensure consistent enforcement of security policies in all services and service consumers deployed within an enterprise? If a security decision is taken to allow access to a specific resource, how do we trace it to a security policy? Enterprise SOA security solutions need to provide easy-to-use mechanisms to answer these questions.[2]

- *Interoperability*   How can we ensure interoperability between different security solutions if standards allow different options for good reasons?

In other words, enterprise SOA security solutions need to take the costs of development and management into account and ensure interoperability. In this chapter and the next we will show you how to do so.

In this chapter, we will present the idea of security as a service. To understand this idea, consider the following: One way of securing services is to implement security for each of them. Since the security is not dependent on the actual service, there will be many common elements in different implementations of security. If this were normal application development, we would extract

---

[1] Kerberos, described in chapter 5, can by itself provide the basis for an enterprise-class security framework. The use of Kerberos across trust domains (enterprises, or even divisions within enterprises) is rare. We need alternate security mechanisms that scale within and beyond an enterprise.

[2] These questions are significant for other reasons as well. Regulations (such as the Sarbanes-Oxley Act in the U.S.) and corporate governance policies require mechanisms that guarantee consistent enforcement of security policies.

this commonality into a library. For the reasons we explained in the first chapter, in SOA it is natural to extract security into a service, so that it can be used by any technology and platform.

Thankfully, there are standards that are developed specifically for addressing this need. These include WS-Addressing, SAML assertions, the SAML protocol, WS-Trust, and AON. Of these, we introduced WS-Addressing in chapter 3. We will describe SAML assertions, the SAML protocol, and WS-Trust in this chapter. AON will be described in appendix E. With the help of these standards, you will learn how to develop security as a separate service so that it can be used for SOA security.

We will start this chapter by introducing the idea of security as a service and how it is useful in securing SOA. Subsequently, we will introduce you to standards that allow security to be used as a service. We will present several use cases to understand how these standards can be used. Finally, we will show you how to implement a security service that uses these standards.

8.1 Security as a service

In the first chapter, we discussed basic security issues. As shown in table 8.1, we've already addressed them except protection against attacks and privacy. Since we will refer to these technologies later in this chapter, let's summarize.

Table 8.1   Review of security technologies described in earlier chapters

Requirement	Technology choices	See chapter
Making and verifying identity claims	Username and password	4
	Username and password digest	4
	Kerberos	5
	Digital signatures	7
	Authentication using JAAS against a variety of repositories	4
Protecting data confidentiality	Point-to-point secure transport with SSL	6
	Selective encryption with shared secrets, PKI, or Kerberos	5 and 6
Verifying data integrity and nonrepudiation	Point-to-point secure transport with SSL	6
	Selective signing with PKI or Kerberos	5, 6, and 7

If all you have are a few simple services, you can build one or more of these mechanisms into each of the service and service consumer implementations. Figure 8.1 depicts this approach.

This approach to securing services is simple to implement. The standard protocols and established practices in security are sufficient to deliver this solution. Consequently, it is easy to understand and develop. In fact, most enterprise applications are built this way even today.

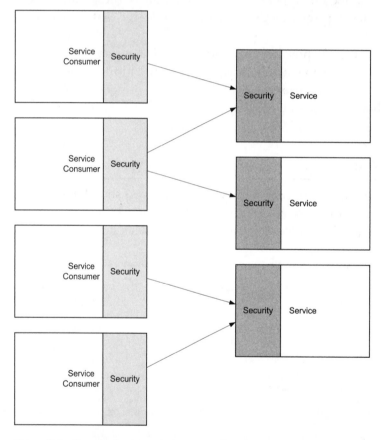

Figure 8.1   Security implemented as part of each service and service consumer. Each service implements its own security, which is invoked as a part of service consumer and provider. For instance, the consumer may add username and password information and the provider may validate them and grant access.

But what if you need to secure a large number of services, as would be the case in any enterprise? Would you still use the same approach?

Consider what happens if you need to secure a large number of services. If we go by the approach shown in figure 8.1, we have to replicate the security enforcement machinery across all services and service consumers. Worse still, if security requirements differ for each application (for example, some services may have stricter security controls than others) then the security machinery in each will end up looking similar with subtle differences, leading to high maintenance costs. In addition, this simple design approach does not lend itself to more advanced use cases. What if a service needs to contact other services when processing a message? It would need to transfer the entire security context to all the service providers, which can be complex.

If you are planning on building an enterprise-class framework for securing a large number of services, you will want to explore ways of shifting at least some of the security enforcement burden from services and service consumers to a shared security service. A shared security service will help you enforce security policies consistently across all services. Figure 8.2 illustrates this approach.

One may argue that separation of security as a shared service is not really necessary to ensure reuse of security machinery; one can always offer the security implementations as libraries that all services and service consumers can reuse. Even though a security service does offer a superior reuse mechanism—one that is independent of programming languages and platforms—note that reuse is not the main reason why we are considering implementing security as a shared service. What we are really seeking to address is the challenge of deploying, managing, and evolving security enforcement mechanisms across a large number of services. A security service can be centrally managed and modified quickly to meet rapidly changing business needs. Security machinery reused via libraries cannot provide the same benefit.

It's one thing to make a case for a shared security service and another thing to implement it. We have to see how we can pull it off. For example, we need to figure out how services and service consumers invoke the security service, how the credentials are communicated, and so on.

We'll discuss the technical feasibility of a security service next. Before we do that, a note on terminology is in order. For reasons that will soon become obvious, we will hereafter stick to the terms *source endpoint* and *destination endpoint* instead of using terms such as service/service consumer, client/server, and sender/receiver.

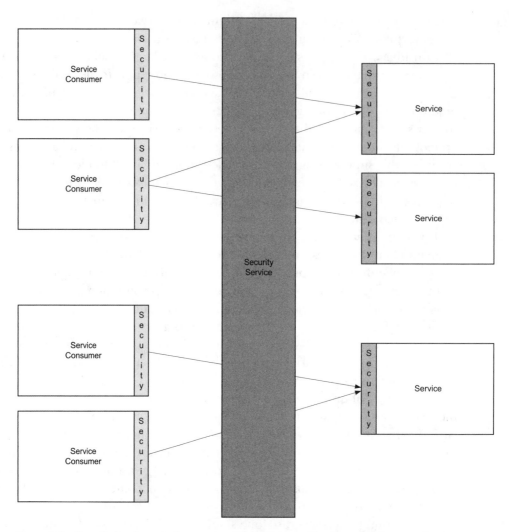

Figure 8.2 Security implemented as a separate service to offload most of the security enforcement burden from services and service consumers. Note that services and service consumers may still handle some security tasks. For example, they may have to understand how to use the security service.

8.1.1 Is a security service technically feasible?

Implementing security as a service is a lot more technically challenging than enforcing security at the endpoints. For it to be technically feasible,[3] we need to address the following questions:

- *Who invokes the security service?* The issue of who invokes the security service seems simple: Whoever needs it will invoke it. What is not obvious is who is supposed to need it. We can say that the source endpoint needs to obtain a security clearance before contacting the destination endpoint. Or, we can say that the destination endpoint needs to validate the credentials submitted by the source endpoint. These choices mean that the security service needs to support different kinds of use cases. For example, a source may simply be interested in getting a service ticket or a destination endpoint may be interested in authenticating and authorizing a request.

- *How is the security context communicated to the destination endpoint?* Endpoints are often interested in the results of security enforcement. For example, a destination endpoint might be interested in knowing the authenticated identity of the caller. Another endpoint might need more than just the identity; it might be interested in knowing the privileges granted to the caller. As you can see, the result of security enforcement is a context that needs to be communicated to the destination endpoint. What constitutes the context varies based on the needs of the endpoint.

- *What is the interface for the security service?* Given the diverse set of use cases and security technologies a security service should provide, it is not easy to come up with an interface that serves all needs. For example, a security service should be able to validate identity claims made using username tokens, X.509 certificates, and Kerberos tickets. Not only that, the interface should allow for securing the communication with the security service itself!

These issues are addressed by various standards, which we will introduce next. Once we understand these standards, it will become clear that a security service is indeed a technically feasible idea.

---

[3] We are not discussing the practical issues in migrating from endpoint-enforced security to a security service. We will discuss them in chapter 10.

8.1.2 Standards for implementing security as a service

A number of standards and technologies need to be brought together when implementing security as a service. We have already introduced some of these technologies in previous chapters. We will introduce the rest here. Table 8.2 lists all of these standards and technologies and provides a pointer to the chapter and section that describes each of them.

Table 8.2 Standards and technologies that make implementation of a security service technically feasible

Standard/Technology	Description	Described in
WS-Addressing	Standardizes SOAP headers for preserving destination endpoint information when routing a message via the security service	3.5
Application-Oriented Networking (AON)	Technology that enables the network to understand application-level messages and even become a security service provider	3.5 and appendix E
Security Assertion Markup Language (SAML)	Provides the syntax for conveying the findings of a security service	8.3
WS-Trust	Describes interfaces for a security service that can issue, validate, renew, and cancel security tokens such as SAML assertions and Kerberos tickets	8.5.1
SAML protocol	Describes interfaces for a security service that returns its findings as SAML	8.5.2

Before we look at SAML, WS-Trust, and the SAML protocol, it helps to look at the possible use cases for a security service. The use case analysis in the next section will help you understand the technical issues in implementing security as a service. This understanding will in turn help you appreciate the motivations behind each of the standards and technologies we listed in table 8.2.

8.2 Analyzing possible uses of a security service

To understand how to create a security service, we have to first understand how it can be used. The possible uses of a security service can be classified into the following five use cases based on how the security service is invoked.

1   Destination endpoint invokes security service out-of-band

2   Source endpoint invokes security service out-of-band

3   Both endpoints invoke security service out-of-band

4   Messages are explicitly routed via the security service by the source endpoint or by a previous intermediary in the message path

5   A smart network device automatically routes messages via the security service

In this section, we will analyze each of these use cases. We will describe the scenario, identify the standards and technologies that can help in the implementation, and evaluate the pros and cons of invoking the security service as described. This exercise will help us identify the different pieces of the technology puzzle needed to create a security service.

Let's start our discussion with a use case in which the destination endpoint invokes the security service out-of-band.

8.2.1 Use case 1: Destination endpoint invokes security service out-of-band

In all the examples we have shown so far, with the exception of in chapter 5 where we discussed Kerberos, the destination endpoint bears the burden of security enforcement. So, the most natural candidate for invoking the security service is the destination endpoint itself. Instead of calling different library functions for executing security-related logic, the destination endpoint can invoke the security service. Let's call this use case 1.

In this use case, the source endpoint is not at all aware of the security service. The source endpoint simply invokes the destination endpoint, which in turn invokes the security service. As the security service is not in the message path, the security service is said to be invoked *out-of-band*. Figure 8.3 depicts this.

Figure 8.3   The destination endpoint invokes the security service out-of-band. The burden of security is moved to a separate service. Still, the destination endpoint (that is, the service provider) must invoke it explicitly.

You will recognize that this use case is quite commonly found if you look at an LDAP server as a security service. An LDAP server provides authentication as a service to server applications that wish to authenticate users contacting them. It also often provides server applications with the information necessary to make authorization decisions, but leaves the final authorization decision to the applications themselves.

The security service we wish to implement needs to provide significantly more functionality than a traditional LDAP server. For example, the security service may need to decide which resources the authenticated source endpoint is allowed to access and for how long. That is, the security service may need to provide authorization functionality, too.

The security service may also need to provide the destination endpoint with additional details about the source endpoint that the security service gets to know when doing authentication. For example, the security service may get to know the source endpoint's location and preferences during authentication. The destination endpoint may need such information for its business logic, consequently the security service will need to communicate this to the destination endpoint.

Furthermore, as we want to provide the security service even over unsecured networks, all communication with the security service needs to be protected. Otherwise, a man in the middle may be able compromise security.

Relevant standards and technologies

Of the standards and technologies described in table 8.2, the following are relevant in this use case:

- *SAML* The security service can express its findings to the destination endpoint in the form of standard SAML assertions.
- *WS-Trust and/or the SAML protocol* These standards specify how the security service can be invoked.

WS-Addressing and AON are not relevant in this use case, as messages are not routed via the security service.

Pros and cons

There are several advantages to the destination endpoint invoking the security service. It is only a small step from the way we have been implementing security. Source endpoints need not even know about the existence of the security service, and need not understand how to interact with one.

The big disadvantage is that every destination endpoint needs to know how to interact with the security service. Furthermore, every destination endpoint is forced to spend time and effort obtaining the security decision. As the number of service requests increases, the load on the destination endpoint increases.

From the perspective of source endpoints, too, this use case has problems. The source endpoints are forced to reveal their credentials to the destination endpoint. This allows destination endpoints to steal and reuse the source's credentials for contacting other services. (We discussed this service-provider abuse in chapter 5.)

The obvious alternative to the destination endpoint invoking the security service is to leave that burden to the source endpoint. Let's discuss that possibility next.

8.2.2 Use case 2: Source endpoint invokes security service out-of-band

In this use case, the source endpoint invokes the security service to get a security token that it in turn submits to the destination endpoint. At the destination endpoint, the security token is examined and appropriate action is taken. Figure 8.4 illustrates this use case.

Figure 8.4   The source endpoint invokes the security service out-of-band. Just as before, security is handled by the separate security service. The burden of invoking it falls to the source endpoint; i.e. the consumer. Since the result should be accepted by the destination endpoint, the security service needs to implement standards such as SAML.

Kerberos operates in a similar fashion. There, too, the client gets a token—a service ticket—which is submitted to the service. The ticket can carry the complete security context in encrypted and signed form. Refer to chapter 5 for an introduction to Kerberos.

Relevant standards and technologies

Of the standards and technologies described in table 8.2, the following are relevant in this use case.

- *SAML* The security token returned by the security service can take the form of a standard SAML assertion.

- *WS-Trust and/or the SAML protocol* These standards specify how the security service can be invoked.

As in use case 1, WS-Addressing and AON are not relevant, as messages are not routed via the security service.

Pros and cons

This use case has a clear advantage over the previous one: It spreads the burden of invoking the security service over the source endpoints. So, this use case scales better than the previous one. In addition, this solution does not reveal the security credentials to the destination endpoint. This prevents the destination endpoint owner from repurposing the submitted credentials to access a different service.

But there are some disadvantages with this use case. Any source endpoint wishing to use the destination endpoint needs to invoke the security service. This increases the programming complexity on the part of the clients, reducing the usability of the service.

In addition, the entire security context that the destination endpoint needs should be available in the ticket. Since the source endpoint cannot be sure what information is required, it will have to carry all the potentially required information in the ticket. This can get bulky as more and more attributes are added to the security context.

One way to take care of the problem of having to carry the entire security context (rather than just the necessary data) to the destination endpoint is to let both endpoints talk to the security service. That possibility is use case 3, which we discuss next.

8.2.3 Use case 3: Both endpoints invoke security service out-of-band

In this scenario, the source endpoint talks to the security service and obtains a security token that provides a partial security context, enough to provide most common information required by any service. If a destination endpoint receives a security token and requires further information about the source endpoint, it will turn to the security service to obtain that information. Figure 8.5 illustrates this possibility.

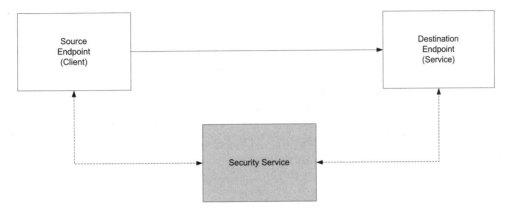

Figure 8.5 Both endpoints invoke the security service out-of-band. As always, security functionality is encapsulated by the security service. Unlike before, both the source and destination endpoints invoke the service, which generates and validates the security tokens.

Relevant standards and technologies

Of the standards and technologies described in table 8.2, the following are relevant in this use case.

- *SAML* The security token returned by the security service to the source endpoint can take the form of a standard SAML assertion. Similarly, when the destination endpoint queries the security service for more information on a source endpoint, the security service's response can be in the form of a standard SAML assertion.

- *WS-Trust and/or the SAML protocol* These standards specify how the security service can be invoked.

As in use cases 1 and 2, WS-Addressing and AON are not relevant, as messages are not routed via the security service.

Pros and cons

While this use case solves a technical problem, it imposes an additional programming burden on both endpoints. This is a general solution that is suitable for several situations.

All the use cases we outlined so far share an essential characteristic: the security service is invoked out-of-band (that is, the security service lies outside the message path). Let us now consider a radically different possibility. The source endpoint (or a previous intermediary[4] in the message path) can submit the message to a security service rather than the destination endpoint.

8.2.4 *Use case 4: Security service as an explicit intermediary*

As we described in chapter 3, SOAP allows intermediaries—nodes other than the source and destination endpoints—to see and act on a message. In this use case, we consider implementing a security service as an intermediary in the message path.

Figure 8.6 illustrates this idea. The source endpoint (or a previous intermediary in the message path) submits the message to the security service. Upon making the necessary checks, the security service in turn forwards the message to the intended recipient.

Figure 8.6   Security service implemented as an explicitly addressed intermediary in the message path. Unlike in previous cases, no endpoint has to invoke the security service. The message is handed off by the source endpoint to the security service, which in turn relays the message to the destination endpoint, after enforcing security.

As the message is being explicitly routed via the security service by the source endpoint (or a previous intermediary in the message path), we say that the security service is acting as an *explicit* intermediary.

Relevant standards and technologies

Of the standards and technologies described in table 8.2, the following are relevant in this use case.

- *WS-Addressing*   As the security service intermediary needs to forward the message to the destination endpoint, the source endpoint needs to communicate the real destination endpoint's address to the security service. This need is fulfilled by WS-Addressing.

- *SAML*   The security service can express its findings in the form of standard SAML assertions.

---

[4] Intermediaries in the SOAP message path are discussed in section 3.5.

WS-Trust and the SAML protocol are not relevant in this use case, as the source endpoint does not invoke the security service separately; instead, the source endpoint simply routes its messages via the security service. A security service implemented as an intermediary will accept arbitrary messages, as it will have to process messages intended for any destination endpoint.

AON is not relevant here unless the security service is hosted on a network device (as opposed to a server).

Pros and cons

The upside is that the security service gets to see the entirety of the messages and not just the source endpoint's credentials. This allows the security service to offer more functionality than was possible in use cases 1, 2, and 3. For example, the security service can scan the messages to look for attacks that target common vulnerabilities in destination endpoints. We will discuss some of the common vulnerabilities in web services in chapter 10.

The downside is that every source endpoint will have to explicitly route messages through the security service. That means increased complexity and dependence on the details of the security service invocation. At the destination endpoint, the situation is not bad unless we want to have two-way messaging. In request-response type scenarios that require both requests as well as responses to be processed by the security service, both endpoints need to be aware of the security service and route messages through it.

There is one additional complexity. As the security service intermediary needs to forward the message to the destination endpoint, the source endpoint needs to communicate the real destination endpoint's address to the security service. WS-Addressing, introduced in chapter 3, can be used for this purpose.

8.2.5 *Use case 5: Security service as an implicit intermediary*

Our issue with explicit routing is increased programming complexity. If we transparently route the messages via a security service, we get all the benefits of explicit routing without programming it in each of the endpoints. It looks like figure 8.7.

Transparent routing is not possible without support from infrastructure such as network devices. If we can program the network devices to force the traffic through a security service, we can make security decisions based on the messages.

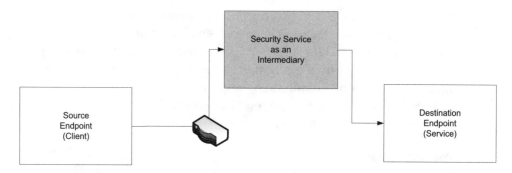

Figure 8.7 Security service implemented as an intermediary in the message path with the help of a network device. It is similar to the earlier case depicted in figure 8.6. The difference here is that the addition of the security service to the message path is done by a network device, without any endpoint knowing about it.

Relevant standards and technologies

Of the standards and technologies described in table 8.2, the following are relevant in this use case.

- *WS-Addressing* Just as in use case 4, if the security service intermediary is to forward the message to the destination endpoint after it examines a message, it needs to know the real destination endpoint's address. WS-Addressing helps in this.

- *SAML* The security service can express its findings in the form of standard SAML assertions.

- *AON* This technology enables network devices to understand application-level context and make decisions on whether to route an application-level message via the security service. Furthermore, the network can itself act as the security service, as you will see when we describe AON in appendix E.

Just as for the previous use case, WS-Trust and the SAML protocol are not relevant, as the security service is not invoked explicitly.

Pros and cons

The big upside, compared to the previous use case, is that endpoints need not be burdened with the task of routing messages via the security service. The downside is also obvious: We need AON devices in order to implement this use case.

This completes our use case analysis for a security service. At the start of this chapter, when considering the idea of security as a separate service (see section 8.1.1), we identified three main technical questions we need to answer. Here are those three questions once again.

1 Who invokes the security service?

2 How is the security context communicated to the destination endpoint?

3 What is the interface for the security service?

We answered the first question by identifying five possible ways in which a security service may be invoked. Let's now shift our focus to the second and third questions. The next two sections (8.3 and 8.4) will show how to address the second question using SAML, a language that allows a security service to express its findings. In section 8.6, we will address the third question.

8.3 Conveying the findings of a security service: SAML

In chapters 3-7, you have already seen one way of decoupling security logic from business logic, albeit not in the form of a separate security service. In the examples shown in previous chapters, all the logic of security enforcement is owned by JAX-RPC handlers that are separate from the JAX-RPC service endpoints that provide business logic for services. Saving the findings of security handlers in a JAX-RPC MessageContext is a common technique that we have repeatedly used in these examples.

For instance, JAASAuthenticationHandler in example 2 (depicted in figure 4.2) saved the authenticated Subject instance in MessageContext because, even though we decoupled the security logic from the business logic, the business logic still depends on some of the findings of the security service.

For example, the BrokerageService in our examples needed to know the identity of the user who is placing an order. It may not just be the user identity that the business logic depends on. Information on the groups the user belongs to, the user's preferences, and the user's location may also be needed. All of this information may become available to the security service when it authenticates a user.

The entity that manages security—be it a security-related JAX-RPC handler or a security service—needs to communicate some of its findings (collectively referred to as the *security context*) to the service endpoint and any other node in the message path that lies downstream of the security service.

When we decoupled security logic from business logic using a JAX-RPC handler, we could convey the findings of the security handler using MessageContext, an in-memory data structure, as the JAX-RPC handler ran in the same process[5] as the service endpoint. The same technique cannot be used when we move the security logic out of the service endpoint process into a separate security service process. We need an alternative technique that does not rely on in-memory structures.

SAML fulfills this need by providing a language for expressing the findings (or assertions) of the security service. In this section, we will introduce SAML and its usage in web services security. In particular, we will describe:

- The structure of a SAML assertion
- Three standard types of statements you can make within a SAML assertion
- The techniques used to protect SAML assertions from forgery, tampering, and replay

In section 8.5, we will also show you the code for a sample security service that uses OpenSAML, an open source library for producing SAML assertions.

Let us first look at the basics of SAML assertions.

8.3.1 SAML assertion basics

As the name suggests, SAML provides a markup language for representing security assertions. These assertions are created by the entity responsible for security enforcement (such as a security service) to convey its findings to other entities that depend on those findings. In this section, we will show you the structure of a SAML `Assertion` element.

Listing 8.1 is an example that shows the structure of a SAML `Assertion` element.

Listing 8.1 A sample SAML assertion

```
<Assertion
  xmlns="urn:oasis:names:tc:SAML:1.0:assertion"          Indicates SAML
  MajorVersion="1" MinorVersion="1"                       version
  AssertionID="MySAMLAssertion1"       ←❶ Identifier for this assertion
  Issuer="http://manning.com/xmlns/samples/soasecimpl/cop"
  IssueInstant="2005-09-19T18:07:08.419Z">                URI identifying
                                          Time at which    assertion
                                          this assertion  ❷ issuer
                                       ❸ was issued
```

---

[5] By *process*, we mean a running instance of a program. Different parts of the same process can exchange data by simply writing to and reading from the same in-memory location. Data exchange between different processes on the same machine or different machines is lot more complicated and requires a data exchange standard.

```
<Conditions
  NotBefore="2005-09-19T18:07:08.419Z"
  NotOnOrAfter="2005-09-19T18:12:08.419Z"/>
```
❹ **Conditions under which this assertion is valid**

```
...
</Assertion>
```
❺ **One or more statements (not shown here)**

A SAML assertion must always have an identifier ❶ and must always say who is making the assertion ❷ and when the assertion is made ❸. A SAML assertion may also explicitly state the `Conditions` ❹ under which it is valid. For instance, in the previous listing, the assertion specifies the time period during which it is valid.

The assertion in listing 8.1 did not say much. That is because we skipped the statements ❺ that make up the meat of the `Assertion`. SAML defines three standard statements you can make within an `Assertion`:

- Authentication statement
- Attribute statement
- Authorization decision statement

We will describe each of these in the following sections, with the help of examples.

8.3.2 AuthenticationStatement: Asserting authentication results

An example of a simple assertion could be user authentication. After a security service authenticates a user, if it wants to provide that information to endpoints (and any downstream node in the message path), it can use this assertion. Listing 8.2 shows how an assertion can say who was authenticated, how, and when.

Listing 8.2 A sample SAML assertion making an authentication statement

```
<Assertion ...>
...

<AuthenticationStatement
  AuthenticationInstant="2005-09-19T18:07:08.379Z"
AuthenticationMethod="...:SAML:1.0:am:password">

  <Subject>
    <NameIdentifier
      NameQualifier="manning.com"
      Format="...:SAML:1.1:nameid-format:emailAddress">
      chap@manning.com
    </NameIdentifier>
  </Subject>
```

Statement about authentication done by issuer

Time when authentication took place

Mechanism used for authentication

Information on the authenticated subject

```
</AuthenticationStatement>

...
</Assertion>
```

In this listing, the issuer of the assertion is stating that a user identified by the email address chap@manning.com has been authenticated using a password-based authentication scheme. We are skipping detailed descriptions of Authentication-Statement (and other statements we discuss in this section), as you can easily decipher the details from the listing. You can refer to the SAML specification (cited in the "Suggestions for further reading" section at the end of this chapter) for complete descriptions.

Consider the example of a security service. When invoked, implicitly or explicitly, it can validate the username and password. When it does, it can use SAML to assert the identity of the user. It can assert even more information, such as the groups the user belongs to, the user's preferences, and the user's location. All this information is part of the security context for a user, which is needed by services to authorize users and customize information for them.

Let us next look at how the security service can assert user's attributes.

8.3.3 *AttributeStatement: Asserting user attributes*

As we mentioned, we need to assert various attributes about the user to reduce the burden of security information on the consumer. An endpoint can use such information to make access control decisions or simply customize its behavior. Listing 8.3 shows how an assertion can state attributes of a subject, in this case, the groups the user belongs to:

Listing 8.3   A sample SAML assertion making an attribute statement

```
<Assertion ...>
...                              A statement about the
<AttributeStatement>    ◁┐     attributes of a subject

  <Subject>
    <NameIdentifier
      NameQualifier="manning.com"
      Format="...:SAML:1.1:nameid-format:emailAddress">     Identity of
      chap@manning.com                                      the subject
    </NameIdentifier>
  </Subject>
```

```
<Attribute
  AttributeName="memberOf"
  AttributeNamespace="http://manning.com/saml/attrns">

  <AttributeValue>authors</AttributeValue>
  <AttributeValue>soasecimpl</AttributeValue>

</Attribute>
</AttributeStatement>

...
</Assertion>
```

| Namespace qualified name of an attribute

| One or more values of the attribute

In this sample, the assertion is stating that the subject, chap@manning.com, is a memberOf two groups named authors and soasecimpl. An AttributeStatement can provide values for any number of a subject's attributes. We have only showed one in this listing.

In addition to asserting a user's identity and attributes, a security service may also have the responsibility of asserting which actions a user is allowed to carry out and which he isn't. Next, let us see how SAML makes that possible.

8.3.4 AuthorizationDecisionStatement: Asserting authorization decisions

The security service may convey the kind of access granted to the subject for various resources using AuthorizationDecisionStatements. Listing 8.4 shows an example.

Listing 8.4 A sample SAML assertion making an authorization decision statement

```
<Assertion ...>
  ...

  <AuthorizationDecisionStatement
    Resource="http://manning.com/ebooks/soasecimpl/"
    Decision="Permit">

    <Subject>
      <NameIdentifier
        NameQualifier="manning.com"
        Format="...:SAML:1.1:nameid-format:emailAddress">
        chap@manning.com
      </NameIdentifier>
    </Subject>

    <Action Namespace="http://manning.com/saml/actionns">
      Annotate
    </Action>
```

Statement about an authorization decision

❶ Identity of the access-controlled resource

❷ The authorization decision

❸ Identity of the subject

❹ Action for which the decision is given

```
. . .
</AuthorizationDecisionStatement>

. . .
</Assertion>
```

The assertion in this example states that the user, chap@manning.com ❸, is permitted ❷ to Annotate ❹ the resource identified by the URI, http://manning.com/ebooks/soasecimpl/ ❶.

An AuthorizationDecisionStatement can record the authorization Decision for more than one Action on a Resource. We have only showed one in this listing.

As you can see from these examples, SAML allows a security service to communicate its findings using three kinds of statements.

1. Authentication statements to indicate that the identity of the caller has been verified by the security service.

2. Attribute statements to indicate the caller's attributes, such as the list of groups/roles the caller belongs to.

3. Authorization decision statements to indicate the actions the caller is allowed to carry out on one or more resources.

At the start of this section, we explained how the decoupling of security logic into a separate security service necessitates a mechanism such as SAML to communicate the findings of the security service to the service endpoint and other nodes in the SOAP message path. There is one more repercussion of moving security logic out into a separate security service. All communication between the security service and the service endpoint now needs to be secured just like any other data on the wire. In other words, SAML assertions are as vulnerable to forgery, tampering, and replay attacks as any other data on the wire. Appendix D describes in detail various techniques you can use to secure a SAML assertion against these vulnerabilities.

There's much more to SAML than what we covered here. An important aspect in the context of a security service is the SAML protocol that specifies an interface for explicitly invoking a security service. We will discuss it in section 8.5.2.

SAML answers a very important question for implementing security as a service: How does the security service communicate its findings (and do so securely) to the service endpoint? You now understand the answer to this question. Let us solidify that understanding by looking at the implementation for a sample security service that uses SAML. Once we do that, we will return to address other challenges in the implementation of a shared security service.

8.4 *Example implementation using OpenSAML*

In this chapter, we are discussing the idea of offering security as a service. So far, you have seen the different use cases for a security service and how the findings of a security service can be represented using SAML.

We are now in a position to implement one of the use cases identified in section 8.2. WS-Addressing, described in chapter 3, and SAML, described in the previous section, are all you need to implement use case 4. In this section, we will show you a sample implementation of this use case.

In the sample implementation shown here, we will create and parse WS-Addressing–defined XML elements using W3C DOM/SAAJ APIs—just as we created and parsed, for example, `UsernameToken` in chapter 3. On the other hand, when it comes to creating and parsing SAML-defined elements, we will use a higher-level API provided by OpenSAML, like we used the Apache XML Security library in chapters 6 and 7 to create and parse elements defined by the XML Encryption and XML Signature standards.

Figure 8.8 shows the components involved in the example and the data exchanges between them. The source endpoint explicitly routes the request to a security service that authenticates requests based on WS-Security `UsernameToken`. If the authentication is successful, the security service adds its findings as SAML assertions and forwards the message to the destination endpoint that is identified by the WS-Addressing headers in the message. We will use the brokerage service you have seen in the examples throughout this book as the destination endpoint.

Even though this example will only illustrate a security service that authenticates usernames and passwords, you can easily extend it using the code shown in previous three chapters to use other authentication schemes, encryption, and signatures.

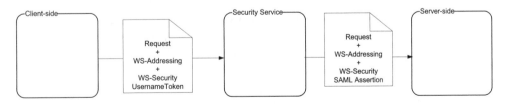

Figure 8.8 Overview of the example used to illustrate the concept of a centralized security service. The message is routed from the client-side to the server-side via the security service. Notice that the username and password token is replaced by the SAML assertion as the message is processed by the security service.

Table 8.3 Steps to run example 6, which illustrates a shared security service

Step	Action	How to
1	Set up your environment.	If you have not already set up the environment required to run the examples in this book, please refer to chapter 2 to do so. `ant deploy` installs all the examples.
2	Set up JAAS configuration.	As the security service will be performing authentication via JAAS, customize the JAAS configuration file, set up the JAVA_OPTS environment variable, and restart Tomcat as described by steps 2, 3, and 4 (respectively) in table 4.1.
3	If it is not already running, start TCP monitor.	Run `ant tcpmon` so that you can observe the conversation. Check the "XML Format" check box to allow `tcpmon` to format shown requests and responses.
4	Run the example.	Run `ant demo -Dexample.id=6`. You should be able to view the request-response messages as they are captured in the `tcpmon` console.

Table 8.3 provides the instructions to set up and run the example.[6]

You should now see the execution of web service calls as captured by `tcpmon`. You will see two requests, one to `/axis/services/proxy` and one to `/axis/services/example6`. The first of these is the request from the client endpoint to the security service, and the second is the request forwarded by security service to the brokerage service.

We will walk through the code that implements the client-side, the security service, and the server side to help you see how all the components come together. Let's tackle the client-side code first.

8.4.1 Client-side implementation

Take a look at figure 8.8 to figure out what we need to do on the client-side. You will recognize that you already know how to do half the job—adding `UsernameToken` to the request. You have seen the code for this chapter 4. The other half of the job is to add the WS-Addressing headers to the request and route the request via the security service. Here we will describe the code for this other half of the functionality.

Figure 8.9 zooms into the full details of the client-side implementation.

In addition to the `ClientSideWSSecurityHandler` that you saw in chapter 4, you can see that we use an additional handler named `AddressingHandler` in this example. There's a little more going on here than just the addition of this new

---

[6] One or more known issues in Apache Axis 1.x prevent this example from running successfully. See appendix A for a description of these issues.

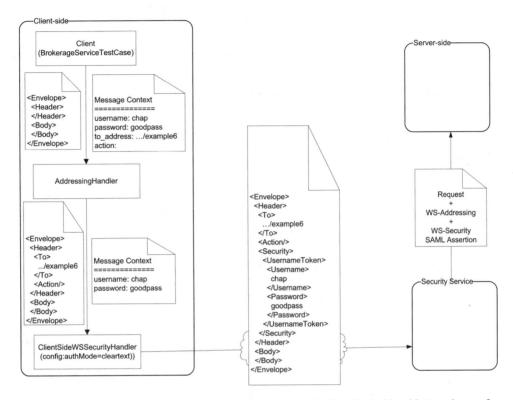

Figure 8.9 Details of client-side implementation in example 6. The client side adds two pieces of information using handlers: the address and the username and password.

handler. There are two additional tasks we are carrying out in this code compared to what you saw in chapter 4. These tasks are:

1. Routing the request to the security service rather than the service endpoint.
2. Preserving the endpoint address using a WS-Addressing header entry.

Let's dive into the implementation details for each of these tasks separately.

Routing a request via the security service

There is no standard way to reroute a request in a JAX-RPC client. In chapter 2, we saw that JAX-RPC provides a client three different ways of invoking a web service. A client can use a pregenerated stub, a dynamic proxy, or the JAX-RPC dynamic invocation interface. In all three cases, JAX-RPC does not provide a standard way to explicitly route a request via an intermediary. In the example shown in figure 8.8, we pregenerated a stub using Apache Axis's WSDL2Java tool and replaced the end-point address in one of the generated files, BrokerageServiceLocator.java, to trick Axis into explicitly routing the request to the security service instead of the target endpoint. This kind of a hack may or may not be possible in other web services engines. In such cases, you will have to configure your network to route the request implicitly to the security service.

Adding a WS-Addressing header entry

Preserving the endpoint address using a WS-Addressing header is accomplished using a JAX-RPC handler named AddressingHandler. As shown in figure 8.9, the client sets up the destination endpoint address and SOAP Action URI values in message context. The AddressingHandler reads these values from the message context and creates WS-Addressing headers, wsa:To and wsa:Action. The code required to do this is similar to the code you saw in chapter 3 for ClientSideWS-SecurityHandler. Instead of username and password, we have the destination endpoint address and SOAP action URI; and instead of a Security header with a UsernameToken element in it, we have To and Action headers to create. Given that you have seen this pattern before, we will skip line-by-line explanation of AddressingHandler here. See example6/AddressingHandler in the example code base if you wish to review the code.

That's all there really is to the client-side implementation. Let us now take a look at the code in the sample security service.

8.4.2 *Security service implementation*

The functionality of the security service in this example can be divided into three parts:

1 Authenticating the request by verifying the username/password provided by the client.

2 Creating a SAML authentication statement and adding it to the WS-Security header.

3 Forwarding the message to the endpoint.

You are already familiar with the code needed to accomplish the first of these three parts—WSSecurityUsernameHandler and JAASAuthenticationHandler described in chapter 4. What you have yet to see is the code for the second and third parts, which we will describe here.

Figure 8.10 zooms into the full implementation details of the sample security service.

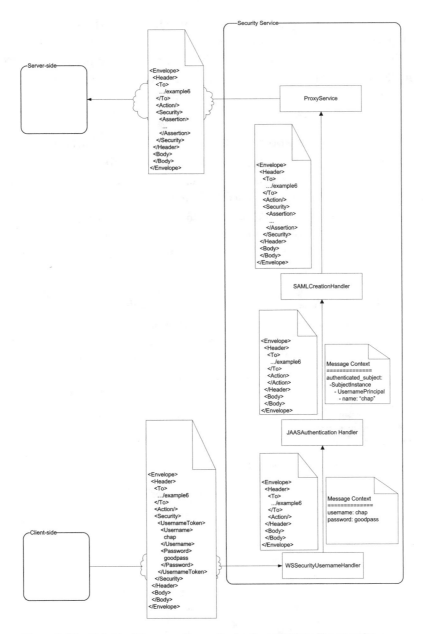

Figure 8.10 Details of the security service implementation. The security service has a JAASAuthenticationHandler to validate the username and password and a SAMLCreationHandler to add the SAML assertion to the message. The proxy service is used to forward the message to the server side.

In addition to the WSSecurityUsernameHandler you have already seen in chapter 4, observe that we have two new components—SAMLCreationHandler and Proxy-Service—that you have not seen before. These two components are responsible for creating SAML assertions and forwarding the request to the service endpoint. We will describe the code that goes into each of these components next. Let's start with the code in the SAMLCreationHandler.

Creating SAML statements and assertions: SAMLCreationHandler

Code in a SAMLCreationHandler is very much like the code in client-side JAX-RPC handlers such as ClientSideWSSecurityHandler, which you have seen before. The authenticated subject information placed in the message context by JAASAuthenticationHandler is used by the SAMLCreationHandler to create a SAML assertion with an AuthenticationStatement in it. Instead of creating a SAML assertion and its contents using low-level DOM APIs, we will use OpenSAML, an open-source library for creating and consuming SAML.

Listing 8.5 Code snippet from SAMLCreationHandler

```
String username = (String) messageContext.getProperty
    (Constants.USERNAME_MSG_CONTEXT_PROPERTY);        Looks up
if (username == null) {                               authenticated
    throw new RuntimeException                         username
    ("Username cannot be null if authentication succeeded");
}

String authenticationMethod = (String)      Looks up authentication
    messageContext.getProperty              method
    (Constants.AUTHENTICATION_METHOD_MSG_CONTEXT_PROPERTY);

SAMLSubject samlSubject = new SAMLSubject();
samlSubject.setNameIdentifier
    (new SAMLNameIdentifier
        (username,
        null,  //optional name qualifier - can be used to    Creates a
            //indicate the domain username belongs to        SAML
        null //optional format URI to indicate name          subject
            //format. e.g., is the name a email
            //address? or a X.509 subject name? or
            //or a windows domain name?
        ));

SAMLAuthenticationStatement authStmt =
    new SAMLAuthenticationStatement();
authStmt.setSubject(samlSubject);           Creates an
Calendar instant = Calendar.getInstance();  AuthenticationStatement
authStmt.setAuthInstant(instant.getTime());
authStmt.setAuthMethod(authenticationMethod);
```

```
SAMLAssertion samlAssertion = new SAMLAssertion();          Creates a SAML
samlAssertion.addStatement(authStmt);                       assertion
samlAssertion.setIssuer(faultActor);

samlAssertion.setIssueInstant(instant.getTime());
samlAssertion.setNotBefore(instant.getTime());              Sets validity interval
instant.add(Calendar.SECOND,validityInterval);              for the assertion
samlAssertion.setNotOnOrAfter(instant.getTime());

SOAPHeaderElement wsaToElement =
    Utils.getHeaderByNameAndActor
        (soapEnvelope,
         Constants.WS_ADDRESSING_TO_QNAME,                  Looks up To
         null, //no specific roles                          address from
         true); //use headers targeted at ultimate dest     WS-Addressing
if (wsaToElement == null) {                                 header
    throw new RuntimeException("To Address not found");
}
String toAddress = wsaToElement.getValue();

SAMLAudienceRestrictionCondition audienceCondition =
    new SAMLAudienceRestrictionCondition();                 Adds AudienceRestriction-
audienceCondition.addAudience(toAddress);                   Condition to assertion
samlAssertion.addCondition(audienceCondition);

securityElement.appendChild                                 Adds the assertion to
    (soapPart.importNode(samlAssertion.toDOM(), true));     WS-Security header
```

The net effect of this code is to produce a SAML assertion element with an Authen-ticationStatement (like in listing 8.2), a validation period (like in listing 8.1), and an AudienceRestrictionCondition (like in listing 8.5).

This completes the description of the code in SAMLCreationHandler. We will not show the code for securing the assertion using encryption and signatures, as you have already seen in chapters 6 and 7 (respectively) example code for implementing encryption and signatures.

Referring back to figure 8.10, there is only one component in the example security service that you have yet to understand: ProxyService. Let's look at that next.

Forwarding the message to the endpoint: ProxyService

The last component of the security service needs to forward the message to the next hop along the message path. In this example, the destination endpoint is the next hop. As we implemented the security service using JAX-RPC handlers in Axis, the last component is a web service implemented in Axis. We have named the web service `ProxyService`, as it simply forwards requests to the destination endpoint and routes responses back to the client.

The `ProxyService` is quite different from the `BrokerageService` you have seen in all the examples until now. We implemented `BrokerageService` as an RPC-style service in Axis. We cannot do the same for `ProxyService`, as the service does not explicitly provide operations that a client can invoke. In `ProxyService`, we simply forward the entirety of the SOAP request message to the destination endpoint and return the resulting response message to the client. We implement `ProxyService` as a *message-style* service in Axis. A message-style service deals directly with the request and response SOAP messages instead of relying on Axis to parse SOAP messages into Java objects on the way in and serialize Java objects into SOAP messages on the way out.

In the rest of this section, we will show you how to implement `ProxyService` as a message-style service in Axis. We will first explain how you can declare a message-style service in Axis. We will then show you the code that goes into `ProxyService`.

To declare `ProxyService` as a message-style service in Axis, we need to first create a WSDD file by hand. We did not do this for `BrokerageService` because its WSDD was generated by the `WSDL2java` tool. If we are deploying the `Brokerage-Service` and `ProxyService` in the same Axis instance, we can simply edit the WSDD file generated for the former and add the following service description to it; otherwise, we can clone the WSDD file generated for the former and replace the service description as shown in listing 8.6.

Listing 8.6 Deployment descriptor for the `ProxyService`

```
<service name="proxy" style="message">
  <handlerInfoChain>
    <handlerInfo classname="...example6.WSSecurityUsernameHandler">
      <parameter name="usernameTokenMandatory" value="false"/>
    </handlerInfo>
    <handlerInfo classname="...example6.JAASAuthenticationHandler">
      <parameter name="jaasAppName" value="soasecimpl"/>
    </handlerInfo>
    <handlerInfo classname="...example6.SAMLCreationHandler"/>
    <role soapActorName=".../soasecimpl/cop"/>
  </handlerInfoChain>
  <parameter name="className" value="...example6.ProxyService"/>
  <parameter name="allowedMethods" value="relayInAxis"/>
</service>
```

Now that we know how to declare `ProxyService` as a message-style service in Axis, let's shift our focus to the code in `ProxyService`. Axis requires methods that provide a message-style service to have one of the signatures shown in listing 8.7.

> **Listing 8.7 Four possible signatures for methods that implement a message-style service in Axis**

```
public Element [] method(Element [] bodies);
public SOAPBodyElement [] method (SOAPBodyElement [] bodies);
public Document method(Document body);
public void method(SOAPEnvelope req, SOAPEnvelope resp);
```

In our declaration of `ProxyService` (see listing 8.6), we only named one method for `ProxyService`, and that is `relayInAxis`. None of the four method signatures allowed by Axis are ideal for this method, as all we want to do is forward the request message to the destination endpoint and return the response we receive from the endpoint to the caller of the `ProxyService`. We do not act on the message in any particular way.

The fourth signature is the one that comes closest to our needs. Even though it provides access to the request and response envelopes, it is not an ideal fit for our needs for the following two reasons.

1   There can be lot more in a SOAP message than just a SOAP envelope. You saw in chapter 7 that a SOAP message can have any number of attachments.

2   Depending on the transport used, there may be special transport-level headers that need to be set. In our example, HTTP is the transport and we need to set an HTTP header named `SOAPAction` for the destination endpoint to correctly process the request.

What we really need is the ability to access the request `SOAPMessage` instance and set the response `SOAPMessage` instance as opposed to just getting access to request and response `SOAPEnvelope` instances. This is what we ended up doing for implementing the `relayInAxis` method:

■   Adopt the fourth signature shown in listing 8.7 but do not rely on the request and response envelopes provided as arguments.

■   Get access to the request message from the message context (the JAX-RPC `SOAPMessageContext` API provides this facility).

■   Relay the request message to the service endpoint using the JAXM API.

- Take the response message returned by the JAXM call and relay it back to the client endpoint by setting it as the response message in ProxyService. The JAX-RPC SOAPMessageContext API does not provide a method for setting the response message. We use a Axis-specific MessageContext method call in this step.

To separate out the axis-specific and portable code, most of the logic in these steps is implemented in a different method named relay. The relayInAxis method simply invokes the relay method and takes care of Axis-specific logic. Both the methods are shown in listing 8.8.

Listing 8.8 Code snippet from the ProxyService implementation

```
public void relayInAxis
  (SOAPEnvelope requestEnv, SOAPEnvelope responseEnv) {

  SOAPMessage requestMessage = messageContext.getMessage();
  SOAPMessage relayResponseMessage = relay(requestMessage);

  ((org.apache.axis.MessageContext)messageContext).
    setResponseMessage
      ((org.apache.axis.Message)relayResponseMessage);
}

public SOAPMessage relay(SOAPMessage relayMessage) {
    logger.debug("received a request to relay");

    try {
        //look up the destination address and SOAPAction
        //from the WS-Addressing headers in the request

        //... this portion of code not shown ...

        //=== now, call the target service ===

        SOAPConnection connToDestination =
            SOAPConnectionFactory.newInstance().
            createConnection();
        URLEndpoint destinationEndpoint =
            new URLEndpoint(toAddress);
        relayMessage.getMimeHeaders().setHeader
            (Constants.HTTP_SOAP_ACTION_HEADER, action);

        return connToDestination.call
            (relayMessage, destinationEndpoint);
    } catch (Exception e) {
        throw createSOAPFault(e);
    }
}
```

How did the `ProxyService` know where to forward the request message? The destination endpoint information is available in the WS-Addressing headers created by the `AddressingHandler` on the client-side. The code required to extract the destination address and action from WS-Addressing headers is quite similar to the code you have seen in chapters 3-7 to extract security tokens from WS-Security headers. We will skip reviewing that portion of the code here.

This discussion completes the security service implementation. Let us move on to discuss the code on the server-side.

8.4.3 Server-side implementation

Figure 8.11 zooms into the server-side implementation.

The server-side implementation in this example needs a handler that can consume the SAML `AuthenticationStatement` provided by the security service and set the username in message context for the benefit of `BrokerageService`.

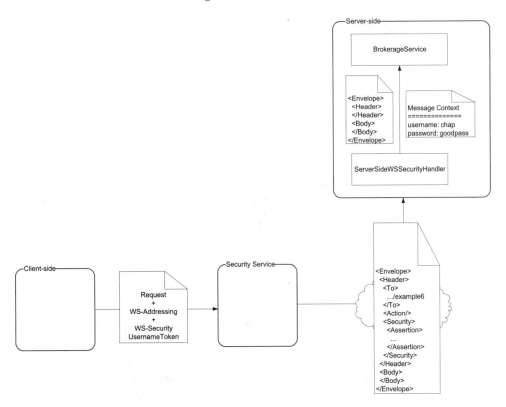

Figure 8.11 Details of server-side implementation. The server-side handler needs to understand and validate the assertion, and finally extract the username and password from the message.

The security service in this example does not encrypt/sign SAML assertions, but as that is to be expected in general, we extend the `ServerSideWSSecurityHandler` you saw in chapter 7 and add to it the code for processing a SAML assertion. The resulting handler code invokes the `processSAMLAssertion` method shown in listing 8.9 whenever it encounters a SAML assertion in the WS-Security header.

Listing 8.9   Code to process a SAML assertion with an authentication statement and set the authenticated subject information in message context

```
private void processSAMLAssertion
    (Element samlAssertionElement,
     SOAPMessageContext soapContext, String faultActor) {
    logger.debug("Processing SAML Assertion");
    try {
        SAMLAssertion samlAssertion =
            new SAMLAssertion(samlAssertionElement);
        Iterator samlStatementsIter =
            samlAssertion.getStatements();
        while(samlStatementsIter.hasNext()){
            Object stmt = samlStatementsIter.next();
            if (stmt instanceof SAMLAuthenticationStatement) {
                SAMLAuthenticationStatement authStmt =
                    (SAMLAuthenticationStatement) stmt;
                soapContext.setProperty
                    (Constants.USERNAME_MSG_CONTEXT_PROPERTY,
                     authStmt.getSubject().
                     getNameIdentifier().getName());
                break;
            }
        }
    } catch (Exception e) {
        createFaultInContextAndThrow
        (soapContext,
         Constants.SOAP_SERVER_FAULT_CODE,
         "Error processing SAML: ",
         faultActor, e);
    }
}
```

This code is self-explanatory so we will not explain it line-by-line. Observe that this code sets the authenticated subject information (username in this example) in the message context, just as the `JAASAthenticationHandler` did in chapter 4. This is so that the `BrokerageService` can use the authenticated user's identity in its business logic. The `BrokerageService` code remains unchanged from what you have seen in previous examples. So, we will not show it here.

This completes our example to illustrate the use of SAML in a security service. At the start of this chapter, when we introduced the idea of a shared security service, three important questions came up:

1　Who invokes the security service?

2　How is security context communicated to the destination endpoint?

3　What is the interface for the security service?

We answered the first of these questions in section 8.2 by identifying five different use cases for a security service. We introduced SAML to answer the second question. We will proceed to the third question next.

8.5 *Standards for security service interfaces*

In section 8.2, we discussed different possibilities for how to invoke of a security service. In three out of the five use cases we discussed, the security service is explicitly invoked by the sender, the receiver, or both. What interface should a security service provide for such explicit invocations? Is there a standard interface security service consumers can rely on?

The answer depends on the functionality you want from the security service. WS-Trust and the SAML protocol (not the same as SAML assertions) are two standards that specify an explicitly invokable interface for a security service. In this section, we will introduce you to both of these standards. But before we do that, we should tell you what to expect and what not to expect from these standards (see callout).

NOTE　*What to expect and what not to expect from an interface for a security service*　In this chapter, you have already seen an example of a security service. We showed you a sample security service that functions as an intermediary to authenticate SOAP requests. We also mentioned that our sample security service can be easily extended to provide additional functionality such as encryption/decryption and creation/verification of digital signatures. Knowing this, you may now have certain expectations about the functionality a security service can provide. Note that we have only shown you so far what a security service can do as an intermediary. Not all functionality that a security service can offer as an intermediary may make sense for a security service that is invoked explicitly. For example, while authentication and authorization are often delegated to a security service using explicit invocation, the same cannot be said of encryption/decryption and creation/verification of signatures. Retransmitting all or substantial amounts of large messages to a security service in order to encrypt/ decrypt/sign/verify signatures is, in general, not considered scalable.

This understanding of the difference in scope between a security service that is offered as an intermediary and one that is offered for explicit invocation will help you appreciate why the interfaces standardized by WS-Trust and the SAML protocol cater to certain kinds of security needs and not to other needs.

We will now briefly introduce you to the interfaces standardized by WS-Trust and the SAML protocol. Let's start with WS-Trust.

8.5.1 *WS-Trust*

WS-Trust[7] describes interfaces for a security service that can issue, validate, renew, and cancel security tokens. In our case, the security tokens we are dealing with are SAML assertions. As you recall, SAML provides only the language to express the security information. Without help of a standard such as WS-Trust, we cannot issue, validate, renew, or cancel any security token.

WS-Trust describes a service called a *security token service (STS)* that issues security tokens. The interface for the STS is designed to meet the requirements of a wide variety of situations. Here, we describe four commonly encountered scenarios:

1   *The client requests a token to access a web service from STS*   A web service client can request that STS issue a security token that can be used to access a web service. When making the request to STS, the client can use WS-Security or transport-layer mechanisms to identify itself. The security token issued by STS in this case can serve as proof of identity, a confirmation of privilege, or even as a key that can be used to encrypt and/or sign messages. For example, the returned token can be a SAML assertion or a Kerberos ticket or a key.

2   *The intermediary invokes STS to do authentication/authorization*   An intermediary such as a web services gateway can intercept requests and invoke STS to check the identity claims made by the client and, optionally, authorize them. If the client claims are authenticated, STS can issue a security token (such as a SAML assertion) to convey its findings to the intermediary that invoked it or to the destination web service.

---

[7] WS-Trust is expected to become more popular as it forms the basis for CardSpace (formerly "InfoCard"), Microsoft's replacement for Passport.

3   *The service endpoint invokes STS to do authentication/authorization*   A web service endpoint can itself refer a caller's security claims to the STS and obtain a statement of findings as a security token.

4   *The intermediary/target service invokes STS to exchange one security token for another*   This is a combination of scenario 1 with scenario 2 or scenario 3. A web service client can submit a security token provided by one STS to an intermediary/target service that in turn consults a different STS. The net effect is that one security token is exchanged for another token that the end service understands and accepts.

As you can see, STS needs a generic interface that can serve different types of security tokens in different kinds of situations. STS's designers met this challenge by coming up with a generic request-response protocol. In this section, we will describe this protocol first at a high level. Subsequently, we will explain the structure of the request and response messages with examples. The examples will be restricted to illustrating the issuance of a new security token. Once you follow these examples, you can look up the WS-Trust specification and easily understand the interfaces for token validation, renewal, and cancellation, which are needed for security service to be invoked by other services.

Let's get started with a high-level overview of the STS interface standardized by WS-Trust.

STS interface

As we described before, WS-Trust defines a standard interface for security services that issue security tokens. Any security service that supports this standard interface is referred to as an STS. Figure 8.12 illustrates the interaction between an STS and a party that seeks to procure a security token from the STS.

The party that seeks to obtain a security token from the STS may be an endpoint (client/server) or an intermediary. In all cases, the party requesting the security token sends a SOAP message containing a `RequestSecurityToken` (RST) element to the STS.

Figure 8.12   Security token service interface defined by WS-Trust: a request for a security token (RST) is met with an RST response (RSTR).

If the STS is satisfied that the caller qualifies for the security token it is request-ing, the STS then responds with a SOAP message containing an RSTR element; if not, it responds with a SOAP fault.

So, the actual details of the STS interface are all in the RST and RSTR ele-ments. We will describe them next, starting with RST first.

RequestSecurityToken (RST)

Before taking a deep dive into the makeup of a RST element, let's look at the big picture. A party requesting a security token from the STS needs to do things in its request:

1   Describe the kind of security token it is requesting. For example, the requestor needs to say whether it wants a Kerberos ticket or a SAML assertion.

2   Prove that it is qualified to get the security token it is requesting. This may simply mean authenticating with the STS using valid credentials.

The first is what an RST element facilitates. The second can be accomplished via WS-Security, using the authentication techniques you learned in chapter 4 (pass-word-based auth), chapter 5 (Kerberos), and chapters 6 and 7 (PKI-based auth). Listing 8.10 emphasizes this division of responsibilities between the RST element defined by WS-Trust and the `Security` header entry defined by WS-Security.

Listing 8.10   Structure of a request to an STS

```
<soapenv:Envelope ...>
  <soapenv:Header>
    <wsse:Security soapenv:actor="...">      WS-Security header
      ...                                    with caller's claims
    </wsse:Security>
  </soapenv:Header>

  <soapenv:Body>
    <wst:RequestSecurityToken xmlns:wst="...">   RST describing the
      ...                                        requested security token
    </wst:RequestSecurityToken>
  </soapenv:Body>
</soapenv:Envelope>
```

Now that you understand the context in which an RST element is used, let's look deeper into the makeup of an RST. Listing 8.11 shows an example RST element.

Listing 8.11 Example of an RST element

```
<wst:RequestSecurityToken xmlns:wst="...">
  <wst:TokenType>
    .../wss/oasis-wss-saml-token-profile-1.1#SAMLV1.1
  </wst:TokenType>

  <wst:RequestType>
    http://schemas.xmlsoap.org/ws/2005/02/trust/Issue
  </wst:RequestType>

  <wsp:AppliesTo xmlns:wsp="...">
    <wsa:EndpointReference   xmlns:wsa="..."
      xmlns:impl=".../samples/soasecimpl">
      <wsa:Address>
        .../axis/services/example6
      </wsa:Address>
      <wsa:PortType>
        impl:Brokerage
      </wsa:PortType>
      <wsa:ServiceName>
        impl:BrokerageService
      </wsa:ServiceName>
    </wsa:EndpointReference>
  </wsp:AppliesTo>

  <wst:Claims Dialect="...">...</wst:Claims>

  <wst:Entropy>
    ...
  </wst:Entropy>

  <wst:Lifetime>
    <wsu:Created>2006-03-16T02:17:41</wsu:Created>
    <wsu:Expires>2006-03-16T02:22:41</wsu:Expires>
  </wst:Lifetime>
</wst:RequestSecurityToken>
```

❶ **Type of requested security token**

❷ **Indicates request goal**

❸ **Service the caller wishes to invoke using issued token**

❹ **Info on claims needed in the requested security token**

❺ **An optional cryptographic key**

❻ **Suggested validity period for the returned key**

Let's walk through the content of the RST element in this example to further understand what goes into an RST.

The TokenType element ❶ indicates the type of security token the caller desires from the STS. Token types are identified using URIs laid down in WS-Security Token Profiles (standards describing the use of a token in WS-Security). In this example, the caller is asking STS to return a SAML 1.1 assertion using the URI reserved by WS-Security's SAML Token Profile.

The RequestType element ❷ indicates what the request is for: token issuance, validation, renewal, or cancellation. In this example, the caller is requesting that STS issue a new token by using the URI shown as the RequestType.

The AppliesTo element ❸ provides a reference to the service the caller wishes to contact using the issued security token. This allows the STS to use its knowledge of the target service provider's policies and determine the type of token to issue. The TokenType element ❶ we seen earlier is optional if the AppliesTo is specified, and vice versa. Both can be specified as well, but in that case, STS is free to override the TokenType requested, as it probably has better knowledge of service policies than the caller. We should point out here the use of elements defined by WS-PolicyAttachment and WS-Addressing, as indicated by the namespace prefixes wsp and wsa, respectively. The AppliesTo element is defined by WS-Policy-Attachment. We will discuss policy-related standards in the next chapter. The EndpointReference element is defined by WS-Addressing as a standard mechanism for referring to a service endpoint. In this example, we are relying on the endpoint address, port type, and service name defined in the service WSDL to create a reference to the service.

The caller asked for a SAML 1.1 assertion in this example, but it didn't indicate the kinds of statements it wants the STS to make, did it? Should the STS issue an AuthorizationStatement along with an AuthenticationStatement? Should it add an AttributeStatement as well? The STS might infer the answers to these questions based on its knowledge of the service provider's policies (assuming the target service is identified using the AppliesTo element, as in this example). Or, the caller can explicitly request from the STS specific kinds of statements using the Claims element ❹. WS-Trust relies on WS-SecurityPolicy to provide syntax for specifying the needed claims. We will discuss WS-SecurityPolicy in the next chapter.

The optional Entropy element ❺ allows the caller to provide a cryptographic key to the STS. We will describe the motivation behind this when describing the STS response.

The optional Lifetime element ❻ can be used by the caller to suggest a length of time for which the returned security token should be valid. The STS may disregard the timeframe suggested by the caller.

In summary, the RST element helps callers of STS to specify the kind of security token they want, the claims they want in the token, and how long they want to use the returned token. All this information is needed by STS to provide a suitable token for the caller. Let's now take a look at what the STS returns in response to an RST.

RequestSecurityTokenResponse (RSTR)

You saw in figure 8.12 that an STS returns an RSTR in response to an RST if the caller is found to be eligible for the requested security token. Before we get into the details of what an RSTR contains, it helps to discuss a few important considerations that went into RSTR's design.

Security tokens can have a lot of information in them. Authentication and authorization statements, information on attributes of the caller, dynamically generated cryptography keys, and signatures to guarantee the integrity of all these items may all be part of a security token. Given this wide range of possibilities, nobody other than the STS and the service for which the security token is intended should assume that they can look into the security token and understand it.

At the same time, there are a few things that callers often need to know about the security token issued by STS. For example, the caller may need to know the type of token returned and its expiry time. If the token returned by the STS provides a dynamically generated key that the caller can use to encrypt the service request, the caller will need a copy of the key in order to do the encryption. In addition, the caller will need the ability to tell the service, "I am encrypting my request message using the key provided to me by STS." In other words, the caller needs the ability to refer to the token returned by STS.

STS needs to provide a lot more than just an opaque security token in RSTR. The example response shown in listing 8.12 will help you understand how WS-Trust accomplishes this.

Listing 8.12   Example of an RSTR element

```
<wst:RequestSecurityTokenResponse>
  <wst:TokenType>
    .../wss/oasis-wss-saml-token-profile-1.1#SAMLV1.1    ❶ Issued security
  </wst:TokenType>                                            token type

  <wst:RequestedSecurityToken>
    <!-- an encrypted and signed SAML assertion -->     ❷ Issued token,
  </wst:RequestedSecurityToken>                              possibly encrypted
                                                             and signed
  <wsp:AppliesTo>...</wsp:AppliesTo>     ◁⌐  Reference to service for
                                        ❸   which the token is issued
  <wst:RequestedAttachedReference>
    <wsse:SecurityTokenReference
      wsu:Id="MySAMLAssertion1Ref1">
      <wsse:KeyIdentifier                ❹ Reference to use if
        ValueType="...#SAMLAssertionID">   the issued token is in
        MySAMLAssertion1                   the same doc
      </wsse:KeyIdentifier>
    </wsse:SecurityTokenReference>
  </wst:RequestedAttachedReference>
```

```
<wst:RequestedUnattachedReference>
  <wsse:SecurityTokenReference
    wsu:Id="MySAMLAssertion1Ref2">
    <saml:AuthorityBinding
      Binding="...:SAML:1.0:bindings:SOAP-binding"
      Location="http://..."
      AuthorityKind="samlp:AssertionIdReference"/>
    <wsse:KeyIdentifier
      ValueType="...#SAMLAssertionID">
      MySAMLAssertion1
    </wsse:KeyIdentifier>
  </wsse:SecurityTokenReference>
</wst:RequestedUnattachedReference>

<!--
<wst:RequestedProofToken>...</wst:RequestedProofToken>
<wst:Entropy>...</wst:Entropy>
-->
<wst:Lifetime>
  <wsu:Created>2006-03-16T02:17:41</wsu:Created>
  <wsu:Expires>2006-03-16T02:22:41</wsu:Expires>
</wst:Lifetime>
</wst:RequestSecurityTokenResponse>
```

⑤ Reference to use if the issued token is not in the same doc

⑥ A token caller can use to prove possession of the issued token

⑦ A random key generated and used by the STS to create ⑥

⑧ Validity period for issued token

Just as we did when discussing an RST example, let's now walk through each of the child elements in the example RSTR to further understand what goes into a RSTR element.

The TokenType element ❶ indicates the type of token issued. In this example, the token issued is a SAML 1.1 assertion.

The RequestedSecurityToken element ❷ contains the issued token, possibly encrypted and signed to secure it from every party other than the service endpoint for which the token is issued.

The AppliesTo element ❸ provides a reference to the service endpoint for which the token is issued, in case the caller asked for a service-specific token.

The RequestedAttachedReference element ❹ provides a reference to the issued token (SAML assertion in this example) for use in documents carrying the issued token.

The RequestedUnattachedReference ❺ element provides a reference to the issued token for use in any document. In this example, the reference provides the identifier of an assertion that can be retrieved from a SAML authority. Attributes on the SAMLAuthorityBinding element describe the protocol, location, and query to use when contacting the SAML authority. You will see more details on the SAML protocol in the next section.

The `RequestedProofToken` element ❻ provides a token the caller can use to prove possession of the token issued by the STS. (Note that this and the `Entropy` element are commented out, as they are not needed in this example. We are only showing them here for the sake of completeness.) This element becomes useful when STS wants to provide the caller and the target service with two different copies of a dynamically generated cryptographic key, each encrypted differently.

You have seen the `Entropy` element ❼ in the RST, and we promised to explain its significance when we got here. Callers who want to ensure that the STS is generating cryptographic keys randomly enough can do so by providing a random key that they themselves generate. When a caller provides STS with entropy, STS has three choices.

1 Adopt the caller provided key as is. In this case, RSTR will not have `RequestedProofToken` and `entropy` elements.

2 Discard the caller-provided key and generate its own. In this case, `RequestedProofToken` is used to convey the generated key.

3 Combine the caller-provided key with another key STS generates itself. In this case, the key generated by STS is communicated using the `entropy` element in RSTR and the computation used to combine the keys is indicated by a `<wst:ComputedKey>AlgorithmURI</wst:ComputedKey>` under `RequestedProofToken`.

The `Lifetime` element ❽ specifies the period of validity for the issued token.

You now understand the STS interface provided by WS-Trust for requesting issue of new tokens. With this understanding, you can easily follow the interfaces described in the WS-Trust specification for validating, renewing, and canceling security tokens. You should certainly read the WS-Trust spec now if you need a complete understanding of the standard for your work. See the "Suggestions for further reading" section at the end of the chapter for a link to the specification.

So far you've seen how WS-Trust can help a security service provide security tokens to callers. If a security service implements WS-Trust, then its callers can request using RST and get a response in RSTR. These interfaces are independent of any security token. For our purpose, the only security tokens we are interested in are SAML assertions. Is there a simpler protocol if we restrict our security tokens only to SAML assertions? It turns out that there is one such protocol, aptly named the SAML protocol, which we will describe next.

8.5.2 SAML protocol

If all we are interested in issuing, validating, renewing, and canceling SAML assertions then SAML protocol is much simpler than WS-Trust. It is often employed in SSO solutions for web applications. Here we will show how it can be used over SOAP.

Like WS-Trust, the SAML protocol proposes a request-response protocol. In this section, we will describe this protocol with the help of simple examples. Let us first take a look at how a request is made in SAML protocol.

Making a request

The structure of a request is simple enough to understand through an example. Here is an example request querying the security service to see if the named subject is permitted to execute the identified resource.

Listing 8.13   Example of a request using SAML protocol over SOAP

```
<soapenv:Envelope ...>
  <soapenv:Header>
    <wsse:Security soapenv:actor="...">         WS-Security header with
      ...                                        caller's security claims
    </wsse:Security>
  </soapenv:Header>

  <soapenv:Body>
    <samlp:Request ...>
      <samlp:AuthorizationDecisionQuery>       Request element
        <saml:Subject>                         defined by SAML
          <saml:NameIdentifier                       protocol
            NameQualifier="manning.com"                         Authorization
            Format="...:nameid-format:emailAddress">            query for the
            chap@manning.com                                    named subject
          </saml:NameIdentifier>
        </saml:Subject>
      </samlp:AuthorizationDecisionQuery>
    </samlp:Request>
  </soapenv:Body>
</soapenv:Envelope>
```

This example is quite straightforward. The caller submits his credentials using the WS-Security header entry and requests that the security service return a SAML assertion with an `AuthorizationDecisionStatement` (see listing 8.4) for the subject identified in the query.

Let's now look at an example response to understand how a security service supporting the SAML protocol can respond to requests.

Receiving a response

The response, just like the request, constitutes the body of a SOAP message. We will skip showing the SOAP envelope, header, and body elements here.

Listing 8.14 Example of a response from a security service supporting the SAML protocol

```
<samlp:Response>

  <samlp:Status>
    <samlp:StatusCode Value="samlp:Success"/>        Indication of the request's
  </samlp:Status>                                    success or failure

  <saml:Assertion ...>
    <samlp:AuthorizationDecisionStatement
      Resource=".../axis/services/example6"
      Decision="Permit">

      <saml:Subject>
        <saml:NameIdentifier
          NameQualifier="manning.com"
          Format="...:nameid-format:emailAddress">      Returned SAML
          chap@manning.com                              assertion
        </saml:NameIdentifier>
      </saml:Subject>

      <saml:Action
        Namespace="...:SAML:1.0:action:rwedc">
        Execute
      </saml:Action>

    </samlp:AuthorizationDecisionStatement>
  </saml:Assertion>

</samlp:Response>
```

As you can see from this example, the security service first states whether the request succeeded or failed, and if it succeeded, returns one or more assertions. For a complete list of status codes, refer to the SAML specification cited in the "Suggestions for further reading" section at the end of this chapter.

Let's recap what you have learned in this section. Implementing security as a service can usher in multiple benefits, but there are a few challenges that need to be tackled to make it possible. One of the key challenges is to define a standard interface that a security service can offer to callers. In this section, we saw two standards, WS-Trust and SAML protocol that address this challenge.

8.6 *Summary*

Up until this chapter, we focused on addressing one security aspect at a time. We did this deliberately to help you understand each of the fundamental building blocks of SOA security. Now that you understand all the fundamental building blocks, we have shifted our focus in this chapter toward figuring out the best way to assemble those building blocks to provide complete solutions that are maintainable, manageable, scalable, and auditable.

The most obvious way to add security to services and service consumers is to build the security logic into every service and every consumer. Such an approach leads to manageability and maintainability problems. So, we considered a different approach: implementing security as a service.

We then looked at some use cases for a security service and figured we need a few more standards and technologies to be in place if we are succeed in implementing security as a service. In particular we showed the need for:

1 Standards/technologies that enable the use of intermediaries, such as a security service

2 Standard ways to communicate the findings of a security service

3 Standard interfaces for invoking security services

In chapter 3, we introduced WS-Addressing and SOAP processing rules for intermediaries to fulfill the first of these three needs. In this chapter, we introduced SAML for the second and WS-Trust/SAML protocol for the third. We also showed you a working example of a security service intermediary using Apache Axis, OpenSAML, and JAXM. If you followed these examples, you can see how we can implement a security service that can issue SAML assertions that can be used by service consumers and providers. Such a service is manageable, scalable, maintainable, and auditable.

A technology that we have often referred to in this chapter, AON, is described in appendix E. AON technology allows the network to be a provider of security services.

Another appendix that adds to the material in this chapter is appendix D, where we describe how to secure SAML assertions against forgery, tampering, and replay.

While the idea of security as a service is indeed technically feasible as you have seen in this chapter, its adoption in the real world is not often easy. Factoring out all the security logic that has been hard-wired into endpoints is impractical. A hybrid approach is needed to realize the benefits of a security service as much as possible, even while accommodating legacy endpoints that take upon themselves the task of security enforcement. We will discuss this topic further in chapter 10.

Several times in this chapter, we made references to the manageability of security solutions. One approach that promises to greatly enhance manageability of SOA security solutions is *declarative security* or *policy-based security*. In the next chapter, we will introduce you to the standards that support such an approach.

Suggestions for further reading

- The SAML specifications are available at http://www.oasis-open.org/committees/ tc_home.php?wg_abbrev=security. In particular, the SAML 1.1 specification described in this book is available at http://www.oasis-open.org/committees/ download.php/3400/oasis-sstc-saml-1.1-pdf-xsd.zip.

- The WS-Security SAML Token Profile 1.1 is available at http://www.oasis-open. org/committees/download.php/16768/wss-v1.1-spec-os-SAMLTokenProfile.pdf.

- The WS-Trust specification was developed by an ad hoc industry group. It is available at http://specs.xmlsoap.org/ws/2005/02/trust/WS-Trust.pdf as an initial public release dated February 2005.

- OpenSAML libraries and documentation are available from http://www. open-saml.org/. The version used in this book is 1.1b.

- Windows CardSpace (formerly "InfoCard"), Microsoft's new digital identity "meta" system based on WS-Trust, WS-SecurityPolicy, and WS-MetadataExchange, is described at http://download.microsoft.com/download/6/c/3/6c3c2ba2-e5f0-4fe3-be7f-c5dcb86af6de/infocard-guide-beta2-published.pdf.

Codifying security policies

9

This chapter covers

- WS-Policy
- WS-MetadataExchange and WS-PolicyAttachment
- WS-Security Policy

In the previous chapter, which marked the beginning of part III, we began exploring how we can create an enterprise-class SOA security solution using the lessons from part II. As a first step, we looked at how to implement a shared security service that reduces the security enforcement burden on endpoints. That solution addresses only some of the challenges in enterprise security. We will address the remaining ones in this chapter and the next. In this chapter, we will focus on three challenges that can be addressed by adopting a declarative approach to security:

1 *Ease of development and administration* There's just too much detail that every service developer and security administrator needs to know in order to effectively secure services. Unless the security framework is easy to use for the developers and administrators, it cannot be successful.

2 *Consistency of security checks* Most enterprises will end up having more than one security service for administrative or historical reasons. When a merger happens between two enterprises, each one's security service may remain operational side-by-side. Furthermore, there may be some endpoints into which security is hard-wired. The challenge in such enterprises is to create and maintain a consistent set of security checks across all the security enforcement points.

3 *Interoperability of security solutions* Security solutions in an enterprise will have to interoperate with the security solutions of the enterprise's customers, suppliers, and partners. Interoperability is not guaranteed even if all the security solutions are 100% standards-compliant. This is because standards allow administrators to make a lot of choices—a security solution in an enterprise may demand 512-bit encryption keys whereas a partner's security solution may only be able to work with 128-bit encryption keys. Obviously interoperability is a concern.

This chapter introduces the concept of declarative security in SOA and shows how you can address these three challenges using security policies in web services. By the end of this chapter, you will understand how to codify and share security policies using standards such as WS-Policy, WS-SecurityPolicy, WS-PolicyAttachment, and WS-MetadataExchange. As some of these standards are not easy to understand, we use examples as the primary mechanism to describe the ideas behind them. You will also learn the shortcomings of these standards and be able to plan for necessary extensions in your use.

We will start off by explaining the declarative approach and why it makes sense for SOA security solutions.

9.1 *Introducing declarative security*

Complexity in programming has been growing over the years. Gone are the days when people armed with the knowledge of a language and a few libraries develop complete applications. These days, developers have to be familiar with several different technologies, standards, and best practices to be effective at their jobs. To complicate matters further, most of the developmental activities that programmers do these days require intricate domain knowledge. Typically, developers do not have this knowledge and need to work with domain experts to develop the solution. Domain expertise is needed in more than the application field. Security, corporate governance, and graphic design are also examples of domains that require specialized expertise.

To help developers and domain experts collaborate without having to fully understand each other's work, most development platforms these days try to separate out concerns. Declarative programming is one mechanism that's often used to separate a concern from the rest of the solution.

Declarative programming takes many shapes. In web application development, a graphic artist can declare the look and feel of various elements in the application using Cascading Style Sheets (CSS). The web application developer simply refers to CSS files produced by the graphic artist to get the right look and feel for each of the elements in the application.

A more complex example would be if we let domain experts declare the rules of the system. Taxation domain expert may codify taxation rules by supplying statements such as "long-term gains on energy stocks are tax-exempt for the year 2006." The declarations are not written in such clear English, but nevertheless, they are separate from the program and available for a domain expert to view, validate, modify, and maintain.

SOA too has several different experts collaborating to develop a solution. In particular, in SOA security, security policies can be developed by people who understand security issues well. If we are to secure services by writing code the way we did in the examples in part II, developers and security experts will have to work very closely with each other. This is clearly not a scalable approach.

Does the idea of security as a service, introduced in the previous chapter, solve this problem? No. Even with a shared security service, developers of each service still need to write the code for interacting with the security service and using its findings appropriately. Instead, if the SOA platforms on which services are hosted allow security experts to declaratively specify the security policies that should be enforced, developers need not work closely with the security experts. Developers can develop services and security experts can set up security policies that should be enforced—the work of both communities will come together seamlessly.

Most web services platforms already support separation of concerns between security experts and service developers. In fact, the latest versions of all leading web services platforms take a policy-driven approach to security, making declarative security not only possible but also the easiest and the most natural way to secure services. If you are developing a service today, you can configure it to be secured by a security policy that was created independently. The security policy may be created by security experts in your enterprises, or you may pick one of the prepackaged security policies provided by your platform vendor. In either case, you are taking a declarative approach to security.

Declarative security can be adapted to varying degrees. The benefits and the complexity involved will differ accordingly. Here are three different degrees to which you can employ declarative security:

1   Internal use within an enterprise to ensure consistent application of security policies by all security solutions used by the enterprise

2   Use at design time to ensure interoperability between the enterprise's security solutions and those of partners/customers

3   Use at runtime to ensure interoperability between the enterprise's security solutions and those of partners/customers

Let us look deeper into each of these use cases, in that order.

9.1.1 *Policy consolidation for planning and consistent enforcement*

Declarative security can be employed internally within an enterprise to ensure that security policies are applied consistently by all security solutions used by the enterprise. An analogy will help you understand this better. If you programmed in the C language, you will remember how you can group the definitions of related constants as a header file and include them in multiple applications using the `#include` mechanism. This mechanism makes it easy to consolidate and manage constants that should have consistent values across multiple applications. It has no bearing on the execution of the code; its use is mainly for maintenance.

Similarly, declarative security can be used to codify and consolidate the security policies in use within an enterprise. Even if we don't use the policies at runtime, this step of codifying and consolidating all the security policies is still useful. In OO modeling, describing the model in a suitable language can help developers understand a problem and make it tractable. Similarly, codified and consolidated security policies are primarily of help in planning and development.

A full description of the process for policy codification and consolidation is beyond the scope of this book. To describe this process briefly, it starts with a cataloguing of the existing services. After that, the security policy of each service needs to be described. The security policies of each service may subsequently have to be evaluated for compliance with government regulations and corporate governance policies. Eventually, the policies for all services are codified and consolidated in a repository. The codification can take place in several different ways, depending on the tools used.

As shown in figure 9.1, security policies are often scattered in compiled forms in different solutions. Converting security policies into declarative statements (that is, codifying security policies) and consolidating them in a repository will help with consistent application of policies across all solutions in an enterprise. As mentioned earlier, creating and managing a policy repository can be the responsibility of a security expert or experts group. It is the responsibility of the developers to make sure that the applications implement these policies.

The developers, without any special tools or frameworks, can read the codified policies for the services and turn them into working code. This is very much like developing code from use cases. If the security policy of an enterprise states that all uses of HTTPS should be with 1024-bit encryption the developer makes sure that his application follows that rule.

This approach clearly is error-prone and tedious. While it still achieves consistency of security checks, it is not easy to develop; in addition, it does not ensure interoperability. If the tools and frameworks support the development process to use codified policies automatically, as shown in figure 9.1, it can make development a lot easier.

To fully realize the potential of declarative security, we need a few standards.

- The language for codifying policies should be a standard. A standard language will help us in creating design-time tools that can read the security policy for a service and generate code or configuration files to implement the policy. It will also help us in creating runtime platforms that can read the security policy for a service and enforce it.

- The protocol to fetch security policy from the policy repository should be standard. A runtime platform that can understand security policies and enforce them can use such a standard to fetch the applicable policy from the repository.

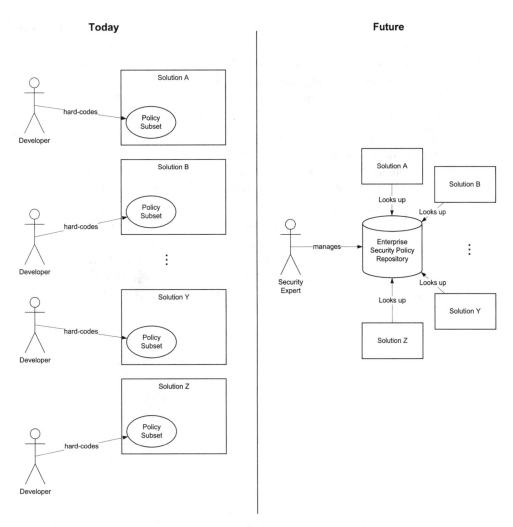

Figure 9.1 Developers today are forced to hard-code security policies into each solution. The vision of declarative security is to allow a security expert to create an enterprise-wide policy repository that each solution in the enterprise can refer to.

The benefits of these standards are ease of use and interoperability. Let's see how to derive these benefits in the next two subsections.

9.1.2 *Use at design time to ensure interoperability*

Declarative security can be used at design/deployment time to ensure interoperability between the enterprise's security solutions and those of partners/customers.

The developer of a service consumer can fetch the security policies of the service provider and his own enterprise, reconcile the differences, and develop the consumer to comply with both policies. Better yet, he can do this using a design-time tool. Recall that we did something similar in chapter 2. We generated a service consumer stub from a description of the service in WSDL. Similarly, a tool can assist the developer in complying with the security policies of all parties involved.

For example, as shown in figure 9.2, when the developer is using his application designer, it may present a choice of authentication mechanisms that are supported by the policies of both parties. The developer may opt for one possibility. Based on that choice, the tool can generate the code required for authentication.

The idea of using security policy declarations at design time to ensure interoperability is simple and therefore attractive. It is not always practical. The security policies of the service provider and/or the service consumer are liable to change over time. In such cases, the solutions on both sides may have to be rebuilt when the policy changes on one side. A runtime mechanism to ensure interoperability will not suffer from this problem. Let's look at that possibility next.

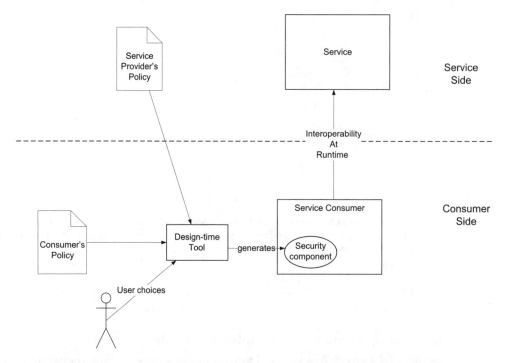

Figure 9.2 A design-time tool can obtain and compare the security policies of both parties, present options that are compatible with both policies, and generate code based on user choices.

9.1.3 *Use at runtime to ensure interoperability*

So far, we've looked at two different ways to use declarative security: consolidate existing policies and validate them, or use at design time to generate code and configuration. We will look at a more advanced way of using declarative security— namely, using it at runtime.

Consider how your browser interacts with SSL-enabled web servers. Each web server may support several different encryption algorithms with different key strengths. Your browser is also capable of communicating at different encryption strengths. Somehow they negotiate the best possible security mechanism to communicate between themselves. Similarly, a service and a service consumer can exchange security policies at runtime and figure out how to interoperate.

The level of sophistication required in this scenario is clearly much higher. It requires security frameworks that can fetch and reconcile the security policies of parties involved in a message exchange, and customize themselves at runtime. Figure 9.3 shows the requirement.

As figure 9.3 shows, the policies of parties involved in the message exchange can be fetched and reconciled at runtime to ensure interoperability. While the sophistication required for this in practice is quite high, the benefits of interoperability are attractive enough to justify the effort.

Let's summarize what you have learned in this section so far. Current-generation SOA platforms allow you to declaratively specify the security requirements of a service. This approach is preferable over coding-in the security requirements into each service because:

1 It helps us hide the complexity of all the technologies that go into SOA security from service developers and administrators. Security experts can independently formulate the security policies that the SOA platforms will enforce.

2 The security policies of the enterprise can be stored and managed centrally, ensuring consistency of security checks made by different solutions in the enterprise.

3 Codified security policies can be used to figure out how security solutions of an enterprise can interoperate with the security solutions of its partners and customers.

These three benefits can be realized in practice to varying degrees. The first benefit is the easiest to realize. Almost every leading SOA platform already supports

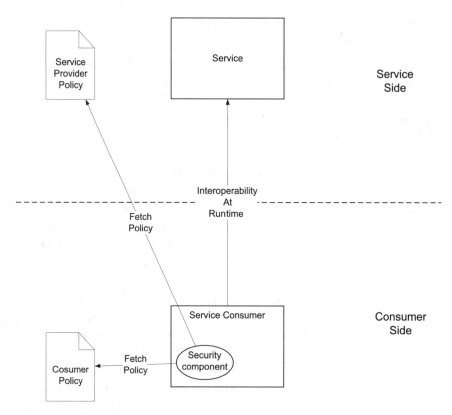

Figure 9.3   Use of security policies at runtime to achieve interoperability between any two parties.

declarative security, helping us hide the complexity of SOA security technologies from service developers and administrators.

The second benefit is a little tougher to realize. Consolidation of security policies using a central repository is easy if there is a standard language for codifying security policies. But all is not lost if there is no standard policy language. Consolidation is still possible, as tools can be created to transform policies expressed in one language into another.

The third benefit is the toughest to realize. A standard policy language is a must if we are to use policies to ensure interoperability. This is possibly why WS-Policy and WS-SecurityPolicy, which, together, define a standard policy language for use in security solutions, seem to limit themselves to addressing the needs of interoperability.

Vendors currently define their own custom extensions to WS-Policy and WS-SecurityPolicy in order to allow you to declaratively specify security for your services. As we cannot possibly describe the extensions created by all leading vendors here, we will restrict the discussion in the rest of this chapter to what the standards cater to now: interoperability.

Before we look into WS-Policy and WS-SecurityPolicy, it helps to first understand the kind of interoperability problems that we seek to solve by codifying security policies. We will dedicate the next section to discussing the interoperability challenges in SOA security.

9.2 *Interoperability challenges in SOA security*

One of the most compelling arguments in favor of SOA is that it lets enterprises reuse software without being inhibited by differences in platforms. Given this promise, designers of enterprise SOA security just cannot wish for a homogeneous environment. Any enterprise-class SOA security solution will have to interoperate with multiple other implementations of SOA security.

To understand the challenge of interoperability in SOA security, let's look at the sources of incompatibility between two implementations of SOA security standards. This analysis will help us understand what kind of policy declarations are required to enhance interoperability. We will use this understanding in later sections when we talk about WS-SecurityPolicy.

9.2.1 *Sources of incompatibility*

Here are the main reasons why two different applications implementing the same SOA security standards may be incompatible:

- The SOA security standards you have learned about in previous chapters leave considerable choice to implementers. Different implementations may make different choices, leading to incompatibility.

- Most implementations do not support all possible choices enumerated by the standards in order to keep the cost of implementation low. This situation leads to possible incompatibilities between one security solution and another.

Table 9.1 goes deeper into the sources of incompatibilities. It may not be an exhaustive list, but it is representative of the incompatibility problems that can arise.

Table 9.1   Causes of incompatibility in web services security solutions

Cause for incompatibility	Description
Choice between transport-layer security and message-level security	Most home-grown web services toolkits still rely on transport-layer security (HTTPS in most cases). Such implementations will clearly not be able to interoperate with endpoints that rely on message-level security enabled by WS-Security.
Third party to trust: WS-Trust STS, certificate authority, Kerberos KDC, SAML authority	There will never be an agreement on a central security authority. Given this, two implementations that rely on different security authorities will find it difficult to interoperate without prior agreement on some common security authority that each party trusts directly or indirectly.
Versions of SOAP, WS-Security, security token profiles, WS-Trust, SSL/TLS, and other applicable standards	As web services standards evolve, implementations will vary in support for different versions of standards. Two implementations compliant with different versions of the same standard will run into interoperability problems unless the higher version implementation is backward-compatible.
Types of supported security tokens	If a service consumer cannot provide a token required by the service provider, interoperability will clearly suffer. Most home-grown service consumers still use username and password for authentication. If a service provider starts requiring the use of digital certificates for authentication, that provider's services can no longer be accessed by service consumers who do not have the ability to use digital certificates.
Inclusion/referral of security tokens and in the case of referral, mechanisms used	WS-Security leaves the choice of token transport to implementers in almost all cases. Security tokens can be embedded or referred to using one or more mechanisms. An X.509 certificate can be referred to by its issuer and serial number or by its X.509 `SubjectKeyIdentifier`. These choices will cause interoperability problems between implementations that do not support all possible referencing mechanisms.
Choice of algorithms, key strengths, transformations, and encoding	Multiple algorithms exist for almost every cryptography related activity we use in SOA security. This choice will lead to interoperability problems, as not all implementations will support every possible algorithm with every possible variation (such as key strength).
Encryption/Signing of only selected parts in a message	Most implementations still only support encryption/signatures on the entirety of message body/message. When working with such endpoints, the other endpoint cannot choose to do selective encryption and signing.
Mechanisms used to refer to protected message elements	The absence of a single mechanism to identify elements in a message has already caused much damage, as we learned in previous chapters. A mix of `ID`/`IDREF` with `wsu:Id`, `Id`, and `xml:id` will cause a lot of interoperability problems.

continued on next page

Table 9.1 Causes of incompatibility in web services security solutions *(continued)*

Cause for incompatibility	Description
Order of encryption and signing	As we discussed in the chapter on signatures, we have the option to encrypt and then sign or sign and then encrypt. There are positives and negatives with both orders. Good implementations should be able to deal with both, but poor implementations that assume one order will break if the other party uses another.
Order of entries in a WS-Security header	It is a little difficult to develop efficient implementations that can access the entries in the security header in random order, as and when required. Implementations may have specific requirements on the order of elements in the WS-Security header.
Use and location of timestamp in a WS-Security header	Timestamps are needed for detecting replay attacks. There are two practical issues in using timestamps. First, clocks need to be synchronized closely. Second, implementations should understand time zone information. Daylight saving time (DST) is not easy to deal with, especially if different countries keep changing the dates on which DST kicks in/out.
Attachment mechanism	We describe the evolution of attachment standards in appendix C. As different implementations are likely to use different standards in the near future, interoperability problems are bound to occur.

As you can see, interoperability problems can stem from different sources:

- Difficulty in implementing choices
- Different choices to solve the same problems
- Evolving standards
- Several optional components to the implementation

There are two different ways to solve these interoperability issues. As we mentioned, we can determine the subset of standards to use based on the security policies of involved parties at runtime, which is not easy to implement and unsuitable for some situations.

A simpler solution is to restrict the choices to a small subset (profile), so that implementers have a better chance of supporting that subset. It is clear that this simpler solution cannot solve the interoperability problem completely, will still have to be left to the implementors. Still, this solution is worthwhile in practice. The WS-I Basic Security Profile specification, introduced next, is a standard that attempts this incomplete but simpler solution to interoperability problems in SOA security.

9.2.2 *WS-I basic security profile*

The Web Services-Interoperability (WS-I) Organization is an industry consortium that seeks to enhance interoperability among web services implementations. WS-I publishes implementation guidelines known as *profiles* for popular web services specifications with the goal of enhancing interoperability. WS-I Basic Profile 1.0 (later split into Simple SOAP Binding Profile 1.0 and Basic Profile 1.1) provides guidelines for implementing SOAP, WSDL, and UDDI. WS-I has also published multiple working drafts of a Basic Security Profile that similarly clarifies WS-Security and associated security token profiles.

Readers of this book will find drafts of WS-I Basic Security Profile very easy to understand. We will not repeating here the long list of rules laid down by this specification. But to help you better understand the basic ideas behind WS-I Basic Security Profile, we will list the kinds of rules you will see in the profile.

- *Elimination of unnecessary choices* WS-I Basic Security Profile prohibits the use of SSL 2.0, since there are known issues in SSL 2.0 that are fixed in 3.0. Implementations can assume that eliminated choices are not used and simplify the code.

- *Establishing best practices* Where possible, the profile establishes best practices. WS-I Basic Security Profile prohibits the use of more than one WS-Security header with the `actor` attribute omitted. These best practices again make the implementations simple.

- *Making type data mandatory* WS-Security does not mandate the presence of type data when different types of values can be used in a particular context. WS-I Basic Security Profile enhances interoperability by making the presence of type data mandatory in such cases. A security token reference must specify a value type.

As you can see, WS-I Basic Security Profile not only enhances interoperability but also makes it easier to develop a security solution by eliminating unnecessary choices and providing clarifications needed to eliminate the gray areas in WS-Security. WS-I Basic Security Profile, however, cannot guarantee interoperability between conforming implementations. This is because not all choice can be eliminated by WS-I Basic Security Profile. WS-I Basic Security Profile, however, cannot eliminate the choice between PKI and Kerberos. Of course, such a choice is required by implementations. This is where WS-Policy and WS-SecurityPolicy come into play. These specifications attempt to provide a comprehensive framework for ensuring interoperability among web services security implementations. We will introduce you to both of these standards in the next two sections.

9.3 *Web services policy framework*

As you know by now, a declarative approach to SOA security can bring three main benefits to an enterprise. It can:

- Simplify the job of service developers/administrators
- Bring consistency to security checks done by different security solutions in the enterprise
- Ensure interoperability with security solutions of partners/customers

Of these three, standards are a key enabler for the last; the other two can benefit from standards too, but are not impossible to accomplish without standards. Currently (at the time of writing this book), standards for declarative security almost exclusively focus on enabling interoperability.

Interoperability of security solutions happens to be a special case of a larger problem. Just like WS-Security, other web services standards that extend SOAP such as WS-ReliableMessaging also leave a lot of choice to implementers in order to ensure applicability in a wide variety of situations. Unless there are mechanisms for ensuring interoperability, it is quite likely that web services implementations that use any of these extensions will not be compatible.

It makes sense to standardize a generic framework for ensuring interoperability. In this section, we will discuss such a framework proposed in WS-Policy and related standards. In particular, we will:

- Formalize the concepts of *policy* and *policy intersection*
- Illustrate WS-Policy with an example
- Describe WS-MetadataExchange and WS-PolicyAttachment, two standards that specify how policies may be fetched

In section 9.4, we'll look at applying this framework specifically to create security policies. Let's start with a discussion of the formal concepts of policy and policy intersection.

9.3.1 *What is a policy?*

The word policy suggests process-related rules and guidelines. The definition of a policy is more formal in the context of web services. In this context, a policy is a machine-readable expression of what is required in a message exchange from a WS-Standards perspective. To understand the motivation behind this formalism, let's look at an example.

Figure 9.4 shows the use of policies for ensuring interoperability in a two-party scenario. In this scenario, party 1 needs to make a web services call to party 2. It does not know the requirements, capabilities, and constraints of party 2. In step 1 of figure 9.4, party 1 fetches the policy of party 2. Party 2's policy tells party 1 how to customize its implementation in order to interoperate with party 2. Party 2 may have the requirement that all parties invoking its services should:

- Sign the body of the request.
- Encrypt the body of the request.
- Encrypt the signature of the body.
- Include a timestamp as the last entry in WS-Security header.

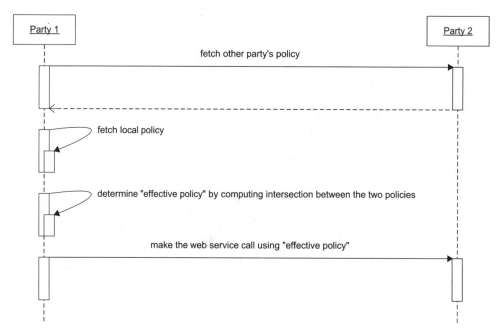

Figure 9.4   Policy-based approach to ensuring interoperability between two parties in a web service message exchange

In addition, it may also have limitations on the algorithms and key strengths it can use for decryption and verifying signatures. Party 2 may only support AES with 128/192-bit keys for decryption.

Party 1 can understand these requirements and constraints by fetching the security policy of party 2. Naturally, it may also have its own requirements and limitations. Party 1's security solution may have its own list of supported algorithms and key strengths that can be used in encryption and signatures. In our example, let's assume that party 1 can encrypt using AES and 192/256-bit keys.

At this point, it is obvious to us that party 1 can only use AES with 192-bit keys for encryption when communicating with party 2. The question is: Can machines make this analysis as well and ensure interoperability?

In the simple scenario illustrated in figure 9.5, party 1 needs to compare its own list of supported algorithms and key strengths with the list provided in party 2's policy and see if the two lists have any common elements. If they do, the two policies are said to *intersect* or be *compatible*. Party 1 can customize its call to party 2 using the *effective policy* determined by computing the intersection between the two policies.

Steps 2 and 3 of figure 9.4 illustrate this process. Party 1 fetches its local policy, compares it with the policy of party 2, and determines an effective policy by computing the intersection between the two policies.

Once an effective policy is computed, party 1 makes the web service call to party 2 using the guidelines in the effective policy. This is shown as step 4 in figure 9.4.

The same mechanism can be used in the opposite direction as well. Party 2 can fetch party 1's policy when receiving responses, compute the intersection between its own capabilities and party 1's requirements/constraints, and customize the way it responds to party 1's request.

Figure 9.5   Illustration of a policy intersection. Party 1's policy states that party 1 can only do encryption using AES with 192/256-bit keys. Party 2's policy states that it can only decrypt text encrypted using AES with 128/192-bit keys. The intersection of the two policies dictates that both parties use AES with 192-bit keys if they are to interoperate.

Comparing two policies, computing their intersection, and customizing a web service on the fly to ensure interoperability is a complex task. Most web services toolkits are not capable of doing this yet. For now, polices need to be used offline to evaluate interoperability between service providers and consumers and to customize producers and consumers at development or deployment time.

Now that you understand the formal definitions of policy and policy intersections, we can introduce you to WS-Policy. We do that next with the help of an example.

9.3.2 *WS-Policy*

The WS-Policy specification provides the basic syntax for expressing policies. Listing 9.1 is an example policy that lays down the text encoding and languages supported by the subject of the policy.

Listing 9.1   Makeup of a WS-Policy

```
<wsp:Policy xmlns:wsp="..../policy" >  ←─ A WS-Policy element

    <wsp:ExactlyOne>  ←┐ ExactlyOne grouping of
                        │ alternatives
      <wsp:All>                              ┐ Assertion mandating a
        <wsp:Language Language="te"/>  ←┘ specific language
        <wsp:TextEncoding Encoding="UTF-8"/>  ←┐ Assertion mandating a      │ Alternative-1
      </wsp:All>                                │ specific TextEncoding

      <wsp:All>                              ┐ Assertion mandating a
        <wsp:Language Language="en"/>  ←┘ specific language
        <wsp:TextEncoding Encoding="iso-8859-1"/>  ←┐ Assertion       │ Alternative-2
      </wsp:All>                                      │ mandating a
                        ┐ ExactlyOne grouping of      │ specific
    </wsp:ExactlyOne>  ←┘ alternatives                │ TextEncoding

</wsp:Policy>  ←─ A WS-Policy element
```

As you can see from this example, a policy consists of one or more policy assertions that can be grouped together as policy alternatives. In this example, there are two policy alternatives. The first requires the use of a language named Telugu (indicated by the language identifier `te`) with UTF-8 as the encoding. The second requires the use of English with ISO-8859-1 encoding.

Putting it all together, here's what this policy is saying: The service/service consumer that is the subject of this policy can understand UTF-8–encoded Telugu messages or ISO-8859-1–encoded English messages.

WS-Policy limits itself to providing the syntax for writing up policies as collections of policy alternatives, each alternative being a collection of policy assertions. It rightly does not go on to enumerate all possible assertions that can be used in a policy. Instead, WS-Policy leaves it up to other specifications to come up with the list of policy assertions that make sense in each domain. The `wsp:Language` and `wsp:TextEncoding` assertions shown in listing 9.1, along with a few other very basic assertions useful for all web services, are standardized by a specification named WS-PolicyAssertions and not WS-Policy. In the security domain, WS-SecurityPolicy specifies the list of assertions that can be used for making security policy assertions.

WS-Policy also specifies an algorithm to compare two policies without understanding the semantics of assertions used in either policy and compute their intersection to a first approximation. We will not discuss the algorithm here. You do not need the details of this algorithm unless:

1   You are developing a policy engine that needs to compare policies and compute intersections.

2   You are creating custom policy assertions for your domain and want to make sure that the approximation made by WS-Policy's algorithm does not lead to incorrect comparison of your custom assertions.

If you fall into either of these categories, you should refer to the WS-Policy specification itself, which provides you with complete details of the policy specification.

In summary, here's what WS-Policy provides:

- A syntax for expressing the alternatives a service/service consumer supports, where each alternative is a collection of assertions that must hold true

- An algorithm for comparing two policies and computing their intersection to a first approximation, even without understanding what the two policies are saying

Did you notice that there is one missing piece in the standards-based solution we have discussed so far for the interoperability puzzle? Let's say you are a service consumer. If you can access the service provider's policy and your own policy, you can use the policy intersection algorithm specified by WS-Policy to compute the effective policy. But how do you access the service provider's policy? This is the topic of the next section.

9.3.3 *Standards for fetching policy: WS-MetadataExchange and WS-PolicyAttachment*

The generic policy framework we are describing in this chapter seeks to standardize the approach for solving the interoperability puzzle in web services. As we just pointed out, one of the important questions that the framework should help answer is: How does one fetch the policies of a party one wants to communicate with? Figure 9.6 shows three possible answers to this question.

1   You can make a request to the other party's metadata service.

2   If you are a service consumer, you can fetch the WSDL of the target service and look for the policies attached to service, endpoint, operation, and message definitions.

3   You can discover the policies of the other party via UDDI.

The first of these possibilities is standardized by WS-MetadataExchange. The second and third possibilities are described by WS-PolicyAttachment. Let us look at both of these standards next, starting with WS-MetadataExchange.

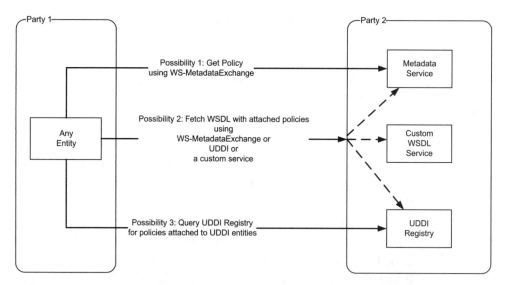

Figure 9.6   Different ways of fetching a policy: query via WS-MetadataExchange or look up policies attached to WSDL/UDDI entities as described in WS-PolicyAttachment.

WS-MetadataExchange

WS-MetadataExchange defines a very simple protocol for querying metadata such as XSD, WSDL, and WS-Policy. Figure 9.7 depicts how a policy document can be fetched using WS-MetadataExchange.

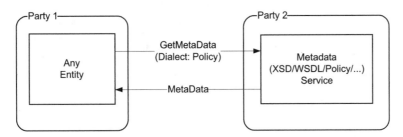

Figure 9.7   WS-MetadataExchange provides a simple protocol to fetch metadata such as XSD, WSDL, and WS-Policy. The `Dialect` element in the `GetMetaData` request is used to indicate what type of metadata is being requested. To fetch a WS-Policy document, the `Dialect` element can be set to a URI that identifies WS-Policy as the type of requested metadata.

As the figure shows, any entity seeking to fetch metadata can use the GetMetaData request defined by WS-MetadataExchange. The Dialect element in the request can be used to indicate what type of metadata is being requested. Listing 9.2 shows an example request in which the Dialect element is set to a URI that identifies the metadata being requested as a WS-Policy document.

Listing 9.2   Sample `GetMetaData` request

```
<Envelope xmlns=".../soap/envelope/">
  <Body>
    <wsx:GetMetadata xmlns:wsx=".../mex">
      <wsx:Dialect>
        http://schemas.xmlsoap.org/ws/2004/09/policy        Request for
      </wsx:Dialect>                                         metadata
    </wsx:GetMetadata>                     Dialect setting to
  </Body>                                  indicate WS-Policy
</Envelope>
```

In this example, the client is requesting for the policy from the server. The server may respond with the response shown in listing 9.3.

Listing 9.3   Sample response to a `GetMetadata` request

```
<Envelope xmlns=".../soap/envelope/">
  <Body>
    <wsx:Metadata xmlns:wsx=".../mex">        Dialect setting
      <wsx:MetadataSection                     to indicate
        Dialect=".../policy" >              ⊲  WS-Policy
        <wsp:Policy xmlns:wsp="...">           WS-Policy         Response with
        ...                                     returned by the   metadata
        </wsp:Policy>                           metadata service
      </wsx:MetadataSection>
    </wsx:Metadata>
  </Body>
</Envelope>
```

WS-MetadataExchange is that simple to use. Observe that WS-MetadataExchange does not assume a policy repository (or registry) that is shared by the service provider and service consumer. Policies can be exchanged by any two parties using this protocol.

Service consumers often have access to a service registry in which service descriptions (WSDL documents) are stored. In such cases, it is possible to eliminate the need for a metadata service by attaching policies to service descriptions. The WS-PolicyAttachment standard specifies how this can be done. We will describe WS-PolicyAttachment next.

WS-PolicyAttachment

WS-PolicyAttachment defines how policies can be attached to WSDL definitions and UDDI entities. We will restrict the discussion here to attaching policies to WSDL, since we have not discussed UDDI in detail in this book.

WS-PolicyAttachment identifies four levels at which policies can be defined for a web service. These are Service, Endpoint, Operation, and Message. Formally, these are referred to as *policy subjects*, as they are the subjects of policy assertions. For example:

1 At the service level, a policy might indicate that all message exchanges need to be logged for auditing purposes.

2 At the endpoint level, a policy might indicate that a particular set of algorithms and key strengths are supported for encryption and signatures.

3 At the operation level, a policy might indicate that a SAML assertion is needed to indicate the privileges and/or preferences of the caller.

4   At the message level, a policy might identify parts of the message that need to be protected with encryption and/or signatures.

The policy to use in a message exchange is a combination of those associated with each of these four levels or subjects. Syntactically, the policy is split into these four portions in WSDL. WS-PolicyAttachment identifies multiple points in WSDL where a policy can be attached for each of these subjects. The endpoint is the subject for policies attached to wsdl:Port, wsdl:Binding, and wsdl:PortType elements in WSDL. The possible points of attachment for each subject are listed in figure 9.8.

WS-PolicyAttachment provides two mechanisms for attaching policy assertions to any element with a WSDL document.

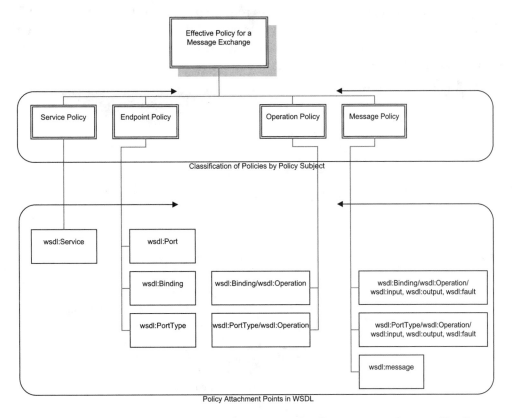

Figure 9.8   To compute the effective policy for a message exchange, one needs to combine the policies attached to four different subjects: Service, Endpoint, Operation, and Message. Policies can be attached to each of these subjects at the attachment points shown in this diagram.

1 Using a child element named `wsp:PolicyReference`:

```
<wsp:PolicyReference
  URI="#OurEndpointPolicy" wsdl:required="true"/>
```

2 Using an attribute named `wsp:PolicyURIs`:

```
<wsdl:binding
  wsp:PolicyURIs="#OurEndpointPolicy"
  ...>
...
</wsdl:binding>
```

The first of these mechanisms is not always legal, since WSDL does not allow extension elements under all WSDL elements. WS-PolicyAttachment provides the second mechanism as well.

In both cases, URIs are used to refer to policy assertions defined elsewhere. For policy definitions that are available as part of the same WSDL document, the URIs take the form of `#Id` where `Id` refers to the policy's identifier as given by its `wsu:Id` attribute. Listing 9.4 shows an example.

Listing 9.4 Attaching a policy to WSDL

```
<wsdl:definitions ... >
  <wsp:Policy wsu:Id="OurEndpointPolicy">          Policy 1 definition
    ...
  </wsp:Policy>
  <wsp:Policy wsu:Id="SecureMessagePolicy">        Policy 2 definition
    ...
  </wsp:Policy>

  ...

  <wsdl:binding name="example1SoapBinding"
    type="impl:Brokerage">
    <wsdlsoap:binding style="rpc"
      transport=".../soap/http"/>
    <wsp:PolicyReference URI="#OurEndpointPolicy"   Attachment of policy 1;
      wsdl:required="true"/>                        endpoint is the subject
    ...
    <wsdl:operation name="createMarketOrder">
      <wsdlsoap:operation soapAction=""/>

      <wsdl:input name="createMarketOrderRequest">
        <wsdlsoap:body
          encodingStyle=".../soap/encoding/"
          namespace="..." use="encoded"/>
        <wsp:PolicyReference URI="#SecureMessagePolicy"   Attachment of policy 2;
          wsdl:required="true" />                         message is the subject
      </wsdl:input>
```

```
      <wsdl:output name="createMarketOrderResponse">
        <wsdlsoap:body
          encodingStyle=".../soap/encoding/"
          namespace="..." use=encoded"/>
        <wsp:PolicyReference URI="#SecureMessagePolicy"
          wsdl:required="true" />
      </wsdl:output>
    </wsdl:operation>
    ...
  </wsdl:binding>
  ...
</wsdl:definitions>
```

Attachment of policy 2; message is the subject

Naturally, the client needs to combine all the subject-specific policies into one policy to understand the requirements of the service.

So far, we have described a generic policy framework for ensuring interoperability in web services. In particular, we

- Described the basic ideas of policy and policy intersection.
- Introduced the syntax provided by WS-Policy for expressing policy alternatives and illustrated it using a few basic assertions defined by WS-Policy-Assertions.
- Illustrated how WS-MetadataExchange and WS-PolicyAttachment can be used to fetch policies.

Now, it is time to look at how this generic framework can be used to ensure interoperability between security solutions. There is only one extension that we need to make the generic policy framework work; we need to standardize the security-related policy assertions we are going to use as part of policy alternatives in a WS-Policy document. WS-SecurityPolicy does exactly this. Let's study it in the next section.

9.4 *WS-SecurityPolicy*

WS-SecurityPolicy provides security-related assertions that can be used in WS-Policy documents to express the requirements, capabilities, and constraints of a web services security implementation. In particular, WS-SecurityPolicy standardizes assertions related to usage of WS-Security, WS-Trust, and WS-SecureConversation.

The assertions defined by WS-SecurityPolicy can be classified into four groups based on the policy subjects they can be associated with.

1 Policy assertions with endpoints as subjects; in other words, security policies that can be set at the endpoint level.

2 Policy assertions with operations as subjects; in other words, security policies that can be set per operation.

3 Policy assertions with messages as subjects; in other words, security policies defined at the message level.

4 Policy assertions that cannot be directly associated with a subject. These assertions can only be nested into other assertions.

Observe that WS-SecurityPolicy does not describe any assertions whose subject is a service. Figure 9.9 further classifies the assertions for endpoints, operations, and messages.

To help you understand the policy assertions, we will show you different kinds of policy examples. We will start with examples of policies defined at the endpoint level.

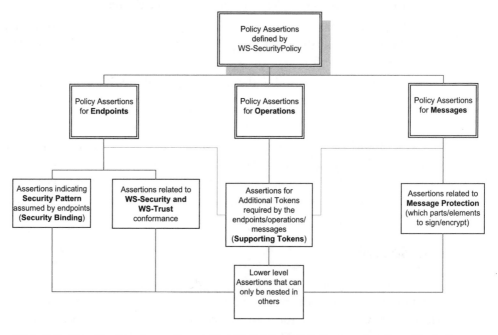

Figure 9.9   Classification of assertions defined by WS-SecurityPolicy based on the subjects they can be associated with: Endpoints, Operations, and Messages

9.4.1 *Security assertions for endpoints*

Before we start to learn the assertions defined by WS-SecurityPolicy for endpoints, it is helpful to understand how the designers of WS-SecurityPolicy approached this problem.

Previously, when discussing the challenges of interoperability between security solutions, we listed (in table 9.1) a large number of potential variations between security implementations that can break interoperability. The task that the designers of WS-SecurityPolicy had on their hands was to come up with policy assertions that unambiguously describe the position a security implementation should take on each possible variation. As there are too many possible variations, the trivial approach of simply defining one assertion per variation will result in a combinatorial explosion.

The designers of WS-SecurityPolicy attacked this problem by recognizing that only a few combinations of these variations are commonly seen in the real world. In fact, most real-world security implementations can be seen as following one of the three security usage patterns shown in figure 9.10.

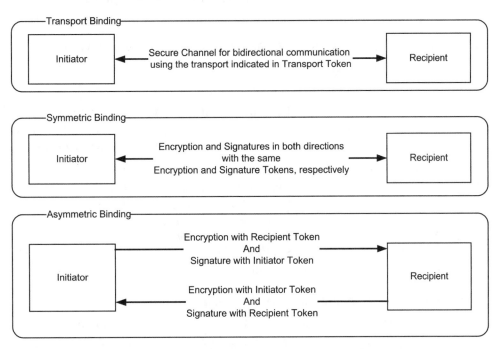

Figure 9.10   WS-SecurityPolicy identifies three common security patterns and defines how security policies should be bound to endpoints in each.

In words, these three possibilities can be described as:

1 Endpoints rely on a secure transport channel (such as an HTTPS channel). Security at such endpoints is in *transport binding*.

2 Endpoints take care of security at a message level and use the same tokens for message protection in either direction (request and reply). Security at such endpoints is in *symmetric binding*.

3 Endpoints take care of security at a message level and use different tokens for message protection depending on the direction of message exchange. Security at such endpoints is in *asymmetric binding*.

For each of these security usage patterns, WS-SecurityPolicy defines assertions for:

- The tokens needed
- Algorithms and key strengths
- Layout of elements in the WS-Security header
- Order of protections such as encryption and signatures
- Other required elements such as timestamps in the WS-Security header

In addition to assertions related to the security usage pattern, WS-Security-Policy defines two other kinds of assertions with regards to an endpoint's security policies.

1 Assertions about the conformance levels required with WS-Security and WS-Trust. We can assert that the other party must be able to resolve various types of security token references defined by WS-Security.

2 Assertions about the supporting tokens we need in addition to the tokens required by each security usage pattern supported by the endpoint. For instance, we may specify that a SAML assertion is needed.

We will look at examples of all these assertions in this section. We will start with examples of the assertions that can be used to specify one of the three security usage patterns described in figure 9.10.

Assertion for security pattern 1: TransportBinding

The security policy of an endpoint that is secured using transport-layer security is described using a `TransportBinding` assertion. As part of the `TransportBinding` assertion, the endpoint can specify the kind of transport-layer security it is willing to accept. It can state that it requires an HTTPS protocol with a specific key strength. Listing 9.5 shows how to put this information in a WS-Policy document.

Listing 9.5   Example of `TransportBinding` in WS-SecurityPolicy describing endpoint-level requirements

```
<wsp:Policy xmlns:wsp=".../policy">
  <sp:TransportBinding                    Asserts transport
    xmlns:sp=".../securitypolicy">        layer security
    <wsp:Policy>

      <sp:TransportToken>
        <wsp:Policy>                      Asserts HTTPS-based
          <sp:HttpsToken/>                point-to-point
        </wsp:Policy>                     secure channel
      </sp:TransportToken>

  ...
    </wsp:Policy>
  </sp:TransportBinding>
</wsp:Policy>
```

This example is quite simple—it says that we are using HTTPS for the transport. Let's next look at an example of the assertions defined for the second security usage pattern described in figure 9.10.

Assertion for security pattern 2: SymmetricBinding

Recall that endpoints that use the same tokens for message protection in both directions (request and reply) are said to be using *symmetric binding*. An example of a token that can be used that way is a Kerberos ticket. Figure 9.11 shows a sample interaction that is secured in both directions using a Kerberos ticket. The source endpoint in this interaction obtains a Kerberos ticket from a WS-Trust STS (described in section 8.5.1).

Listing 9.6 shows how the service provider shown in figure 9.11 can assert that service consumers must use a Kerberos ticket issued by a specific WS-Trust STS to encrypt/sign messages to and from the service provider endpoint.

Listing 9.6   Example of `SymmetricBinding` in WS-SecurityPolicy describing endpoint-level requirements

```
<wsp:Policy>
  <sp:SymmetricBinding>
    <wsp:Policy>
```

```
<sp:ProtectionToken>                                    Policy on protection
                                                        token in both directions
    <sp:IssuedToken
      sp:IncludeToken=".../Once" >

      <sp:Issuer>
        <wsa:EndpointReference
          xmlns:wsa="..." xmns:impl="...">
          <wsa:Address>.../sts</wsa:Address>
          <wsa:PortType>impl:Issue</wsa:PortType>
          <wsa:ServiceName>                                        ❶  Requires
              impl:IssueService        Details of the                 protection
          </wsa:ServiceName>           issuer—an STS in                token from
        </wsa:EndpointReference>        this example ❷                particular
      </sp:Issuer>                                                     Issuer

      <sp:RequestSecurityTokenTemplate>          Template of
        <wst:TokenType>                          the request
          ...#Kerberosv5_AP_REQ                  for obtaining
        </wst:TokenType>                          a protection
        ...                                       token
      </sp:RequestSecurityTokenTemplate>

    </sp:IssuedToken>
</sp:ProtectionToken>
                                          Asserts signature
                                          before encryption
<sp:SignBeforeEncrypting />
<sp:EncryptSignature />              Requires signature
</wsp:Policy>                        to be encrypted
```

In listing 9.6 we are asserting that the initiator should use a token issued by a specific STS ❷. The IncludeToken attribute on the IssuedToken ❶ element needs further explanation. This attribute can take four different values to indicate the different possibilities described in table 9.2.

Table 9.2 Possible values of the IncludeToken attribute defined by WS-SecurityPolicy

URI[1]	Description
.../Never	The security token must never be sent along with the message. It must always be referred to using an external reference. Refer to an X509 certificate by issuer and serial number (or other external reference mechanisms for certificates) instead of embedding the certificate.

[1] To keep the text in the table readable, we have only shown the last component of the URIs. Replace "..." in the URIs with http://schemas.xmlsoap.org/ws/2005/07/securitypolicy/IncludeToken

continued on next page

Table 9.2   Possible values of the `IncludeToken` attribute defined by WS-SecurityPolicy *(continued)*

URI[1]	Description
.../Once	Only include the token in the first message from the initiator to the recipient. For all subsequent messages in either direction, refer to the token using an external reference.
.../AlwaysToRecipient	Always include the token in messages from initiator to recipient. Never include the token in messages from recipient to initiator.
.../Always	Include the token in all messages in either direction.

[1] To keep the text in the table readable, we have only shown the last component of the URIs. Replace "..." in the URIs with http://schemas.xmlsoap.org/ws/2005/07/securitypolicy/IncludeToken

Figure 9.11 is an example of the assertions defined for the third security usage pattern described in figure 9.11.

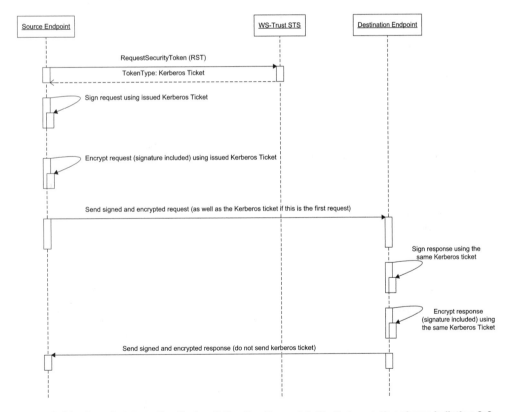

Figure 9.11   Sample interaction that satisfies the SymmetricBinding assertion shown in listing 9.6.

Assertion for security pattern 3: AsymmetricBinding

Recall that asymmetric binding, as opposed to symmetric binding, is where the endpoints use different tokens for message protection depending on the direction of message exchange. Figure 9.12 shows a sample interaction that fits into this pattern.

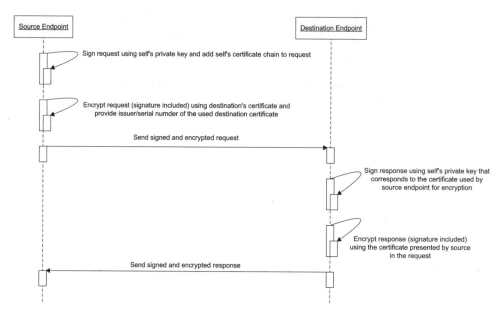

Figure 9.12   Sample interaction that matches the `AsymmetricBinding` assertion shown in listing 9.7

Listing 9.7 shows how you can use the `AsymmetricBinding` assertion defined by WS-SecurityPolicy to require the use of two different X.509 certificates—one belonging to the source endpoint and another belonging to the destination endpoint—for protecting request and response messages.

Listing 9.7   Example of `AsymmetricBinding` in WS-SecurityPolicy describing endpoint-level requirements

```
<wsp:Policy>
  <sp:AsymmetricBinding>
    <wsp:Policy>

      <sp:InitiatorToken>          Requires initiator's
        <wsp:Policy>               certificate chain in
          <sp:X509Token        ▽   all requests
```

```
                sp:IncludeToken=".../AlwaysToRecipient">
                  <sp:WssX509PkiPathV1Token10/>
              </sp:X509Token>
          </wsp:Policy>
        </sp:InitiatorToken>

        <sp:RecipientToken>
          <wsp:Policy>
            <sp:X509Token
              sp:IncludeToken=".../AlwaysToRecipient">
                <sp:RequireIssuerSerialReference/>
            </sp:X509Token>
          </wsp:Policy>
        </sp:RecipientToken>

        <sp:SignBeforeEncrypting />
        <sp:EncryptSignature />

      </wsp:Policy>
    </sp:AsymmetricBinding>

    ...

</wsp:Policy>
```

Requires initiator's certificate chain in all requests

Requires identification of recipient's certificate by issuer and serial number

Requires signature before encryption

Asserts that signature should also be encrypted

In all three security usage patterns, we need to deal with interoperability issues that can arise out of mismatches in algorithms and key strengths between different endpoints. The next assertion we discuss is designed to deal with this problem.

AlgorithmSuite assertion

Instead of defining one assertion per algorithm and key strength combination, WS-SecurityPolicy groups commonly used combinations of algorithms and key strengths into *algorithm suites*. An endpoint can assert its support for one or more suites using the AlgorithmSuite assertion. We can specify the following snippet under the Policy element to state that the endpoint supports the Basic algorithm suite with 256 bits of key strength.

```
<sp:AlgorithmSuite>
  <wsp:Policy><sp:Basic256/></wsp:Policy>
</sp:AlgorithmSuite>
```

The AlgorithmSuite assertion can be nested in any of the three security usage pattern assertions we have defined previously: TransportBinding, Symmetric-Binding, and AsymmetricBinding.

We will next discuss the Layout assertion, which can also be nested in any of the three security usage pattern assertions we have defined previously. It is only useful when a WS-Security header entry is used to provide message-level security.[1]

Assertion related to layout of elements in the WS-Security header entry

In chapters 3-8, you have learned a lot about security tokens that can be included as part of a `Security` header entry in a SOAP message. In these chapters, we have also talked about the ordering of tokens in the `Security` header entry. In chapter 6, when introducing the security tokens used for encryption, we told you that the `ReferenceList` of elements that have been encrypted must be prepended to the `Security` header entry to make the decryption process easy for receivers of the message. But standards cannot always mandate a specific order of elements in the `Security` header. At the same time, implementations may be limited in their ability to handle elements in arbitrary order; for the sake of simplicity and/ or efficiency, implementations may assume particular layouts of elements within the `Security` header.

So, if we want to ensure interoperability between arbitrary security implementations, we need a standard way to declare the capabilities and constraints of either endpoint in handling different layouts of elements in the `Security` header entry. WS-SecurityPolicy makes this possible by defining a `Layout` assertion. This assertion can be used to specify four different kinds of layouts, as described in table 9.3.

Table 9.3   Four possible layouts that can be asserted using WS-SecurityPolicy

Layout name	Description
Strict	This layout is probably the easiest to handle for WS-Security implementations. Tokens are declared before they are used, signed elements within the WS-Security header appear before their signature, and `ReferenceList` occurs before any of the `EncrypedData` elements within the WS-Security header are referred in the list.
Lax	Elements can occur in any order as long as the WS-Security spec is not violated.
LaxTimestampFirst	Same as Lax except that the first entry in the WS-Security header must be a `wsu:Timestamp` element defined by WS-Security
LaxTimestampLast	Same as Lax except that the last entry in the WS-Security header must be a `wsu:Timestamp` element defined by WS-Security

---

[1] Note that a message secured using a point-to-point secure channel such as HTTPS can also have a WS-Security header entry in it.

If we want to specify the layout to be strict, here is how we can do it.

```
<sp:Layout>
  <wsp:Policy><sp:Strict/></wsp:Policy>
</sp:Layout>
```

One of the elements in the WS-Security header we discussed in table 9.2 is `wsu:Timestamp`. Let's next look at assertions related to that.

Timestamp assertion

WS-Security defines but does not mandate the inclusion of a `Timestamp` element. It is almost always desirable to include it. Implementations that want to make the `Timestamp` element mandatory can do so using an assertion defined by WS-Security-Policy. Using this assertion is quite simple: Just nest an `<sp:IncludeTimestamp/>` element in the `TransportBinding`, `SymmetricBinding`, or `AsymmetricBinding` assertions, whichever is declared in the endpoint's policy document.

So far, we have seen assertions related to the three security usage patterns described in figure 9.10. As we described previously, there are two other kinds of endpoint-related assertions that WS-SecurityPolicy defines.

- Assertions about the conformance levels required with WS-Security and WS-Trust
- Assertions about the supporting tokens we need in addition to the tokens required by each security usage pattern supported by the endpoint

Let's next look at the assertions related to conformance with WS-Security and WS-Trust.

Assertions related to conformance with WS-Security and WS-Trust

WS-SecurityPolicy defines assertions that an endpoint can use to declare the conformance it requires with WS-Security 1.0/1.1 and WS-Trust 1.0. As we said before, these assertions become necessary because several options defined by these specifications and implementations may or may not support all options.

WS-Security provides options for referring to a security token. A security token can be embedded within a request or simply referred to using some token identification mechanism. Let's say an endpoint prefers to refer to X.509 certificates by issuer name and serial number as shown in the following:

```
<wsse:SecurityTokenReference>
  <ds:X509IssuerSerial>
    <ds:X509IssuerName>
      CN=Prasad Chodavarapu,OU=Authors,O=Manning,...
    </ds:X509IssuerName>
```

```
     <ds:X509SerialNumber>
        1120945714
     </ds:X509SerialNumber>
   </ds:X509IssuerSerial>
 </wsse:SecurityTokenReference>
```

How does such an endpoint declare that a client endpoint will need the capability to resolve references to certificates based on issuer and serial numbers? The solution is straightforward: The endpoint should declare in its policy that any party seeking to interact with it must support security token references based on issuer and serial number, as defined in WS-Security 1.0. The following assertion does this:

```
<sp:Wss10>
  <wsp:Policy>
    <sp:MustSupportRefIssuerSerial/>
  </wsp:Policy>
</sp:Wss10>
```

This example should have given you a good idea of how WS-SecurityPolicy seeks to solve the interoperability problems that arise out of options defined by WS-Security and WS-Trust. Table 9.4 shows the complete list of assertions defined by WS-SecurityPolicy for declaring conformance with various optional aspects of WS-Security 1.0/1.1 and WS-Trust 1.0.

Table 9.4 Assertions defined by WS-SecurityPolicy to declare conformance with WS-Security 1.0/1.1 and WS-Trust 1.0 specifications

Specification name and version	Top-level assertion element defined by WS-SecurityPolicy	Assertions that can be nested
WS-Security 1.0	Wss10	MustSupportRefKeyIdentifier MustSupportRefIssuerSerial MustSupportRefExternalUri MustSupportRefEmbeddedToken
WS-Security 1.1	Wss11	MustSupportRefKeyIdentifier MustSupportRefIssuerSerial MustSupportRefExternalUri MustSupportRefEmbeddedToken MustSupportRefThumbprint RequireSignatureConfirmation
WS-Trust 1.0	Trust10	MustSupportClientChallenge MustSupportServerChallenge RequireClientEntropy RequireServerEntropy MustSupportIssuedTokens

Most of the assertions listed in table 9.4 have self-explanatory names so we will not be describing them in detail here. Refer to the WS-SecurityPolicy specification if you need formal definitions for each of these assertions.

Let's now discuss the last class of WS-Security defined policy assertions that can be attached to an endpoint. These assertions let an endpoint mandate the presence of supporting tokens in addition to the tokens required by the security usage pattern supported by the endpoint.

Supporting token assertions

WS-SecurityPolicy defines four kinds of supporting tokens, as described in table 9.5.

Table 9.5   Four types of supporting tokens defined by WS-SecurityPolicy

Supporting token type	Description
`SupportingTokens`	Tokens included in addition to the token required by the security usage pattern (binding). The inclusion of tokens may necessitate the signing/encryption of more parts.
`SignedSupportingToken`	Same as `SupportingTokens` with the additional assertion that the supporting tokens must be signed using the mechanism described in the security binding. In the case of transport binding, no signing is necessary, as the binding does not use message-level signatures.
`EndorsingSupportingToken`	Same as `SupportingTokens` with the additional assertion that the supporting token should sign the signature produced by the security binding. In the case of transport binding, the endorsing token should simply sign the timestamp in the WS-Security header, as the binding does not produce a message-level signature.
`SignedEndorsingSupportingToken`	Combination of `SignedSupportingToken` and `EndorsingSupportingToken`.

Suppose an endpoint wants to specify that we need a SAML 1. 0 token as defined in the SAML Token Profile 1.0 for WS-Security. Here is how it can do so:

```
<sp:SupportingTokens>
  <wsp:Policy>
    <sp:WssSamlV10Token10
       sp:IncludeToken=".../Always" />
  </wsp:Policy>
</sp:SupportingTokens>
```

Now that you understand several assertions that can be used to describe the security policy of an endpoint, let's look at the security assertions that describe message-level policies.

9.4.2 Security assertions for messages

Up until now, you've seen how WS-SecurityPolicy–defined assertions can be used to specify the requirements, constraints, and capabilities of an endpoint. In this section, we will describe how message-level policies can be defined using the assertions defined by WS-SecurityPolicy.

WS-SecurityPolicy provides assertions to mandate:

1 **Signing**: There are two different kind of assertions that can be made about signing:

  1.1 *Signing of specific parts of a message*   You can sign the entirety of the SOAP body or headers identified by their namespace and, optionally, names.

  1.2 *Signing of selected elements in a message*   The elements to sign can be identified using XPath.

2 **Encryption**: There are two different kind of assertions that can be made about encryption:

  2.1 *Encrypting of specific parts of a message*   You can encrypt the entirety of the SOAP body or headers identified by their namespace and, optionally, names.

  2.2 *Encrypting of selected elements in a message*   The elements to encrypt can be identified using XPath.

3 **Presence**: Specific elements, identified by their XPaths, can be mandated using assertions defined by WS-SecurityPolicy.

Listing 9.8 illustrates all of these assertions.

> **Listing 9.8 Example of WS-SecurityPolicy assertions that describe message-level requirements**

```
<wsp:Policy
  xmlns:wsp=".../policy"
  xmlns:sp=".../securitypolicy" >

  <sp:SignedParts>
    <sp:Body/>
    <sp:Header Namespace=".../addressing"/>
  </sp:SignedParts>
```

Requires signing of body and all WS-Addressing headers

```
<sp:SignedElements xmls:wsu="...">
  <sp:XPath>//wsu:Created</sp:XPath>        Requires signing of all wsu:Created
  <sp:XPath>//wsu:Expires</sp:XPath>        and wsu:Expires elements
</sp:SignedElements>

<sp:EncryptedParts>               Requires entirety
  <sp:Body/>                      of message body to
</sp:EncryptedParts>             be encrypted

<sp:EncryptedElements>
  <sp:XPath xmlns:soapenv="..." xmlns:ns1="...">      Requires encryption
    /soapenv:Envelope/soapenv:Header/ns1:h1/ns1:secret   of elements
  </sp:XPath>                                          identified by XPath
</sp:EncryptedElements>

<sp:RequiredElements>
  <sp:XPath xmlns:soapenv="..." xmlns:ns1="...">      Mandates presence
    /soapenv:Envelope/soapenv:Header/ns1:h1           of elements
  </sp:XPath>                                         identified  by XPath
</sp:RequiredElements>

</wsp:Policy>
```

Let's discuss the assertions defined by WS-SecurityPolicy for declaring operation-level policies.

9.4.3 *Security assertions for operations*

In table 9.5, we have seen `SupportingTokens`, the only types of assertion defined by WS-SecurityPolicy that can be associated per operation. There is nothing further to add here about the assertions for operations.

In the past few sections, you have learned about the assertions defined by WS-SecurityPolicy. Table 9.6 summarizes the material we covered.

Table 9.6 Recap of WS-SecurityPolicy

Policy subject	Assertion topics
Endpoint	Security usage pattern (binding) Conformance with WS-Security and WS-Trust Supporting tokens
Message	Signing of message parts/elements Encryption of message parts/elements Required elements
Operation	Supporting tokens

As we stated before, WS-SecurityPolicy is new, complex, and incomplete. We will discuss its limitations in the next section.

9.4.4 *Limitations of WS-SecurityPolicy*

We started this chapter with a vision of declarative security. Any declarative security mechanism has two facets: One is external and supports interoperability and negotiation. Another is internal, which lets an implementation be derived from those declarations. Clearly, WS-SecurityPolicy only aims for the external facet. As yet, it is not suitable for generating a security implementation by itself. We cannot specify the LDAP directory to be used for authentication. SOA security vendors rely on proprietary extensions to fill this void.

Even when we are declaring to others the kind of security we are implementing, WS-SecurityPolicy falls short. We cannot specify the CA to be used for certificates. We can say we need a SAML token, but we cannot specify that the SAML token must contain an authorization assertion. There are several other small details that are needed by a security policy statement but are not covered by WS-SecurityPolicy.

It is worth noting that there are other standards that focus on codification of specific kinds of policies. A standard named XACML (Extensible Access Control Markup Language) provides a language to codify access control policies. XACML is not widely adopted so we will not be covering it in this book.

To summarize, WS-SecurityPolicy supports declarative security that is comprehensive enough for interoperability and negotiation, despite falling short in providing details for a full implementation.

9.5 *Summary*

This chapter covers one of the emerging topics in SOA security management. The standards described in this chapter, WS-Policy and WS-SecurityPolicy, are not yet widely used. Yet, several vendors are working on incorporating these standards into their tools.

Let's recap what we learned in this chapter. Declarative security is driven by three different goals: interoperability among applications, enforcing security policies consistently across several different security solutions in an enterprise, and ease of application development. Of these, the standards currently address only the first goal: interoperability.

Interoperability challenges arise from the choices that applications make in implementing standards. We can eliminate the unneeded choices by adhering to

WS-I Basic Security Profile. By itself, it will reduce the complexity of implementation addressing most common requirements.

When our requirements go beyond WS-I Basic Security profile, we can declare the security we need using WS-SecurityPolicy. If you followed the chapter so far, you should understand the details of WS-SecurityPolicy: how to read the policy statements, how to exchange them with another application, and how to even specify a policy with the right syntax.

The standards we have described in this chapter are all very recent and are not yet widely used. It is very likely that they will evolve further to meet real-world needs. We expect future enhancements or modifications to be incremental in nature; the effort you have put in into understanding this chapter should prove to be useful.

Over time, we can expect support from toolkits and solutions to make your job of dealing with security using declarative means easier. For instance, policy discovery, exchange, negotiation, and security decisions can be handled by a framework, without involving any code from the developer side.

This concludes the discussion of standards in implementing security in SOA. Chapter 10 will focus on the real-world issues in implementing solutions built on these standards. We expect more standards to emerge in SOA security over time; the ones we've discussed so far will form the core of SOA security.

Suggestions for further reading

- "WS-I Basic Security Profile Version 1.0" is available at http://www.ws-i.org/Profiles/BasicSecurityProfile-1.0.html. At the time of writing this book, the Basic Security Profile is still a working group draft dated March 29, 2006.

- The WS-Policy and WS-PolicyAttachment specifications are submissions made to W3C by an ad hoc industry group. The specifications are available at http://www.w3.org/Submission/WS-Policy/ and http://www.w3.org/Submission/WS-Policy-Attachment/. The drafts available at the time of writing this book are dated April 25, 2006. The "W3C Team Comment" on these submissions is available at http://www.w3.org/Submission/2006/06/Comment.

- WS-MetadataExchange is a specification developed by an ad hoc industry group. It is available at http://specs.xmlsoap.org/ws/2004/09/mex/WS-Metadata-Exchange.pdf as a public draft dated September 2004.

- Web Services Security Policy Language (WS-SecurityPolicy) Version 1.1 is a specification developed by an ad hoc industry group. It is available at http://specs.xmlsoap.org/ws/2005/07/securitypolicy/ws-securitypolicy.pdf as a public draft dated July 2005.

- Apache Neethi, at http://ws.apache.org/commons/neethi/index.html, is an open source Java library to create, parse, normalize, merge, and intersect policies compliant with WS-Policy.

- Support for declarative security and WS-Policy in BEA WebLogic Server 9.1 is described at http://edocs.bea.com/wls/docs91/webserv/security.html #210122.

- Support for declarative security in Web Services Enhancements (WSE) 3.0 for Microsoft .NET is described at http://msdn.microsoft.com/webservices/default. aspx?pull=/library/en-us/dnwse/html/newwse3.asp and http://msdn.microsoft. com/webservices/default.aspx?pull=/msdnmag/issues/06/02/wse30/ default.aspx.

- Layer 7 Technologies sells a SOA policy compliance manager named Secure-Span Manager. According to the product page available at http://www.layer7tech. com/products/page.html?id=4, SecureSpan Manager audits policy compliance in addition to supporting authoring and sharing of policies.

Designing SOA security for a real-world enterprise

This chapter covers

- Securing diverse services
- Deployment architectures
- Vulnerability management

We started this book by identifying three new approaches—message-level security, security as a service, and policy-driven security—that address the challenges SOA introduces in security.

Part II (chapters 4-7) described all the technologies and standards related to message-level security. Making and verifying identity claims, protecting data confidentiality, and verifying data integrity were described there. Chapter 8 explored the idea of offering security as a service. Chapter 9 focused on declarative, policy-based security.

By now you know enough about SOA security, both technology- and standards-wise. Still, if you want to design SOA security solutions for real-world enterprises, you need to know more. In particular, each enterprise has unique requirements that influence the overall SOA security solution. One enterprise may be concerned about high availability and disaster recovery capabilities, perhaps due to the high cost of application unavailability. Another may be focused on return on investment (ROI) and demand a low-cost solution. As an architect, you should translate these unique needs into technical guidelines.

In this chapter, we are going to provide insight into the process of developing security solutions that respect the constraints in an enterprise. While the other chapters in this book discussed a concrete technology that solves a specific problem, this chapter identifies the standard problems that you might face when designing security solutions in an enterprise and discusses the approaches typically used to solve these problems. In other words, this chapter will not provide silver-bullet answers; instead, it provides enough information for you to come up with your own answers.

We will begin by classifying the real-world challenges for SOA security solutions into different categories:

1   *Enterprise software requirements*   Most developers, including those who are developing security products, do not realize the complexities of enterprise software development, several of which are nontechnical. In section 10.1, we will provide the details of these challenges and how to address them in your solution.

2   *The kind of services we are securing*   In this book, we deliberately chose simple services when illustrating SOA security concepts. In real life, the services to secure are lot more complex and varied. In quite a few cases, it may not be easy to see how you can apply the security techniques we discuss in this book. In section 10.2, we discuss how you can secure different kinds of services you are likely to find in the real world.

3 *Deployment requirements* So far, we did not consider the impact of network design in SOA security solutions. We simply assumed that a security service can be located on any host that can be reached by the client and/or server. In the real world, the location of a security service is an important element of security design that needs to take into account network design and user locations. We also need to take into account organizational and legal structures that can have an impact on where the security service can be located. In section 10.3, we will discuss deployment scenarios that consider all these factors.

4 *System requirements* We have not covered performance, availability, scalability, and robustness. Even though these are generic requirements, we will discuss them in the context of SOA security frameworks in section 10.4.

5 *Threat of attacks* Every service implementation, including the implementation of the security service itself, may have a few known and unknown vulnerabilities. We will tell you in section 10.5 about XML-specific vulnerabilities and how you can defend your services against attackers looking to exploit them.

Let's start with the enterprise software requirements and see what kind of challenges they pose for a security solution.

10.1 Meeting the demands of enterprise IT environments

Most software developers fail to appreciate the complexity of enterprise software. They cannot understand why a simple software solution costs so much to deploy. The IT processes seem downright archaic, unsuitable for developing quality software. It is easy to write software that works; so why is it so complex to put together, say, a simple database-backed website?

In reality, there are several steps before any solution can be used by an enterprise. The following questions are asked before rolling out a database-backed website: How is the database managed? How is the application deployed? How is it updated? How do we train the users? How do we take care of hardware failures? Similar questions need to be answered before rolling out any enterprise SOA security solution.

Instead of answering these questions one by one, we will provide the general concerns that enterprises have for their application, so that you can answer them effectively. Typically the enterprises quantify these concerns using TCO (total cost of ownership). The aspects of the solution that impact the TCO:

- Catering to a large and diverse user base
- Designing for long life cycles
- Ensuring robustness
- Designing for manageability
- Integrating with diverse legacy applications

We will first describe the need for catering to a large and diverse user base and explain how it impacts the design of enterprise SOA security solutions.

10.1.1 *Large and diverse user base*

Typically, enterprise software is used by people with different technical backgrounds. For example, senior managers in a logistics company—people with deep knowledge of logistics (their business domain) but less familiar with application security—may need to use several applications. The process managers who use the computer frequently may need in-depth knowledge of the applications and yet may have only a limited understanding of the security solutions. Warehouse operators and truck drivers are likely to use less software.

In short, we have a large number employees with differing job descriptions using software for their specific duties at different locations. Naturally, this imposes several constraints on the way we develop a security solution.

To start with, the diverse user base makes it difficult to train anyone in security awareness. The security solution will have to be simple enough to be used by everybody. As the saying goes, "assume stupidity on part of the internal users, and maliciousness on part of the external users." That means, if any mistake can be made by users, assume that they will make it. If you make the password schemes complex, assume that they will write down the passwords. Also, be aware that you cannot prevent social engineering-based[1] security compromises without proper training.

How can we make a simple security solution really secure? One way is to have strong audit measures by monitoring for unauthorized requests or unusual num-

---

[1] Social engineering attacks are ones where hackers trick people into providing access control information. We cannot address them using technology alone. A well-designed security solution can take care of these attacks in multiple ways; for, example, by making password sharing difficult or alerting users of possible security violations, and so on.

ber of requests, unusual times of requests, or unusual patterns of requests. This monitoring can lead to proactive security management, such as temporary revocation of privileges or manual verification of the user activities.

The other way we can increase security is by *multifactor authentication* where we require users to present multiple pieces of evidence to identify themselves. For example, as shown in figure 10.1, we may require users to present a key generated by a hardware token along with their username and password.

Theoretically, multifactor authentication will improve security only if the multiple pieces of identification users present are qualitatively different from each other. For example, if the user simply presents two different passwords, that does not enhance the quality of security. A password is something the user knows. If the user can in addition present evidence that he is in possession of something—a hardware token that generates a different key every minute or a smart card that has an embedded digital certificate—the quality of security is certainly higher than what we get with a simple password-based scheme.

We need to be wary of any solution that is complex, as it will make logistics, training, and support difficult. For example, if we go in for two-factor authentication, we have the additional burden of distributing and managing hardware tokens or smart cards. That is why we should try to stick to mechanisms that are familiar to our users. As always, security and convenience impose opposing constraints on the solution, and the existing corporate culture will provide guidance on how to strike the right balance.

The next challenge in enterprise-class solution development is the need to design for long life cycles.

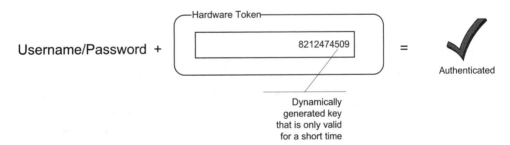

Figure 10.1 Example of two-factor authentication. In this example, username/password (something you know) is combined with a key generated dynamically by a hardware token (something you have) to create two-factor authentication.

10.1.2 *Long life cycle*

Most of us are surprised to find how old some applications in enterprises are. Some enterprises have back-end applications from the '60s. Others are just now migrating from Windows 98. This is in sharp contrast to most developers, who always want to use the latest tools and technologies. Why is that? And, what lesson is there for our security solution?

The complexity of IT in enterprises is such that they need to manage systems carefully. Any introduction of new software will have to be accompanied by extensive testing, training, and support provisioning. Since the cost of introduction and upgrade is so high, it may take six months, whereas a developer can upgrade his systems within six hours.

What this means to us solution developers is that we need to design our upgrade processes carefully. In this regard, separating the security concerns into declarative information can make upgrades easy. Be aware that we still have to go through the full cycle of testing, as we mentioned earlier. As a part of this upgrade, users should not require new training. Some of the techniques we have shown earlier, such as JAAS, can help isolate the changes to new libraries and new configuration files.

The long life of applications also requires us to make our implementation choices carefully. For example, we should choose technical standards, libraries, and vendors with a long-term perspective of viability, availability of source code, and support. We have to make sure that we can support our solution for a long time.

Another important requirement for enterprise-class solutions is robustness. Let's discuss this requirement next.

10.1.3 *Robustness*

For an individual, an application crashing may result in loss of data and time, causing inconvenience. For enterprises, this is not mere inconvenience; it may cause serious process disruption, resulting in irate customers, a warehouse full of unshipped goods, idling flights, and unhappy shareholders.

While any process disruption is bad, a security process disruption can be even worse. For instance, a solution that depends on a crucial resource such as a credential store can render every application inaccessible when it crashes. With such serious consequences, we must make sure that our solution is robust; that is, it works even in the event of unexpected failures. Here are some ways we can make our security solution robust.

First, we must follow standard application development guidelines to make the applications robust. Usual causes of crashes can be unstated and unreasonable limits on the resources. For example, if you program assuming only 10 people are going to access the system, what if an emergency forces 100 people to access the system? This can cause the system to repeatedly crash, making the situation even worse. One way we can make sure this will not occur is by gracefully dropping the additional users without application thrashing.

Second, we need to provide fault-tolerant systems. When a primary instance of an application goes down, a secondary instance should quickly come up and take over. There are a few standard ways of doing this regardless of what the application is. The approach to use will depend on details such as the amount of time it takes to start the application, the amount of state that the application keeps, how the state is kept, whether the application can gracefully recover from loss of state, and so on.

Enterprise SOA security solutions should also gracefully degrade and employ fault-tolerance mechanisms in order to be robust enough for use in real-world enterprises.

Next we will discuss the manageability requirements that enterprise solutions must satisfy.

10.1.4 Manageability

Manageability refers to the ease with which applications can be managed. Important aspects of enterprise application manageability include the ease with which administrators can provision applications for use by a large number of users, monitor the health of applications, and do maintenance activities such as creating backups and installing patches.

An enterprise-class SOA security solution needs to pay attention to all of these issues. For example:

- The security solution should integrate with existing corporate directories so that user provisioning need not be repeated.
- It should be easy to provision the use of the security service by a large number of services.
- It should be possible to federate the creation and maintenance of access control rules.
- It should be possible to monitor the security service using any of the popular application monitoring frameworks such as IBM Tivoli or HP Open-View. By *monitoring*, we mean more than just a routine check to ensure

that the security service is up all the time. We also mean SLA checks to see that the service is responding as required and auditing to ensure that the service is not accessing or consuming more resources than it should.

- Tools should be available to integrate the security solution with other infrastructure in the enterprise. For example, it should be possible to redirect notifications generated by the security solution to pagers of administrators.

Another challenge that enterprise-class solutions often have to meet is the need to integrate with diverse legacy applications. Let us discuss this requirement next.

10.1.5 *Integration with diverse legacy applications*

As we described, due to the long life cycle of applications, enterprises accumulate applications built on different technical platforms. A typical enterprise will have a mix of applications running on mainframes, Unix servers, and Windows desktops. Any security solution we build must be able to work with all these systems. That is:

- Any existing application should be able to use our security solution.
- If the security solution relies on assets that are managed by legacy applications, it must do so without requiring replication.
- If the security solution needs to interoperate—invoke other applications— it should be equipped to do so.

In section 10.3.2, we will describe different strategies you can use to secure legacy services.

In this section, we have discussed challenges and requirements all enterprise solutions must address. We have also discussed the impact of these challenges on the design of an enterprise SOA security solution. In the next section, we will focus on the strategies you can use when securing different kinds of services in an enterprise.

10.2 *Securing diverse services*

Although we have been assuming that a service is just that—a service—up to this point in this book, different kinds of services may need different security strategies. For example, the strategy we would use to secure a new service that is being developed from scratch on a web services platform may be different from the strategy we would use to secure a service that wraps a legacy application running

on a mainframe. It is important for enterprise SOA security architects to understand the kinds of services that need to be secured and the strategies that work
well for each kind of service.

In this section, we will discuss three broad kinds of services:

1 Services developed from scratch
2 Services wrapping legacy applications
3 Services that are composed of other services

For each kind of service, we will explore the strategies we can employ when securing them. Let's start with a discussion of the strategies we can use for services
developed from scratch.

10.2.1 *Services developed from scratch*

Typically, most enterprises build services on top of their existing applications as
they start moving to a SOA-driven enterprise. In new projects, it is likely that they
develop services entirely from scratch. Securing such services is simpler than
securing the legacy services.

Remember security is a part of the overall SOA strategy. High-level SOA
security strategy should be coming from the SOA governance team in your
enterprise. If you are part of the team assigned the responsibility of coming up
with a security strategy, here are some of the guidelines you can use when
developing a security strategy for new services:

1 *Identify the user repository* If there is already a corporate standard directory server, plan on using it. For testing and experimenting reasons, you
   may want to have your own directory server. It can be set up as a replicated slave server, making it useful immediately for the server authentication needs.

2 *Classify the authorization roles early on* Even if you have limited physical
   roles, plan on having as many logical roles as required. For example,
   even if the services you wish to secure only distinguish between two roles,
   say admin and authenticated, you can introduce as many roles as logi-
   cally required. Instead of a single role called admin, we can introduce
   multiple roles depending on what they administer: app admin, domain
   admin, system admin, and so on. This early separation of roles helps us
   later when we reconcile this security model with an external security
   model. We will describe what we mean by reconciling security models in

section 10.3.2 when we discuss strategies for securing services that wrap legacy applications.

3 *Develop a security framework* This framework may come from your vendor or from your team. It should support at the minimum following:

3.1 Securing a new service should be done without adding more code. It should be possible to use a declarative facility for that.

3.2 Managing security for a service should be easy. We should be able to change the role required to use a service without having to understand the code.

3.3 The framework should support auditing and logging as well. This helps us fine-tune the security implementation in practice. Often these services are already a part of the security requirements.

3.4 Whether you deploy security as a separate service or as a part of each service depends on your particular requirement. It is important to centrally maintain the code that manages security so it can be audited and tested thoroughly.

These guidelines help you in figuring out a specific security strategy for services you are developing from scratch. Next, let's explore the strategies you can use for securing services that wrap legacy applications.

10.2.2 *Services wrapping legacy applications*

Most of the services in the current generation of SOA implementations come from wrapping existing legacy applications. In fact, SOA is seen as a way for these applications to participate in modern workflows. Without SOA, these applications cannot provide the useful business logic they contain in a readily usable form.

There are many ways we can wrap legacy applications to offer services, each constraining the security strategy differently. Let's look at what technical choices we have in developing the services before discussing the possible security strategies for each of those choices:

■ *In-process library* If the legacy application is a stand-alone application, we can add another library to the application that can "talk" SOAP over HTTP and translate SOAP calls into function calls. This approach can work well for custom applications despite the complexity of development and management.

- *Messaging mechanism* Some applications have a document- or message-centric interface. They take requests in the form of a file in an input directory or as messages in a queue and produce responses as files in an output directory or as messages in queues. We may expose the capabilities of such applications as web services. For example, we can create WSDL bindings and declare FTP or message queue providers (such as JMS or IBM MQ Series) as the transports. Alternatively, we can create a wrapper that generates the files in input directories or messages in input queues upon receiving a service request and translates output messages to service responses. The wrapper may need to handle more complex situations. For example, the application may only respond to a request message after a long time, while the service invocation may have to be modeled as a synchronous request/response for reasons beyond your control. Messaging and Business Process Management (BPM) tool vendors (such as IBM, TIBCO, BEA, and Oracle) address these complexities by providing tools that make this kind of wrapping easy.

- *Existing API* The application may offer an API that can be used to build services. If an application already offers a CORBA interface, we can easily adapt it to implement web services. Or, if there is a network interface providing application services, we can do a protocol translation to offer them as SOAP-based web services.

- *Mimicking the end user* Some applications may not have the right interfaces or facilities for developing the services. If a partner's application offers only a web-based interface, you will have to resort to screen-scraping. Some old mainframe applications may offer only a tn3270 interface (a cursor-based interface). In that case, we write a library that interacts with the application to mimic the end user and use that as the basis for a creating a service.

Figure 10.2 depicts how wrapper services work, abstracting away the details of strategies used to wrap a service interface on top of a legacy application.

Figure 10.2 A service wrapping a legacy application to provide a service. In fact, there are tools typically provided as part of an ESB platform that can wrap the existing functionality and offer it as a service. This wrapping can convert message format, as well as protocol; in addition it can combine multiple functions into one service.

As you can see, there are three entities in the picture. The first is the client. The second is the wrapper or the proxy for the service. The third is the actual application implementing the service. As we discussed earlier, sometimes the second and third entities may lie in the same application. In any case, we can assume that the communication between the wrapper service and the legacy app is secure. Thus, we only have to see:

- How the client can invoke the wrapper service
- How the wrapper service can transform the security context, if any, to the legacy app

The material you have seen in the book so far describes how to tackle the first challenge. The second challenge involves reconciling the security model of the service with that of the back-end application. By security model, we mean the notion of users, roles, authentication, authorization, encryption, and nonrepudiation.

> **NOTE** *Reconciling security models* Security models in different applications can have different views on users and roles. In the security model of one application, each user may have only one role, and in the security model of another application, each user may have multiple roles. The user and role names themselves may be different. Or, roles with the same name may semantically differ. For example, an expert role could mean different sets of permissions in different applications.
>
> When we reconcile the security models of two applications, we map the users or roles of one model to those of the other. If traceability is important, each username in the first application must map to one and only one username in the other. If traceability is less of a concern than other factors such as simplicity and licensing costs, it may be acceptable to map roles defined by the security model of the first application to roles defined by the security model of the second application. When mapping roles, we want to achieve a semantically meaningful mapping, where roles in one application get equivalent roles in another application.

In reconciling the security models of the wrapper service and the back-end application, there are three choices:

1. We can completely manage the security in the wrapper service itself.
2. We can map users in the wrapper service to users in the application.
3. We can let the application manage the complete security.

To illustrate these choices in security models, we will examine some sample scenarios next.

Legacy application with no security model

In the simplest case, the underlying application may not have any security model. It may be relying on the network or the machine infrastructure to enforce security. For example, several Unix applications use file permissions to handle security traditionally. As shown in figure 10.3, in this scenario, we can completely manage the security in the service itself.

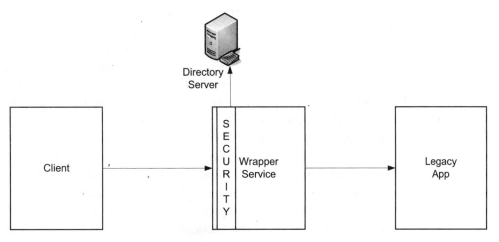

Figure 10.3   Security may be completely taken care of by the wrapper service if the legacy application delegates security away to the underlying infrastructure.

The wrapper service will have to address all aspects of security including authentication and authorization mechanisms per the overall SOA security guidelines.

Let's now consider a sample scenario of a legacy app wrapped by a service interface and see what security strategies make sense.

Home-grown application with simplistic security model

Here is a common scenario you might encounter: A department, to satisfy its own need, develops a small web application. Over the years, the application evolves, adding new functionality that the users require. Since it is built on early-generation web technologies, it might not support the security model that the corporation approves. It may have a simple model of authenticated, superuser, and guest roles, with every user mapped into one or more of those roles. It may have its own user management system that lets the admin create users and grant roles. As shown in figure 10.4, to reconcile security models of the wrapper service and the legacy app in this scenario, we can map users in the wrapper service to users in the application.

The corporate standards typically dictate the use of a more fine-grained set of users and roles backed by a user directory. Since the application has the built-in logic for users and roles, we must map the corporate standard into the application model. One popular choice is to create three internal users in the service called authenticated-user, superuser, and guest-user, each one registered with the back-end application with the appropriate role. After suitable authentication and authorization, each incoming user is mapped into one of the internal users. The back-end application is invoked using these internal users.

The mapping of the users to these limited roles depends on the security framework we are using. If we are using LDAP-based authentication, we can create the roles in the directory itself. If we are using a security service, the SAML assertion can provide the role in the header as we discussed in earlier chapters.

There is a precedent for this kind of security model management. Most database-backed web sites map web users to a single generic database user. They do not depend on the database user model for authenticating and authorizing the users. This technique lets them pool database connections in the web application.

There are drawbacks to this approach. If the back-end legacy application maintains its own auditing, your user mapping will render it useless. For example,

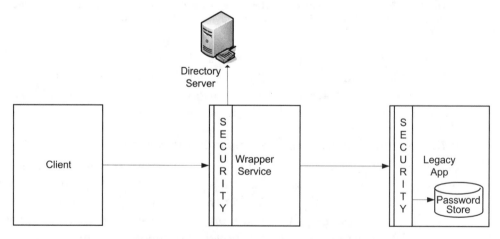

Figure 10.4 Where legacy applications come with a home-grown security model, the wrapper service needs to map its security mechanisms to those of the legacy application.

the back-end application will show a large number of accesses from authenticated-user, which in reality are from several different users. If we want to analyze user accesses, we must now rebuild auditing facilities at the wrapper service access point. In addition, the diagnostic messages or the informational logging messages from the back end may not be useful under this gross mapping scheme.

If the response of the back-end application depends on the actual username, we should provide the username as is. In that case, we cannot use this mapping technique. Instead, we need to provision all the users in the application, then use one-to-one mapping. Or, if the back-end application uses a directory, we need to synchronize it with the corporate directory.

Let's consider yet another sample scenario of a legacy app wrapped by a service interface and see what security strategies make sense.

Home-grown application with flexible security model

Several applications being developed these days support pluggable authentication systems. Some of the application servers even support completely externalized declarative support for authentication systems.

We can envision two different ways to use the flexibility of the security model in the legacy application.

1   We can implement the security entirely in the application and invoke the service without any security precautions. This approach will not work if the wrapper service needs the assurance of the client's name or role. As we will discuss later in this chapter, in case of DoS attacks, the entire burden falls on the legacy app to filter out bogus requests.

2   As shown in figure 10.5, we can use a separate security service that can be used by the wrapper service as well as the legacy application. Since there is only one authentication source, we do not have any reconciliation issues. The wrapper service can use the user and role information not only in any computation, but also to filter out any bogus requests. The legacy application can obtain the authenticated user and role information from the security service before computing its response. If the legacy application provides the portfolio total amount for the client, it needs the person's name to be verified before computing the total.

Next we will discuss the security strategies you can use in another commonly found scenario: a wrapper providing a service interface to capabilities found in an enterprise resource planning (ERP) application.

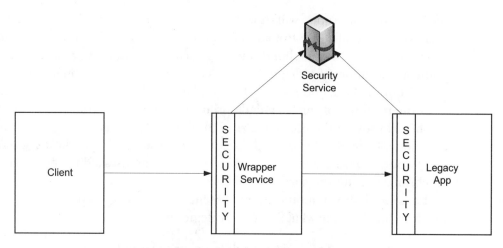

Figure 10.5 Where a security mechanism can be plugged into the legacy application, the wrapper service may establish a security context in an external security service for subsequent use by a custom security plug-in in the legacy application.

ERP application with hard-wired security model

Large ERP applications come with sophisticated user models which support user hierarchies, groups, and good management tools. An ERP application can offer desktop applications, web applications, and command-line interfaces and its security model must support each type of application. In addition, it provides standard interfaces via libraries, network protocols, and message buses for getting the data in and out of the application and invoking the functionality provided by the ERP.

Since ERPs offer such complete security models, it is preferable to use one of them. If ERP packages need to be integrated, especially using services, we face the problem of mapping the security model of one application to another. If both applications use one source for authentication and authorization, this is a simple task. Typically we need to reconcile the user information between two different directories and our choices range from synchronizing the two directories using tools to reconciling user information as we discussed for other legacy applications. Vendor solutions for solving this problem are typically referred to as *identity management solutions*.

So far, we have discussed the security strategies you can use for services written from scratch and services that wrap legacy applications. Let's now look at the security strategy for services that are composed of other services.

10.2.3 *Services composed of other services*

When we are wrapping applications in services, we may be doing more than simple proxying. We may be orchestrating multiple applications to produce a response to a service request. What we are creating in such cases is a composite service—a high-level service that brings together the capabilities of several lower-level services.

Composition of services can happen in different ways. A simple composition may merely transform and collate the data from multiple services. More sophisticated composition can selectively invoke services based on the outcome of other services. In more complex scenarios, composition can involve additional business logic and invocation of alternate services to elicit the best possible response. Figure 10.6 illustrates a sample composite service.

Securing composite services can be complex. For instance, in figure 10.6, the composite service has to invoke services A, B, C, and D to provide a response. Who can invoke the composite service is determined by who can invoke A, B, C, and D. One choice is to make the composite service simply relay the user credentials (for example, username and password) to services A, B, C, and D. If a client is allowed access to all the required services he is allowed access to the composite service. This model does not preserve the atomicity of the composite service. That means that after service A is invoked, if service B rejects the credentials, we would have to roll back the effect of invoking A.

An alternative is to define the security policy of the composite service conservatively as an intersection of services A, B, C, and D. After authenticating the user, we can carry the context to each of these services so that the access is granted to the client. This approach takes more effort to build security for the composite service. The benefit is that the atomicity of the composite service is not broken due to security violations.

As you can see, in every scenario, there are multiple security strategies you can choose from. You will have to evaluate the trade-offs associated with each possible strategy and pick one that you are comfortable with.

So far in this chapter, we have discussed two of the topics enterprise SOA security architects must be familiar with. We discussed the demands of enterprise IT environments and their impact on SOA security design. We also discussed a number of security design strategies for different kinds of services commonly encountered in enterprises.

Next, we will discuss the challenge of coming up with the right deployment architectures for SOA security solutions.

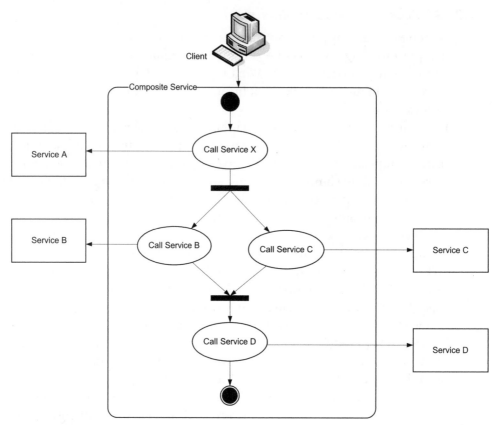

Figure 10.6 Example of a composite service. Different approaches are possible when securing composite services such as this. No one approach is suitable in all situations.

10.3 *Choosing a deployment architecture*

Until now, we have dealt with services, service consumers, credential stores, and security services as if their relative locations did not matter. This abstraction was deliberate. Focusing on logical characteristics of entities and ignoring their relative locations helped us reduce the complexity often seen in the real world, for the purpose of teaching. Now, we are going to address the location question—where in the network does each service belong?

Location has a significant bearing on the design of a SOA security solution for a real-world enterprise. This is generally true for any enterprise solution. Designers of enterprise solutions see the impact of location in multiple ways:

- The solution may fix the relative locations of certain entities. If you are offering a solution over the Internet, users are going to be accessing the application over the public network. We exercise little control over the public network. If the users are the general public, you cannot even ask for a VPN-based solution. When designing security solutions for services offered to the public, we have take into account the fact that unauthorized users can potentially attack and gain control over the servers hosting public services.

- Entities whose locations are not fixed by the solution need to be placed in appropriate locations by design. This task can be complex; in some cases, we may have to break an entity into multiple physical components so they can be placed in locations appropriate for each. Or, we may have to deploy multiple instances of the same logical entity in different locations for performance and availability reasons.

- When we break up a logical entity into multiple components at different locations or when we redundantly deploy a logical entity in multiple locations, we run into additional design work that we would not have considered until then. When doing redundant deployments of a credential store, for example, we have to worry about keeping the stores in sync.

In addition to these challenges, security, performance and availability requirements need to be taken into account when answering the "what goes where" question. The solution to what goes where is commonly referred to as the *deployment architecture*.

In the rest of this section, we will discuss deployment architectures for SOA security solutions. Figure 10.7 depicts the challenge of what goes where in the context of a SOA security solution.

In the figure, on the left side are the entities in our problem domain:

- Services offered for use within the enterprise intranet, services offered to the public, services offered to partners, and services offered by partners
- Service consumers within the enterprise, in partner firms, and from the public at large
- Credential stores (directories)
- Security service

On the right side are the possible locations for these entities. At a high level, possible locations are:

- Enterprise
- Partners
- Managed service providers
- Public at large

As you can notice, these locations are not atomic. Some can and should be divided if we are to succeed in coming up with the right deployment architecture. To do this division, we need to identify locations that have unique needs/capabilities or pose unique challenges. The enterprise may need to be further divided into regions, with each region consisting of a headquarters, branch offices, and data centers. A data center may in turn need to be divided into multiple locations for security reasons.

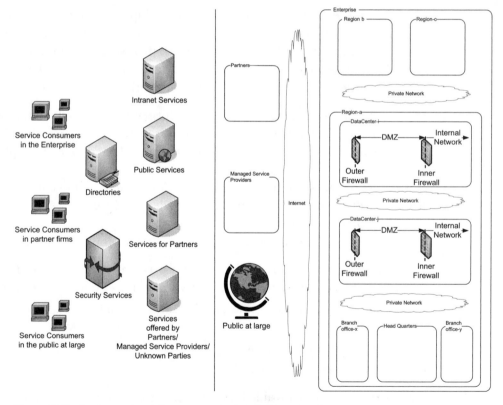

Figure 10.7   Deployment architecture puzzle: What goes where? Match the entities on the left with the locations on the right. Break up or duplicate entities as required.

Some of this division may be omitted if the basis on which further division can happen is inconsequential when discussing the deployment choices for a use case (or a class of use cases). This is what we will do as we consider three important classes of use cases.

The three classes of use cases we consider here are

1   Security for services offered within an enterprise intranet
2   Security for services offered to the public at large
3   Security for services offered to partners or hosted by partners/managed service providers.

We will start our discussion with the intranet use cases.

10.3.1 *For securing services in the intranet*

One would think that the deployment architecture for securing services within an enterprise intranet would be quite simple. Firewalls will not get in the way and one can assume that all entities live in a single large network. This simplistic view turns out to be misleading.

The distributed and federated nature of twenty-first century enterprises makes intranet network topologies quite complex. Administrative and legal boundaries, the multiplicity of data centers, and the lack of IT support staff at small branch offices, can all have a significant impact on the deployment architecture for a security solution. We will discuss the impact of each of these factors, starting with the simplest possible case of an enterprise with just one data center and one office.

Simple case: One data center, one office

Assume that the enterprise intranet consists of just two locations, a data center and an office, as shown in figure 10.8. All the services are hosted out of the data center. So are the security service and the credentials repository. Service consumers can exist both in the office (user applications acting as service consumers) and in the data center (one service depending on another).

The exact form of security service can vary. It can be a server-based solution or a network device (such as an AON device described in appendix E). Interaction between services/service consumers and the security service can take any of the five forms described in sections 8.2.1 through 8.2.5.

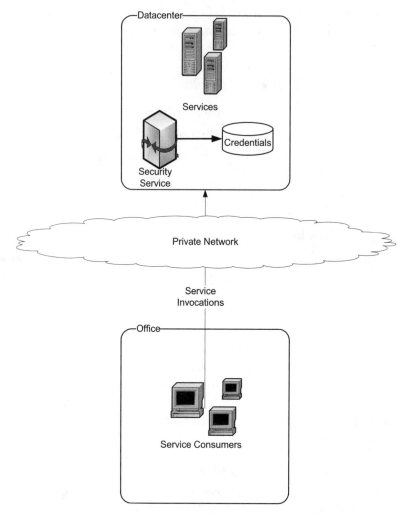

Figure 10.8   A simplistic view of an enterprise intranet consisting of one data center and one office. How services/service consumers interact with the security service is deliberately omitted from this figure, as multiple possibilities exist.

Catering to the needs of small/remote branch offices

It is common for enterprises to have a large number of branches. For example, you see banks opening branches in supermarkets and oil companies owning gas stations in remote areas. It is difficult to place qualified IT people in these branches. Any task that requires complex configuration and maintenance is an operational challenge in these offices.

Let's see what kind of support these branch offices need. Some desktop applications used in a small/remote branch office might be consumers of services offered within the enterprise intranet. That means these service consumers need to be configured with at least the location of a registry that houses metadata for services offered within the enterprise. This configuration needs to be updated if and when the registry location changes. In addition, if some of the consumers require security policies to be configured beforehand, a mechanism is needed to keep the preconfigured policies up-to-date. This is clearly a challenge if IT support staff is not available in the branch office.

A possible solution to this problem is shown in figure 10.9.

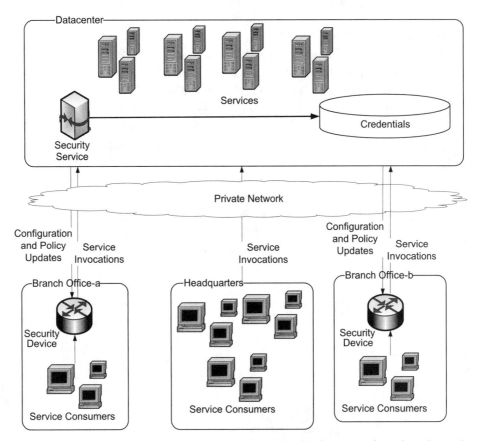

Figure 10.9 A remotely configurable security device (either hardware or software) can be used as client proxy. This technique comes in handy in small/remote branch offices that lack IT support staff.

If we place a remotely configurable security device (either hardware or software) at each small/remote branch office, we need not maintain the security policy configuration in each of the desktop applications acting as service consumers. The security device can be periodically updated with the latest security policies, based on which it can appropriately secure each service invocation emanating out of the branch office.

There are several choices for implementing remotely manageable client proxies. We can use a remotely managed server running client proxy software. We can use tools from middleware vendors to develop and manage this server. We can also use an AON. We can expect these tools to support, at the minimum, remote configuration and monitoring.

Adding a second data center

An enterprise may rely on more than one data center for multiple reasons. Every office can be served from the closest data center to provide fast responses. Enterprise operations can be kept up and running even if disaster strikes in one of the data center locations. Adding a second data center brings additional complexity.

Each data center may house its own credential stores and security service. In such a case, we need to set up mechanisms for replicating credentials and security policies between the data centers as shown in figure 10.10. All LDAP directories support replication between multiple instances of the same make. If you use directories from different vendors in different locations, you will need to build your own replication mechanisms unless all vendors support LDAP Duplication Protocol

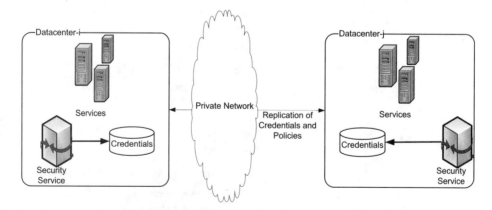

Figure 10.10   When using multiple data centers, enterprises need to replicate credentials and policies across all data centers.

(LDUP). How you replicate security policies will depend on where you store them. If you are using a service registry to store your policies, you will need to check with your registry vendor to understand how you can replicate registry contents between multiple instances.

Managing trust between autonomous units or regions

Multinational companies have autonomous units in different countries or regions to satisfy legal requirements in each location. The strength of relationships between autonomous units can vary from enterprise to enterprise. In most cases, there is a trust established between autonomous units so that they can use some of each other's services over a private network. Trust between these enterprises—established by accepting each other's digital certificates, Kerberos tickets, or other mechanisms—needs to be maintained and managed as both enterprises evolve as shown in figure 10.11.

There is no one specific technique for trust management, as requirements will vary widely between enterprises. Here, technology plays only a limited role; there is a need for defining and managing security processes to establish and manage this trust.

We have so far discussed possible deployment architectures for securing services in the intranet. Let's now discuss the deployment architectures for securing services offered to the public.

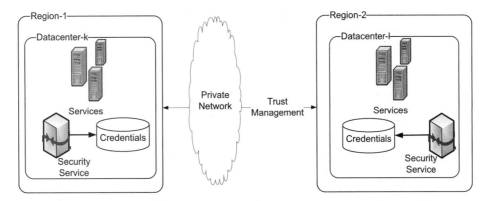

Figure 10.11 Trust relationships between multiple autonomous units of an enterprise need to be maintained. A trust relationship may be based on acceptance of security tokens issued by each other's security service for invocation of specific services shared between the units.

10.3.2 *For securing services offered to the public*

We have seen in the previous section how, contrary to our initial expectations, deployment of a security solution for intranet services can get quite complex. The situation is the opposite for deployment of services offered to the public. Thanks to the popularity of web applications, most techniques needed for securely deploying services offered to the public, for instance firewalls and the demilitarized zone (DMZ), are well understood. There are a few new questions to be answered before we can decide on specific deployment architecture for publicly offered services. We will cover these later in this chapter.

Before we proceed we need to introduce two common techniques—one from network security and another from web application deployment. A good understanding of these techniques is needed to follow the rest of the discussion in this section.

Introduction to firewalls

A firewall is a network device that filters traffic passing through it based on rules set up by the firewall administrator. To understand firewalls, you need to understand how a network works.

An application message, such as a SOAP request addressed by one endpoint to another, gets split into one or more packets by the network. Each packet carries a part of the data in the application message, plus addressing information and other control fields (such as a checksum). The addressing information within a packet is different from what we understand as that at an application level. The endpoint URI for a service call is not part of the addressing information in packets that make up the service call. Instead, all that is available at the network layer is

- Source and destination IP address
- Transport (not to be confused with what we call transport in the case of web services) protocol, typically TCP or UDP
- In the case of TCP and UDP, source and destination port numbers

As a network firewall filters one packet at a time, the filtering rules you provide to a firewall can only be based on information available within a packet. The kinds of rules firewalls can use for filtering

1   Allow any TCP packet addressed to port 80/443 of 192.168.1.2 (my web server's IP address).

2 Allow any TCP packet addressed to port 25 of 192.168.1.3 (my mail server's IP address).

3 Allow all packets whose source IP address is 192.168.1.x (my internal subnet). This rule allows internal hosts to send packets out.

4 Disallow attempts to establish a new inbound TCP connection (TCP SYN) except those allowed by rules 1, 2, and 3.

5 Allow all TCP packets not covered by rule 4 so my internal hosts can receive responses on connections they have initiated.

6 Disallow all other packets.

Figure 10.12 illustrates the combined effect of rules 1, 2, and 4. As you can see, firewall rules can be used to block all packets except those that we specifically allow to come in or go out of our internal network.

Introduction to DMZ

It is no good stating that we will firewall every application. There are always a few applications that need to be exposed to the outside world. For example, a mail server is always needed to receive emails from customers, partners, and the general public. As no piece of code is ever perfect, we need to prepare for the eventuality of an attacker gaining complete control over the machines hosting publicly accessible applications. A security hole such as a buffer overflow in an application can allow an attacker to execute arbitrary code on the server and obtain, in lots of

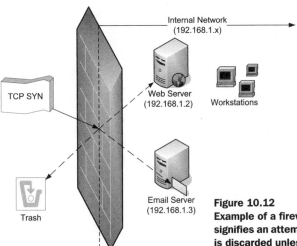

Figure 10.12
Example of a firewall rule: An inbound TCP SYN that signifies an attempt to establish a new TCP connection is discarded unless it is destined to the web server or email server.

cases, privileged access. A common technique used to defend against compromise of publicly exposed applications is to place them in a separate subnet called the DMZ.

Applications in a DMZ can receive packets from anywhere—from within the enterprise intranet or from a public network. Applications in a DMZ cannot, in general, initiate connections to nodes within the enterprise intranet. The damage an attacker can cause is limited even if he assumes complete control over a machine within the DMZ.

There are multiple ways to implement a DMZ. Figure 10.13 shows a popular implementation strategy. Two firewalls are used in this strategy:

1 An outer firewall that only allows connections to specific applications hosted in the DMZ

2 An inner firewall that only allows new connections one way—from an internal network into the DMZ but not the other way around

One or both firewalls may additionally do Network Address Translation (NAT) from publicly known IP addresses to private IP addresses. This further enhances security.

In practice, limited exceptions are made to allow applications within the DMZ to access specific applications within the intranet that they depend upon. It is common to punch a hole in the inner firewall to let a web server access a database within the internal network, as shown in figure 10.14.

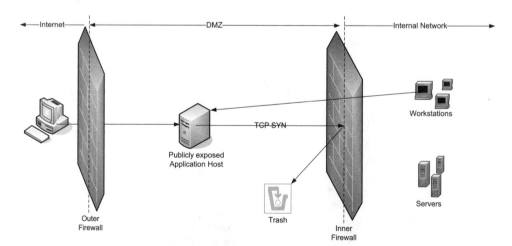

Figure 10.13 DMZ implementation using two firewalls. The inner firewall discards any attempts by DMZ hosts to initiate a new connection into the internal network.

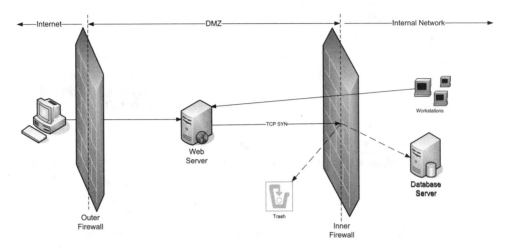

Figure 10.14 **A web server located in the DMZ is often allowed to initiate a connection to a database server within the internal network, as it is a more secure choice than moving the database server as well into the DMZ. Connection initiation attempts by the web server in the DMZ to any internal application other than the database server will be discarded.**

Although this seems, at first sight, to be a serious dilution of the concept of DMZ, this is a better choice than placing all the needed applications into the DMZ. We could have placed the database server as well in the DMZ, but this is not a good alternative, as the database server would get opened up for direct attack.[2]

In some cases, punching holes in the inner firewall can be avoided if the direction of connection establishment can be reversed. If the application in the internal network can be made to establish a connection to the application in the DMZ no hole would be needed in the inner firewall. The DMZ application can then use the connection established by the internal application for all subsequent communication.

Deployment of publicly exposed web services

Now that you understand the concepts of firewalls and DMZ, it is easy to see how a security solution should be deployed for publicly exposed services.

As the public web services will themselves be hosted in the DMZ, a security service protecting them will also have to be in the DMZ. This service should protect the

---

[2] This is true even if we do not allow direct access to the database server in the DMZ across the outer firewall. An attacker who gains control of another machine in the DMZ can launch a DoS attack on the database server by flooding it with TCP SYNs.

public services by validating incoming requests against a schema, scanning the requests for commonly used XML attacks, then authenticating and authorizing the request. This kind of security service is a *web services security gateway.*

Where should the credential store (directory server) for authentication be deployed? The directory server should be within the internal network, as placing it in the DMZ will expose it to direct attacks. A specific hole needs to be punched into the inner firewall to let the security service in the DMZ contact the directory service in the internal network as shown in figure 10.15.

There is another important and interesting question to answer here. Where should the enterprise's private key be stored? If the inbound messages received by the security service are encrypted, the security service will need access to the enterprise's private key in order to decrypt incoming messages. It is not a good idea to permanently store the enterprise private key in the DMZ, as it could be stolen more easily. The key needs to be protected by placing it in the internal network.

When the security service requires the private key for decryption, it can fetch the key from the credential repository in the internal network. The security service should not remember the private key for too long, as the key can be stolen if the security service itself is compromised.

A more secure option is to rely on a service offered from within the internal network to decrypt incoming requests. That way, the enterprise private key never

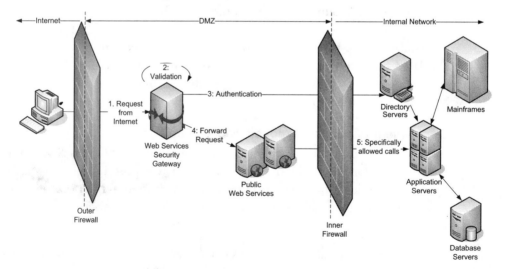

Figure 10.15 Example deployment architecture for securing services offered to the public.

leaves the internal network. Another hole needs to be punched into the inner firewall to let the security service in the DMZ contact the decryption service in the internal network. Or, the decryption service can initiate a connection to the security service in the DMZ and the latter can use the established connection to invoke decryption services.

You now have a good idea about possible deployment architectures when securing services in the intranet and when securing services offered to the public. Let's look into the possibilities when securing services offered to/by partners.

10.3.3 *For securing services offered to/by partners*

Partners are different from the general public or internal members. They get controlled and limited exposure to the enterprise. Not all partners are alike. We will consider three kinds of partners for discussion in this section.

1 Large partners providing their own services for the enterprise's benefit in addition to consuming services offered by the enterprise.

2 Small partners without much IT infrastructure to speak of. We can assume that these partners do not offer any services of their own. They simply consume services offered by the enterprise.

3 Managed service providers which host services for use by the enterprise. They do not consume any of the services provided by the enterprise.

Not all partners of every enterprise will fit into one of these three classes perfectly. We just picked these three to illustrate the deployment choices available when integrating with partners. Figure 10.16 shows a deployment option each for these three classes of partners.

Small partners with little IT infrastructure of their own may not have the ability to satisfy the security policies of the enterprise. For example, a small partner may not have a security solution in place that can encrypt parts of a message that need to be kept confidential. In these cases, the enterprise can require its small partners to place a security agent that will help them comply with the enterprise security policies in their networks. The security agent can take the form of a device (such as an AON) that can be remotely managed. This will keep the burden on the small partner to the least amount necessary.

Requests secured by a security agent at the partner's site can be trusted and routed directly to web services offered for partners. Requests emanating from large partners who do not use the enterprise's security agent will have to be first screened by a security gateway in the enterprise DMZ.

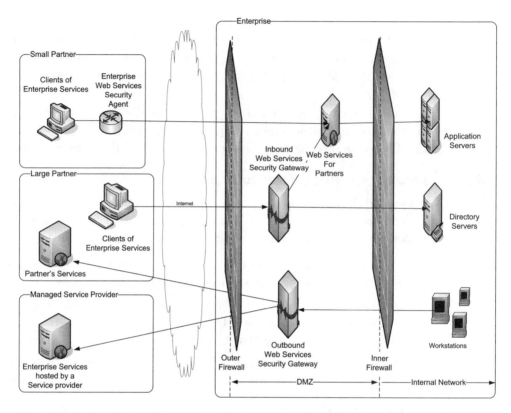

Figure 10.16 Security solution deployment for offering services to partners and consuming partner services. Note that we have not shown the security solutions used internally by each of the partners or managed service providers.

Requests to partner-provided services or services hosted by a managed service provider will also have to adhere to the enterprise's security policy. When we say security policy here, we are referring to the policy for outgoing messages. In figure 10.16, we illustrate a logical separation between a security gateway for inbound messages and a security gateway for outbound messages.

In this section, we described the possible deployment architectures for securing services in the intranet, services offered to the public, and services offered to/ by partners. We will next look into another important challenge enterprise SOA security practitioners face: making the security solution industrial-strength.

10.4 *Making the solution industrial-strength*

SOA is becoming an important part of IT strategy. One of the prerequisites of widescale deployment of SOA is that it should be industrial-strength. That is, corporations can rely on it to support business needs. Security solutions for SOA should support the same goals. In this section, we will examine what it means to make a SOA security solution industrial-strength and how we can achieve that goal. In particular, we will describe how you can address performance, scalability, and availability requirements. We will start with a discussion of performance issues.

10.4.1 *Performance*

Everybody likes their systems to perform well. Unfortunately, compared to the tightly coupled systems that are typically replaced by SOA, performance of SOA systems lags behind. This is a big concern for enterprises embracing SOA. Fortunately, there are several ways to increase the performance of systems based on SOA. In this section, we are going to confine ourselves to only those that increase the performance of the security solutions.

One clear guideline about improving the performance is this: unless we know where the performance bottleneck is, we cannot develop an efficient solution. Speeding up a task that takes 50 percent of overall time by 10 percent has more impact than speeding up a task that takes 10 percent of overall time by 50 percent. Therefore, we should start optimizing once we have good metrics on where time is being spent in the total solution.

Next, let's consider what you can do when you encounter a performance bottleneck.

Hardware solutions

There are several tasks that are part of a security solution that can effectively be done in hardware. Hardware offers increased performance in multiple ways, at a cost of increased complexity. Special-purpose hardware can be faster than general-purpose processors, since it can be optimized specifically to do the task it is designed for. At a minimum, it offloads the burden from the main processor, allowing it to do other tasks. It introduces additional complexity—the program or the processor needs to know which task to delegate to the hardware. If the program needs to do the delegation, it needs to be explicitly coded. In some specific cases, the processor can invoke the hardware device without explicitly being asked.

The best candidates for hardware acceleration are ones with very well-understood requirements. For example, point-to-point encryption is well understood and is expensive enough to benefit from hardware acceleration. Indeed, several special-purpose hardware chips offer SSL in hardware. These have been in use since even before SOA—and are applicable in SOA security as well—to provide network-level encryption.

Not all time-consuming activity can be done in hardware. Typically the difficulty lies in coming up with a problem that is well defined and can be done in hardware more efficiently so that the overall solution can be faster. There are only so many tasks that fit this description. One recent approach is to expand the range of tasks that the hardware can do by making hardware programmable.

One such example, as discussed in appendix E, is AON. AON solutions can be programmed to do well-defined horizontal tasks (that is, those that do not require deep domain knowledge): security, auditing, content-based routing, load balancing, and so on. We can only expect the increased use of such special-purpose hardware to provide well-understood generic services that are customizable for a situation. The complexity these days lies in customizing and maintaining the total SOA solution. With enough attention to these problems, hardware solutions may become more and more usable.

Software solutions

Hardware-based solutions for improving performance are not always applicable. Improving the design and implementation of the solution in software can often improve performance to the required levels. Here are some of popular techniques:

- *Credential caching*   One of the tasks of security is to authenticate and authorize the users. Most of the time, this necessitates a user-to-role map lookup in an external store. We can speed up access to the credential store considerably using various techniques. For example, we can maintain a local cache that keeps all user credentials. With machine memory being cheap, this often is a workable solution. We can also keep this cache as needed, building it up as we go along. Caching may weaken the overall security of a solution. Vulnerability in the service may be exploited by an attacker to access the cached credentials. A common strategy is to not remember sensitive parts of the credentials, such as passwords, while retaining relatively less sensitive information in the cache.

- *Replication of the authentication source*   In a distributed organization, authentication and authorization can happen at different locations. If the credential store is not local, it can take time to invoke. A standard technique is to replicate this store locally using well-established methods (for example, using LDAP replication).

- *Maintaining the state* Imagine you're logging in to a system using a password. Once you log in, each interaction happening in that session assumes the same security context. In the case of web services, since there is no state, each service call needs to be authenticated explicitly. If we can keep state somehow, we can avoid establishing the security context each time. If we are hand-coding the application, we can use tokens that can be passed between the client and server, much like cookies in the HTTP protocol. WS-SecureConversation formalizes this in the context of web services.

- *Using SAML* We can set up the framework in such a way that the security context is always maintained with the request by using SAML. Thus, we can ensure that multiple services have access to this information. In composite services, it is particularly important to use this mechanism since multiple services may require this information.

This is not an exhaustive list of possible optimizations. As mentioned, any optimization must start with a performance profile of the application. Most of the standard optimization techniques work well for security solutions, too. In particular, XPath evaluations cause serious performance degradation in applications. We can handle this in two different ways: by reducing the complexity of XPath expressions that need evaluation and by using libraries that reduce XPath evaluation cost.

Let's take a look at what scalability means for a SOA security solution, and how we can achieve it.

10.4.2 *Scalability*

As the performance and load requirements on the application keep increasing, we need to make sure the application can handle it by adding more resources. If we configure a system to handle 1000 users and if it had to handle 10,000 users, we need to make it work by adding more hardware resources—additional memory, additional disks, additional machines, and additional network infrastructure.

Normally scalability is achieved through adding more machines. We can make use of more machines effectively only if we can partition the problem in such a way that each machine can be engaged in solving a part of the problem. There are three ways we can engage multiple machines:

1   *Horizontal partitioning*   To engage multiple computers, we can do a horizontal portioning of the problem, where different parts are solved by the different machines. By separating security as an independent task, we can dedicate a machine for it. We can further subdivide the task of security to achieve greater scalability, which comes at a cost. We need to pull together the answers from multiple services to generate the answer for a security service. The communication costs can exceed the benefits of the scalability. In addition, there are natural limits to horizontal partitioning; there are only so many subtasks that the security service can be divided into.

2   *Vertical partitioning*   A better approach to scalability is to partition the problem vertically. In this approach, we replicate the service in multiple nodes and direct clients to services so that all the machines are used. That is, we map the incoming requests to appropriate instances of the service. This mapping can take place in multiple ways. We can do this mapping statically—requests for users whose usernames start with A-M on one machine and N-Z on another machine. Or, based on incoming IP number, we can map the users to a specific machine. A more complex dynamic allocation can take into account the load and availability information of each machine to allocate the task to a lightly loaded and available server. In any case, as the number of service requests increase, we can increase the number of machines to provide better response.

3   *Replication of crucial resources*   One specific case of vertical partitioning is when we replicate credential stores closer to where we are authenticating. This can provide needed scalability when these stores become the bottlenecks.

If we separate security concerns into a service, we can easily make it scalable. Even if we build security into each service, we can replicate essential parts to provide the scalability. This scalability needs synchronization among the replicated resources, which is not difficult to do.

We have so far discussed how to address performance and scalability concerns of an enterprise when securing its services. Let's now discuss another important concern any enterprise will have when deploying a SOA security solution: availability.

10.4.3 *Availability*

If we make every service implement security, we must make sure that security works all the time. If not, applications stop when the security solution does not work. Thus, availability of security solutions is important in an enterprise.

There are standard ways to ensure high availability. If there is a critical resource such as a directory service or a token-granting service that is the central piece in a security resource, it should be configured for high availability. For instance, if we are depending on some files, we can use highly available storage solutions such as storage area network (SAN). If we are depending on a critical data source, we can set up a hot spare, which needs to be kept in sync with the main server. If we have a critical service, we can run it in a cluster that manages one machine as a backup for the other.

This concludes our description of possible approaches for performance, scalability, and availability requirements for a SOA security solution. These are very important concerns in real-world deployments, and any enterprise SOA security architect should have experience dealing with them.

Despite all our effort, we know that no security solution can be perfect. We can proactively develop defensive practices that reduce the damage that attackers can cause. In the next section, we will address under this issue by looking at how we manage vulnerabilities in our solutions.

10.5 *Vulnerability management*

As indicated at the beginning of the book, we have not been discussing security holes introduced by poorly written code. For example, we have not focused on the possibility of a buffer overflow in a service implementation. In the real world, you need to worry about such vulnerabilities in your services, service consumers, intermediaries, the security service itself, and any other services/libraries you depend on. Here we will briefly discuss the kinds of vulnerabilities you need to guard against and common techniques to do so. In particular, we will discuss:

- Common vulnerabilities in any software that hackers usually seek to attack
- XML-specific vulnerabilities
- A workflow process you can use to stay on top of vulnerabilities in your services/security solution

Let's start with a discussion of common vulnerabilities in any software that hackers usually seek to attack.

10.5.1 Common vulnerabilities

Code in SOA implementations, like any other code, is vulnerable to certain common forms of attack. Thanks to the focus on security brought about by numerous virus attacks in recent years, common vulnerabilities in code are well understood by the security community. Techniques and processes to defend against common vulnerabilities are also well understood. Here is a representative sample of common vulnerabilities and techniques to defend against them.

Vulnerability to buffer overflow attacks

Buffer overflow is probably the most commonly exploited security hole. This problem occurs when a program preallocates fixed buffers to deal with inputs and processing. Under certain circumstances, by carefully crafting the input, the program can be made to write and access beyond those preallocated buffers and trick the system into violating security constraints. The references listed at the end of this chapter will help you understand this topic in greater detail. What we will briefly mention here are the techniques to guard against buffer overflow vulnerabilities.

A first line of defense against buffer overflow attacks is provided by some of the modern programming platforms. Java, for example, internally checks all array access for bounds violations. Array bounds checking also happens internally when managed code is executed in .NET.

All this checking certainly causes performance degradation. But most applications can afford to pay this cost. For high-performance applications that cannot afford the cost of automatic bounds checking, you will have to rely on the programmer's skill to make sure that buffer overflows do not occur. You can choose to have a second line of defense, though.

Assume that your application does indeed have a buffer overflow vulnerability and try to minimize what an attacker can do after successfully exploiting the vulnerability. Never give an application more privileges than it really needs. Configure vulnerable applications to be run using accounts that do not have administrative privileges. This way, the amount of damage an attacker can cause is limited.

On Unix you can further limit the damage by running an application in a `chroot` jail. See the references listed at the end of this chapter for information on what a `chroot` jail is and how you can set it up.

Vulnerability to SQL injection attacks

Most business services rely on a database. If a service composes an SQL query using data provided by the caller without vetting the data first, it runs the risk of an SQL injection attack. The following query is composed by a `BankAccount` service to implement a balance query operation.

```
"select balance from account where accountId = '" + accountId + "'";
```

The implementer of this service expects that the caller will provide an `accountId`, as shown here:

```
<queryBalance>
  <accountId>account123</accountId>
</queryBalance>
```

A malicious caller may guess the details of this implementation and try submitting the following instead as `accountId`.

```
<queryBalance>
  <accountId>
    account123';
    update table account set (balance) values (1000000)
      where accountId='account123';
    select balance from account where accountId='account123'
  </accountId>
</queryBalance>
```

If the service implementer is naïve and uses the caller-provided `accountId` as is when composing the SQL query, the composed query will now consist of three SQL statements:

```
select balance from account where accountId = 'account123';
update table account set (balance) values (1000000)
  where accountId='account123';
select balance from account where accountId='account123';
```

As you can see, the malicious caller is able to update the balance in an account to a million dollars! These are known as *SQL injection attacks* and are representative of a large class of attacks that take advantage of applications that do not sanitize input before using it.

The only effective antidote to SQL injection attacks is in the hands of programmers; security administrators can only ensure that no more privileges than necessary are granted to an application in the database security configuration.

Almost every database access API provides a safe way of binding user input to placeholders in an SQL query. Quotes and special characters are escaped or handled

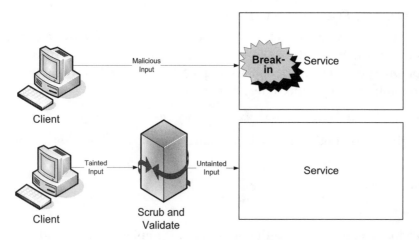

Figure 10.17   All inputs should be treated as tainted and scrubbed before using them in a service. This is especially true of any data that forms a part of a command or program.

appropriately if a programmer uses such APIs. Java programmers should use a PreparedStatement with placeholders instead of composing a Statement using string concatenation. Figure 10.17 shows the architecture for general input validation.

Programming languages such as Perl also provide facilities to mark all input as tainted and disallow direct use of suspect data. Programmers can only remove the taint attached to an input data item by extracting a specific pattern of characters from it. In the balance query code shown previously, the accountId provided by the user can be sanitized by picking only the first substring of alphanumeric characters using a regular expression such as [a-zA-Z0-9]+.

Vulnerability to distributed denial of service (DDoS) attacks

There is not much most applications can do when hit with a flood of concurrent requests from multiple points in the network. Almost all software crumbles under such an attack, resulting in DoS to legitimate users.

To cope with DDoS attacks, applications need to be able to quickly distinguish between legitimate requests and others. The faster this check can be made, the more an application can stand up to a DDoS attack. Unfortunately the rate at which an application can screen requests can be exceeded by the rate at which bad requests are coming in. Filtering needs to happen early and at multiple access points to the network, as shown in figure 10.18. Every access point into the network hosting the application needs to be equipped with firewalls that can filter good traffic from bad. Several network vendors provide products that can do this job effectively.

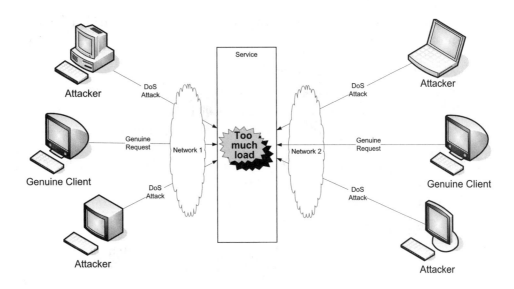

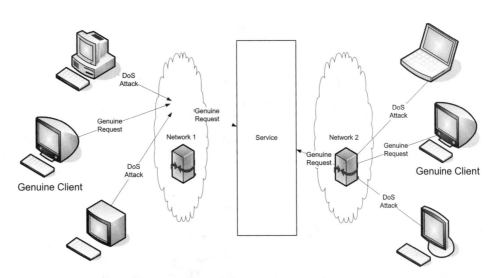

Figure 10.18 The top half of this picture shows how a DDoS attack can be launched by flooding a service with requests from a large number of clients. The bottom half of the picture shows a strategy for coping with DDoS attacks. By filtering traffic generated by DoS attackers early and at multiple access points, the impact of DDoS on a target service can be eliminated.

So far, we've discussed common vulnerabilities that are found in any software. Let's next discuss specific vulnerabilities that XML-based web services may possess.

10.5.2 XML-specific vulnerabilities

In addition to the vulnerabilities that SOA software shares with every other piece of code, there are a few more that are likely to be specific to SOA. Almost all SOA implementations involve a lot of XML processing, and XML brings its own set of new vulnerabilities.

The biggest source of vulnerabilities in XML lies in the facility for defining internal and external entities. Entities are declared within a Document Type Definition (DTD). An internal entity in a DTD is like a named constant in a program.

```
<!ENTITY constant1 "value1">
```

An external entity in a DTD is like an `include`/`import` statement; it allows the DTD to get a part of its contents from external sources.

```
<!ENTITY importFromFile SYSTEM "/some/file/path">
<!ENTITY importViaHttp SYSTEM "http://... ">
```

Once an entity is defined, it can be referenced using the syntax `&entityName;`. Two types of potential attacks are reported in the use of entities: *entity recursion attacks* and *external entity attacks*. We will describe each separately.

Entity recursion attacks

It is possible to define one entity's value by referring to another.

```
<!ENTITY constant1 "value1">
<!ENTITY constant2 "&constant1; and value2">
```

Any reference to `constant2` now expands to `"value1 and value2"`. It is possible to quickly build up large amount of text:

```
<!ENTITY constant1 "value1">
<!ENTITY constant2 "&constant1;&constant1">
<!ENTITY constant3 "&constant2;&constant2">
...
<!ENTITY constantN "&constantNminus1;&constantNminus1">
```

By defining the value of `constantN` as a concatenation of two `constantNminus1` values, we have employed recursion to build 2^{N-1} repetitions of `constant1`. This constitutes a vulnerability in the following sense.

An attacker can submit an XML document with an internal DTD subset that employs the recursive definition trick shown here to exhaust the memory resources available to the recipient's program. Note that recursion allows one to generate exponentially growing output with input that only needs to grow linearly. In our example, an attacker can generate 2^{32} repetitions of `constant1` simply by defining $32+1$ constants recursively. The attacker's program does not require much memory to generate input that will exhaust the attacked program's memory resources.

External entity attacks

Almost every XML parser allows you to plug in an external entity resolver that can resolve external entity references. A naïve implementation of a resolver that simply resolves any external reference is bound to introduce vulnerabilities, such as the following:

- An attacker can use the external entity resolution facility available in multiple services to launch a DDoS attack.

- An attacker can bring down the performance of the attacked program by making it repeatedly access a limited system resource, such as /dev/random (a random number generator that can cause a performance hit if accessed very frequently) or c:\con\con (a path that crashes Windows 98 when accessed).

- An attacker may use an echo service to read files on the target service that he does not otherwise have access to.

A security-conscious implementation of an external entity resolver will limit resolution to a limited set of known locations.

Guarding against entity attacks

To rule out the possibility of entity attacks, SOAP explicitly prohibits the presence of DTD (and processing instructions) within a SOAP message. If your SOAP-processing engine is compliant with the SOAP specification, it should not be vulnerable to entity attacks.

If your SOA software accepts any XML input other than SOAP messages, you may need to turn off entity expansion altogether to completely secure yourself against entity attacks.

Validating XML inputs to guard against other XML attacks

In security enforcement, it is always a good idea to ban everything first, then allow a few trusted entities. This principle should be applied, where possible, when accepting XML inputs. If schema definitions exist for the XML inputs your services accept, validate incoming XML against those schemas. Schema-based validation is expensive, and you may see a performance hit when you introduce validation into your processing. If the performance hit you are seeing is unacceptable, evaluate the use of high-performance validators that are available in the market.

Despite that, two important limitations of schema-based validation need to be kept in mind.

1. Schema-based validation is not always possible. To develop a schema, one needs to know the structure of a document in its entirety. This is not always possible. For example, if you are developing a routing service for B2B documents, you may not understand the entirety of every possible B2B document. You may only know and care about the fields that provide the basis for routing decisions in your service. In such cases, use other XML validation techniques that you find to be applicable. You may employ a rule-based validation scheme that validates just those parts of each document that you know and care about.

2. Schemas represent theoretical limits on the structure of a document and do not impose the practical limits that a security service would want. A schema may allow any number of repetitions of a particular element in an XML document. In reality, the XML parser that processes the document may have practical limits on how many repetitions it can handle, depending on how it parses the document. A streaming parser may process an arbitrarily high number of repetitions, whereas a DOM parser may have restrictions imposed by memory. It is desirable to impose some practical limits on XML inputs—no messages larger than 2 MB—if you suspect that your services may not handle larger inputs well.

As you can see, validation of XML messages is turning out to be a specialized area. XML security appliances in the market address this area well. For a list of vendors, see appendix E.

Thanks to the focus on security in the last few years, enterprises have a much better understanding of how to stay on top of vulnerabilities that are common in software. Next we'll discuss a workflow process enterprises use to fix vulnerabilities promptly and regularly.

10.5.3 *Vulnerability remediation workflow*

Security experts recognize that there will always be many more vulnerabilities in our code than we recognize at any point. Guarding against vulnerabilities is not a one-time activity. It obviously requires constant vigilance. It is important to

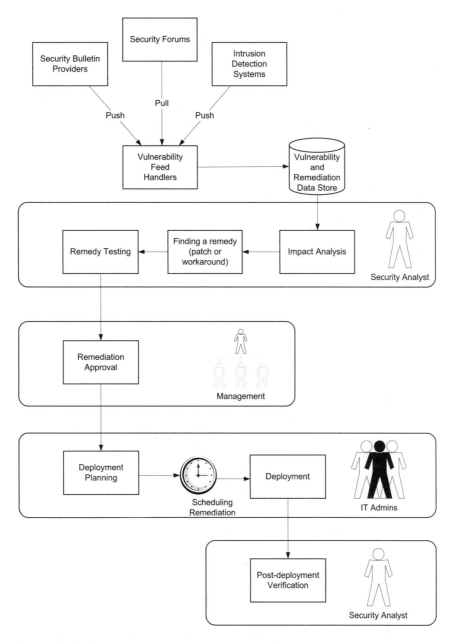

Figure 10.19   By following a well-managed vulnerability remediation workflow, you can reduce the threat posed by vulnerabilities. This picture shows the steps involved in a vulnerability remediation workflow and the personnel who need to participate in it.

institute a process for patching up vulnerabilities when they are reported. Vulnerability remediation is an important workflow within an IT organization. Figure 10.19 depicts this workflow.

Activities that are part of this workflow are

1   Scouring security-related forums for reports on new vulnerabilities

2   Assessing the impact of each reported vulnerability

3   Finding a workaround or locating a patch

4   Testing the workaround/patch

5   Planning a deployment

6   Getting approval for deployment

7   Scheduling deployment of the workaround/patch

8   Verifying the effectiveness of the workaround/patch once it is deployed

Figure 10.19 identifies the owner of each step in a typical enterprise. In a large enterprise, this workflow needs to be managed by tools. Manual management can be cumbersome, as the number of resources and management processes is too great.

10.6   *Summary*

Developing a SOA security solution for an enterprise is not easy. One needs to combine all of the ideas introduced in the previous chapters with the right implementation and deployment choices to create a solution that fits the needs of the enterprise. In this chapter, we tried to give you a good idea of the challenges you are likely to face and the choices you have when designing a SOA security solution for real-world enterprises.

We first explained the demands enterprise IT environments place on software solutions. An enterprise SOA security solution must be usable by a large and diverse user base, must remain usable over a long time, must be robust, and must be easy to manage. In addition, as most enterprises are likely to have a mix of services—some developed from scratch, some that wrap legacy applications, and some high-level services that compose lower-level services—we explained the variations in strategies you can use for securing these different kinds of services.

We also discussed myriad considerations that can go into designing the deployment strategy for a SOA security solution. We discussed methods of deployment in an enterprise—with branch offices, with partners, and to the general public.

The deployment scenarios differ in how elements of the solution can be placed in the network.

While the issue of DoS attacks is not the focus of this book, we discussed a few issues that can affect security—in particular, we showed how XML-based attacks work and how to protect applications from them.

One warning: This chapter merely touched on issues that come up when developing an enterprise-class SOA security solution. Unlike other chapters, we cannot offer a fully working concrete example here. The best way to use this chapter is to understand your particular problem in the terms explained here. With enough practice, you will be able to extend the lessons in this chapter to solve your security problems.

This chapter completes our book on SOA security. By reading this book, you have come to understand that SOA security is quite different from typical application security. Fortunately, SOA standards help you build good secure solutions.

If you are with us thus far, you have learned the standards through simple examples, along with the underlying technologies. You also have seen the different options for full-fledged frameworks and several practical challenges. Depending on your responsibilities, you can use this knowledge directly in building a security solution for your application; or you can use it in formulating SOA security strategy for your enterprise based on vendor tools and products. In either case, we hope the information you've learned from this book—the standards, code explanations, and underlying technologies—will help you on your way to mastering SOA security.

Suggestions for further reading

- CICS (Customer Information Control System) transaction server, first introduced in 1969, is still used by a large number of enterprises for core business services that require very high performance and reliability. CICS applications are a good example of legacy applications that will be wrapped as services. CICS Transaction Server 3.1 introduced support for web services. WS-Security is supported, too. See http://publib.boulder.ibm.com/infocenter/cicsts/v3r1/topic/com.ibm.cics.ts31.doc/dfhws/wsSecurity/dfhws_WSSecurity.htm.

- SAP R/3 is an enterprise resource planning (ERP) application a large number of enterprises use for managing their business. SAP R/3 is a good example of a legacy application around which services may be wrapped. Interestingly, SAP is promising to support web services natively in their software, as part of an initiative named Enterprise Service Architecture (ESA). ESA is described in detail in *Enterprise SOA: Designing IT for Business Innovation*, by Dan Woods and Thomas Mattern, published by O'Reilly Media, Inc. in April 2006. ISBN: 0596102380.

- *Writing Secure Code*, by Michael Howard and David LeBlanc (Microsoft Press, 2002) describes the precautions you need to take to avoid vulnerabilities to buffer overflow, SQL injection, and other such attacks. This ISBN is 0735617228.

- *Practical Unix and Internet Security, Third Edition*, by Simson Garfinkel, Gene Spafford, and Alan Schwartz, is a good reference for understanding firewalls and chroot jails, in addition to many more security topics. This book was published by O'Reilly Media, Inc. in February 2003.

- Section 10 of RFC 3023 lists some of the possible vulnerabilities in XML processing. The RFC is available at http://tools.ietf.org/html/3023.

- The example of an entity recursion attack shown in this chapter was constructed and reported by Mark O'Neill as described at http://www.vordel. com/ knowledgebase/vordel_view5.html.

- Gregory Steuck Security Advisory #1, 2002 describes how external entity resolution may introduce several vulnerabilities. See http://www.securityfocus.com/ archive/1/297714.

Limitations of Apache Axis

In most ways, Apache Axis is a very successful open source project in Java. Axis 1.x is probably the most widely used Java-based SOAP toolkit that is not tied to any particular J2EE application server. Unfortunately, Axis 1.x suffers from limitations that make some of the example code in chapters 6, 7, and 8 fail. In this appendix, we will describe these limitations. We will also briefly describe a new generation of Axis, Axis2 and tell you what you can and cannot do with it right now.

A.1 Buggy implementation of W3C DOM API in Axis 1.x

Axis does not correctly bind data in a SOAP message to an object tree as defined by the W3C DOM API. This causes failures in other XML-processing libraries (such as XPath interpreters and XML encryption/signature libraries) that assume a W3C DOM-compliant object tree. We have reported two such issues as AXIS-2125 and AXIS-2163 in the Apache bug database for Axis 1.x. In the rest of this section, we will explain these issues in greater detail.

SAAJ provides a standard API for programmers to create, parse, and manipulate SOAP messages. You have seen the use of several classes defined by this API in the code examples discussed in chapters 2-8. The SOAPMessage, SOAPPart, SOAPEnvelope, and SOAPElement classes from the javax.xml.soap package are all defined by SAAJ. Axis 1.x supports SAAJ APIs alongside its own custom APIs for dealing with SOAP messages programmatically.

SAAJ allows programmers to deal with data in a SOAP message as if it were a tree of objects. In other words, SAAJ provides its own DOM API for dealing with SOAP documents (messages). For good reason, SAAJ allows programmers to use either or both of the following DOM APIs when dealing with a SOAP message:

1   One is SOAP-specific, making it easy for developers to deal with SOAP-level constructs. This API is defined by SAAJ itself using classes such as the ones listed previously in this section.

2   The second is the generic W3C DOM API that is defined independently of SOAP to manipulate any XML document:

There is a reason why SAAJ allows the use of generic W3C DOM API. Given W3C DOM's large mindshare, which comes from being the first to market, W3C DOM API is still the lowest common denominator that most XML-related libraries assume. Programmers using SAAJ also often need to use generic XML-processing infrastructure such as XPath interpreters and the XML Encryption/Signature libraries.

This infrastructure currently assumes the availability of an object tree that can be inspected and modified using the W3C DOM API.

For historical reasons, W3C DOM API is filled with a large number of methods that overlap in functionality. This makes W3C DOM API implementation a very tedious for task developers. Axis developers avoided some of this tedium by using tricks that pass the examination of a Java compiler and the Axis unit test suite but fail when exercised by arbitrary code.

In Apache Axis 1.4, if you inspect the source of the `getAttributes()` method in the `org.apache.axis.message.NodeImpl` class, you will find that attributes of an element (only element nodes can have attributes) are not created with the right ancestry. The attributes returned by `node.getAttributes()` are not created in the same document as the node to which they belong! Instead, the attributes returned by this method are created in a dummy document. This results in the situation shown in figure A.1.

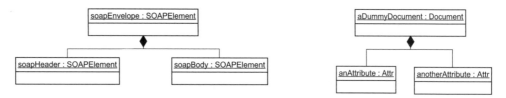

Figure A.1   Faulty W3C DOM structure created by Axis 1.x. Observe that attributes belong to a dummy document and not to the SOAP Envelope document.

Problems such as these trip up the code in XPath interpreters and the XML Security libraries we use in chapter 6, 7, and 8.

A.2 *Axis2 does not support JAX-RPC handlers*

The Apache Axis team has recently released a new generation of Axis named Axis2. Axis2 seeks to deliver much higher performance than Axis 1.x by taking advantage of improvements in XML-parsing technology. Axis2 also supports asynchronous interactions by nonblocking clients. These and a number of other improvements make Axis2 technically superior to Axis 1.x.

Axis2 is not as widely adopted as Axis1.x for the following reasons.

- Axis2 reached the 1.0 milestone quite recently. It will be some time before mindshare of Axis2 in the development community reaches anywhere near that of Axis 1.x.

- Axis is not backwards compatible with Axis 1.x. The packaging and configuration mechanisms are quite different in Axis2.

- Support for JAX-RPC/JAX-WS standards is partial. JAC-RPC/JAX-WS handlers are not supported. Axis2 does provide its own handler API, though.

In spite of all the differences between Axis 1.1 and Axis2, working with Axis2 will not prove difficult for readers of this book. In fact, the same should apply for users of any web services toolkit, not just Axis. The conceptual understanding we provide in this book will hold you in good stead, no matter which toolkit you use to get your work done.

WS-SecureConversation

Consider a front-end application that uses SOAP message exchanges to invoke the services offered by a back-end application. If you have read chapters 3-8, you already know how to secure these message exchanges. Using WS-Security, the front-end and back-end applications can add security tokens needed for authentication, encryption/decryption, and signing/verifying signatures *to each message*. Observe that we are emphasizing the need to add the required tokens to each and every message. Is this really necessary? If the front-end application is going to exchange a series of SOAP messages with the back-end application, is it possible to authenticate just once, or exchange the keys used for encryption/decryption and signing/verifying signatures just once?

For performance reasons, the answer to these questions should be "yes." But SOAP, for good reasons,[1] does not by itself provide a mechanism to tie a message to a past message. That is, SOAP is a stateless protocol. However, a SOAP extension is free to introduce a mechanism to tie together a series of message exchanges into a "conversation." WS-SecureConversation is one such extension, and its purpose is to provide for the establishment and maintenance of a security context across different messages in a conversation.

As you would expect by now, WS-SecureConversation introduces a new WS-Security header element named `SecurityContextToken`[2] (in a new namespace defined by the WS-Conversation spec). This element can be used to carry an identifier that identifies the security context in which the message is being sent. Listing B.1 shows an example in which WS-SecureConversation enables the reuse of a previously established symmetric encryption key.

Listing B.1   Reuse of a previously established symmetric encryption key using WS-SecurityConversation

```
<soapenv:Envelope ...>
  <soapenv:Header>
    <wsse:Security>

      <wsc:SecurityContextToken wsu:Id="sct-1"          ❶
          xmlns:wsc=".../ws-secureconversation.xsd">  ◁❷
        <wsc:Identifier>WSSC-1</wsc:Identifier>   ◁❸
      </wsc:SecurityContextToken>
```

---

[1] SOA proponents value the simplicity stateless protocols provide, which explains why SOAP was designed as a stateless protocol. It is easier to consume a context-independent or stateless service, as the consumer only needs to make one message exchange with the service.

[2] This token is similar to a cookie in HTTP.

```
          <xenc:ReferenceList>
            <xenc:DataReference URI="#EncryptedData-1"/>      ❹
          </xenc:ReferenceList>

       </wsse:Security>
     </soapenv:Header>

     <soapenv:Body>
       <xenc:EncryptedData Id="EncryptedData-1" ...>
         ...
         <ds:KeyInfo>
           <wsse:SecurityTokenReference>
             <wsse:Reference URI="#sct-1"
               ValueType=".../sct"/>              ❺
           </wsse:SecurityTokenReference>
         </ds:KeyInfo>
         ...
       </xenc:EncryptedData>
     </soapenv:Body>
   </soapenv:Envelope>
```

In this example, the SecurityContextToken element ❶ in the Security header entry is establishing the message as part of a conversation. The SecurityContext-Token element and its child elements are defined in a namespace ❷ specified by WS-SecureConversation.

This message is marked as part of a secure conversation identified by the Identifier WSSC-1 ❸. The identified conversation may have already included one or more previous messages. We assume that one of those previous messages established a dynamically generated symmetric key for data encryption. This is unlike listings 6.8-6.10. Remember, in those, we were

- Using an EncryptedKey element in the WS-Security header to establish a dynamically generated symmetric key for encryption.
- Using a ReferenceList element under the EncryptedKey element to declare what elements are encrypted by the key.

In contrast, here, we skip the EncryptedKey element needed to establish a key and directly use a ReferenceList element ❹ to declare what elements in this message are to be decrypted by the recipient using a previously established symmetric key.

In addition, the EncryptedData element needs to identify the key used for encryption, as we do not have an EncryptedKey header. It can do this using an embedded KeyInfo element ❺, which in turn can refer to the key established at the start of current secure conversation. As you can see, the ValueType attribute on the `Reference` indicates that we are referring to a `SecureContextToken` (SCT) and the URI attribute indicates which `SecureContextToken` element we should pick up the secure conversation identifier from.

You now know how to use WS-SecureConversation to eliminate key transport at all times except at the start of a new conversation. You can similarly use WS-SecureConversation to eliminate the need to send security tokens for authentication with every message.

Refer to the WS-SecureConversation specification listed in the "Suggestions for further reading" section at the end of this appendix to learn more about

- How a new conversation can be established
- How a key can be set up for use throughout the conversation
- How the key can be changed periodically
- How new keys can be derived using the originally established key

Suggestions for further reading

The WS-SecureConversation specification, as originally developed by an ad hoc industry group, is available at http://specs.xmlsoap.org/ws/2005/02/sc/WS-SecureConversation.pdf. This specification is now worked on by a standards body and can be found at http://www.oasis-open.org/committees/tc_home.php?wg_abbrev=ws-sx.

Attaching and securing binary data in SOAP

In chapters 6 and 7, you saw how to encrypt and sign a message or parts of a message. The techniques you learned there allow you to encrypt and sign any data that is part of the SOAP message. As you recall from chapter 2, XML does not allow binary data. What if you want to send binary data with SOAP? And how do you encrypt and sign such data? We will answer these questions in this appendix.

XML does not allow arbitrary bytes (more precisely, octets, as the size of a byte isn't guaranteed to be 8 bits on some rarely encountered platforms) to be included in element content. Only characters defined by the Unicode character set (excluding a few) are allowed using a character encoding scheme such as US-ASCII and UTF-8. This helps keep the text character of XML, allowing XML code to be inspected by humans using text editors.

But what if we want to include binary data (data containing arbitrary octets) such as certificates, signatures, compressed data, encrypted text, and images? We introduced a common trick, namely base64 encoding, to encode arbitrary bytes into character data, in chapter 4. Such encoded data can be embedded in XML, as seen in multiple places in chapter 4-7.

Using base64 encoding presents its own problems in a few common cases. It bloats data to four thirds of its original size. This is fine if the data to encode is only a few kilobytes, but when it comes to dealing with large amounts of data (such as images), the size increase leads to an unacceptable performance penalty. The extra computational cost to encode and decode large amounts of data is also a concern (although it pales before the cost we're already paying in most cases for encryption).

Multiple approaches have been proposed to address these concerns. They differ in their impact on the encryption and signature techniques that are already in use. In this appendix, we are going to show the two most popular approaches currently vying for adoption: SOAP with Attachments (SwA) and SOAP Message Transmission Optimization Mechanism (MTOM). We will especially look at their impact on how we encrypt and sign SOAP messages.

C.1 SOAP with Attachments (SwA)

These days, all of us are familiar with the concept of attaching files to email messages. For a long while, it was not possible to attach files to email. Email messages were restricted to consist of text (and that, too, using 7-bit characters only with no more than 1,000 characters per line). A standard named *Multipurpose Internet Mail Extensions (MIME)* changed all that. For the purposes of our discussion here, MIME provided two significant features (among other things):

1   A way to package arbitrary data items into a single message.

2   A way to declare metadata about the data items within the MIME package, such as the relationship among the items in the package (for example, are they alternative representations of a same item or are they simply disparate items packaged together), the type of data within each item (is it text, HTML, or a GIF image), and how each item is encoded (7-bit text, 8-bit text, base64-encoded text, or binary data).

Although MIME seems to have been designed explicitly for use in email applications (as the name reflects), it was found to be of use in other applications as well. SwA takes advantage of MIME to attach arbitrary data items to a SOAP message. Listing C.1 shows a simple example.

Listing C.1   Example of an SwA message

```
Content-Type: Multipart/Related;          ←❶
  boundary=_MIME_boundary_;         ←❷
  type=text/xml;                  ←❸
  start="<request60914@our.brokerage.com>"    ←❹
Content-Length: ...
                    ←❺
--_MIME_boundary_      ←❻
Content-Type: text/xml; charset=UTF-8             ❼
Content-Transfer-Encoding: 8bit
Content-ID: <request60914@our.brokerage.com>
                    ←❽
<soapenv:Envelope ...>
  <soapenv:Body>
    <ns1:createAccount ...>
      <firstName>...</firstname>
      <lastName>...</lastName>
      <identityProof type="driversLicense"            ❾
        href="cid:request60914.jpg@our.brokerage.com"/>   ←❿
    </ns1:createAccount>
  </soapenv:Body>
</soapenv:Envelope>
--_MIME_boundary_      ←⓫
Content-Type: image/jpeg                   ⓬
Content-Transfer-Encoding: binary
Content-ID: <request60914.jpg@our.brokerage.com>

...JPEG image bytes...
--_MIME_boundary_--      ←⓭
```

SwA requires the MIME message to be declared at the transport level as consisting of multiple related parts using `Multipart/Related` as the main content type declaration ❶. In this example, we assume HTTP as the transport protocol, and an HTTP header named `Content-type` is used to declare the body as a `Multipart/Related` message. Observe that a blank line is used ❺ to separate the HTTP headers from the MIME message in the HTTP message body.

MIME relies on a boundary marker string ❷ to separate different items in a multipart message. The boundary string used should not occur anywhere within the contents of any part.

In `Multipart/Related` messages, one of the parts is identified as a root so that applications know which part to process first. The `type` parameter ❸ should provide the content-type of the root part. In our case, the type is `text/xml`, as our root part is a SOAP envelope. Each part in the MIME package is required to be identified using a `Content-ID` or a `Content-Location` header. In `Multipart/Related` messages, a `start` parameter ❹ can be used to identify the root part using its `Content-ID`. If the `start` parameter is not specified, the first part is assumed to be the root.

The start of a message part ❻, ⓫ is indicated by two dashes (`--`), followed by the boundary marker we declared in the transport-level `Content-Type` header. Each MIME part has its own MIME headers ❼, ⓬. A blank line indicates the end of MIME headers for the following part ❽. SOAP `Envelope` ❾ is the first part in this example. In this case, the body consists of a request to create an account in our brokerage. The second part in this example is a JPEG image. Notice that we declare the content encoding for the JPEG image in this part to be binary ⓬.

Where necessary, references can be made in the SOAP message to content in other parts. For example, we are here referring to the JPEG image attached as the second MIME part. The `Content-ID` of the referred part is converted to a URI using `cid:` as the prefix, and the `href` (hyper-reference, used so widely in HTML) attribute is used to establish the reference ❿.

The end of a MIME multipart package ⓭ is marked using two dashes (`--`), followed by the boundary marker we declared in the transport-level `Content-Type` header and two more dashes (`--`).

That is how any binary data can be attached to a SOAP message. Let's understand the pros and cons of this mechanism before going to the alternate approach.

C.1.1 *Issues with SwA*

SwA is often criticized for two reasons:

1 MIME attachments break the idea of SOAP messages being XML. Because all implementations make that assumption, they break when confronted with a non-XML message. Or, they have to be retrofitted to accommodate the possibility of MIME packaging. Use of the XML Encryption and XML Signature standards in WS-Security now needs to be reviewed to see what enhancements are needed to secure attachments as well.

2 An application needs to scan through a part looking for the boundary marker in order to locate where the part ends. The scan obviously takes a few more computational cycles than would be required if we knew the part's length in advance.

An alternate attachment scheme known as *Direct Internet Message Encapsulation (DIME)* attempted to address the performance problem. It did not address the bigger issue with attachments: their impact on WS-Security. At the same time, attempts to marry SwA with WS-Security gained momentum, and this has led to the abandonment of DIME. The Web Service Interoperability (WS-I) organization picked SwA over DIME.

There are multiple ways to standardize support for SwA in WS-Security. We will look at the most popular choice next.

C.1.2 *WS-Security SwA Profile*

A WS-Security profile has already been defined for securing attachments made using SwA. The underlying ideas are quite simple.

- Use `cid:` URIs to reference attachments.
- Define new transforms to distinguish between the possible targets when referring to an attachment: the attachment's content as well as its MIME headers or just the attachment content.
- Define canonicalization algorithms for MIME headers and attachment content.
- Sign all attachments or use an application-specific mechanism to detect malicious addition or removal of new attachments.

Although these ideas seem simple, they may not be widely implemented, as SwA may itself be replaced by a competing standard named MTOM. We describe MTOM next.

C.2 SOAP MTOM

An alternative way of marrying attachments with WS-Security has emerged, in the form of SOAP Message Transmission Optimization Mechanism (MTOM). MTOM considers the use of attachments as merely a pragmatic way of representing parts of a SOAP envelope over the wire, and asks applications to pretend that attachments are present inline in XML in base64-encoded form. That is, by the time applications see the message, the attachments are no longer there; they are contained within the message. This minor adjustment in the way we look at attachments brings back the pure-XML character of SOAP messages without sacrificing the size advantage that binary attachments give us over inlined base64-encoded data.

How does MTOM impact WS-Security? An application that relies on WS-Security to secure attachments will have to first create the pure XML form of the message (or in the case of a receiver, recreate it from the attachments received on the wire). Once this is done, the application can pretend that attachments are not even used.

How do the applications know where to inline each attachment? The XML-binary Optimized Packaging (XOP) specification, which MTOM relies on, defines an `xop:Include` element to indicate where each attachment (identified by its Content-ID using the `cid:` URI scheme) should be included in the original XML document.

XOP/MTOM are not restricted to MIME attachments; they allow other schemes of packing an XML document along with the pieces extracted out of the XML document for optimization in transmission. In the case of MIME-based attachments, the `Content-Type` information for each attachment is preserved using an `xmlmime:contentType` attribute, where the `xmlmime` prefix refers to a special namespace established by a specification that standardizes how media types can be assigned to binary data in XML.

Listing C.2 shows all of these ideas in action.

> **Listing C.2 An example SOAP message serialized as a MIME message, in accordance with MTOM**

```
Content-Type: Multipart/Related;
  boundary=_MIME_boundary_;
  type="application/xop+xml";
  start="<request60915@our.brokerage.com>"
  startinfo="text/xml; action=\"\""     ◁—❶
Content-Length: ...
```

```
--_MIME_boundary_
Content-Type: application/xop+xml; charset=UTF-8 ;       ❷
   type="text/xml; action=\"\""
Content-Transfer-Encoding: 8bit
Content-ID: <request60915@our.brokerage.com>

<soapenv:Envelope ...>
  <soapenv:Body>
    <ns1:createAccount ...>
      <firstName>...</firstname>
      <lastName>...</lastName>
      <identityProof type="driversLicense">
        <xop:Include
          xmlns:xop="http://www.w3.org/2004/08/xop/include"
          xmlns:xmlmime="://www.w3.org/2004/11/xmlmime"      ❸
          xmlmime:contentType="image/jpeg"
          href="cid:request60915.jpg@our.brokerage.com"/>
      </identityProof>
    </ns1:createAccount>
  </soapenv:Body>
</soapenv:Envelope>
--_MIME_boundary_
Content-Type: image/jpeg
Content-Transfer-Encoding: binary
Content-ID: <request60915.jpg@our.brokerage.com>

...JPEG image bytes...
--_MIME_boundary_--
```

XOP mandates the use of `application/xop+xml` as the `Content-Type` ❷ of the root part. This aids in detection of XOP-optimized transmissions. In addition, XOP requires us to preserve the `Content-Type` and `SOAPAction` header values from the original message using a `type` parameter as part of the `Content-Type` value.

As we have seen with SwA, `Multipart/Related` messages can provide the root part's `Content-ID` using a `start` parameter ❶. Another optional parameter, `startinfo`, can be added to further aid the recipient in processing the envelope. Here, we are providing the `Content-Type` and `SOAPAction` header values from the original message in `startinfo`.

If you compare the MTOM wire representation example shown here with the SwA example shown previously, you will find only a few trivial changes. Instead of using `text/xml` as the root part's type, we are using `application/xop+xml`. We added `startinfo` to the MIME headers. And, we added `xop:Include` ❸ as a child of the `identityProof` element instead of directly adding an `href` attribute to it. The main difference is how applications process it.

In this appendix, you have seen two standards, SwA and MTOM, that address how attachments can be made in SOAP. While attachments made to SOAP messages in compliance with SwA can be encrypted and signed as specified by the SwA profile, MTOM makes encrypting/signing attachments no different than encrypting/signing SOAP messages without attachments. Practitioners of web services security who care about interoperability in the short run will need to understand and implement the WS-Security SwA profile. Others can take advantage of MTOM and do nothing special when encrypting/signing SOAP messages with attachments.

Suggestions for further reading

- The SOAP with Attachments (SwA) specification, a W3C Note, is available at http://www.w3.org/TR/SOAP-attachments.

- RFCs on MIME that are relevant in the context of SwA: 2045, 2046, 2047 and 2387. You can look up a RFC by its number at http://tools.ietf.org/html/.

- The expired Internet Draft Specification on DIME is available at http://msdn.microsoft.com/library/en-us/dnglobspec/html/draft-nielsen-dime-02.txt.

- WS-I "Attachments Profile Version 1.0" is available at http://www.ws-i.org/Profiles/AttachmentsProfile-1.0.html.

- The WS-Security SOAP with Attachments Profile is available at http://www.oasis-open.org/committees/download.php/16672/wss-v1.1-spec-os-SwAProfile.pdf.

- The XML Binary Optimized Processing (XOP) specification, a W3C Recommendation, is available at http://www.w3.org/TR/xop10/.

- The MTOM specification, another W3C Recommendation, is available at http://www.w3.org/TR/soap12-mtom/.

D

Securing SAML assertions

In chapter 8, we introduced SAML assertions that can be used to communicate the findings of a security service. Since service endpoints depend on SAML assertions to identify users and make other security decisions, we should secure those assertions, too, in particular against the following threats:

- *Forgery and tampering* An attacker may submit a completely forged assertion. Or, he may tamper with the information in an assertion created by the security service. In use case #2 we described in section 8.2.2, the source endpoint can add an `AttributeStatement` (or alter it) in the assertion returned by the security service to make itself a member of the administrators group.

- *Replaying* An assertion can be captured and reused by an attacker. The attacker might replay the original message that has an assertion in it as is, or reuse the captured assertion as part of a different message.

- *Privacy* The user's privacy may be violated if an assertion includes more details than a service endpoint really needs or if a MIM grabs the details in the assertion by eavesdropping.

In the next section, we will look at detecting forgery and tampering of SAML assertions.

D.1   *Detecting forgery and tampering*

To detect forgery and tampering, we can use the same techniques we discussed in chapter 7 to verify the integrity of messages. Any receiver of SAML assertions should only accept those assertions that are signed by their issuers. A SAML `Assertion` is like any other XML element; it can be signed by the issuer using the same signing mechanisms we described in chapter 7. A small technicality makes signing of SAML assertions slightly more complex than it should really be.

Recall that we need the ability to refer to an element in order to include its digest as part of `SignedInfo`. In chapter 7, we saw how we can refer to any element using its `wsu:Id` (or simply `Id` for elements defined by the XML-Signature and XML-Encryption specs) attribute value. As SAML `Assertion` elements already have an attribute named `AssertionId` that is declared as an identifier by the SAML schema, there's now a dilemma when referring to an `Assertion`. Which identifier attribute's value should we use to refer to a SAML `Assertion`?

Use of both `wsu:Id` and `AssertionId` attributes is not a good idea, as it can lead to confusion and inconsistency. Use of just `wsu:Id` is not possible, as the SAML schema requires an `AssertionId` on every `Assertion`. Use of just `AssertionId` is also not a clean solution, as the signature verifier will now need to look for three different attributes—`wsu:Id`, `Id`, and `AssertionId`, depending on what the referred element happens to be.

To get around this problem (and probably for other good reasons as well), the SAML profile for WS-Security defines a roundabout way of referring to SAML assertions from `SignedInfo`. Instead of referring to the assertion from within `SignedInfo`, the profile recommends a `Reference` to a `SecurityTokenReference` (STR) that in turn refers to the `Assertion`, as shown in figure D.1.

In this scheme, the `SecurityTokenReference` element identifies the `Assertion` by its `AssertionId` and creates for itself a `wsu:Id` that can be referred to from `SignedInfo`. Here is an example:

```
<wsse:SecurityTokenReference wsu:Id="MySAMLAssertion1Ref1">
  <wsse:KeyIdentifier  ValueType="...#SAMLAssertionID">
      MySAMLAssertion1
  </wsse:KeyIdentifier>
</wsse:SecurityTokenReference>
```

Note that the `KeyIdentifier` element in this example is defined in the WS-Security namespace rather than the SAML namespace. WS-Security establishes the notion of a `KeyIdentifier` as an opaque string that uniquely identifies a security token. The `ValueType` attribute indicates the type of token being identified. See figure D.1.

Listing D.1 is a sample signature that protects the integrity of a SAML Assertion.

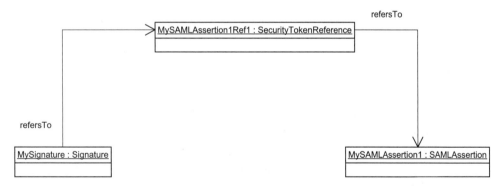

Figure D.1 Two levels of indirection are recommended when signing a SAML assertion. `Signature` **refers to a** `SecurityTokenReference` **that in turn refers to the signed SAML assertion.**

Listing D.1   Example of a signature over a SAML assertion

```
<saml:Assertion AssertionID="MySAMLAssertion1">          ❶ SAML assertion
  ...                                                        to protect
</saml:Assertion>

<wsse:SecurityTokenReference
     wsu:Id="MySAMLAssertion1Ref1">
  <wsse:KeyIdentifier                                     ❷ STR referring to SAML
    ValueType="...#SAMLAssertionID">                         assertion in ❶
      MySAMLAssertion1
  </wsse:KeyIdentifier>
</wsse:SecurityTokenReference>

<ds:Signature>
  <ds:SignedInfo>
    ...
    <ds:Reference URI="#MySAMLAssertion1Ref1">            Reference to
      <ds:Transforms>                                   ❸ STR in ❷
        <ds:Transform
          Algorithm="...#STR-Transform">                 STR dereference
          <wsse:TransformationParameters>             ❹ transform
            <ds:CanonicalizationMethod
              Algorithm=".../xml-exc-c14n#"/>
          </wsse:TransformationParameters>
        </ds:Transform>
      </ds:Transforms>

      <ds:DigestMethod Algorithm=".../xmldsig#sha1"/>
      <ds:DigestValue>...</ds:DigestValue>
    </ds:Reference>

  </ds:SignedInfo>
  ...
</ds:Signature>
```

From chapter 7, you will readily recognize the key elements in this code. The SignedInfo element contains a Reference ❸ to the SAML assertion that needs to be protected. As shown in figure D.1, this reference happens in an indirect way. The Reference in ❸ points to a SecurityTokenReference (STR) element ❷ that in turn points to the SAML assertion ❶ we want to protect.

There is one key piece of this listing that you have not seen before—an STR dereference transform ❹. Here is why it is needed here. As the Reference ❸ in SignedInfo points to an STR ❷ rather than the Assertion ❶ we want to protect, we need to employ an STR dereference transform to indicate that the DigestValue ❺ is computed after dereferencing the STR.

To summarize, you can use signatures to protect a SAML assertion, as it is just another XML element. Because standards say that you should refer to a SAML assertion via an STR, you will need to apply an STR dereference transform when computing the digest that goes into the signature's `SignedInfo` element.

Next we will describe how we can protect SAML assertions against replay attacks, where the attackers capture and replay an assertion.

D.2 Defending against replay attacks

SAML assertions are susceptible to different kinds of replay attacks. A MIM may capture an assertion in whatever form it was transmitted and reuse it. He may replay the original message that has the captured assertion in it as is, or reuse the captured assertion as part of a different message. Note that an attacker can replay signed and encrypted assertions as well. He does not need the ability to decrypt the captured assertion or forge a signature.

A malicious service provider can capture an assertion submitted to it and resubmit the assertion to a different service without the subject's permission.

There are a several strategies to defend against replay of SAML assertions, but all have limitations. In this section, we will present four strategies:

1   Reduce the validity period of the assertion

2   Restrict the audience for the assertion

3   Confirm message origination

4   Use `AssertionId` as nonce

We will also describe the limitations of each. You can combine some or all of these strategies in your implementations to get the best possible defense against replay attacks.

D.2.1 Strategy 1: Reduce validity period

In listing 8.2, you saw that a SAML assertion's validity can be constrained by a time window. We can take advantage of this constraint and reduce the window of opportunity for replay attacks by narrowing the validity period of assertions to a short period of time.

This technique still cannot fully prevent replay attacks. A replay can still be made within the small validity period we set on each assertion. Furthermore, there are practical constraints that prevent us from reducing the validity period to a small value. For example, we have to account for the fact that the clocks of the assertion issuer and receiver may not be in exact sync; or we may have to support asynchronous services.

On the other hand, this is a simple strategy to use, and a good practice to always use.

D.2.2 *Strategy 2: Restrict the audience for the assertion*

The issuer of an assertion can explicitly identify the audience for an assertion. This would eliminate the possibility of assertions being replayed by an attacker or by a malicious service provider to services other than the one for which the assertion was originally issued.

Listing D.2 shows how the audience for an assertion is constrained.

Listing D.2   Example of `AudienceRestrictionCondition`

```
<Assertion
  xmlns="urn:oasis:names:tc:SAML:1.0:assertion"
  MajorVersion="1" MinorVersion="1"
  AssertionID="MySAMLAssertion1"
  IssueInstant="2005-09-19T18:07:08.419Z"
  Issuer="http://manning.com/xmlns/samples/soasecimpl/cop">

<Conditions
  NotBefore="2005-09-19T18:07:08.419Z"
  NotAfter="2005-09-19T18:12:08.419Z">
  <AudienceRestrictionCondition>
    <Audience>
      http://localhost:8000/axis/services/example6      ❶
    </Audience>
  </AudienceRestrictionCondition>
</Conditions>

  ...
</Assertion>
```

This example is self-explanatory. To restrict the audience for an assertion, we simply add an `AudienceRestrictionCondition` child ❶ to the `Conditions` element. An `Audience` element, consisting of a URI, identifies each of the parties who are expected to rely on this assertion. If an `AudienceRestrictionCondition` is set within an `Assertion`, any party that is not listed as an `Audience` should refuse to accept the `Assertion`.

Note that this strategy cannot prevent replay attacks against parties identified as the intended audience for the assertion. For attacks against everyone else, this strategy works well.

D.2.3 Strategy 3: Confirm message origination

SAML makes it possible for recipients of an assertion to figure out which parts of a message surely originate from the subject identified in an assertion. This facility is known as *subject confirmation*. It aids us in detecting replay attacks in which the attacker incorporates an assertion from a previously captured message into a different message.

A security service that issues SAML assertions can enable subject confirmation in two different ways. Table D.1 summarizes these and discusses the conditions under which each of them is most suitable.

Table D.1 Methods for confirming that an assertion's subject is the one that created parts of a message or the entire message

Confirmation method name	Description	Key pair used in signature	Suitable if
`sender-vouches`	The security service that issues the assertion signs those parts of the message that it can vouch for as originating from the Subject identified in the assertion.	Security service key pair	Security service is in a position to verify that it securely received a part of or the whole message directly from the Subject identified in the assertion
`holder-of-key`	The security Service that issues the assertion certifies a key as belonging to the assertion's Subject. The subject in turn signs the parts of the message it is sending using the key certified by the security service.	Key pair of the subject identified in the assertion	Security service is not in the message path to sign the message itself

SAML facilitates both of these confirmation methods using a `SubjectConfirmation` element that can be added to a `Subject` element in an assertion. We will discuss both these methods next, starting with the `sender-vouches` method.

Subject confirmation method 1: sender-vouches

If the security service that is issuing a SAML assertion is in a position to vouch for the integrity of an entire message or particular message parts, it can convey this information to the receiver by signing those parts and setting the `Subject-Confirmation` element as shown in listing D.3.

Listing D.3   Example of a subject with `sender-vouches` subject confirmation method

```
<Subject>
  <NameIdentifier
    NameQualifier="manning.com"
    Format="...:SAML:1.1:nameid-format:emailAddress">
    chap@manning.com
  </NameIdentifier>
  <SubjectConfirmation>
    <ConfirmationMethod>
      urn:oasis:names:tc:SAML:1.0:cm:sender-vouches
    </ConfirmationMethod>
  </SubjectConfirmation>
</Subject>
```

NOTE   *Who is the sender in "sender-vouches"?* The word sender in `sender-vouches` may be confusing. In this context, sender actually refers to the sender of the SAML assertion—that is, a security service—and not the original sender of a message.

This subject confirmation method is applicable if the security service can somehow make sure that it securely received a part or whole of the message directly from the subject identified in the assertion it is issuing. For example, a subject may use a VPN or SSL/TLS to securely send a message to the security service. Or, a subject may sign the entire message or particular message parts using a key that can be verified by the security service as belonging to the subject.

But what if the security service is not in a position to vouch for the integrity of message contents? For example, the security service may not be in the message path. In such cases, the `holder-of-key` method is more suitable for subject confirmation.

Subject confirmation method 2: holder-of-key

A subject might obtain an assertion for later use out-of-band (like in Kerberos). In this case, the security service cannot vouch for the integrity of message contents, as it does not receive the message content from the subject. The security service can still facilitate the receiver's task of identifying message parts that can be trusted to have originated from the subject named in a SAML assertion. The security service can do this simply by adding the subject's key information to the assertion. Receivers can then trust any parts signed using the key in the assertion as originating from the subject named in the assertion.

Listing D.4 shows how this method of subject confirmation is conveyed in a SAML assertion.

Listing D.4 Example of a subject with `holder-of-key` subject confirmation method

```
<Subject>
  <NameIdentifier
    NameQualifier="manning.com"
    Format="...:SAML:1.1:nameid-format:emailAddress">
    chap@manning.com
  </NameIdentifier>
  <SubjectConfirmation>
    <ConfirmationMethod>
      urn:oasis:names:tc:SAML:1.0:cm:holder-of-key
    </ConfirmationMethod>
    <ds:KeyInfo>
      <ds:KeyValue>...</ds:KeyValue>
    </ds:KeyInfo>
  </SubjectConfirmation>
</Subject>
```

To make the job of a receiver easy when using the `holder-of-key` confirmation method, a sender can simply refer to the key specified by a SAML assertion's `SubjectConfirmation/KeyInfo` instead of repeating the key information in its signatures. This way, the receiver is saved the additional task of determining which signatures in a message use the key specified by a SAML assertion. Listing D.5 shows this technique.

Listing D.5 Example of a signature whose `KeyInfo` points to a SAML assertion

```
<ds:Signature>
  <ds:SignedInfo>
    ...
  </ds:SignedInfo>

  <ds:SignatureValue>
    ...
  </ds:SignatureValue>

  <ds:KeyInfo>
    <wsse:SecurityTokenReference>
      <wsse:KeyIdentifier
        ValueType="...#SAMLAssertionID">
        MySAMLAssertion1
      </wsse:KeyIdentifier>
    </wsse:SecurityTokenReference>
```

```
      </ds:KeyInfo>
    </ds:Signature>
```

Confirming message origination prevents replay attacks in which the attacker reuses an assertion with a different message than the one in which it was originally used. This strategy is certainly a lot more powerful than the previous one, which could only defend against replays to services that were not listed as the audience for an assertion. Of course, the extra power comes at the cost of additional complexity. Strategies 1 and 2 were definitely much simpler to understand and use than this strategy.

The biggest limitation of this strategy is that it cannot defend against replays of the entire original message as is. In fact, it is very difficult to protect against replays of original messages as is. The next strategy strives to address this challenge.

D.2.4 *Strategy 4: Use AssertionId as a nonce*

The strategies we have described so far cannot avoid replays of a captured message as is. To avoid replay attacks of this kind, we need to include a nonce in the assertion. Recall from chapter 4 that a nonce is a number used once; that is, a number that will not be repeated. The service will need to remember the nonce values used in the last m minutes and reject any assertions with a repeating nonce value or with an issue instant that goes back more than m minutes.

Neither SAML nor WS-Security currently provides a standard way to communicate nonce values. In the case of an assertion issuer (security service) that does not cache and reuse SAML assertions even when contacted repeatedly with the same credentials, the AssertionId can effectively work as a nonce. But if the assertion issuer caches and issues the same assertion more than once, we cannot use this strategy.

Of course, none of these four strategies would guarantee protection against replay attacks unless we use signatures as discussed before to detect tampering of assertions. An attacker can simply change the timestamps, audience restrictions, and nonce values before resubmitting an assertion if the assertion is not protected against tampering by signatures.

To recap, we can use multiple strategies to prevent replay attacks. We have discussed four strategies here. While the last of these strategies, using AssertionId as a nonce, is the most watertight, it is not always applicable. In such cases, the remaining strategies can all be combined to reduce the opportunity for attackers. Strategy 1 of reducing the assertion's validity period is always a best practice and helps even when strategy 4 is applicable by reducing the time window during which a repetition of nonce needs to be detected.

Let's now consider the third and final security aspect we promised to discuss here.

D.3 *Protecting confidentiality and privacy*

SAML assertions contain information on subject identities, attributes, and privileges. Some or all of this information may need to be protected. In addition to clearly sensitive information such as bank account numbers, SAML assertions may carry often-shared identifiers or attributes such as email addresses that still need to be safeguarded from falling into the wrong hands, such as spam agencies.

There are two very different aspects to these concerns: confidentiality and privacy. Confidentiality is easier to tackle. We can use the encryption techniques discussed in chapter 6 to guarantee that sensitive information is not readable by third parties. Privacy, as we noted in chapter 1, is a lot tougher to guard.

A web service endpoint that should only be accessible to adults only needs assertions stating the age of a user. The security service need not reveal the real identity of the user. One way of attempting this is through the use of pseudonyms in assertions. Pseudonyms by themselves do not provide complete anonymity. This is because inferences can be made by correlating information from multiple assertions. We will not cover privacy protection in more detail here, as it is outside the scope of this book.

Application-Oriented Networking (AON)

In chapter 8, we discussed the idea of security as a service. In the working example we showed you there, we explicitly routed messages via the security service. Explicit routing is not always possible. First, you may not have access to the source code of the service and service consumer to add the routing logic. Even when you do have access to the source code, you may not want to add routing code into each endpoint, as it can lead to maintenance problems when you need to switch security service locations or introduce load balancing between multiple security service instances. Wouldn't it be nice if the network could somehow be configured to route every message (or select messages that meet some criteria) via the security service?

Transparent routing of application messages via intermediaries is not a new idea. IP packets destined for port 80 (the default HTTP port) are often intercepted by routers and redirected to web caches using techniques such as Web Cache Coordination Protocol (WCCP). Similarly, it is possible to set up a network element such as a router to transparently intercept packets based on source and destination IP addresses and port numbers and route them via intermediaries such as a security service.

But what if we want the network to intercept SOAP messages only and route them via a security service? A regular network device cannot do that, as network devices, in general, do not understand application-level messages. Network devices deal with packets, which every application message gets split up into. Unless a network device can collect and assemble information from multiple packets that belong to the same application message, the device cannot distinguish a SOAP message from any other message.

If we assume that an intelligent, application-aware network device can collect and assemble information from multiple packets that belong to the same application message, can such a network device itself act as a security service instead of routing messages via a security service? For that matter, why only a security service? Can the network device provide other application-level services such as validation, transformation, visibility, caching, content-based routing, and application-aware load balancing?

Vendors such as Cisco and IBM DataPower can offer almost of these features in a new product line referred to as AON. AON is about a lot more than just security, but security is a key offering, and good support for security standards exists even in the first generation of AON products. For example, with Cisco AON, you can

- Extract identity claims made using a wide variety of mechanisms—be they transport-level mechanisms such as HTTP Basic Authentication or SSL Peer Certificate or message-level mechanisms such as WS-Security with a User-name token, Kerberos ticket, X.509 certificate chain, or SAML assertion.
- Authenticate the extracted identity claims against an LDAP directory or using Kerberos.
- Authorize service calls using LDAP groups or custom rules.
- Encrypt/decrypt all or select parts of a message using XML Encryption and WS-Security standards.
- Sign or verify signatures for all or select parts of a message using XML Signatures and WS-Security.
- Validate a message against a supplied schema.
- Update the message to add security context.

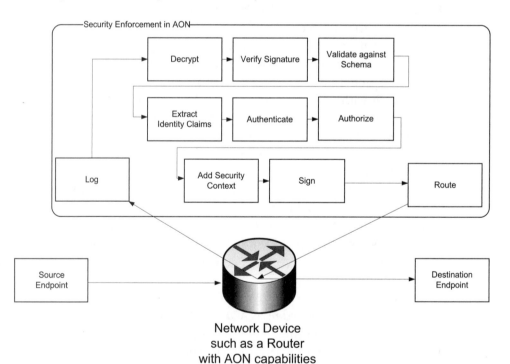

Figure E.1 **Security services implemented as an implicit intermediary with the help of an AON-capable networking device.**

Higher-end AON devices, such as the diagram in figure E.1, are even tuned for some of these tasks with the help of special hardware for cryptography, XML parsing, encryption, and signatures. This makes AON a very interesting choice for implementing a security service.

A complete description of AON is obviously beyond the scope of this book. If you are interested in knowing more about AON, look up the references cited in the "Suggestions for further reading" section.

Suggestions for further reading

- "The Network's New Role," Taf Anthias and Krishna Sankar. ACM Queue, May 2006. Pages 38-46 discuss the ideas behind application-oriented networking.

- Cisco's application-oriented networking product page is at http://www.cisco.com/go/aon.

- DataPower (acquired by IBM), Sarvega (acquired by Intel), Layer 7 Technologies, Reactivity, and Forum Systems are some of the firms selling XML security devices. The home pages of these firms are at http://www.datapower.com/, http://www.sarvega.com/, http://www.layer7tech.com/, http://www.reactivity.com/, and http://forumsys.com/ respectively.

index

MORE TITLES FROM MANNING

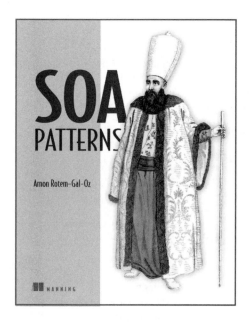

SOA Patterns

    by Arnon Rotem-Gal-Oz
    ISBN: 1-933988-26-6
    400 pages
    $49.99
    June 2008

Becoming Agile

Adapting and applying Agile in an imperfect world

    by Greg Smith
    ISBN: 1-933988-25-8
    400 pages
    $44.99
    June 2008

For ordering information go to www.manning.com

LASZLO in Action

by Norman Klein, Max Carlson,
   with Glenn MacEwen
ISBN: 1-932394-83-42
550 pages
$44.99
December 2007

Test Driven
Practical TDD and Acceptance TDD
for Java Developers

by Lasse Koskela
ISBN: 1-932394-85-0
544 pages
$49.99
October 2007

For ordering information go to www.manning.com

MORE TITLES FROM MANNING

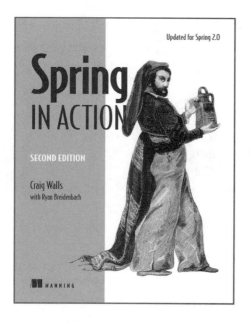

Spring in Action, Second Edition
  by Craig Walls
      with Ryan Breidenbach
  ISBN: 1-933988-13-4
  768 pages
  $49.99
  August 2007

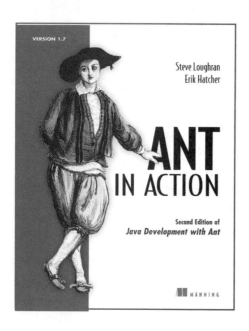

Ant in Action
Second Edition of Java Development with Ant
  by Steve Loughran and Eric Hatcher
  ISBN: 1-932394-80-X
  600 pages
  $49.99
  July 2007

For ordering information go to www.manning.com